Prof. Marvin Alisky
ASU
Political
Science

D1617532

AFRICAN STUDIES SERIES
General Editor: J. R. GOODY

DEPENDENCE AND OPPORTUNITY

OTHER BOOKS IN THIS SERIES

DEPENDENCE AND OPPORTUNITY

POLITICAL CHANGE IN AHAFO

JOHN DUNN
Lecturer in Politics, University of Cambridge

A. F. ROBERTSON
Director of the African Studies Centre, University of Cambridge

CAMBRIDGE UNIVERSITY PRESS

Published by the Syndics of the Cambridge University Press
Bentley House, 200 Euston Road, London NW1 2DB
American Branch: 32 East 57th Street, New York, N.Y.10022

© Cambridge University Press 1973

Library of Congress Catalogue Card Number: 73–79303

First published 1973

ISBN: 0 521 20270 1

Printed in Great Britain by
Western Printing Services Ltd
Bristol

TO THE ANCESTORS, CHIEFS AND PEOPLE
OF AHAFO
AND TO THEIR DESCENDANTS

CONTENTS

LIST OF MAPS AND TABLES

PREFACE

We have benefited greatly from discussions with our academic colleagues in Cambridge and the University of Ghana, Legon. We owe a particular debt to the sponsor of our study, the African Studies Centre at Cambridge, and to its Directors Audrey Richards and Jack Goody. Robertson's work was financed by the Social Science Research Council and latterly by a Trinity College grant from the William Wyse Fund. Dunn's work was assisted by grants from the Smuts Fund and from King's College, Cambridge and made possible by the grant of a year's leave from his college duties to teach in the Political Science Department of the University of Ghana. We must record our gratitude to all these bodies for their support.

Each of us, in carrying out the study and writing his share of the text, is aware of a few prominent debts which must be acknowledged specifically. Robertson would like to thank Malcolm Ruel, Peppy Roberts, Luciano Pavignano and Enid Schildkrout. Dunn wishes particularly to thank Susan McKaskie, George and Paulina Ofosu Amaah and Quentin Skinner.

We greatly appreciate the enormous amount of assistance which we received from many members of the Ghanaian public service. Our even more obvious debt to the people of Ahafo is acknowledged elsewhere. Several of them expressed their conviction that our study would bring us immediate wealth and rapid promotion. If we are less sanguine, our dependence on the good-will and good counsel of our Ghanaian friends will be clearly apparent in the following chapters.

Cambridge   J.D.
January 1973   A.F.R.

xi

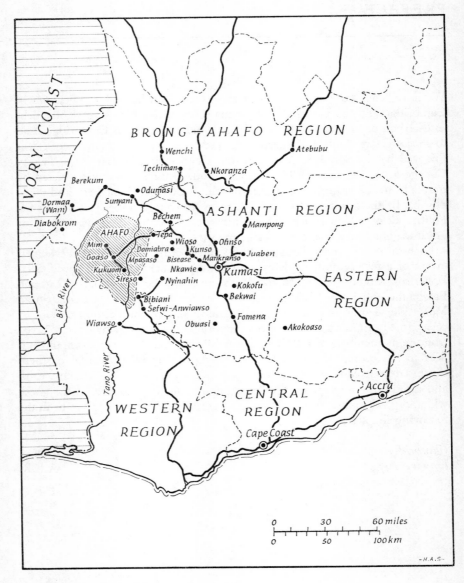

Map A   Southern Ghana

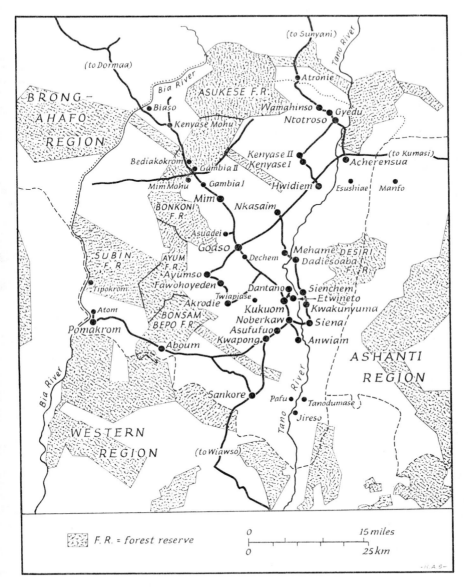

Map B Ahafo

CHAPTER I

INTRODUCTION

Ahafo, like most other inhabited sections of the globe today, is not what it used to be. The ecological and demographic shift from a virgin forest thinly peopled with hunters to a huge cocoa plantation and timber stand producing massively for the world market has come in its entirety within the span of a single life. It has come, too, from the outside. No one living in or visiting Ahafo over the last few decades could fail to realise that the area was being transformed. Yet transformation is not in itself necessarily obliteration. Ahafo was not a blank sheet of paper on which the world market and the colonial state were free to scribble as they pleased. It was not inert matter in the hands of an active agent. The political energies and even perhaps the political aspirations of many in Ahafo today are still in part shaped by beliefs about the proper description of shadowy social relations in the forest before the white man came. What men today believe that Ahafo used to be is still at times (though plainly not at all times) a consideration which informs their vision of what they wish it to become. Probably no one in Ahafo would care it to revert in its entirety to how the forest was in 1896, when the British Hausa column moving through Ahafo was unable to prevent dozens of domestic slaves deserting their masters in its wake.[1] Few indeed can now remember what this meant and perhaps equally few could now imagine what it would mean. But then the Catholic population of Belfast or or Londonderry have no wish to revert to the social and political conditions which prevailed before Strongbow landed. An ideal past and an ideal future are not any less toughly and emotively related because the actual past as a whole is not a condition to which anyone would choose to revert.

In writing about political change and its meaning in Africa in recent decades it has not proved easy for scholars, whether from West, East or from Africa itself, to hit upon a range of focus which captures convincingly the integrity of current political action. Constitutional pieties, ideological incantations and *mafioso* vendettas at the level of the national government have tended to be balanced by a cosy picture of small town communal entertainment at the local level. In part these difficulties have been a product of the conditions of research. But it seems likely that overall it has been the prior enthusiasms and anxieties of the researchers which have made it so hard for them to pick out the most revealing segments for analysis. The exigencies of decolonisation, the hasty concerns of comparative government and the austere professional caution of anthropologists have certainly illuminated many aspects of African politics. But it seems just, by now, to insist that there are many aspects which they do not appear to have found any clear means of illuminating. Between *Creating Political Order* and *Social Change at Larteh, Ghana*[2] there remains a wide gulf of plain ignorance and incomprehension and it does not perhaps any longer require particular cynicism to suppose that it is in this gulf that much of the meaning of African politics is to be found (if found it ever is). There are two drastically separated facets of national political action in an African state today. The first of these is the relationship between the postcolonial state apparatus and the agencies, political and economic, on the world market against which it attempts with greater or less energy or skill or dedication to protect the interests of its subject population. It is impossible to exaggerate the importance of this facet; but since the people of Ahafo have yet to find any way of affecting it, nothing which we have to say in the present book can hope to do much to illuminate it. The second facet, the relationship between the postcolonial state apparatus and the subjects whom it in part controls lies more within our scope. But, taking our stand within Ahafo and looking upwards, we have not concerned ourselves with the state as the trustee of the national future of Ghana, squinting sympathetically or unsympathetically down the barrel of the administration to see why its subjects make such an elusive target. Politically the perspective which we have adopted is in some respects a populist perspective, *l'arbre vu du côté des racines* as Victor Hugo put it.[3] But we have not adopted it out of any simple conviction as to the location of political virtue or intelligence – that the 'people' know how to rule Ghana. (Do the 'people' know how to rule Britain? Does anyone know how to rule Britain?) The reason why we have taken our stand within Ahafo and looked upwards is not the belief that bureaucrats or parliamentarians or army officers are wicked and peasants virtuous, but the blanker, if epistemologically less precarious reason that Ahafo is there. It was important for the purposes which we have had in mind that it should have been an area of something like the scale and population which it has – not somewhere as large as Ashanti or as small as Larteh. But the order of approximation was very rough and the grounds for it extremely vulgar: a matter of how large was the area for which it was possible to study the administrative records and the current political activities and institutions within a limited time and of how small an area within which we expected to reveal these political activities at a sufficiently complex level to permit some analytical progress with them. The initial grounds for our choice of Ahafo are of little importance compared with the judgement whether or not it did in fact prove an area of a scale suitable for revealing the processes in which we have been interested.

What we have attempted to understand is a process of transformation in which we have endeavoured to see neither end of the causal relationship, local or national, as simply an inert or a wholly predictable force. We have assumed that there are many aspects of Ahafo identities, and less intimately of Ahafo roles, which have resulted from external pressures, as well as some aspects which have survived these pressures without drastic amendment. But we have also assumed that a great many (and probably rather more) aspects of them have resulted from a process of active response by Ahafos and by those who came to Ahafo from the outside over these decades. By the same token we have attempted to explain how far the external pressures of colonial moralism or national aspiration over these same decades have been interpreted and changed by the active character of this response. The present of Ahafo, especially in political terms, is very different from its more distant past; and it is for obvious reasons the present which we have had best opportunities for investigating and assessing. But we have tried above all to grasp how this present has become the legitimate inheritor, through Ahafo passion and action, of this historical past. As an ambition this plainly represents a studied confusion of academic genres, of history, anthropology and political science. How far it has been successful it is no longer for us to judge. But at least it should be clear that this confusion is not inadvertent, that it is indeed the point of our collaboration.

An obvious advantage of this approach may be worth emphasising, as may its even more obvious converse disadvantage. Anthropologists are bound by professional etiquette (and fitted, it is to be hoped, by personal disposition) to take seriously the values of those whom they study. In the analysis of national politics in Africa it has been a major difficulty for investigators to decide whose values it is wholly appropriate for them to take seriously. Should it, for example, be the formal criteria of liberal democracy or the salvationary hopes of socialist prophets, or the less articulated hopes of poor peasant farmers or urban petty traders? Excessive commitment to some simple image for the location of political virtue has recently been largely replaced, in Hegelian antithesis, by a pervasive cynicism as to the possibility of political value becoming localised in African political structures at all. This attitude may be less innocent than its predecessor; but it is not obviously any less offensive. To define politics stolidly in terms of who gets what when how is to ignore the pervasively relevant and altogether more fundamental question of just *why* this should be the pattern of distribution which is maintained. By looking at the complex net of dependencies and opportunities running from Accra (and abroad) down to the hamlets and compound houses of Ahafo, and seeing the scope for action and the possibilities for and limitations on moral solidarity at all these levels, an image may be formed of the distribution of influence and responsibility in the framework of Ahafo's politics. Such an image may lack the moral clarity of purely localist or purely national perspectives (my hamlet right or wrong – the army right or left). But it may nevertheless be more salutary for the moral imagination, whether African or foreign, to have to admit that such an image, however vague in initial outline, is closer to where it ought to begin to work than the bland or histrionic foreign archetypes so plentifully on offer. At the least it might be a better starting point from which to attempt to reflect on the possibilities and impossibilities of building political community in Africa. This is not a humble hope and it may well be judged a misplaced one. Even at best it must be balanced against the obvious disadvantage of the approach which we have chosen. By refusing to confine ourselves either to the present or to the past, we have necessarily constructed a work in which the parts are heterogeneous and in some respects potentially confusing to a hasty reader. To insist doggedly on complexity is always to risk the charge of having simply failed to elicit clarity. Books, as John Burrow has memorably noted, do not have to be isomorphic with their subjects: bald if on Caesar, devious if on Harold Wilson, muddled if on Ahafo. Several of the chapters contain both historical and observational materials and are not divided up neatly into sections labelled 'history' and 'observation'. The decision to allow this amalgam to remain was not dictated by the conclusions reached but by a necessarily subjective judgement as to what did or did not illuminate the processes by which contemporary roles and attitudes were created and (by virtue of doing so) what exactly these roles or attitudes now were. On balance we have been more anxious to suggest the illumination which can derive from this change in focus than to bring back a single and splendid snapshot of some arbitrarily chosen subject.

It is often said today by sensitive students of African local politics that the accumulation of precise information about such topics is a perilous enterprise because it is so likely to get into the hands of (and presumably to be put to use by) those powerful external interests which do not have the interests of Africans at heart. The argument for ignorance is seldom an overwhelming one in any of its variants in social affairs. It is also far from obvious from the viewpoint of the manipulated whether a little knowledge is in any general way any less dangerous than a lot. But whatever the general desirability of 'Area Handbooks for Africa', it is hoped at least that the focus of the present work on the disparities between external ambitions as they come to Ahafo and the fate which befalls them on their domestication there may serve to discourage, rather than to promote, fantasies of the transformation or even of the effortless manipulation of an inert material.

*

4

The collaboration on which this book is based has involved no very clear-cut division of labour. Before either of us left for Ghana we discovered a congruence of interests and have hoped from the outset that our experience could be combined usefully, particularly in the task of finding out as much about Ahafo as possible in the time available to us. Purposely our approach has not shown much regard for disciplinary boundaries, indeed insofar as we may be categorised as social anthropologist and political scientist our research and the preparation of this book have involved us in substantial role exchange. In this process the social anthropologist has discovered public records and the administrators and politicians of the capital, while the political scientist has accustomed himself to living for lengthy periods in a small forest town and conversing with his neighbours. Aware that we have been studying a very complicated political field we have made a point of knowing each other's business and at times have found that two heads may be more reassuring, if not necessarily more reliable, than one.

For both of us our research has involved documentary study and field investigations. Developing a sense of historical continuity extending back some seventy years, and tracing the relationship between Ahafo and the various political centres, have involved examination of public records in London, Accra, Kumasi and Sunyani. By the courtesy of the Commissioner for Local Government and with the kind co-operation of the various local officers we have been allowed to examine open files in the Goaso District Office and the three Local Councils. This has given us privileged access to contemporary information which we have attempted to use with due respect. It must be noted that government attitudes towards enquiry into political and social processes were, during the period of our study, liberal and broad-minded to an extent quite uncharacteristic of other times and other places; we are gratefully aware of how much our research has been facilitated by this prevalent mood of tolerance for academic inquisitiveness. It is very probable that much of the paper accumulated during seventeen years of local government in Ahafo and now stored in an outhouse in Goaso may not survive archival selection and the thirty year restriction on public documents; a student may therefore feel justified in searching through such records with some care if he is given the opportunity. Much the same is true of the legal and local administrative papers which remain in Goaso. There has certainly been much elimination of 'redundant' material already, although it is difficult to assess the extent of this. It is well known that a large proportion of the documents relating to the years of Convention People's Party rule were destroyed at the time of the February 1966 coup d'état.

Our study of contemporary political process has been confined to three years, 1968–71, conspicuously a period of political transition in Ghana. In 1969 a representative Constituent Assembly was convened by the police-

5

Dependence and opportunity

military junta to approve a new constitution for the Second Republic, and shortly afterwards authority was handed over to the popularly elected government of Dr Busia's Progress Party. The moods of resignation and scepticism, deepened by the disgrace of the N.L.C. chairman in 1969, and of hope embodied in the untarnished reputation of Dr Busia, were all experienced in varying degrees by the people of Ahafo. Nationally there was much introspection and self-criticism focussed on public enquiries into the political and financial trustworthiness of a number of eminent men. Although caution may not have been dispelled there was a mood of candour both in Accra and in Ahafo, an indulgence in the luxury of expressing political opinion which could ill be afforded in the years before 1966. In conversation we were frequently reminded that such frankness would have been impossible in the mutual mistrust of the Nkrumah era, particularly as it was often inferred in Ahafo that we were 'from the government' no matter how much we tried to cast our roles in more independent terms.

The period from March to August 1969 was one of extremely active political manoeuvre, both nationally and in Ahafo itself. Opportunity for inspecting and for understanding political allegiance in the making was plainly extremely favourable in this time. But several features of the election campaign and its background meant that our opportunities for inspection and perhaps for understanding also, were more favourable in some directions than others. One of the authors had become a relatively close friend of one or two of the Legon academics who played a prominent part in the organisation of Dr Busia's campaign and was thus much better informed about the strategies adopted on a national scale by this party and about the problems which it encountered than he was able to become in respect of other possible or actual national political parties. Whatever effect it had on his sympathies as an observer, it does not seem likely on reflection that this perspective had any very distorting impact on the interpretation of what took place in Ahafo. More important and more accidental was the fact that the house in which both the authors stayed throughout their time in Ahafo became one of the major centres for organising the Progress Party campaign in the Asunafo constituency. Since the District Secretary of the Party lived in the next door room to the one which was occupied in succession by the authors and since he was on very good terms with the authors long before he occupied this office, it was natural for us to be presented with a much richer and less formal sense of what the local organisers of the party were up to than could have been open to us under any other conditions. Some of the less edifying aspects of the campaign were apt to be discussed outside the bedroom window in the early hours of the morning, while the two leading candidates for the Progress Party nomination met for the first time in our room. But such contingent conveniences of this location were plainly balanced by the tendency for us to

6

become associated with the Progress Party as a political interest, particularly in the minds of their active opponents. Extensive efforts were made to offset this, one major asset in the attempt being the unwavering aversion of our Krobo assistant to the Progress Party and his excellent contacts with their opponents. (He was offered a major organisational position in their party in the constituency.) But partly because of the difference in the political styles of the two parties discussed in the text, a contrast in tone between the respectable and the mildly raffish, and partly because of the intractable physical location of our room, it is certainly true that both our knowledge and our understanding of the political activities of those who led the National Alliance of Liberals' campaign was less intimate than in the case of their opponents. It has been necessary to exercise considerable discretion in the precision of our descriptions of behaviour known to us which was in breach of the electoral laws. On balance we do not believe that the accounts of the behaviour and purposes of one side as presented is any more or less reliable than that of the other. But it is important that this is a matter of judgement and that we did *know* less about one side than about the other.

We have both been uncomfortably aware of our slow and inadequate progress in learning the vernacular, and of the need for linguistic competence in understanding and interpreting the subtleties of political interaction. Our attempts at coming to grips with this consisted mainly of interviews structured with some care, and the extensive (but always overt) use of portable tape recorders. The interviews were essentially open-ended, and only those conducted with the Ahafo chiefs could in any sense be described as a set. These consisted of a series of meetings, never less than two and in one case as many as seven, with each of 26 of the 28 chiefs. The chief was invariably interviewed in the company of at least one elder and in many cases meetings involved a full session of the stool council. Partly intentionally and partly by force of circumstance we have been concerned with the public, not the private face of the chief. These meetings could generate a memorable sense of occasion, involving such preliminaries as the pouring of a libation to the stool ancestors, gods and fetishes. At times they acquired a momentum of their own, the interview being transformed into a series of forceful and illuminating political statements. The set was incomplete in that the question guide was not rigorously applied and that it proved impossible to meet the chiefs of Pomakrom and Siena because of communications problems.

In a relatively unstructured way we also interviewed as many of the people who were concerned in the present or in the past with Ahafo politics as we could. These included cabinet ministers, Members of Parliament and parliamentary candidates, regional and district administrators, local council personnel and many others. We also interviewed the elders, town committee members and other prominent citizens of Goaso, the administrative and commercial centre of Ahafo. Although the frame of reference for our study has been the Ahafo communities, in matters of detail we have devoted attention specifically to Goaso, our home town. A lengthy questionnaire was applied quite rigorously in the interview of 32 men and 26 women, selected somewhat arbitrarily from the people of the town with the assistance of the local government house register. The sample was chosen without much statistical finesse, its representative nature being judged very much by rule of thumb. Subsequently it provided a valuable guide in the assessment of contemporary political attitudes. As with all our interviews, each was recorded in full and translated with the aid of our research assistants.

It will be apparent that our observation of Ahafo has depended to a large extent on hanging on the words of our informants. For this reason quite lengthy periods were spent painstakingly reconstructing, translating and transcribing tape-recorded interviews and meetings. We selected very carefully from a quite impressive list of applicants a 33 year old interpreter/assistant, Mr J. Omersu Kwablah, who has subsequently contrived to make a career out of the bizarre occupation of assisting students in the field. Our main criteria for this choice were his wide knowledge of Ghanaian languages, his relaxed proficiency in public relations, his sound geographical knowledge of Ahafo gained during service with the Co-operative movement and (as a southerner by birth) his relative disengagement from local politics. After some time Mr Omersu developed a helpful understanding of our research interests, and a patient sympathy for our at times frenetic pursuit of meanings. While we depended heavily on his linguistic tutorship we avoided confining our exploration of certain perplexing terms, ideas and values to conversation with him alone, and have always taken advantage of the interest and patience of our English-speaking friends in Ghana. We were also able to rely on the competence of our clerk and copy-typist Mr Alex Amoako-Attah, particularly where the need to observe meetings and other events very closely warranted the deployment of all available eyes, ears and pens. The interest of one of us in public decision making[4] intensified our scrutiny of certain events, and it could be said that one by-product of this obsession was to sensitise our assistants and ourselves to the minutiae of political interaction generally.

Although we may feel that we have explored many different ways of learning about Ahafo, our research must inevitably manifest many shortcomings. Some of these we may ascribe to shortage of time and resources, others to inadequacies in our own perceptions and field methods. Perhaps it would be fair to say, however, that throughout our research we have repeatedly reminded each other of our cardinal concern for as clear a presentation of as wide a range of views of Ahafo politics as possible. In our fieldwork we were concerned that these values should be elicited with the minimum of interference from our own constructions and preconceptions. It is our hope that at least some of these voices from the present and the past have survived the rigours of interpretation and will speak candidly for themselves in the following chapters.

CHAPTER 2

CHANGING COMMUNAL IDENTITIES

The identity of Ahafo, in political as well as geographical terms, derives in large measure from the Tano river, which rises near Techiman in central Ghana and flows out into the Juen lagoon over 150 miles south, on the Ghana/Ivory Coast border. The Tano has provided the main orientation for settlement and today the population of Ahafo is concentrated in the wide valley around its central reaches. The Bia river, running a parallel course through the forest thirty miles to the west, is very different; it is a boundary marker which relatively few Ahafos have actually seen, whereas the Tano is a focus for human interests and a source of political growth. Named after Tano or Ta Kora, the most important of the Ashanti terrestrial gods,[1] its waters are treated with great ritual respect and many of the fetishes closely associated with the establishment and growth of the Ahafo communities are alleged to have been discovered in the river. However contentious the political integration of Ahafo may be, there is much to suggest to the people who live around the Tano that they belong to a quite distinctive place.

Ahafo provides a lush and potentially rich environment. It is an area of dense forest and savannah woodland, well watered with an average annual rainfall of 60 to 80 inches, and the forest ochrosols are soils well suited to cocoa, the prime cash crop of the region. Some 20 miles west of the Tano the forest is sparsely settled, and herds of elephants still pose a threat to the establishment of new farms. The forest extends in a pattern of reserves and shelter-belts, protecting the farms on the south from the annual incursion of dry harmattan winds. Boundaries to the south and east are more open, reflecting the two main axes of communication into the district. The district and regional boundary with Ashanti, defined in 1959, runs through the Disiri forest reserve and an area of relatively sparse settlement 15 to 20 miles east of the Tano.

The settlement of Ahafo is supposed to date from the middle of the eighteenth century when isolated communities, primarily concerned with hunting and the gathering of forest produce, were established. These origins are still expressed in the geographical and political relationships between communities, but Ahafo is very much a product of the cocoa era in Ghana. The crop was first exploited in the hills to the north of Accra in the first

decade of this century, and expansion has subsequently followed the wide belt
of suitable soils which extend westwards into the Ivory Coast. The cocoa
frontier now runs through Ahafo from north to south, turning it into what
Caldwell has called 'the rural boom area of Ghana'.[2] It has all the attributes
of a new immigrant population, youthful, heterogeneous and increasing
rapidly. In 1960, 81,589 people were enumerated, indicating a 300 per cent
increase since 1948.[3] More than two thirds of the present inhabitants were
born outside Ahafo, mainly in neighbouring Ashanti, and as many as 16 per
cent are immigrants from countries adjacent to Ghana, notably Upper Volta.
Ninety-one per cent of the population are under 45 years of age, and the high
proportion of males to females (147:100) is indicative of recent and extensive
immigration. The Ghana census records that in these respects Ahafo is
second only to the rapidly expanding area around the new port of Tema.
The relatively low population density in Ahafo (about 50 persons to the
square mile) suggests that the saturation point in immigration has not yet
been reached; indeed, as we have seen, the frontier of settlement is still
advancing into the western forest.

One cannot, of course, learn very much from the census data about the
dispersion of settlement or the nature of community growth. The pattern,
typical of the Akan area, is one of close nucleation of dwellings into villages
and towns, the largest of these being Mim (population about 8,000). Although
there are many very small hamlets scattered throughout Ahafo, community
growth is still in terms of the proliferation of courtyard houses separated by
narrow streets. The largest and longest-established towns and villages are all
situated within about ten miles of the Tano river, and it is within this area
that the native Ahafo people are concentrated. The many less permanent
residents are categorised as 'strangers' (*ahoho*), a collective term for various
kinds of immigrant. Some are landholders from Ashanti and southern Ghana
who commute back and forth to Ahafo and rely on caretakers – also immigrants – who work their land on a share-crop basis. Others are seasonal
labourers working for the Ahafo farmers and resident stranger-farmers.
The interests of the Ahafos and the strangers are to some extent opposed, in
that the Ahafos fear that local wealth is being drained away to other parts of
Ghana while the strangers are continually on their guard against economic
and political exploitation by the natives. The two categories are to some extent
segregated spatially, the Ahafos around the Tano river and the newcomers
in more recently established, politically subordinate villages and in 'camps'
out near the forest frontier. Most strangers are reluctant to become involved
in local politics, partly because they recognise the prior claims of the Ahafos
and partly because their own political interests remain closely associated with
their own home communities. This is indicative of the enduring significance
of the Akan idea of citizenship, the individual's assurance that no matter

where he may travel he will continue to belong to a particular community and may enjoy economic and political rights there which he can not expect to acquire easily elsewhere.

It is essentially priority of settlement and formal citizenship which distinguishes the Ahafos from the strangers, rather than homogeneity of ethnic or other identities. The Ahafos form the political core of the district, both with regard to the expansion of settlement and the extent to which they dominate the local political arena. However the distinction between stranger and citizen is in reality relative and imprecise. Many Ahafos will concede: 'we are all strangers here', an acknowledgement that settlement in the area is little more than two centuries old and that unlike other Akan areas Ahafo has no autochthons. The fact that the origins of all settlers can be traced to communities outside the district is an important political principle, and remains significant even when the relationship with the 'parent' community is no longer actively maintained.

The origins of Ahafo settlement is a subject fraught with political significance. Throughout the district, conflicting versions of history seek to express and validate contemporary political alignments.[4] A more objective account can draw on only scanty evidence for years prior to 1900. Settlement seems to have been largely a by-product of conflict during the eighteenth century between the rival Akan states of Ashanti and Denkyira, and of the expansion of Ashanti after the defeat of Denkyira in the epoch-making battle of Feyiase (1701). At the height of its power, Ashanti was a politico-military confederation of states united around Kumasi, whose paramount chief became the Asantehene (the suffix *-hene* denotes a chief). The declared allegiance of the other five paramount chiefs to him was the principle on which the confederation of states depended. In the latter half of the eighteenth century further campaigns extended the Ashanti sphere of influence beyond the territory of the six states in an expanding empire of provinces, 'protectorates' and tributaries.[5] The wing-chiefs of the Kumasi state played a prominent part in these campaigns and were rewarded by their paramount chief (alias the Asantehene) with control of tracts of land in what is now Brong–Ahafo Region. They were entitled to collect tribute, place their hunters and settle their subjects in these 'Kumasi Islands'. Today, seven of the Kumasi chiefs claim parts of Ahafo and assert their rights to demand rents and allocate land. To them Ahafo has no corporate political identity, it is a motley of allotments extending into the western forest.

The Ashanti Confederacy was primarily a military union and its political coherence was apparently much greater in war than in peacetime. Towards the end of the nineteenth century when the main threat was the encroaching authority of the British, Ashanti control over tributary areas apparently weakened. Meanwhile there was a growing self-awareness among the Ahafo communities, and eventually they felt able to resist the demands for tribute from their Kumasi overlords. After a series of skirmishes they routed a Kumasi force and, aware of the threat of reprisal, made a Treaty of Friendship and Protection with the British in 1896. Just as the Ashanti states had formed themselves into a military alliance to challenge Denkyira, so the Ahafos had united around the leadership of Kukuom (see Map B) to confront the Ashantis. This constitution, in which Mim and Noberkaw held senior right- and left-wing positions, was recognised by the British authorities, and in the eyes of all but the disaffected Kumasi chiefs Ahafo became an independent state with Kukuomhene as paramount chief. In 1901 the British abrogated the Ashanti Confederacy and until it was re-established in 1935 the Ahafo chiefs enjoyed autonomy and independence.

During seventy years of political vicissitudes, the main opposition of interests within the district has involved Kukuom and Mim. Paramount chief until 1935, Kukuomhene's authority was eclipsed by Mimhene, who prospered in the renewed association with Kumasi when the British re-established the Ashanti Confederacy. In 1958 Kukuomhene was restored to the status of paramount by the Convention People's Party government, and the Ahafo state was revived. Deposed for the next eight years, Mimhene again acquired the upper hand when the C.P.P. government was ousted in the coup d'état of February 1966, and Kukuomhene's paramountcy was abrogated. In this political see-saw, the other Ahafo chiefs have allied themselves, with varying degrees of conviction, with the two principals. Today a group of seven acknowledges the pre-eminence of Kukuomhene and advocates the re-establishment of the independent Ahafo state. Nineteen others form a less coherent group favouring the incorporation of Ahafo within the wider Ashanti union. Although Mimhene is their informal leader, few of them would support his elevation to the status of paramount chief. They feel that Ahafo should be a division of the Ashanti state, but unanimity on a constitutional framework is lacking. Details of this dispute will be elaborated later and its political significance in many contexts discussed. The many rival versions of local history may be interpreted as attempts to validate the various competing interests involved in this schism. The Kukuom faction, bitterly opposed to the idea of incorporation within Ashanti, argue that their ancestors were originally immigrants from Denkyira, the historic rival of Ashanti. Predictably, most of the pro-Ashanti chiefs trace their origins to Kumasi. Both factions, however, are in agreement that it was the abundance of forest produce in Ahafo which induced the original settlers to stay, regardless of their origins. Local semantic interpretations of the word 'Ahafo' play on this theme – the political and historical point-of-view always being made explicit. For example Dantanohene, an advocate of the political independence of Ahafo and Kukuomhene's paramountcy, explained:

'There were so many monkeys here and they were sold at half-a-crown each, so people said that this was a place where things were very abundant – *ade a eye fo*. When you go to Ahafo, things are very abundant indeed. Everything was made cheap to encourage people to settle here.'

The pro-Ashanti faction regard the word as an expression of their responsibility to the Asantehene, who himself explained:

'The hunters and their families increased and became "Ahayofuo" for the king. The word "Ahayofuo" has now been corrupted as "Ahafo" and that is why this part of Ashanti is known and called Ahafo, i.e. land occupied by hunters "Ahayofuo" for the Asantehene.'[6]

It is interesting that the Ahafo chiefs tell a great deal about the early days of Ahafo settlement in their histories apropos of constitutional alignments within and beyond the district, but say relatively little about what was, in objective terms, the period of most drastic change – the expansion of the cocoa industry into the area. This economic revolution, discussed in detail in chapter 3, dates from 1905,[7] and is still in progress today as the line of cultivation advances through the forest to the west. We may construe that the cocoa industry changed drastically many of the premises of community organisation. Its political repercussions are a basic theme of this book. Hitherto the Ahafo community had been a close, protective cluster of dwellings surrounded by a narrow belt of subsistence plots and connected to distant centres by forest tracks. Economic interest in the forest was in terms of its natural produce, the game, snails and rubber trees. With the advent of cocoa, and afterwards the timber industry,[8] interest in the resources of the forest became much less diffuse and more territorial. Land itself became valuable and boundaries a matter of political contention. Eastern Ahafo has been carved up into rich timber concessions and cocoa farms; a flood of immigrants, initially from the Kumasi area and subsequently from progressively further afield, has turned the Ahafos from gatherers of forest produce to landholders. The transition from small, dispersed and relatively mobile camps to permanent towns with stoutly defended marches is still very much in progress, and its implications are of very great importance to an understanding of current politics. Although much of this can only be a matter for surmise, the most important features of settlement history and consequent political development are well known to the Ahafos themselves and much discussed by them.

A cardinal theme in the expansion of settlement is the migration of the founders of a new community from some other established community within or beyond the Ahafo. This is usually named, and great political significance may be attached to the move. However, a broad distinction may be made in historical terms between those whose departure was voluntary and sanctioned by the parent community and those who left as fugitives; and in political terms between those currently acknowledging their political sub-ordination to the parent community and those asserting their independence. The recognition that one community has 'hived-off' from another does not necessarily imply subordination although, as we shall see, it may become a political issue. Priority of settlement is often used to argue political claims, yet the fact that very many of the 28 communities regard Sienchem as the first town to be established in Ahafo seems to have done little to enhance its political stature. Geographically, Sienchem seems a very probable original focus of Ahafo settlement. Of the principal communities it is the closest to Kumasi, lying some 54 miles due west of the city. What was once an import-ant forest track ran eastwards from Sienchem into Ashanti, providing access for settlers and a route for the export of forest produce. Situated centrally on the east bank of the Tano, Sienchem was probably both a bulking-point for game and a hub for the spread of new hunting camps out in a wide arc into the forest on the west bank of the river. There the east–west line of com-munication from Ashanti met the trade route from the north to the coast, providing a new axis for the spread of settlement and – as Kukuomhene's historical account makes clear – diminishing the economic and political significance of the Kumasi orientation. Communities in the vicinity of Sienchem were probably established earlier than the towns of the north east of Ahafo which was later a focus of settlement for the first of the cocoa farmers. Early this century the main eastward line of communication became the present road from Goaso through Acherensua which strikes the Kumasi–Sunyani road near Bechem. Some recognition is given to these two distinct foci of Ahafo settlement in two named sub-district divisions, *Asutifi*, meaning the upper reaches of the Tano, and *Asunafo*, the lower reaches (see Map A). To the Ahafos this distinction is a very loose one, although it has proved to be of some value in the demarcation of constituency and local authority boundaries.

The situation of the main Ahafo towns reflects their original establish-ment as hunting camps, small communities strategically sited for hunting and gathering expeditions into the forest, rather than for their agricultural suitability. A forest clearing or a secure, well-drained hill slope, ready access to springs or streams and to a main line of communication seem to have been the main requirements. Most of the Ahafo communities are supposed to have been named after features of their immediate environment, a nearby stream (Ntotro-*so*, Goa-*so*), a grove of trees (Nkasaim) or a river crossing (Etwineto). Some allusions are more graphic:

ANWIAMHENE: 'Because the river Tano caused floods the people moved from that first place to here, they came here to where it was sandy and decided to stay here, saying that flooding could never effect this place . . . When a hunter shot an animal another would appear and sit there looking at him. They said 'here animals sit staring at people' – '*hwe me haa*'. This was later [corrupted to] Anwiam.'

Many local accounts of the early settlement of Ahafo mention the relative isolation of these hunting communities. In his account of the establishment of his town, Kwakunyumahene suggested that the authorities in Kumasi, who had a vested interest in the game collected in Ahafo, regarded this as a matter of policy. He explained that his ancestors' settlement near Sienchem interfered with the hunting in the area and restricted the amount of meat available for porterage to Kumasi:

'The Asantehene . . . instructed them to go and stay several miles further away from the other hunters. If they persisted in staying in the middle there they would make him die of starvation. He told [them] to go as far away as possible from the other hunters so that they would not be impeded.'

The change from a predominantly hunting to a cash-crop economy has important implications for the political identity of the Ahafo community. Broadly speaking the movement, by no means complete yet, has been away from the conception of interests radiating out into the forest from a residential core, towards the idea of lineal boundaries demarcating territorial sovereignty. When a chief says 'the white man showed us our boundaries' we may assume that he is referring to an era of political and economic change in which the cultivation of cocoa has been a dominant influence. Today the community is still a settlement nucleus in the real sense, a compact unit of dwellings surrounded by the high forest trees which shelter the cocoa farms. It is a centre from which the townspeople make daily excursions out to their farms, and it is a nucleus for economic and demographic growth. As population expands within the residential core, so new farms are established increasingly further afield. The townsman's view of his community may be interpreted in terms of concentric circles set in the forest. In the middle is the town itself, increasing over time from a cluster of small huts to a grid of streets with substantial courtyard houses. Beyond this built-up area is the wider circle of subsistence and cocoa farms, expanding outwards into the forest. This cultivated belt is an interesting transitional zone in Akan cosmology, having neither the close 'social' ethos of the town nor the absolute 'antisocial' extensiveness of the virgin forest.

The radial thrust of the farms into the forest is the community's frontier where wild animals and dense vegetation continually threaten to encroach on the glades where the young cocoa is planted. In the most populous parts of Ahafo these circles of settlement form contiguous patterns; at some point the territorial expansion of the community is arrested by an encounter with an alien community in the forest, and a political boundary must be recognised. In reality, the two communities are unlikely to be strangers to one another, for they will probably have been connected for a long time by a forest track. By facilitating outward movement this line of communication will have distended the two circles of settlement into an hourglass shape, and will ultimately have exposed the point of contact between them to public view.[9] Land litigation suggests that the cutting of a track between two communities implies the recognition of a boundary point somewhere along its length, regardless of the extent of cultivation. A stream, a rock or some other suitable marker is agreed upon, and each community undertakes responsibility for the maintenance of the track to that point. A chief is thus said to have 'owned' a track, or part of it. These radial lines of communication are still more salient indicators of the limits of economic and political interest than the demarcation of boundaries by circumferential lines. Nkasaimhene explained:

'Formerly there were no boundaries. When the white man came we made tracks with cutlasses. We made a track from Nkasaim to Hwidiem, and Goaso made a track to Nkasaim, and from Goaso to Kukuom. The boundaries were reckoned from the middle of each track for each chief. This was during my lifetime ... Our boundary with Goaso was put at Agyebire, and the white man asked if Goaso and we agreed. This is how it is now.'

Krom is the common Ahafo term which we translate here as 'community'. A more general translation is 'town', but like *oman* ('the body politic'[10]) its semantic range is wide and its use contingent. In one sense it is 'home' (as in *meko ne krom*, I have come home), in another it is the physical settlement nucleus, and thirdly it is the political unit constituted by this nucleus. It expresses the individual's commitment and incorporation but it is also an idealised view for, in objective terms, *krom* is a large, populous and politically superior settlement such as the capital of a state. Used in the context of a small, politically humble settlement, *krom* has clear connotations of aggrandisement, and its people use the term even if their community is classified objectively as *akura* (village) or even *osese* (camp). In a thesis on changing settlement patterns in Ashanti, S. A. Darko has observed: 'indeed, although he might be living in a village, yet a person might not like to be referred to as *okuraseni* (villager), a derogatory term, which also suggests rusticity'. Darko also notes 'the great sense of belonging the Ashanti had towards their *nkurow* (towns)', and the corollary, the need for every Ashanti to have a community he could call his own.[11] These distinctive meanings, particularly the sense of integration and of aggrandisement, should be borne in mind where we have used the word community to translate *krom*.

In a more objective sense, krom, akura and osese are expressive of a continuum of settlement growth which is of fundamental importance to any interpretation of politics in Ahafo. Defending 'my sub-chief of Sankori' against the political claims of the distant chief of Techiman, the paramount chief of Ahafo, Kukuomhene, could explain in a letter to the District Commissioner at Sunyani as early as 1906: 'the town Sankori was a mere hunting camp . . . and these people's children and grandchildren extended the camp into a town, which is now under me'.[12] However, a clear distinction must be made between the expansion of the nuclear community itself, and the growth of separate, subsidiary communities by outmigration. It is reasonable to suppose that outward development from an isolated settlement nucleus must eventually involve extensive daily commuting for some residents, which will in turn encourage the building of temporary accommodation out of town. More recently, this tendency has been fostered by the immigration of share-croppers and groups of tenant farmers who cannot conveniently be accommodated in town, or who find their status as 'strangers' there irksome. The authorities in the town will be anxious to assert the political subordination of the subsidiary community from the outset, particularly if its own citizens are involved. A move out from the security of the parent community is no casual matter and requires the permission of the chief and his elders as well as their propitiation of the venture. 'Emigrants' of this kind will almost certainly be tied to the community by bonds of kinship. The superiority of the parent community is expressed symbolically in many ways, for example in the 'carrying of fire' from a hearth in town to the new site in the forest. Local accounts suggest that a subsidiary community may be established for other than economic reasons; Mim Mohu grew around the dwelling of the priest of a god associated with an impressive rock outcrop in the forest not far from Mim.

This pattern of expansion, real or supposed, is a major source of political intrigue in Ahafo. As dependence on the parent community decreases, so the threat of political segmentation grows. The establishment of subsidiary communities also has interesting implications on the question of boundaries. A chief of one of the 28 Ahafo stools, asked to describe the limits of his land, will call off points around the perimeter of an imagined circle; although he may mention such natural features as streams and boulders he will refer mainly to small camps and villages. The boundary is not so much a line as a series of points of expansion, and can therefore be difficult to express on a map. Anwiamhene, for example, defined his boundary thus:

'I have a boundary with Tano Dumase at a village called Kofi Boakye. My boundary with Asufufuo is at Betinko. The Noberkaw boundary is at Bepoko. The boundary with Sankore is Betenasua, a stream, and the river Tano is my boundary with Kwawuduma Sreso.'

It is very rare for a road or pathway to be mentioned as a boundary for any-thing other than a farm for, as we have seen, communities tend to grow *around* the lines of communication. Ultimately the boundary of a com-munity is marked by its furthermost farms, as Ayumsohene's account suggests:

'Asaseka, a river, is my boundary with Mimhene. I make my farms up to there. The boundary then passes through the forest to Beposo, Wasa, and Akosa, Subinso, Kotiagon and so to the river Bia on the left side. Someone went there to Wamaso and made his farm.'

Here we may see the dynamism of boundaries at the minimal level. A farm normally has defined width rather than defined length,[13] and an enquiry about its size will bring the response 'so many poles'. This does not refer to the archaic English unit of area but to a lineal measurement – supposedly the distance between two telegraph poles.[14] A farmer has the right to cultivate out along the line allocated to him until his progress is arrested by the farm either of a fellow townsman or of someone from an adjacent community.[15] Certainly, the development of the cocoa industry in Ahafo is making boundaries more specific, as population pressure and the awareness of land as an economic resource increase. In the community as a whole, boundary litigation reflects the contemporary interest in the value of land reserves.

The importance of ecology is clearly expressed in the moral values of the Ahafo community. The citizen's interests are, as it were, centripetal within the circle of settlement described above, the centre itself being his own domestic hearth. This inward orientation seems to find expression in the architecture of the courtyard house, a style of family dwelling which pre-dominates in the established town. Made of swish and daub or landcrete blocks faced with cement, the plain outside walls of the house, with small shuttered windows, confront the other buildings of the town. Inside, verandahs and open doorways look out over the courtyard which is the focus of domestic activity. The component units of the often sizeable matrifamily household have private rooms around this area, but in the middle women prepare food, children play and the men meet to talk and drink. For the individual, this is the focus of all that is familiar, moral and secure. The surrounding nucleus of settlement is somewhat less so, being an aggregate of similar family units with specific and at times conflicting foci of interest of their own. Wider social categories may divide the community, sometimes territorially, on the basis of extended matrifamily membership or, more commonly in Ahafo, according to community of origin. Established towns also have a particular quarter called the *zongo* where most of the resident 'strangers' live. Ultimately there is the contrast between the 'social' nucleus of settlement and the surrounding forest, which is 'antisocial', alien and dangerous. The moral solidarity of the *krom*, the community, has many expressions including the jealously guarded rights of citizenship, the serving of the gods and fetishes proper to the town, and the corporate rituals performed by the chief, elders and family heads which express ancestral relationships and community growth. All these are part of the political identity of the individual and the community in Ahafo, and are of enduring significance in contemporary politics.

The Ahafos regard the political organisation of their communities as in part a product of the pattern of growth just described. The basic model for political structure is one characteristic of the Akan area; communities are aggregated into a hierarchy of units (*aman*, s. *oman*) culminating in the state, led by a paramount chief (*omanhene*). Margaret Field, writing of the southern Ghanaian state of Akim-Kotoku, has described the oman at this level as 'a confederation of stools, which may or may not be contiguous', and adds: 'since the people of one town are usually united around one stool, it is also said, with considerable accuracy, that an oman is a confederation of towns'.[16] This dictum would certainly be recognised as valid in Ahafo. Political relationships which, notably in the case of Ahafo, do not necessarily parallel the residual rights in land, form a pattern of allegiances and responsibilities in which relationships laterally among structural equals are expressed ideally in terms of affiliation to a common overlord. There is a theme of confederation running through the hierarchy which apparently provides scope for a continual re-evaluation of constituent political relationships. If the concept oman is expressive of the discreteness of political units, the much-used term *kroye*, usually translated as 'unity', is expressive of their integrity. The political process in Ahafo, if not among the Akan people generally, involves balancing the two, seeking communal goals within the context of a wider community of interests. This process is expressed differently in political interaction at different levels, but may be identified as clearly within the village community as within the state itself. The community consists mainly of a set of segments, each led by a senior man, united by economic and territorial interests of the kind already described, and acknowledging the superior authority of a headman or chief. The fundamental importance of the principle of matrilineal descent in Akan social organisation has been clearly established by anthropologists; this holds good to a very large extent in Ahafo in spite of its demographic heterogeneity and the fact that it lacks the lengthy heritage of the more established parts of Ashanti. It is maintained that community leadership is vested in the matrilineal descendants of the person or family group of original settlers. Many of the histories which are told to validate current alignments trace the political core of the community to a brother and sister, that is, the founder of the community and the woman who provided his heirs. However, the histories also acknowledge that rules of exogamy imply the presence in the community of members of other lineages from the outset. Lineage segments in which senior elderships are now vested are often traced back to the wife of a founding ancestor. A former chief of Noberkaw explained:

'In Ashanti here when a village is founded it is usually governed by two sections or families. The first one is the *odikro* [headman] ... and the second one is the *Krontihene* [chief counsellor] ... The family of that Krontihene may be the family of the wife to the chief, who came with him and formed the place or the village. Or the Krontihene may be of the family of the man who came next to the chief ... But in most cases it is mainly depending on the wife of that chief that a Krontihene is found. In the case of Noberkaw ... the family of that Krontihene was a wife to Noberkawhene. This woman was called Nana Kwama and the first man was Nana Acquah. It was this Nana Acquah who married Nana Kwama and brought her to settle at Noberkaw.'[17]

In spite of the dominance of the matrilineal principle it is interesting to note that in Mim and Sienchem accession to chiefship passes from father to son. A few aman in Ashanti follow this rule, notably Bantama, and Mimhene argued that this was primarily attributable to their military origins. Stationed in their frontier posts in the forest, away from their matrifamilies, they had little alternative but to pass the leadership on to their own sons. However, political establishment is not a strictly male prerogative; we have already noted the importance of wives and sisters, but the distant town of Pomakrom is an example of a community founded and led by a woman.[18] Cardinall describes in vivid terms his meeting with this lady, Poma:

That evening Poma told me how her village had come to arise. She had accompanied an Ashanti expedition against some of the Ivory Coast tribes, and on their return had obtained leave to settle on the Bia. It obviously was good hunting country, both for meat and snails, and the river afforded the opportunity of plenty of fishing. One companion a female, remained with Poma; and some young men had cleared a little farmland and had built a hut for them, before leaving the two behind.
Poma's real reason for stopping I could not learn. However, she was determined to found a village, and with this in view made the rule that no man should marry either of them or any other girl who might join them; that men could stop only a while in the village, and would have no rights at all over any children born as a result of the inevitable intercourse between them and the village women ... Her scheme succeeded, and I believe there were some two hundred inhabitants in the village when I visited it.[19]

The chiefship was apparently vested in her son and has since passed matrilineally to male holders. Pafu, a small community on the west bank of the Tano near Sankore, is the only village with a female head in contemporary Ahafo.

It is some time before a new community acquires the political dignity of a stool (*nkonnua*), and the cognate title of chief (*ohene*) for its headman. Until then the settlers depend on the patronage of a parent community and on supernatural protection. As Ayumsohene put it: 'formerly the fetishes were the chiefs of Ahafo'. In Ahafo the stool, symbol of both the territory and the political heritage of the community, is commonly reckoned to have been 'carried in' from the parent community. No standard political significance can be attached to this act, for in some cases it is taken to represent dissociation and in others affiliation. There is an apparent illogicality in the establishment of the first legitimate stool. The coherence of the political community and the individual's claim to office are held to depend on the existence of the ceremonially blackened stool of at least one ancestral predecessor. Implicitly, the establishment of the stool involves the recognition of a 'chief' who never reigned. The rationale for this is that the stool is an offshoot of a pre-existing parent community and that ultimately the greatest stool of all – the golden stool of the Ashantis – was brought down from heaven. With the death of each chief the oman accumulates a collection of ceremonial blackened stools which were once the personal property of their incumbents; '*the*' stool is reckoned to be the stool of the chief with the highest reputation, not necessarily the founder, and may be referred to by his personal name. Thus one may be told: '*ne din kaa akonnua no ho*' – 'his name remained on the stool'; Kukuom is described as 'Attechi's stool', Mim as 'Ntokor's'. Each new chief is ceremonially lifted onto this stool – without actually touching it – by his senior elders, a ritual which very clearly expresses their sanctioning and supporting role. This also implies that the original establishment of the oman depended not only on the superior political authority of the parent community but also on the concurrence of the elders of the other co-resident families. One Goaso elder described a historical episode in which the first chief was challenged on the banks of the Goa river as he was carrying in the stool which was to symbolise his office; the other elders gathered round and after some discussion gave their consent to its installation. Such are the sentiments of 'confederation' associated with Akan political communities.

The implication is that the stool which is 'carried in' must be the blackened stool of an ancestor of the first officeholder. This means that a family stool is taken out of the parent community, ideally on the sanction of the chief and elders of that community, in order that the new oman may be set up. At the same time the pattern of succession is firmly instituted and the political bond with the parent community asserted. The headman, *odikro*, is now designated chief, *ohene*. In reality, the bond with the parent community may not be recognised – such is the stuff of politics. A family decamping from the parent community, dissociating itself after some political struggle, is reckoned to have carried its ancestral stools with it and used them, unilaterally as it were, to set up an independent oman. This is the basis of Kukuomhene's claims to legitimacy.

Although an odikro is advised by the senior men of the community, an ohene is expected to have a formally constituted council of stool elders. Elderships, in order of superiority, are commonly assumed to have been vested in the families of settlers who followed the founder into the community. According to the model of Ashanti political organisation described by Busia,[20] all citizens were represented on the Stool Council by their family elder. It is doubtful whether this applies to Ahafo even as an ideal; certainly in many stools there are families without such representation and stool councillors who hold briefs for no particular lineage. It is difficult to generalise about the structure of the politico-familial units which supposedly comprise the stool community. Very few Ahafo chiefs described the groups comprising their communities as *abusua*, families; Kwaku-Nyumahene, for example, discussing the three segments of his town from which elders were selected, used the word *akuo*, which could be translated as 'associations'. Their variable composition is doubtless attributable to the vagaries of lineal growth, the absorption of 'strangers' over time, and accommodation to particular local circumstances. Formerly in the Akan states – certainly not today – lineage ranks could be increased by the incorporation of people of slave stock. The extent of such incorporation is almost impossible to establish because of the impropriety of discussing such origins. Although it is probable that political segments in smaller communities are simple minor matri-lineages, it is clear that in larger towns the abusua may be an aggregate of immigrant groups united by fictional kinship ties. Very occasionally one of the eight major Akan matriclans (*nton*) constitutes the basis for such a grouping; thus members of the Aduana clan are represented on the Kwapong Stool Council by their elder, called the Aduanahene. It seems more common, however, for a family segment to take the name of its community of origin, real or supposed; the two principal family units in Goaso are called Boadi (the name of a small town near Kumasi) and Nkoranza.

However it may be composed, this politico-familial unit is an important focus for loyalties within the community, even if it does not form a territorially compact unit. It is composed of the separate extended families, each with its own head, living together in the various courtyard houses. Its focal point is the house of the elder of the segment, where the heads of the various domestic units meet, just as the chief's house is the focal point of the community at large. The unitary political importance of the household is no less for the stranger families. No community in Ahafo consists exclusively of incorporated family segments. Although citizenship is a distinct and valued status, the stranger (*ohoho*) is regarded as essential to the organisation and growth of the town. As Kukuomhene observed, 'not all the people who establish a town come at the same time'.

One may detect a series of basic political identities for the Ahafo citizen which reflect the different levels of his incorporation within the community. There is his immediate family, cloistered in its courtyard house. There is the wider community segment, a group of households represented by an elder on the chief's council. There is the very clearly demarcated unit of the town itself, led by a headman or chief, and beyond that there is the aggregation of dependent communities within the limits of the stool. It seems important to draw attention at this point to the danger of dismissing these identities as 'traditional' in the sense that they are no longer relevant. They reflect geographical, economic, architectural and other features which are as 'contemporary' as the modern administrative and party political identities which we shall introduce shortly.

Today the government recognises twenty-eight of the Ahafo communities as stools, officially (if temporarily) co-equal. It regards them as severally responsible for all the smaller communities and as in aggregate co-extensive with the current territorial limits of the Goaso Administrative District. The precise nature of these political allegiances and the limits of territorial sovereignty are unspecified. The recognition of the twenty-eight stools is a government interpretation of precedent based on an accumulation of documentary evidence. The lack of clear structural continuity in the political interrelationships of the Ahafo communities has been a source of embarrassment to colonial and postcolonial governments alike. Compared with the more orthodox Ashanti states, they have found Ahafo as a political entity a parvenu and ill-organised affair. For their part the Ahafo chiefs would acknowledge the normative inadequacy of their interrelationships, but would argue that if theirs is not a state in the proper sense of the word it is a state in the making. The point at issue among them is the constitutional shape of such a state. In the meantime the government has been obliged to classify, in something approaching a conventional Akan idiom, the most eminent of the Ahafo communities in a manner both politically uncontentious and administratively expedient. To the chiefs themselves this appears as something of an imposed truce but in a broader perspective nothing more than a stage in a protracted political process.

Table 1, based on several government documents, is indicative of earlier stages in this process of political growth. Column A, the twelve signatories of the Treaty of Friendship and Protection with the British, may not be a complete list of the politically eminent communities of the time, but is the best available indication of early political interrelationships. These twelve communities are clustered round the centre of Ahafo, supposedly the focus of original settlement. On the document they appear collectively as components of 'Asunafo Ahafo', and it is notable that no community in the area currently described as Asutifi is represented. It is probable that Asutifi was only sparsely populated at this time, and developed some twenty years later when cocoa became established as a cash crop. Certainly, communities in this area feature prominently in the 1932 list (column B). Later lists follow the expansion of cocoa cultivation and the development of timber company roads into the north west, and although they are not yet recognised formally as stools the villages listed at the foot of column E are very much involved in the process of aggrandisement. It is notable that the headman of Bediakokrom, for example, is referred to in many recent official documents as '*ohene*', chief.

The central position of Kukuom (1959 population 2,876)[21] in the earlier-established part of Ahafo is reckoned to have a direct bearing on its acquisition of the paramount chiefship at the end of the last century. Kukuom was a convenient meeting point for the Ahafo communities when they decided to resist the Kumasi demands for tribute. In spite of its earlier prominence, Kukuom did not develop, either as a settlement nucleus or in terms of its dependent villages, as rapidly as many other communities in Ahafo – particularly its old rival Mim (population 6,805). The prosperity of Mim has been enhanced by the location in the town of a large European-operated timber company. In contrast to Kukuom, the town itself has expanded into a substantial network of streets and, of perhaps greater political significance, it has become the gateway to the settlement of the densely forested north west. Noberkaw (832) has a long history of alliance with Mim, expressed in their statuses as respectively the left- and right-wing chiefs of the former Ahafo state. Noberkaw is typical of the older towns in central Ahafo which have not shown such a marked response to the cocoa boom as the other, more recently established communities. The town sprawls untidily and it is recognised that its poorer sandy soils are less fertile than other parts of the district. Sienchem (513) also shows very modest growth economically and demographically, mainly because it has been by-passed by the modern lines of communication into Ahafo; its political decline in recent decades is a source of great frustration to its chief. The other older communities which earlier enjoyed political eminence have also had to struggle to sustain relative political growth: Dadiesoaba and Mehame, near-neighbours on the banks of the Tano river; Dantano (798) which, although small, has considerable stature as the principal political satellite of Kukuom; Anwiam, another small and somewhat isolated community to the south on the banks of the Tano; Fawohoyeden and Kwapong, former hunting camps thrusting out into the forest to the west.

The political eminence of Goaso is largely attributable to its pivotal position

25

TABLE I *Political growth in Ahafo*	*Signatories of 1896 Treaty of Friendship and Protection*	*List of Ahafo villages, prepared by D.C. at Goaso, 1932*	*List of Ahafo villages, Ahafo District Record Book, 1937*
	A	B	C
	Kukuom	Kukuom	Kukuom
	Mim	Mim	Mim
	Noberkaw	Noberkaw	Noberkaw
	Akrodie	Akrodie	Akrodie
	Sienchem	Sienchem	Sienchem
	Dadiesoaba	Dadiesoaba	Dadiesoaba
	Kwapong	Kwapong	Kwapong
	Mehame	Mehame	Mehame
	Goaso	Goaso	Goaso
	Fawohoyeden	Fawohoyeden	
	Anwiam	Anwiam	Anwiam
	Dantano	Dantano	Dantano
		Sankore	Sankore
		Acherensua	Acherensua
		Kenyase I	Kenyase I
		Kenyase II	Kenyase II
		Ayumso	Ayumso
		Ntotroso	Ntotroso
		Nkasaim	Nkasaim
		Hwidiem	Hwidiem
		Wamahinso	Wamahinso
		Aboum	Aboum
		Asufufuo	Asufufuo
		Etwineto	Etwineto
		Gyedu	Gyedu
		Kwakunyuma	Kwakunyuma
		Pomakrom	Pomakrom
		Siena	Siena
		Sawereso	Sawereso
			Tipokrom
			Bediakokrom
			Biaso
			Mim Mohu
			Kenyase Mohu

Sources

Column A: Treaty of Friendship and Protection made at Kukuom, 2 May 1896, copy in the possession of Kukuomhene.

Column B: List of Ahafo villages, appended to letter from D.C. Sunyani to Chief Commissioner Kumasi, dated 11 Sept. 1932, GNA, file D.103.

Column C: List of Ahafo villages, Ahafo District Record Book, vol II (1927–51), GNA, ADM 49/5/7.

Column D: From Native Courts (Ashanti) Establishment Order n. 8, 1953 (LN 448/53), detailing members of the panel for the Ahafo Native Court.

Column E: Membership list, Kukuom–Ahafo State Council, Goaso District Office, File L.52, dated 17 July 1958.

Column F: As above.

Column G: List supplied by the District Administrative Officer, Goaso, April 1968.

Native Court Panel Members in 1953	*List of towns and villages represented in the Kukuom (Ahafo) State Council, 1958*	*Wing chiefs (Gd.C. chiefs) in Kukuom (Ahafo) State Council*	*Towns recognised by the government as stools today*
D	E	F	G
Kukuom	Kukuom	Kukuom	Kukuom
Mim	Mim	Mim	Mim
Noberkaw	Noberkaw	Noberkaw	Noberkaw
Akrodie	Akrodie	Akrodie	Akrodie
Sienchem	Sienchem		Sienchem
Dadiesoaba	Dadiesoaba		Dadiesoaba
Kwapong	Kwapong		Kwapong
Mehame	Mehame		Mehame
Goaso	Goaso		Goaso
Fawohoyeden	Fawohoyeden		Fawohoyeden
	Anwiam		Anwiam
	Dantano	Dantano	Dantano
Sankore	Sankore	Sankore	Sankore
Acherensua	Acherensua	Acherensua	Acherensua
Kenyase I	Kenyase I	Kenyase I	Kenyase I
Kenyase II	Kenyase II	Kenyase II	Kenyase II
Ayumso	Ayumso		Ayumso
	Ntotroso	Ntotroso	Ntotroso
Nkasaim	Nkasaim		Nkasaim
Hwidiem	Hwidiem		Hwidiem
Wamahinso	Wamahinso		Wamahinso
	Aboum		Aboum
	Asufufuo		Asufufuo
Etwineto	Etwineto		Etwineto
	Gyedu		Gyedu
	Kwakunyuma		Kwakunyuma
	Pomakrom		Pomakrom
	Siena		Siena
	Tipokrom		
	Bediakokrom		
	Biaso		
	Mim Mohu		
	Kenyase Mohu		
	Gambia I		
	Gambia II		

between Mim and Kukuom. The colonial government's decision to establish itself mid-way between these two rivals has greatly enhanced the material and political growth of Goaso, and has given it a reputation as the node for the diffusion of modern influences into Ahafo – much to the irritation of such neighbours as Ayumso. Goaso (population 3,454) is now 'the D.C.'s town', headquarters of the administration and all the principal government departments. The colonial government was primarily responsible for moving Goaso earlier this century from its original site on the steep hill overlooking the Goa river to a new location several hundred yards away on the gentler southern slopes of the spur. Today the main road into Ahafo broadens out into a wide metalled main street, characteristic of all southern Ghanaian towns with a modicum of civic pride. The 'New Town', predominantly the home of the Goaso natives, stretches up the hill in a grid of neatly planned streets towards the government offices and bungalows and the spacious grounds of the clinic. The chief and the Goaso elders nearly all live in this area sometimes described as 'Ashanti New Town' to distinguish it from the *zongo*, or stranger-quarter, which extends south from the main road down the hill into the valley. The zongo buildings are not much less substantial or well-tended than those in the 'New Town', nor is it exclusively inhabited by 'strangers'. By all accounts the most substantial and gracious two-storey house in town, the residence of one of Goaso's most eminent citizens, is technically in part of the zongo. In the zongo proper, many of the disadvantages of location such as proximity to the town refuse and night-soil facilities are offset by such conveniences as easy access to the 'Henderson Box' water supply. The market and lorry-park, foci of daily activity in the town, are both adjacent to the zongo. Many shops line the main street, ranging from branches of the principal banks and a well-stocked stationer and newsagent to the palmwine booths characteristic of the very smallest villages. The west end of the town, where the main road branches to Mim, Ayumso and Kukuom, is dominated by the local council headquarters, a complex of buildings including the magistrate's court, staff bungalows, offices, storerooms and the council hall itself. However important it may be as the seat of government in Ahafo Goaso, like any other town in the district, is essentially a community of farmers. Early each morning large numbers of people may be found making their way out to the farms which surround the town. Some claim to travel out as much as ten miles, usually to a small camp or outlying village. It is an interesting reflection on the matrimonial habits of the Akan that the next most common reason Goaso citizens give for regular travel is commuting between the residences of husband and wife. Like most Ahafo towns Goaso has many drinking places, and it also boasts a wide range of churches, mosques and other places of worship.

Sankore (population 1,970) is something of an oddity among the Ahafo communities. Dominating the south of Ahafo it has many connections with Sefwi in Western Region, nevertheless it is as insistently part of Ahafo as are two other outlying communities to the west, Pomakrom (342) and the rapidly growing town of Aboum (842). In the north east, the growth of Acherensua (2,010) has undoubtedly been favoured by its location on the main road into Ahafo and the relatively easy access this affords to both Sunyani and Kumasi. Although it can boast the only secondary school in the district, its neighbour Hwidiem (2,920) has the only hospital plus bank agencies and other important facilities such as a police post. Hwidiem's aspirations to leadership among the Asutifi group of towns is strenuously challenged by Kenyase I which, for its part, can boast the Local Council headquarters. Separated only by a small stream, Kenyase I (2,169) and Kenyase II (3,374) have a history of persistent rivalry, the precedence of the former being challenged quite effectively by the more rapid growth and prosperity of the latter. Ntotroso (2,920) is another would-be leader of Asutifi which has flourished with the expansion of cocoa into the district. Its smaller close-neighbour Gyedu is politically unusual in that although it is recognised as an independent stool by the government, it is so effectively dominated by Ntotroso that its chief today admits subordination to Ntotrosohene. The northernmost Ahafo town Wamahinso stoutly disavows any such claims; well known as a base for Kumasi farmers operating in the district, it has a strikingly neat and affluent appearance, with generously metalled roads and elegant buildings. Nkasaim (2,208) is an older town whose equivocation about its Asutifi or Asunafo identity, particularly apropos of Local Council membership, reflects the imprecise nature of this distinction. Its growth has undoubtedly been sustained by its proximity to the main road, an advantage denied to the smaller isolated villages of the central area, Etwineto, Siena, Kwakunyuma, Asufufuo.

Of the many hundred communities not currently reckoned as stools, there is a sharp distinction between the permanent, rapidly expanding towns characteristic of the north west and the small camps scattered throughout the district. A further distinction must be made between communities with a strong native or permanently resident core, and those which primarily consist of temporary accommodation for the impermanent 'stranger-farmers'. Dechem, some four miles south of Goaso of which it is a subject village, is of the former kind, its substantial tin-roofed courtyard houses arranged in small streets to one side of the main road to Kukuom. In contrast Asuadei, set back from the main road to Mim some three miles north of Goaso, is a sprawl of mainly thatched, temporary dwellings; its status as a subject village of Mim or Goaso is equivocal and there is uncertainty as to whether its headman can be regarded as a citizen of Ahafo. The headman of Dechem, who likes to call himself chief – 'Dechemhene', would be indignant if his 'town' were described as a 'camp'. Although small, Dechem has a definite identity of its own and ideals of aggrandisement which have involved it in direct political confrontation with Goaso on several occasions.

Among the established, politically eminent communities there is a very keen awareness of a corporate Ahafo identity. The present regional and district boundaries certainly express this, and are, reciprocally, regarded as definitive of the political integrity of Ahafo by its citizens. Certainly, there are chiefs in Ahafo who reckon that land further to the east should be included within the district, just as there are chiefs within Ashanti who claim tracts of Ahafo. There is likewise equivocation about the inclusion of communities to the north and there have also been doubts about the border to the south east, partly attributable to the importance in that area of southern and easterly lines of communication to Wiawso and the important mining town of Bibiani. Nevertheless the Ahafo identity remains quite strong among the villages there, expressed for example in the insistence of communities on the eastern bank of the Tano that they belonged to the district and should be included within the Kukuom Local Council area, rather than a more accessible council area outside Ahafo.

In the eyes of the government the integrity of Ahafo is recognised in the form of the 'Goaso Administrative District' whose boundaries also serve as a Regional Planning Area, a Local Authority District and an organisational unit for most ministries, government agencies and national voluntary associations. It is officially recognised as a distinct 'Traditional Area' for purposes of administering chiefship. Although from a local point of view Ahafo is essentially a loosely bonded group of developing communities, its people have come to regard these official boundaries as definitive of territorial limits in a wide range of economic and political contingencies. The government's demarcation of boundaries around and within Ahafo has changed often enough to confuse the most informed citizen. The independent state of 'Asunafo–Ahafo' was the first unit to be given formal recognition by the colonial authorities, with Kukuom, Mim and Noberkaw as the three component Divisions. The Goaso Administrative District has been in existence (with the exception of the First World War years) since 1914, but its limits were not defined with any precision until 1959.[22] The Regional Office to which the Ahafo District Commissioner has been responsible has shifted from Kumasi to Sunyani twice. The wider administrative district of Kumasi West became, with the local government reform of 1952, the District Council area to which Ahafo belonged, and Ahafo itself became a Local Council area divided into twelve wards. In spite of a national drive to rationalise and cut down the number of Ghanaian local authorities, pressures of population warranted the division of the Ahafo Local Council area into the Asutifi and Asunafo Council areas (1962), and then the division of Asunafo into Goaso and

Kukuom areas (1965). The definition of local authority areas and the de-marcation of ward boundaries placed the Ahafo communities in a changing framework of political units. Many petitioned vigorously for or against their inclusion in a particular unit; in 1966 Akrodiehene successfully pressed for the transfer of his community to the Goaso Council area. The first parlia-mentary constituency followed the Kumasi West District limits with the exclusion of the Atwima Council area. The south east corner of Ahafo on the east bank of the Tano was included in the Atwima/Nwabiagya constitu-ency, but in 1964 was reincorporated in the Asunafo constituency which, together with the new Asutifi constituency, followed the then Local Council boundaries in Ahafo.

In 1959 Ahafo was included in the new Brong–Ahafo Region, an area which had previously constituted more than half of Ashanti Region. The external political orientation of Ahafo, whether it should be part of Ashanti or an independent unit in the association of Brong states, has added a new dimension to the schism of interest among the 28 Ahafo chiefs. The pro-Ashanti faction would deny very strongly that the Brong–Ahafo connection is anything more than a political convenience for their rivals: 'Previously there was nothing like Brong–Ahafo. If we said Ahafo we meant Ahafo, if we said Brong, that was Brong' (Gyeduhene); 'Ahafo is within Ashanti, not within Brong at all' (Kenyase II hene). Such points of view do not deny the unity of Ahafo. Even Mimhene, the most staunchly pro-Kumasi chief, went so far as to suggest that Ahafo, with its boundaries widened eastwards into Ashanti and northwards into Brong, could be a viable region in its own right. Here, however, we may see traces of the confusion between the boundaries of traditional political units and modern administrative units, a subject to which we shall return shortly.

The importance of the Ahafo identity appeared frequently in interviews and discussions. Citizens would say without equivocation 'I am an Ahafo'. In spite of his pro-Ashanti orientations, Fawohoyedenhene could explain: 'When the people of Kumasi come here they are called strangers. But if an Ahafo man meets an Ahafo man here, they are not strangers.' These senti-ments were in fact embodied in the constitution of the Ahafo state. A State Council resolution of 1961 noted that an Ahafo citizen was so regardless of his movement from stool to stool, and therefore could never be taxed as a stranger within the district.[23] The solidarity of Ahafo has also been expressed in terms of contraposition to adjacent peoples. Stools around the Ahafo periphery have, at various times, struggled against the predations of neigh-bouring states, for example Mim against Wam in the north, and Kukuom against Nkawie in the east.

In spite of their political preferences most Ahafos feel closer affinity to Ashanti than to Brong. Many emphasised the linguistic connection: 'I won't

Dependence and opportunity

join [the Brongs] because I am an Ashanti-speaking man. They are quite different people, they are Brongs. We have a boundary between Brong and Ahafo . . . I can't join them because I am a different man' (Mimhene). Others remarked on the economic and geographical importance of Kumasi to Ahafo: 'Kumasi is the centre of the country, if you need anything you have to go there' (Ayumsohene). The nature of the Ahafo identity was expressed in these terms by Mr S. K. Opoku, a former C.P.P. Member of Parliament in Ahafo:

'My tribe is Ashanti, for Ahafo is not a tribe. We all travelled here from Kumasi. But I would say I am an Ahafo. By tribe we are Ashantis, but in administration, even since the colonial days when the Assistant Commissioner was in Sunyani, all administrative matters were taken to Sunyani . . . For administrative purposes we are more closely related to Sunyani than Ashanti.'

Sunyani is significant only as a regional administrative centre, a base for the circuit court, the Regional Officer and the police; as Goasohene observed: 'I don't go to Sunyani unless I have trouble.' Although the Ahafos were anxious to distinguish themselves from the Ashantis they would readily realign their identity with the Ashantis when confronted by other, more alien peoples. The tenor of this may best be conveyed by an extract from a conversation with Gyeduhene:

'When someone comes from Teppa, ten miles away, in Ashanti to meet me, I know him as a stranger. I also know the person from Upper Volta as a stranger because he has not been here for a long time. But if you stay in the town for a long time you are included among the townspeople.'
Q. 'Would you treat the stranger from Teppa, and one from Bolgatanga [Upper Region] the same?'
A. 'I know the man from Teppa as an Ashanti, and so I will deal with him differently than the person from the north. I will welcome them both, but the things I discuss with my fellow tribesman will be different from the things I discuss with the Upper Volta man. I know that when I am in trouble the Teppa man, as an Ashanti, will never run off and abandon me. But the Upper Volta man, when there is trouble, can even tell the troublemakers how to get at me.'

In interpreting the way in which local people are aware of an Ahafo identity, it is important to remember that boundaries in a circumferential, linear sense still do not have great meaning. Consensus about these territorial limits is certainly secondary to the notion of unity among the various component communities. Nevertheless, the need to define the corporate identity of Ahafo in precise cartographic terms has increased as the economic interest in land has changed, as population has increased, and as the region as a whole has been subdivided for various administrative purposes. Boundary issues have always been about small peripheral communities and the nature of their

32

political affiliation. This may be taken to include modern interrelationships about which there is ostensibly nothing 'traditional', as a complaint raised by Sankorehene in 1964 suggests. Co-operative societies in two villages subject to Sankore had been grouped, for administrative convenience, with the Sefwi–Wiawso district branch of the United Ghana Farmers Co-operative Council in Western Region. Sankorehene observed: 'Undisputably, Farmers Council deliberations are not the concern of chiefs, yet much as traditional boundaries are concerned, I feel it is incumbent upon me to clarify a point which seems to offset routine principles.' He felt this was the thin end of the wedge and that 'I shall only have myself to blame when I may one day be told that those areas never fall within my area.'[24] At times the District Officers have been as assiduous as the chiefs in guaranteeing the district's marches. In 1965, for example, the Sunyani and Goaso District Commissioners exchanged indignant letters over what each regarded as the intrusion of the other into the village of Atronie, which appears to have been shuttled back and forth across the district boundary at least twice.[25] As disputes have arisen the administration has always seen the precise mapping of agreed boundaries as the only effective solution. The limits of Ahafo were set most precisely when the boundaries of the new Brong–Ahafo Region were defined in 1959. It was readily assumed in Ahafo that this administrative boundary also set the limits of the Ahafo paramountcy, although no such congruence was necessarily intended. The regional boundary has been used to consolidate land claims to the south against the 'intrusions' of Sefwi stools in the Western Region, to the north between Mim and the Brong stool of Wam and, most insistently, against the chief of Nkawie in Ashanti, whose tribute-collecting excursions on the east bank of the Tano have roused the Ahafo chiefs on a number of occasions. Dr A. A. Y. Kyerematen has discussed the bearing of administrative boundaries on land claims in some detail, citing a 1940 lawsuit involving Acherensua. The Asantehene's 'B' and 'A' courts both found that Sir Francis Fuller's demarcation of a boundary between Acherensua and Akwesiase did not constitute a land settlement, but on appeal the Chief Commissioner's Court (Ashanti) reversed the decision. The unsuccessful defendants had contended that Fuller's boundary was not a demarcation of private lands but 'an administrative boundary between two political groups known as the Ahafos and the Odumasis'.[26]

One may detect two broad, converging processes in the recent political development of Ahafo. On the one hand there is the growth of local communities and the consolidation of political relationships among them, within Ahafo and in the region at large. On the other hand there is the definition of political units on a national basis, a segmentation of Ghana for administrative and other purposes dating from the establishment of colonial overrule

33

and becoming progressively more intensive during this century. One might typify the former process as the growth of an Ahafo state, the latter as the development of Local Councils with their component wards, or the demarcation of parliamentary constituencies. It would be misleading to characterise either as exclusively 'traditional' or 'modern', nevertheless the two political processes are quite dissimilar. The local one may be seen to involve growth, both in terms of the aggrandisement of communities and the establishment of political associations of different orders – stools, divisions and states. Even political fission implies growth, two stools or divisions where one existed before. The national process essentially involves subdivision for administrative convenience or in the interests of democratic representation and is sometimes, but not always, congruent with pre-existing units. Local accounts of this usually commence: '. . . then the government split up Ahafo'. It is interesting to reflect that such a statement would be in effect a contradiction of the confederate principles of precolonial Akan political organisation where unity (*kroye*) was – and still remains – a cardinal political interest. One should also recall that the local process has been concerned with a pattern of relationships among communities, whereas the national units are territorial in intention, if not always in effect.

The convergence of these processes can help to explain the complexities of political action in present-day Ahafo. Why are the neat, democratic organisations of modern government so often misconstrued or subverted in the arena of local politics? It is apparent that they become engaged in competitions of local interest over which they can exert little control and which are beyond the expectations of their central government designers.

Today the Ahafos, particularly the younger and better educated, have a quite sophisticated awareness of their district in a wider geographical, ethnic and political context. Theirs is, after all, a cosmopolitan society and for all but the elderly, modern communications permit quite extensive participation in the affairs of the world at large. At the time of writing, about fifty pence will take oneself and one's baggage to Kumasi by minibus within three hours, and for an excursion to Accra one need only budget two or three pounds. The children of moderately successful cocoa farmers attend schools throughout southern Ghana and kola traders come and go between Ahafo and the far north. The inheritance customs of the patrilineal peoples north and south of the matrilineal Akan area are discussed with interested detachment. The affairs of the nation as a whole are followed keenly on transistor radios and in a town like Goaso 200 to 300 national English-language newspapers may be sold daily. There can be few Ahafos who lack an awareness of the geographical and political unity of Ghana, although familiarity with the name dates shortly before independence in 1957. The names of minority groups which comprise the peoples of southern Ghana are reeled off with ease, although peoples of the north may be described collectively as 'N.T.s' (Northern Territorials) and trans-Voltaic Ghanaians to the east as 'Ewes'. The extent to which Ghana is perceived in an international context is less clear, although disputes in which the nation becomes involved can evoke strong feelings of partisanship among ordinary folk. The identity of the Ivory Coast, whose frontier is a mere 40 miles from Goaso, seems imperfectly understood. In common parlance it is 'France', or 'French territory', which can make it difficult to distinguish, in conversation, from Upper Volta in the north.

No doubt in response to the influence of the mass media, the political parties and such bodies as the Centre for Civic Education, the national Ghanaian identity has great currency. It appears, for example, in the libations recited on formal occasions by the Ahafo chiefs: 'Ahafo is part of Ghana – long live us all!' (Kukuomhene). Accra is clearly identified as the political focus of the nation from which order and change emanate and the ultimate goal of local pleas and petitions. It is there that 'the Big Men sit' and the power (*tumi*) of government is concentrated. A major line of political communication is seen to extend from Goaso to Sunyani and to Accra, a pattern which could be said to reflect the 'parent community' theme of the traditional political order. The movement of messages depends on a 'patron' in each place, the Administrative Officers in Goaso and Sunyani and a Member of Parliament or government official in Accra. The pro-Ashanti chiefs would regard Kumasi as an alternative intermediate point of communication, with the authority of the Asantehene second only to that of the central government in Accra.

Interpretations of the meaning of 'government' – *aban* – is a recurring theme of this book. It may be helpful to outline some of these ideas now, as they emerge from discussion with the chiefs and people of Ahafo. Some caution is necessary because, since the advent of national party politics around the mid-1950s, people have been thoroughly catechised on the nature of government, democracy, national political participation, and the like. Direct questions – 'what is the government? what does it do for you?' – tend to elicit well-rehearsed responses: 'the government is the people . . . it makes rules for us . . . it buys our cocoa . . .' These responses are certainly illuminating, but insight into local values must also depend on allusions of a more conversational nature.

The subject of untiring discussion in Ahafo, the government is sometimes treated in very diffuse terms – 'every man is an arm of the government' – and on other occasions as if it were a single individual. Figuratively it may be 'our mother' (*ye obaatan*), or, more specifically, identified with the Head of State: '*Nkrumah aban*'; '*Kotoka Aban*' (the post-February 1966 government of the National Liberation Council). Apter[27] and others have discussed

35

in detail this personalised view of political power, notably in the case of Nkrumah, and its apparent relationship with the traditional role of the chief. Between the populist and autocratic extremes, however, there are other interpretations which see the limits of government as the hierarchy of modern institutions extending to the Local Councils and occasionally to the Town Development Committees or, more narrowly, as confined to the ministries and other central bodies in Accra. The contingency of these interpretations and the fact that such roles as the District Officer should appear to elude clear definition are undoubtedly expressions of the political changes of recent decades.

If *aban* is essentially the central government, closely associated with Accra, its lower echelons and agents in the rural areas are seen in a more ambiguous light. However, chiefship and traditional institutions generally would never be catagorised 'aban', because government in these terms is clearly perceived as an innovation, a superstructure deriving from colonial overrule. Of the traditional era it is said: 'in those days we had no government' (Dadiesoabahene); 'in Ashanti the Asantehene looked after us . . . The whites came and showed us how to govern' (Hwidiemhene). One Goaso citizen summarised the present situation thus: 'the government is different from the stools' (*aban no nko wo nkonnua noho*). The distinction is often strongly asserted by the chiefs themselves: 'the government has no voice in chieftaincy affairs'. . . 'the chiefs have no voice in government affairs' (Fawohoyedenhene). However, it seems that this discontinuity is a normative view and other chiefs are aware of the reality of the government's superior authority over them. Sometimes it is even spoken of as a kind of 'super-chief' to be 'served' (*som*) as one might a traditional paramount: 'We serve the government through the Asantehene' (Asufufuohene).

For the chiefs and ordinary people alike, *aban* is beyond direct personal access. This may derive in part from the earlier image of an aloof and cloistered colonial government, enclosed within the walls of Cape Coast Castle as well as other forts in Kumasi and Accra. However, this segregation is no novelty in itself, for the use of intermediaries is a cardinal idiom of traditional Akan politics. No common man could hope to put his case personally before his paramount. Similarly the government today can not be approached directly but requires the services of an intermediary or a carefully prepared and channelled written petition. Perhaps it is his role as mediator in processes of communication which makes for the ambiguous view of the District Officer as being both part of, but apart from *aban*. However extrinsic and intangible the government may be in popular perception it is not reckoned to be divine. Although he may elicit respect, the District Officer is no priest. Although government is profane and discussed with little awe it has, in the political realm, ultimate power (*tumi*), an attribute recognised even by those expressing populist sentiments: 'the government is here to serve us . . . the government means we have representatives, you report to the representative if someone is annoying you . . . What I am saying is that I fear[28] the government, but at the same time I am part of the government' (Dantanohene). Conversational references to this aspect of government are frequent: 'power is in the government's hands', 'everything belongs to government' or – more realistically – 'the government has the power because it has the soldiers and police. They can do anything without raising a protest. Nothing is impossible to the government. . .' (Dadiesoabahene). Power is not exclusive to *aban*, for even a village chief has a modicum of 'tumi'; it seems that its hierarchic properties are recognised, and indeed one Ashanti loyalist in Ahafo observed that the government had undoubtedly more power than the Asantehene and marginally less power than God.

These properties doubtless derive in large measure from the early military associations of colonial government. Members of the older generation in particular make reference to the civilising and peace-keeping role of government: 'the government bring peace to us. If there is a battle somewhere the police will be called on to settle it. If someone takes his cutlass and kills his neighbour he is charged and then killed. This is how they help us.' In a mildly paternalistic way, government is held to 'look after us all here'. Younger and more educated generations have a more detailed understanding of the organisation and functions of government. Those who read newspapers and have participated in party politics speak quite knowledgeably about parliamentary representation, ministerial responsibilities or the role of President. In general, however, the duties (*adwuma*) of government are interpreted mainly in terms of the satisfaction of personal and local needs, criticism centring on its parsimony in this regard. 'The government has done nothing for us here' is something of a slogan in Ahafo, and local politicians of all persuasions have continually played on the theme that the colonial and subsequent governments have consistently neglected the district or particular communities within it. The lack of schools, hospitals, metalled roads and other facilities is set against the apparently large contribution of Ahafo's wealth to the national exchequer. In terms of personal needs the economic role of the government seems to be paramount: 'it buys our cocoa', says the farmer; 'it pays my salary and gives me a pension', say teachers, clerks and other civil servants, including immigrants from the north in relatively humble local authority employment.

Two further attitudes to government merit comment here. First, as much of the foregoing may have indicated, literacy and education are closely associated with the organisation and processes of *aban*. Speaking to anyone in a position of authority in Ahafo quickly conjures up an impression of the problems of dealing with the paperwork bureaucracy. Asufufuohene explained: 'When the government wants us to do anything it sends us a letter.' On our visits around the district, chiefs and others would seek our advice on the most effective way of communicating their needs to the government. With face-to-face confrontation with the government ruled out, transactions are essentially in writing. The petition is thus by far the most common means of political expression in Ghana today; the profusion of these documents, embellished with many signatures and thumb-prints, continues to assure a good living for the many local professional scribes. Petitions are usually channelled through the district and regional offices but in extreme cases personal participation will extend to escorting the envelope to Accra and assuring that it is placed in the hands of someone whose appearance is sufficiently imposing. There is a reciprocal flow of letters from the government, passing through the regional and district offices, often being rephrased in transit to increasee their immediacy and local relevance. General communications will be addressed to 'the chief and people' of the various communities and are read out and interpreted with varying degrees of accuracy at public meetings. In particular cases an individual may be summoned to the district office to have the contents of a letter explained to him.

It is now well known that legitimacy of a status or project is ultimately conferred by inscription in 'the government's books' (*aban nhoma*). Chiefs are aware that accession and deposition must be gazetted in Accra and that no political battle is won until the government has committed itself to paper. It seems that literacy must remain a central definition of any distinction which may be made between traditional and modern political values.

The other view of government which merits some comment here concerns several complex and at times equivocal interpretations of it as a place where issues are discussed (parliament) and to which local representatives (parliamentary members) are sent. Apart from those who have sophisticated knowledge of formal democratic processes, the Ahafos seem to regard their Member of Parliament primarily as a delegate and only then – if at all – as one who is engaged in national decision-making processes. His main value is that he may 'speak directly to the government', a frequent comment which again suggests the extrinsic view of *aban*. This may reflect the importance of the delegate or intermediary in traditional politics, one who is sent to a political centre to express the point of view or plead the case of the community. Certainly, the value of a representative is not assessed in terms of what he might contribute to debate, but in terms of the amenities he can extract from government for his people. Although in Ahafo experience of parliamentary democracy has been limited to little more than a decade the political potential of the M.P.'s role is quite clearly perceived, and in popular estimation the government's failure in the past to favour the development of the district is attributed at least in part to the inadequacy of local representatives. The loss of M.P.s during the period of military rule (1966-9) was lamented: 'At the moment we have no voice in Accra.'

Although the member is pre-eminently a delegate, parliament as a whole is certainly conceived of as a kind of decision-making body or council. A few saw this as the central function of *aban*: 'Government is when we come together, when one man says this and another man agrees.' If traditional political organisation in any way informs judgements of *aban*, then the idea of counsel and corporate decision making is no novelty. In practice, however, the discreteness of modern government and experience of its apparently arbitrary rule in both precolonial and postcolonial Ghana may have led people to feel that if discussion takes place at all it is contained within its own inscrutable walls. Again, the representatives themselves may understate the importance of debate in fulfilling their parliamentary role; explaining the government's failure to provide an amenity which has been requested an M.P. will tell his people: 'I have put your request to the government, but they have not agreed to build the school for us . . .'

The roles of the M.P. and the District Officer will be discussed in detail in later chapters, as will the political parties which have obviously had momentous implications for the relationship between the Ahafo people and their government. Of the parties, it may be sufficent to note here that of all institutions they have been least amenable to clear categorisation by ordinary folk, being ambiguously 'of the people' and 'of the government'. It has been said that the parties, notably the Convention People's Party, have served to centralise and nationalise local political interests and activities, but the extent to which they have also been a medium for parochial conflict and the polarisation of local political identities should not be underrated. Experience of party politics as an idiom of conflict at all levels has led many Ghanaians to regard them as 'dangerous'. After the 1966 coup d'état many in Accra and in the countryside were concerned to see party opposition contained within 'proper' bounds. Chiefs in particular were doubtful at the wisdom of committing themselves to one party (as they had done in the past). This was in part a reflection of the norm that the chief should be the moderator rather than the director of public opinion, and in part an acknowledgement that parties involved a contract between the (common) people and the government which should be of no concern to the chief.

The theme of political 'discovery', the encounter between the ideas, interests and leaders of Ahafo on the one hand and Ghana or the Gold Coast on the other, runs through this book. This process of mutual discovery, a product of economic growth and national political development, can not adequately be described in terms of simple local/national, traditional/modern dichotomies. As we shall see in due course, the old and the new cannot be sorted out into neat complementary or contraposed institutions, ideas and actions. Indeed, their confusion at various levels in Ahafo has multiplied rather than inhibited the opportunities for political action within the district. Uncertainty or equivocation about formal political structures may, however, lead to dilemma, widening the scope for political negotiation while at the same time obscuring the goals for political action. The case of Ahafo very clearly illustrates the danger of presupposing a stable 'traditional' base from which political 'modernisation' has proceeded. Political institutions are relatively short-lived, there is no long-standing heritage to defend. Vigorous political argument may be couched in conservative terms but in longer-established parts of Ashanti Ahafo is still regarded as parvenu. Only political goals in a broad sense remain fairly constant: individual and corporate advancement reckoned in terms of the economic and demographic growth of communities. An important feature of Ahafo politics is that the political structures, 'traditional' or 'modern', in terms of which this advancement is negotiated are in themselves imprecise and fluid. Whether it be the organisation of a State Council of chiefs or a Town Development Committee, political action is directed both towards the establishment of institutional norm and to the negotiation of individual status.

CHAPTER 3

ECONOMIC DEVELOPMENT OF AHAFO

a. COCOA

In 1910, the first year in which cocoa constituted the single most valuable export commodity of the Gold Coast,[1] the total tonnage of cocoa beans exported was some 23,000.[2] In the 1970/1 main crop season, production for the district of Goaso alone was some 35,400 tons.[3] The production of cocoa is by no means the only economic activity in Ahafo today which is dependent on the vagaries of the world market. But it is certainly the branch of commodity production which directly involves by far the largest proportion of the population and it has played the dominant role both in the growth of population and in the expansion of settlement which Ahafo has seen in the present century. If Ahafo was in origin, as Ashanti diplomacy still insists today, a sort of New Forest for the Asantehene, a vast *chasse gardée* for the provision of game to Kumasi, the forest has largely been transformed over the last half century (at least outside the forest reserves and to some degree even inside them) by the advent of a highly specialised agriculture. As early as 1916, the money supply required in Ashanti as a whole was assumed by the administration to be a direct function of the size of the cocoa crop. The volume of specie allocated to banks in Kumasi through the West African Currency Board was based on the Chief Commissioner of Ashanti's estimate of cocoa crop prospects for the year.[4] Even today the most important regular political decision taken by the national government, as far as the vast majority of the Ahafo population is concerned, is the fixing of the producer price of cocoa. Because the State Cocoa Marketing Board is a government monopsony, it is in a position to set a virtually absolute ceiling on the gains which Ahafo can make from its major product, irrespective of the price which this would secure upon the world market. The only effective impediment to this control is the transporting of cocoa across the border to the former French territory of the Ivory Coast, an idea extensively canvassed by the administration in the years before the present road network was established,[5] but one which is now illegal. Producer prices are fixed in the Ivory Coast too; but they have for some time been fixed, because of a guaranteed access to a protected European market, at a substantially higher figure than in Ghana. The illegality of cocoa smuggling is reflected in the

41

Dependence and opportunity

setting-up of a number of police barriers on roads leading towards the Ivory Coast border, not in themselves perhaps impassable barriers to the smuggler but significant elements in the costing of the enterprise. Since cocoa is a bulk crop and one in the case of which transport costs form a large part of the total cost of production, the difference between Ghanaian and Ivory Coast prices precludes head-loading the crop over great distances. Smuggling over the border (a continuation of trading by another name) has been a consistent practice of the Wams and Ahafos ever since the conquest of Ashanti.[6] But, in the case of cocoa, factor costs and transport conditions conspire to favour a considerable degree of control over the surplus generated in Ahafo's most valuable production by the government and its servants, whether in their public or their private capacities. The coming of cocoa has peopled the forest and made Ahafo rich but it has also made Ahafo very dependent, at first directly, but later more mediately on the vagaries of the world commodity market, and very directly indeed on the colonial government of the Gold Coast and later on the national government of Ghana and on their respective servants. In the old days the Ahafo may have been subjects of the Ashanti Golden Stool; but it was a suzerainty which can seldom have lain heavily on most of them, an etiolated legal fact in the wild expanse of the forest. When the Ahafos united under Atekyi to win their freedom, all that they needed to do at most was to defeat an Ashanti warband. Today they are wealthy and 'enlightened' to a degree that no one could have dreamed. But no latter-day Atekyi could make them independent now as they were made briefly then, whatever his success against more modern warbands. If modernity is to be measured by wealth and health and education and communications, by the transition from hunter-gathering and subsistence agriculture to agricultural commodity production, then it has been largely the coming of cocoa which has made Ahafo modern. But, in becoming modern, Ahafo has also become strikingly dependent on the national government.

Cocoa was brought to Ahafo by the colonial government – and brought in some haste – within a few years of the suppression of the Yaa Asantewa rising. But it was certainly not grown by the colonial government when it got there. Nor would it have been at all easy for the government to have ensured that it should be grown at all. Even if the British administrators had had the will to do so, they could hardly have established in a largely uninhabited forest a cocoa version of the 'Culture System' by which the Dutch compelled the teeming population of Java to grow their rice. It cannot even be claimed that the Ahafos were forced into commodity production, either as peasants or labourers, as many East African subjects of the British crown found themselves, by the imposition of governmental direct taxation. The Ahafos were wheedled into production for the market. They were not *driven* into it. Their entanglement with the world cocoa market was not a form of external violence done to them (as the military conquest of Ashanti might well be represented, even from the Ahafo point of view). It was, rather, the outcome of their own energetic action. Accordingly the medley of rational resentment and potentially paranoid suspicion which the recognition of their extended political dependence on the central government evokes among the Ahafos is in some respects accentuated by their own elaborate complicity in the process which established the dependence. Because cocoa has been the medium through which their dependence was established and because it is the focus of their present political discontents, they are denied the opportunity of escaping from these even in fantasy by a return to the distant and less dependent past. Having helped to forge their own chains the Ahafos cannot readily escape all responsibility for their dependency. The commitment to cocoa is a commitment to a future of greater welfare – of more comfortable dependence. It is not compatible, even in the most disordered imagination, with the abolition of dependence or with anarchy. Many in Ahafo, as in most other places, are at times nostalgic. But it would require an austere fanaticism, and one utterly alien to local temperaments, to be at all comprehensively reactionary. What is regretted politically today is not that a longed-for past has failed to return but that a desired future has yet to arrive.

The pattern of economic growth centred on the production of cocoa, while making Ahafo relatively rich and dependent, has certainly not created by itself any very effective tendencies to the diversification of production. Other products do emerge from Ahafo, one of them, timber, in very considerable volume and for massive economic return. But there is little linkage between the production of these and that of cocoa. On the London commodity market the cocoa produced in the Goaso district in a favourable year is worth many millions of pounds. But the only significant industrial unit in the whole of Ahafo still remains the Mim Timber Company's sawmills at Mim and the prospect of self-sustained economic growth seems infinitely distant. It is certainly correct to see the cocoa farmers of Ahafo, like those of the rest of Ghana, as Polly Hill has so graphically insisted,[7] as engaged in capitalist production. If the system of capitalist production on the world scale is aptly seen as a set of shackles, then it is undoubtedly the Ahafos who have riveted the chains upon themselves. The colonial government had little more in the way of a coherent scheme for the prospective economic development of Ashanti after the conquest than the Ashantis themselves may be presumed to have had. What ideas the colonial government did have centred on the driving of the railway through to Kumasi, the focus of a characteristic medley of concerns including the provision of a transport outlet for the Ashanti Goldfields mine at Obuasi.[8] The main products of Ashanti were seen as being kola and rubber, the former still traded by donkey caravans along the traditional northern trade routes to the Islamic savannah areas on the southern fringe of the Sahara[9] and the latter sufficiently valuable to be worth transporting by head-loading to Kumasi from the western forests.[10] Both kola and rubber grew wild in profusion in the western forests – only a quarter of the kola crop being picked in a year according to the administration's estimate in 1902.[11] Prospects for the profitable cultivation of cocoa, coffee and cotton were thought initially to exist only in the vicinity of rail or river transport.[12] If this view was held at all strictly, the prospects for Ahafo were not enticing. The railway at Kumasi was a considerable distance away and, although the possibility of using the Tano river to float timber was investigated with some care a few years later,[13] the basic impediments to navigation proved to be too various and substantial for anyone to consider it seriously as a possible avenue for the transport of cocoa. However, this careful scepticism was by no means universal within the administration. An undue emphasis upon it necessarily understates, for better or worse, the degree of administrative complicity in the coming of cocoa to Ahafo. The Commissioner for the Western District in 1904 had not merely made efforts to impress upon the chief of his area the prospective gains from the cultivation of cocoa – and done so in the teeth of considerable local scepticism, based firmly on a grasp of the comparative costing of gathering rubber.[14] He had also gone so far as to order the chiefs to clear land for demonstration cocoa farms and to plant these.[15] His plans were impeded by the unreliability of essential supplies from Kumasi. Urgent pleas, first made in October 1904, for the despatch of large quantities of cocoa seeds for the chiefs to plant had to be repeated in December and again two months later in February 1905, by which time a number of chiefs had actually completed the clearing of their farms.[16] In addition to supplying the seeds the Commissioner hoped to offer adequate technical advice to secure the success of the initial establishment of the chiefs' demonstration farms. His February request for an urgent despatch of the necessary seeds was accordingly accompanied by one for the provision of a book (or at the very least of some instructions) on cocoa planting and care.[17] In September 1905 the new Commissioner for the Western District was in a position to despatch two books of instructions of the required type to Mim through the hands of the Kukuomhene.[18] During a visit to Ahafo at the end of the preceding month the Commissioner had noted for the first time

a cocoa farm at Mim in which about 2,300 yearling trees were planted. They looked extremely healthy but were planted too close together. The owner of the farm is going to thin them and transplant ... There seems to be an opening for this industry. The Government might supply seeds at Kumasi free of charge and I will see if I can get two or three men to go to Aburi for scientific instruction in planting, pruning and the preparation of cocoa. The Government are always glad to take such men free of charge and give them assistance.[19]

But in January 1906 the same Commissioner took a far less sanguine view in his annual report:

Cocoa: farms were planted through the instrumentality of Capt. Pamplin Green at many places. The few I have seen were flourishing. Little as I would wish to minimize the importance of this industry, it is essential for its success that the first crop should be a financial success to their owners. From my experience in the Eastern Province of the Colony, the cost of transport will be too heavy for the industry to pay and the sale of the cocoa cannot be anything but a disappointment to the producer. I am informed the price of a carrier with rubber from Odumasi to Kumasi is 12/6. A charge like this where only 16/- is obtained for a load of cocoa would soon I fear cause the people to relinquish their efforts in planting. Moreover with further charges from Kumasi to the coast it is doubtful whether as much as 16/- a load would be paid by the merchant to the producer. In these circumstances I would suggest it is only in the country round Kumasi and in the immediate vicinity of the railway that we try at present to start the industry. I do not myself relish trying to encourage and bolster up the hopes of growers when it is apparent in these outlying districts the profit to them will be small, if any.[20]

The ambivalence of local administrative commitment to the expansion of cocoa planting which the juxtaposition of these two successive judgements shows persisted for several decades. One aspect of it was irreproachably disengaged and manipulative in concern. Colonies, once acquired, ought properly to be productive. Only in this way can they reliably pay even for the expenses of their own administration and policing, let alone furnish the handsome returns on invested energy and public capital which even the most altruistic colonisers are apt to take pleasure in, when these happen to be available. No system of production can continue to function over time within the framework of commercial capitalism unless it yields on balance a clear profit. On Commissioner Fell's calculations the costs of transport would guarantee that the production over most of the Western Province of Ashanti could not yield a profit at all – let alone one in which the returns on invested labour might be expected to equal those of rubber-gathering or even of snail-collecting. But there was always another dimension of potential uneasiness in the administrator's relationship with his charges besides this. When Fell observed that he did not 'relish' encouraging growers to expend their labours for clearly negative returns he was not simply expressing apprehension that there might be hell to pay when the growers found out. He was also asserting that he found it emotionally uncomfortable – because visibly morally unattractive – to lead his charges astray in this fashion. From the viewpoint of the Department of Agriculture in Accra or even of the Governor of the Colony the ups and downs of the world cocoa market could be viewed with long-term equanimity. But local administrators were obliged by their day-to-

Dependence and opportunity

day situation to take a more direct and individuated view of what these fluctuations meant to the lives of their charges. The realisation that cocoa prices did not cover the costs of production severely disrupted the local administrator's sense that his role was simply an extended exercise in doing his subject population a favour.

By January 1906, however, the introduction of cocoa to the people of Ahafo had already been performed and it was already too late for such anxious second thoughts about the prospects for the long, sometimes stormy, but still eminently viable marriage between the two. From this time on cocoa played an increasingly dominant role in the government's preoccupations with Ahafo. It was for most of the colonial period more of an incentive to co-operation between the two than it was a focus for conflict. But it was always a potential basis for conflict; and its association with the fluctuations of the world commodity market gave a persisting edginess to the activity of co-operation despite the extended interludes of massive local enrichment which resulted from it. In time, too, it brought to Ahafo not only elaborate economic differentiation, the creation of a large range of specialised economic roles, but also, through the control of land and the exploitation of peasant borrowing, complex new structures of class stratification and intricate new forms of clientage to accompany these and to form, in due course, effective new agencies of political mobilisation. In the year following Fell's report, a year in which the export of cocoa from Ashanti trebled,[21] cocoa seed was introduced on an even larger scale and the Chief Commissioner claimed that almost every village had its nursery.[22] In 1908 a 'Native Travelling Instructor' from the Department of Agriculture reported on the exceptional richness of the soil in Ahafo and Wam and the good prospects for cocoa and rubber cultivation there.[23] The next year saw the first serious argument for the establishment of a new administrative district with its headquarters in Ahafo, a proposal supported by emphasising the heavy planting of cocoa and the prospective prosperity of the area.[24] Several small cocoa farms in the forest were described by the Provincial Commissioner to the Director of Agriculture at Aburi as flourishing in June; and in July the instructor, Martinson, on a second visit reported the farms as well-maintained and proposed that an instructor should be sent to the area in November for a brief period to teach the farmers about fermentation and curing, since they were about to produce their first crop. By 1910, Martinson felt able to predict, solely on the basis of farms which he had visited personally, that Ahafo would in a few years be producing more than 320 tons of cocoa,[25] a quantity which would have represented more than half the total cocoa exports of Ashanti three years earlier.[26]

Such dramatic expansion raised other problems besides those of simple anxiety over transport costs. 'Strangers' from Kumasi were reported to have

46

come to the Western Province and to be spreading rumours that cocoa was an unprofitable industry and that the farmers who cultivated it would be unable to sell their crops.[27] Some farmers were sufficiently discouraged to neglect their farms and allow them to become overgrown. The Omanhene at Kukuom was instructed briskly to 'advise such that this is mischievous and untrue. There will always be a market for properly prepared cocoa and the trade will be a profitable one.' Furthermore, the Commissioner insisted with resolute optimism, 'As roads are improved and transport becomes cheaper the profit will increase.' Accordingly the Omanhene was instructed to send to all villages under his suzerainty in which cocoa had been planted and to order them not to listen to such foolish advice. Next month Martinson on his yearly tour of inspection came upon what might have been a more fundamental cultural obstacle to the advent of economic rationality. A man was arrested in Ahafo for pretending to cure cocoa pests by 'fetish medicine' for a fee, and boasting of the powers of his 'medicine'. The Provincial Commissioner in this case was sufficiently alarmed to send the alleged offender off to Kumasi to be 'confronted' by Martinson in the presence of the Chief Commissioner himself and to receive exemplary punishment if the charges against him should be fully established.[28] It is hard to imagine such administrative interest being aroused, had the potential beneficiaries of the cure been human beings rather than cocoa trees. The incident clearly indicates both awareness of and uneasiness over the precarious plausibility of cocoa-farming as an economic and social trajectory into a secure and prosperous future. Sardonic economic propaganda and fetish irrationalism seemed almost equally menacing threats to the realisation of such a future. But they were not recurrent threats. Neither outside agitators nor inside charlatans continued to plague the virtuous (if gullible) farmers. When Martinson visited Mim in the October of 1912 he was able to report that the farms were kept well cleaned, though the fermentation was not yet conducted with adequate skill.[29] In August the following year a visiting Commissioner, assessing the consequences for Ahafo of the Omanhene Braimansu's vigorous but unsuccessful campaign against Chief Beditor of Mim, noted that Kukuom itself was virtually the only settlement in Ahafo to have diminished in size in recent years and that it was now only in the area around Kukuom that cocoa was not being cultivated extensively.[30] Enhanced administrative commitment to Ahafo, with the establishment of the new district headquarters there in 1914, offered the long-term prospect of more effective aid to the farmers. The Acting Superintendent of Agriculture visited cocoa farms in Goaso with the Provincial Commissioner and arrangements were made for him to tour cocoa farms throughout Ahafo in the company of the Kukuom sword-bearer.[31] The District Commissioner in Goaso was instructed to select a cocoa learner from Ahafo for training at Aburi.[32] In January 1915 the

Curator of Agriculture distributed raintree seeds to all D.C.s in Ashanti as offering the most effective shade trees for the protection of cocoa.[33] By this time Ahafo had acquired major commitments in cocoa production. Plentiful young cocoa was reported in 1914 at Ntotroso, Kenyase, Goaso, Acherensua and Mim, while the cocoa at Hwidiem was actually bearing and 60 bags of it were sold at 13s a bag.[34] Despite the low prices of the war years a small quantity of cocoa was being grown by 1918 even at Sankore, Kwapong and Aboum in the depths of the forest.[35] In February 1919 the Kukuom elders, recovering from the blighting effects of Braimansu's belligerence, thought it worth their while to propose to the visiting Provincial Commissioner, the building of a road from Kukuom, through Dadiesoaba and Mamfu to Teppa, to be transformed in due course into a motor road, in order to carry their cocoa to Kumasi at a moderate transport cost.[36] The Commissioner was not very sanguine and urged upon them the possibility of selling the cocoa at a profit across the border with the French territory, a proposal which he repeated at Mim, where 2,000 loads were waiting for sale.[37] By 1920, the year in which the cocoa price reached its highest level before 1947,[38] the Chief Commissioner of Ashanti had come to recognise a government duty to push a motor road through to Ahafo in order to render the cocoa grown there profitable, citing the Kukuomhene's claim that the Governor had made a promise to do so when they met at Tanodumase.[39] In April 1923 the D.C. proposed the implementation of the suggestion regularly advanced by the people of Sienchem to cut a road from Sienchem to Mpasaso in the Central Province of Ashanti, with the assistance of labour provided by the D.C. in Kumasi, maintaining that this would greatly assist the inhabitants of Kukuom and the Ahafo towns by cutting the distance along which they had to transport their cocoa from four days head-loading to two or two and a half, and enabling them to sell it direct to the 'Firms' at Kunso.[40] By 1924 a lot of cocoa was grown in Ahafo but the costs of head-transport made it only marginally profitable and standards of cultivation remained poor.[41]

Up to this point Ahafo's experience of cocoa had certainly not been altogether a happy one; but it was still at a stage when 'the misery of being exploited by capitalists was nothing to the misery of not being exploited at all'.[42] No movement to hold up cocoa stocks was found in Ahafo in December 1923, the farmers being only too glad to find buyers, even though prices fell as low as 3s a load at Acherensua, where two years subsequently prices reached as high as 12s a load.[43] The crucial importance of transport costs in restricting investment up to this period can be seen in the sharp rise in interest produced by the approach of motor roads from 1925 on and the extended government advisory activities which accompanied these. By the time that the slump hit world cocoa prices in the 1930s, reducing them for five years to levels lower than they had plumbed in the present century,[44] the motor roads had reached Goaso, Mim and Kukuom and integrated the economy of Ahafo firmly into the world market. Efforts to hold up cocoa in Ahafo to secure higher prices began in 1931 on a small scale.[45] By 1927 the prices of cocoa on the London commodity market were relayed weekly to D.C.s by telegram throughout the buying season.[46] In 1931 the representative of Cadburys judged that a European stationed in Ahafo would be in a position to buy up to 800 tons of cocoa in the first year of his residence and more thereafter.[47] By 1936 the Goaso district alone produced 3,400 tons of cocoa (worth over £10,000).[48] Because of the complementary relationship between cocoa and the growth of certain food crops, notably plantains and cocoyams, there is still much production for subsistence in Ahafo. But with the advent of the motor roads subsistence production relapsed permanently into an ancillary role within a way of life shaped by production for the market. The political identity of Ahafo today is dominated by the extent of its specialisation in cocoa production. As a direct contribution to the establishment of this identity the major colonial offering was no doubt simply the construction of roads. Once the roads were there the forces of the market could be left to redesign Ahafo by themselves.

But between this, on its own terms triumphant, consummation and the initial hopeful introduction of the crop twenty-five years earlier, the administration's benign sponsorship of the cocoa tree had presented it despite itself in a notably unflattering light. A careful economic paternalism was an intrinsic component of the self-image of the administration as it evolved in Ashanti and one which retained plausibility for its members for a remarkably long time. It was a component which it required considerable moral agility to preserve unscathed during the years between 1914 and 1921, when the world market displayed other facets than those highlighted by liberal imperialism. In 1911 those who warned the farmers of Ahafo that cocoa would prove an unprofitable crop were readily identifiable as troublemakers. The thought of the waste of virtuous labour which their mischievous lies might cause came to the Commissioner with a genuine moral shock: 'It would be disgraceful if on account of such foolish advice persons who have spent much time and labour on the planting of cocoa farms were to abandon their plantations.'[49] But by October 1914 the Provincial Commissioner found himself obliged to 'preach everywhere' the reasons for the current low price of cocoa and the certainty of its eventual rise.[50] In 1916 the volume of cocoa exports from Ashanti as a whole fell, despite a rise in the crop yield, because prices had fallen so discouragingly.[51] The Western Province in 1917 showed (at least in the pages of its Commissioner's reports) a proper docility in the face of this experience: 'The natives generally are somewhat dispirited by their failure to find a market for their cocoa this season but they fully realise the situation and bear their disappointment philosophically.'[52] In the following year the Commissioners found great difficulty in many parts of Ashanti because of the continuing low prices in persuading the farmers not to abandon their farms.[53] In the Goaso district at the beginning of the 1920s most of the farmers were claimed to be heavily in debt because of being unable to sell cocoa for three or four years, the prices offered being too low even to cover transport costs. Cocoa brokers took advantage of this situation and a representative of the Department of Agriculture found that many farmers had mortgaged their crops for three or four years ahead.[54] Reporting on a three-week tour of instruction in Ahafo, from Sankore to Acherensua in June 1921, the Superintendent of Agriculture found reassurance in the fact that

a good local Cocoa Instructor can do a very great deal towards getting the Native Farmers to work despite the bad conditions. In one area here depression is as bad as it could possibly be – no cocoa has been sold for years, thousands of loads are either lying moulding or else being burned in villages and transport costs are far and away beyond what the cocoa price justifies. Yet the native farms are not utterly neglected.[55]

In these conditions the point of 'getting the Native Farmers to work' had plainly transcended the vulgarly economic and become a largely self-justifying end.

In practice price depressions acute enough to render the production of existing farms uneconomic have never persisted for long enough to impair permanently the plausibility of cocoa-farming as a field for investment. Even today profits earned in more metropolitan and sophisticated sectors of the Ghanaian economy are apt to be redeployed to some extent into investment in cocoa-growing for a variety of social and economic reasons.[56] A cocoa farm is still a more reliable store of real wealth than a bank account in a rapidly inflating currency. During the late government of Dr Busia, Bafuor Asei Akoto, the former leader of the National Liberation Movement (N.L.M.) sought the reward for his past devotion strenuously in Accra by competing with energy (and success) for some of the more remunerative import licences in the gift of the government. The rewards of national political success can be dizzy. But it seems likely that the huge cocoa farm which he owned at one of the villages on the Mim–Biaso road with its labour force of many dozens will provide a more durable economic base for his family in the next few years than his more dramatic recent capital accumulations. Many of the largest cocoa farms in Ahafo represent the product not of autonomous local class formation but the import of external rural capitalists and rural proletarians. The capital and the labour tend to come from different areas and some of the labour is indeed employed by Ahafo capital. Ahafo is not *merely* a colonial dependency of Ashanti metropolitan capital with a large and impoverished immigrant population from Northern Ghana, the Ivory Coast and Upper

Volta thrown in for it to employ. But it is certainly true today that social stratification in Ahafo is not the product of the internal dynamics of a given community but rather an elaborate palimpsest of external and internal social relations in which categories of social identity, linguistic, geographical and cultural, are criss-crossed by categories of class situation. The contemporary social stratification of Ahafo in terms of class above all, but also to a considerable degree even of status and power, has been a product of the development of Ahafo as a cocoa-growing area. But the political perception which has resulted from this process has always been compelled to articulate many other factors than the simple control over land, capital and labour.

For these reasons it would be simplistic to assume that the historical impact of cocoa on the political structures of Ahafo can be identified in solely economic terms. But it would be an even greater distortion not to insist that the key political fact about Ahafo today as against three quarters of a century ago has been the appearance of forest land as an increasingly scarce factor of production in what has been over the period in question more often than not a markedly profitable process of production. The political triviality of Ahafo in 1896 was directly linked to its character as largely uninhabited virgin forest. What made it politically trivial then – its virtual economic worthlessness – has been what has made it increasingly politically important and economically prosperous for the last five decades. The emergence of rent for land over the ten years prior to 1912 reflects the emergence of forest land as a significant economic asset. Previously land rights had been a simple analogue of political duties and there were no important distinctions in respect to them between strangers and citizens. Politically acceptable strangers could farm lands and politically unacceptable – disloyal or disobedient – citizens could lose their effective land rights by being banished. Shifting food cultivation established no lasting capital assets. But by 1912 commodity production for the market had necessitated the adoption of rather different practices. In Ashanti as a whole stranger-farmers had spent both money and labour on establishing cocoa farms from which they could expect to secure profits spread over several years. In return a rule had become accepted that a stranger-farmer, without in any way disturbing ultimate title to the land, would enjoy security of tenure as long as he continued to pay a 'customary' rent of a third of his crop to the stool. In the Western Province stranger-tenants evicted on political grounds – 'for disloyalty' – had come to be paid compensation, though the Provincial Commissioner, left slightly behind by the developing customary law, doubted sagely if perhaps without precise meaning, if they were 'strictly entitled' to it.[57] The liability to rents or tributes on the produce of the land was not at this point extended to cocoa, foodstuffs or kola in the case of newcomers from the 'same tribe' as that of the landowners, though even these fellow-tribesmen were subject to tribute for snails, palmnuts, palmwine and rubber. Members of the community itself continued to be granted land at the permission of the chief without liability for tribute on the produce but with the general obligations towards the stool – debt-liability and service in particular – which membership of the community imposed.

Whether in the form of land-rentals or of tributes assessed on cocoa or cocoa trees, such control over land access provided novel and attractive opportunities for chiefs to accumulate revenue. The Provincial Commissioner felt obliged to reject the request made by the chiefs of the Western Province in January 1913 to levy tribute on all cocoa produced, insisting sternly on the distinction between the gathering of wild produce in the forests and the cultivation of permanent crops. But he acknowledged of course the legitimacy of agreements to exact rent for access to the land by strangers.[58] The boundaries between tribute and rent were even further blurred by the Chief Commissioner's minute that in the Central Province he had established a rule that stranger-farmers who were farming cocoa land without a formal rental agreement were liable to a tribute of one tenth of their produce, either in cash or in kind. By 1914 a standard rate of cocoa tribute at 1d per tree on land not farmed by the owners seems to have been agreed. Such merit as this regulation might have had in what the Director of Agriculture optimistically identified as 'ordinary times'[59] disappeared briskly in wartime conditions. By August 1917 even such a vigorous exponent of chiefly accumulation as the Ahafo's long-term foe Kobina Kufuor of Nkawie had commuted the payments for the large cocoa plantations on his lands around Bibiani to a single sheep per plantation.[60] The Kumasi Council of Chiefs in the same year appeared equally ready to accept the need to reduce the burden of tribute dues. No effort was made to standardise the rates for several years after this until a time when higher cocoa prices had revived administrative ambitions to establish native authorities as viable agencies of local government with properly kept public treasuries, drawing on a clearly defined tax base. The Chief Commissioner circulated a set of draft cocoa-tribute laws in October 1925 to all districts, making clear that the requirement to pay all tribute to the Head Chief, irrespective of the actual ownership of the land, was designed simply to promote the establishment of Native Treasuries.[61] (Ahafo was in fact singled out a year or two later as an example of one of the areas in Ashanti in which the Omanhene did actually own all the land.[62]) The Kukuomhene and his Council duly signed the cocoa-tribute laws in July 1926.[63] With the exception of areas of overlapping jurisdiction (like a case over the Sankore sections of the Bibiani concession which required the efforts of two D.C.s and three chiefs to adjudicate in 1928)[64] these cocoa-tribute bylaws of 1926 provided a clear and predictable basis of title and obligation for some years. But the clarity of title was wholly dependent on the comparative simplicity of the Ahafo constitution in this period.

With the restoration of the Ashanti Confederacy in 1935 reasonably clear and unequivocal titles to land in return for regular payments gave way to a massive Kumasi *Reconquista*. Land which had been virtually devoid of value at the time when Kumasi suzerainty was first broken by Ahafo skirmishing now provided to the vigorous and enterprising Kumasi overlord pickings even richer and more reliable than the informal and formal exactions of metropolitan legal proceedings.[65] Political authority which had in its earlier incarnation been largely a title to the profits of 'justice' and a share in a few especially valuable commodities (ivory and, later, rubber in particular) which could be gathered in the forest now became an instrument for expropriating a substantial part of the surplus of capitalist agriculture. It was, too, an exceedingly blunt instrument and one for which the shadowy history which furnished its legal basis could hardly in principle serve to define with any great precision. Both to the communities of Ahafo and to the dismayed British administrators standing by, the streams of competing bailiffs from Kumasi carried with them all the reassurance and the moral charm of a swarm of locusts.[66] In 1937 both the Akwaboahene and the Hiahene of Kumasi commenced a drastic campaign to accumulate cocoa tribute from Ahafo, the Hiahene going so far as to visit Kukuom for the purpose against the express orders of the Asantehene.[67] The administration attempted hastily to establish two principles. Cocoa tribute (a form of economic rent) ought not to be levied on citizens of the Kumasi division, whether or not they owed allegiance to a clan chief other than the one whose land they were farming, because the land properly belonged to the Golden Stool and not to the clan chiefs. Strangers from the Colony or even from Ashanti itself outside the Kumasi division, might be made to pay tributes as such but citizens of the Kumasi division ought only to be responsible for rum money or a sheep in token of their political recognition of obligations towards the clan chief whose land they were taking up. Secondly, and more importantly, the cocoa tribute for land access ought to be treated as a form of public money, belonging ultimately to the Golden Stool and to be spent either by the central political authority of Ashanti as a whole or else by local agencies of development in the local area, neither of which represented roles which the clan chiefs of Kumasi could plausibly fill.

But it was the colonial administration which had restored the Confederacy and it was simply not politically possible for the Asantehene to expropriate the clan chiefs of Kumasi from what they collectively and actively considered to be their rights. The factional structure of Kumasi politics provided no ready counterweight for the alienation of the whole of such a prominent group. Those who stood to gain directly from such an alienation, the hapless Ahafos, were scarcely political allies of any consequence in Kumasi itself. The power of Kumasi accordingly was re-established in Ahafo, not merely as

53

the effective vehicle of administrative intentions which could have made the journey equally well by previous routes, but also as the reconstitution of a formal political subordination which in the conditions of capitalist agriculture had become an instrument of pure exploitation.[69] The fact that the making of new cocoa farms in Ahafo had largely ceased by 1940 for the war years was a direct product of a decision by the Asanteman Council in the light of war prospects and the cocoa market to encourage food-farming and to prohibit any expansion of cocoa production.[70] The indirectness of the rule in this case in no way blurred its adaptation to the purposes of a political unit of imperial scale. But the vigorous competition between the clan chiefs over the division of the spoils between 1938 and 1940, the elaborate arrangements which the administration and the Asantehene were obliged to make to mediate the conflicting claims of the clan chiefs and the sharp demand for places in the tribute-extraction network had no obvious relation to the interests either of Ahafo as an area or of the imperial government.[71] The application to one of the clan chiefs to become 'one of your Cocoa Tribute clerks at Kenyasi in the Ahafo district as I am staying there and I know all the strangers on the land' had less the flavour of meritocratic competition for the lowest and most indirect rung of the imperial bureaucracy than of a discreet bid to enrol in a protection racket.[72]

Direct taxation of cocoa producers by immediate authority became much more elaborate in the period from 1950 onwards. The creation of organs of local government for promoting development led to a certain conflict of interest between Kumasi traditional authorities and modernist agencies of local representation. By 1952, for example, the Ahafo Area Committee was attempting to prevent the representative of the Oyokohene of Kumasi from collecting cocoa-tribute revenue within Ahafo.[73] By 1955, when a group of Ahafo cocoa farmers organised under the banner of the Cocoa Purchasing Company and appealed directly to the Prime Minister in Accra against the cumulative depredations to which they saw themselves as subjected, the less regular expenses imposed by the 'atrocious chiefs' (notably the Kukuomhene) were almost swamped by the list of payments accruing to the Local Council or other modern agencies of communal representation: fees for farming in forest reserve areas, basic rates, and special levies for particular development projects.[74] The sharp conflicts all over the area in 1957/8, in Nyamebekyere and Asuadei, in Kukuom and Kenyasi, over the payment of special levies clearly became involved in the political struggle to impose C.P.P. control, as well as being affected by a drastic decrease in the cocoa crop in the 1957/8 season.[75] But they also involved complex issues of local citizenship and its duties in which the liability of stranger-farmers to pay both cocoa tribute (because they did not belong to the community) and special levies voted by a majority in the attempt to promote the development of the community

54

Economic development: Cocoa

(because they grew their crops within its jurisdiction) was forcefully de-
nounced as discriminatory. The development of modern local government,
even with the precarious tax base allotted to it by the central government,
was severely complicated by such anomalies. A system in which citizenship
and land tenure were originally linked intimately at a time when land was of
little economic value had many inequitable results when land became a
decidedly scarce resource. Strangers were second-class landowners in 1957,
not because they were substantially easier to dispossess of the trees with which
they had industriously and rationally mixed their labour, but in the paradoxical sense that, although they were in effect owners of full usufructuary
rights, they were so only on condition they paid permanently a higher level of
tax for the privilege. As late as 1957, however, the Ashanti Confederacy was
still very much in operation and it could still not be claimed that all direct
local expropriation from the cocoa farmers of Ahafo was disposed, however
inequitably, within the area. Indeed even the traditional privileges of the
Ahafo chiefly caretakers of Kumasi interests were by no means reliably
secured. In December 1957 the chiefs of Mim, Hwidiem and Asufufuo,
among other Ahafo chiefs, complained directly to the Asantehene that the
clan chiefs had not been remitting even the share of the spoils to which local
chiefly authorities were customarily entitled. The Akwaboahene alleged that
he permitted representatives of the local chiefs to accompany his cocoa-tribute
collectors on their rounds in order for them to keep check on the totals
realised. But the general tenor of the Kumasi chiefs' response was scarcely
designed to dispute that the rules had been enforced in a somewhat intermittent
fashion. The Asantehene contented himself (though he can hardly have contented the Ahafo petitioners) with the injunction that the clan chiefs and their
caretakers, both of whom he asserted were perfectly well aware of the rules
governing the division of stool revenues, should meet together and arrive at
more adequate arrangements for the rules to be implemented.[76] Shortly after
this case the creation of the Brong–Ahafo Region and the raising of the
Kukuomhene once again to the paramountcy of Ahafo restored a situation in
which the proportion of the cocoa surplus extracted by traditional authorities
was once again fully at the disposal of traditional authorities within the locality.
It may be doubted whether all the disbursements made by the State Council
under this scheme (such, for example, as the substantial payment to the evicted
C.P.P. Member of Parliament, B. K. Senkyire, to assist him to pursue his legal
studies in England) were any more obviously an equitable use of Ahafo wealth
than that previously made of it by the Akwaboahene or the Hiahene. But it did
present advantages solid enough to convince even some of those who were
most eager within the last few years to restore the formal hierarchy of the
Confederacy within Ahafo once again of the merits of retaining control over
the funds of Ahafo within the boundaries of Ahafo itself.

Dependence and opportunity

Over the years, however, it has not been the rent which strangers have been required to pay in order to obtain title to the usufruct of cocoa land which has represented the largest expropriation of surplus from the producers. From the point of view of Ahafo and of its permanent resident population as a whole government taxation of cocoa production has represented a much more drastic and, for most of the time, a far more sharply resented drain on the accumulation of capital than the seepage of cocoa revenue to metropolitan Ashanti. Within the area of Ahafo itself two separate forms of accumulative activity served to part the physical producers of cocoa from much of the eventual value of their product, in both cases with elaborate effects upon the internal social stratification of the area. The import of a substantial labour force to work the accumulated land of earlier Ahafo residents or of wealthy Ashantis who possessed the capital to take up land in the area served for much of the period from the late 1920s on as a very blunt instrument for the extraction of surplus value. Perhaps even more significant in the development of present-day political relationships in the area was the complicated network of dependence and advantage produced by cocoa broking in the period before co-operative societies were created throughout the area and the Cocoa Marketing Board was instituted as a government monopsony. As a field for rapid capital accumulation and for the display of entrepreneurial skill it was for some time unequalled. A marketing mechanism was created *de novo* in notional competition with European firms like Cadburys and Frames within a remarkably short space of time. Ahafo brokers operated elsewhere in Ashanti and held partnership houses in Kumasi.[77] Complex and fluid partnership arrangements were evolved and a measure of reliability over time established even in these highly informal arrangements. In March 1928, for example, a single day's hearings in the Goaso court involved five cases of claimants attempting to recover unpaid balances of cocoa account, involving sums totalling over £250. In the 51 civil cases heard before the court in the first quarter of 1929, no less than 35 were concerned with debt claims arising out of the cocoa-purchasing arrangements. By contrast in the same court in the first quarter of 1936, three of the 14 cases heard arose out of non-payment of wages to cocoa labourers and only one case appears to have arisen directly out of the organisation of cocoa purchasing.[78] From this time on such conflicts virtually disappeared from the court lists. The sums which changed hands in such partnerships were often substantial – as much as £600 within a season.[79] A few prominent brokers enjoyed a sort of apprenticeship in one of the European buying agencies. Such a prominent future Kumasi cocoa entrepreneur and political dignitary as C. E. Osei can be found visiting Goaso with an empty lorry in December 1926 as a representative of Frame's Buying Agency.[80] But for the most part, even though the cocoa was to pass through the hands of the European firms before it left the country, the initial collection of the crop from the farmers and its transport to motor road heads was organised by African initiative through individual brokers with sub-agents posted throughout the cocoa-growing areas.[81] The economic outlook of the political administration was too paternalistic to look on the creation of this entrepreneurial network with much warmth. Commissioners tended frequently to regard the European firms of the Kumasi Chamber of Commerce as lacking in social responsibility because of their insistence on using the roads (so painfully constructed by local communal labour under the strenuous instruction of the Commissioners themselves) under conditions which ensured that they would suffer heavy damage.[82] But the firms in the last resort were in a position to secure powerful external backing. When Mr John Cadbury and 'Mr Cadbury' himself visited Sunyani in February 1929 no one in the administration was under any illusion that the visitors were not fully comparable in importance even with the Governor of the Colony.[83] By contrast indigenous cocoa brokers in Ahafo who were amassing large concentrations of property through a systematic proffering of advances on crops at very low prices enjoyed no externally furnished immunity from the moral scorn of the administration.[84] The profits of the European cocoa agencies (unlike the physical destruction wrought by their lorries) represented for the Commissioners nothing morally more complicated and equivocal than the realities of the world market. But the discovery that many African cocoa brokers were making 100 per cent profits on their advances over a few months or, in the less prosperous times, were foreclosing on the mortgages of hundreds of farms evoked sharp moral condemnation from the administration.[85] The world market stood in large measure above morality, as far as the colonial view of it went; but D.C.s acquired a sharp eye for the more inequitable features of the market as a distributive system within Ahafo itself. The remedy at first favoured by the government was the establishment of co-operatives.[86] None of these had as yet been formed in Ahafo by September 1931;[87] but over the next two decades a large proportion of Ahafo farmers did become organised in this way and, although co-operatives did not altogether obviate the difficulties of protecting the interests of illiterates against literates – the post of co-operative secretary being notoriously a swift path to economic success – they clearly did serve to bring prices paid to producers somewhat closer to prices paid by exporters. D.C.s had no love for the market as such – middleman being very much a term of opprobrium – and they were happy to assist in the establishment of a marketing system which, whatever its inefficiencies from the viewpoint of producers, at least did not explicitly benefit too many local residents who failed to contribute directly to production.

This physiocratic view of economic virtue fitted very aptly with the marketing institution which was eventually to serve as the most effective channel for extracting the cocoa surplus from Ahafo. During the decade of cocoa seasons from 1949/50 to 1959/60 the proportion of total receipts from cocoa sales by the Marketing Board which was paid out by them for cocoa purchases was only once greater than three quarters and on some occasions it was less than half. Apart from comparatively low operating and transport costs, a large part of the gap between receipts and expenditures was paid over directly to the government in the form of increased export duties on cocoa.[88] Much of the residue was either loaned directly to the government or held as a substantial operating surplus in government stocks. This remarkable mobilisation of the cocoa surplus was achieved through an institution established during the Second World War, first as the West African Cocoa Control Board, to ensure a guaranteed market for the cocoa crop during wartime conditions,[89] and continued into the postwar period as a mechanism for guaranteeing more stable producer prices.[90] The decision to continue the operation of the Board was taken explicitly in the light of the direct links between potential political unrest and the intolerable marketing conditions for cocoa producers which the report of the Commission on the Marketing of West African Cocoa had identified in 1938 as the causes of the massive cocoa hold-up of 1937. The use of the C.M.B. as an instrument for the extraction of the cocoa surplus, allied to the increase in cocoa export duties, undoubtedly marked by 1960 (at least in its own eyes) a shift in the location of economic virtue from producers to a government committed to massive development expenditure. Price-stabilisation was still presented as a service to the industrious and rational farmer. But since the prices were for such an extended period of time so drastically below those which could have been obtained on a free market, considerable scepticism developed in the cocoa areas towards the idea that the government's policy did in reality have the effect of doing them a favour. The initial colonial conception of price-stabilisation as an aid to the propitiation of political discontent became under these novel circumstances considerably transformed. The economic morality of the colonial government had always been nervously paternalist. The economic morality of the Nkrumah government by contrast had by 1960 become much more ebulliently paternalist. During the struggle against the opposition National Liberation Movement (N.L.M.), the fact that the government retained control over such a large proportion of the cocoa surplus had provided a keen stimulus to the organisation of political opposition against the C.P.P. government. Being a stimulus which was provided impartially to all the cocoa-growing areas, it cannot of itself suffice to explain why Ahafo, unlike a number of other areas of what was then Ashanti, was in fact successfully incorporated into the N.L.M. electoral alliance. But it certainly did constitute an important and perhaps an essential basis for political mobilisation against the governing party within the bounds of Ahafo. By 1960, though, these battles were effectively lost or won and the machinery of C.P.P. political control was well ensconced. As a government the C.P.P. regime saw itself as investing resources generated by cocoa production in the national interest in the effort to expand and diversify future economic production; it saw itself not as spending the farmers' money on the comparatively prosperous industrial proletariat or the still more prosperous scions of the political class, but as putting money which the farmers would only have blued on larger and drunker funeral celebrations[91] to the use of constructing a modern economy and an economy, moreover, released (somehow) from the toils of neo-colonialism. From Ahafo the identification of who stood to gain from this redistribution was less flattering, sharpened as it was by a more vivid and committed sense of who it was who indisputably stood to lose from it, however extensive its eventual beneficiaries turned out to be.

Taxation had of course been an inflammable issue throughout the history of the cocoa industry in the Gold Coast. Like most other colonies the financial situation of its administration caused regular anxiety. Direct taxation raised the spectre of massive political resistance, an eventuality which the conquerors of Ashanti in particular were extremely anxious to avoid. Indirect taxes were less immediately incendiary; but in conditions in which the administration had very little clear information about the structure of costs in the production and marketing of commodities, export duties were potentially more disruptive and, above all, less predictable in their political and economic effects than were import duties. Proposals had been advanced as early as 1906[92] for the imposition of export duties on kola nuts, cocoa, timber and several other commodities but they had been rejected by the Secretary of State for the Colonies as unnecessary and 'improper'. In October 1915 the proposal to impose an export duty on cocoa was advanced once more as an expedient for replenishing the depleted wartime finances of the administration and for maintaining the interest charges on the construction of the railways.[93] The Chief Commissioner of Ashanti gave full support to the idea in the conditions of modest prosperity which prevailed at the time, though he did draw attention to the risk that imposing an additional payment would in fact – in the event of a slump, which he did not expect until after the end of the war – deter the farmers from bothering to gather their crop.[94] When the decision was eventually taken in September 1916 to impose the tax at a rate of a farthing per pound, the Governor explicitly recognised that it had been taken without any serious knowledge on the part of the government of the structure of costs in cocoa growing in the extremely various types of farming conducted at the time.[95] For all practical purposes the administration was compelled by its sheer ignorance to treat the cocoa-producing sector as a 'black box', the internal mechanism of which it was beyond the capacity of the Political Service and the Department of Agriculture to ascertain with any attempt at precision. Since it was

59

agreed even by the representatives of the European merchants[96] that the tax would be passed on in its entirety to the growers, all that the administration was in a position to do was to keep an anxious watch on the response of the growers and to modify the duty hastily, as the Governor's powers enabled him to do, if the initial rate proved to be a sufficiently powerful disincentive to bring production to a halt and to lead to the beans being left to rot on the trees.[97] Accordingly the Colonial Secretary took pains to issue urgent instructions to Commissioners a week before the duty was formally imposed to observe the growers' response and to inform the central administration at once, 'if possible, by telegraph', if the growers showed any sign of abandoning production. The tax was not a particularly popular one (few taxes are) and it was criticised at regular intervals by unofficial members in the Legislative Council.[98] But it was plainly less unpopular than any form of direct taxation would have been at all likely to prove; and, as Governor Guggisberg argued with some impatience in 1924, although it had certainly been true that the incidence of the tax had initially been firmly on the growers, it did not appear to be true that the reduction in the tax in 1922 had been passed on to them by the merchants with anything like the same alacrity.[99] It is not difficult to see why the Cocoa Marketing Board, on its eventual creation, provided a more satisfying instrument for the expression of this economic morality than the use of taxes on produce sold on a notionally free market. The fiscal requirements of the government were no less well protected; but the residuary beneficiaries at the same time could be guaranteed to consist predominantly (at least as far as the law was observed) of virtuous producers and not of commercial parasites. The political context within which Governor Guggisberg operated was of course more constricted than that surrounding President Nkrumah and his advisers. But both their overt dedication to the economic advantage of the colonial territory and their distaste for those whom they perceived (aptly enough) as its exploiters were recognisably similar to Guggisberg's. The economic paternalism of the postcolonial state had enormously wider scope than that of its colonial predecessor; but the continuities between the two were too striking from the viewpoint of producers for the conveniences of wartime marketing arrangements (the guaranteed prices) to transform by themselves the state apparatus from a lackey of foreign capital to a dependable agent of local interests. However authentic the public commitment of either the colonial administrators or their anticolonial successors, the experience of producing cocoa in Ahafo, as elsewhere in Ghana, has not been an experience of effective popular control over a representative political authority. The economic paternalism of both regimes has generated a widespread (and far from unrealistic) sense of economic dependence on the (as it often seems, miserly) largesse at the disposal of the state. The people of Ahafo do not ask what they can do for their country. They ask what its government (*aban*) will do for them. They ask, too, with discreet humility. In these matters discretion has been found over the last quarter of a century to represent much the better part of valour.

Cocoa, then, has subjugated Ahafo to the will of the state more intimately and predictably than a mere preponderance of military force could have begun to do by itself. But has also had elaborate effects upon the internal social stratification of the area. Some precolonial economic and social statuses were directly suppressed by the administrative and judicial action of the British. Domestic slavery and debt-bondage (pawning) were widely prevalent in Ahafo, as they were elsewhere in Ashanti, at the time of the British conquest in 1896. The process by which they were extirpated was gradual and the initiatives of the Commissioners often decidedly gingerly.[100] Even today the position of young children living in the households of distant and more prosperous relatives (and obliged in return for the food which they eat to carry out whatever labour is required of them) is scarcely compatible with a model of labour allocation confined to the sale of labour power by free adults on a market. But even in this case labour which is today not allocated in strictly market terms (or a public responsibility within the community) is clearly labour within the household. Apart from domestic and communal labour, virtually all productive labour in Ahafo is now either furnished by family members or purchased. The non-familial labour force in cocoa-production is recruited to a number of different statuses. Labourers paid a daily or weekly rate are available in many places. Other labourers are employed on a seasonal or annual basis for a fixed sum in addition to tools, some items of clothing and their upkeep for the period involved. Large numbers of farms are cultivated on the basis of share-cropping.[101] By now cocoa-farming is by no means the only form of employment open to the landless labourer in Ahafo, but it is still substantially the largest source of employment. A distinctive characteristic of Ahafo social stratification is thus the presence of a large dependent and often migrant or semi-migrant labour force, most of which is recruited from outside the Akan areas, much of it from outside the territorial limits of the state of Ghana itself.[102] The recruitment of this labour force was a protracted process and one which, in the nature of things, did not leave extended traces in the records of the administration.

The slow progress of communications in Ahafo served to check the influx of northern labour in substantial quantities until the mid-1920s, when the approach of motor roads began to increase local enthusiasm for planting cocoa. Many immigrant labourers had settled to the north of Ahafo a decade earlier, bringing with them complex problems of social adjustment and public order. A major riot between the local inhabitants and the Mossi

61

community in Teppa in 1916, in which a dozen people were severely injured, echoed events in Bechem and a number of other similar areas of the Western Province within a space of ten days and greatly worried the Provincial Commissioner.[103] 'Aliens' were identified as a major problem in Ashanti as a whole, responsible, as Dr Busia's government was to present them (on the professional authority of Durkheim), for at least two thirds of the crime committed, and 'truculent to the native chiefs'.[104] (In Teppa, in fact, as even the Commissioner agreed, the native chief in question had been quite as much to blame as the head of the Mossi community.) In Ahafo as a whole there were only 116 Muslims recorded in the 1921 census, a fair index of how limited the influx of northern labour had yet become by this date, though in itself a spectacular increase on the lonely pair of the faithful recorded in 1911.[105] The official intelligence report for 1926 noted that there were still no *zongos* in the district of Ahafo.[106] By 1929, however, zongos were recorded at Hwidiem, Kenyase II and Goaso,[107] while the Goaso zongo inhabitants had become sufficiently identified as citizens of the town to agree to participate in communal labour.[108] The problems of authority within Kenyase II's zongo required the mediatory energies of Kenyase's Chief and the Goaso Seriki Zongo (zongo headman) in addition to those of the D.C. himself for their resolution and were noted by the latter to be 'the first Seriki palaver in the district'.[109] The problems posed by the existence of separate heads for the Mossi and Hausa communities in the two Kenyases were resolved by recognising the status of each community's head but subordinating one to the other.[110] Early in 1930 the D.C. reported the N.T. (Northern Territories) communities as intending to build distinct zongos in four villages in Ahafo, though hindered in the attempt by their lack of disposable income and by the new building regulations which prescribed more durable building materials than the traditional swish.[111] But even at this point the D.C. judged the number of immigrants from the north who were permanently resident in Ahafo as very small. In the 1931 census, the population of Ahafo was divided between 13,300 Ashantis (representing presumably all those of Akan origin) and 2,336 Nkramos – northern immigrants of putatively Muslim culture.[112] Much the greater part of these immigrants was male: even in the administrative headquarters of Goaso only a fifth of the 200 Nkramos recorded were females.[113] Both the speed and the extent of this immigration were linked to the impact of the new roads upon the expansion of cocoa-production. Its drastic effect on economic specialisation and on social stratification within the area was soon noted. From 15 to 20 per cent of the population of the area was estimated in 1931 to leave their villages in search for work every season for an average period of six months and for a maximum of a year at a time. 'Farm or cacao work attracts the men from the North to the district. Palm-wine cutting, swish-

building and the cacao trading take the young men away from the district.'[114]
The farmer, the Provincial Commissioner noted in a 1932 report,

who ten years ago walked 60 or 80 miles with his family carrying the cocoa crop
to market is today a gentleman of leisure owning several farms, employing
immigrant labour to do the work in the farm and selling his produce in his own
village when the price suits him. Ten years ago the immigrant labourer was
almost unknown but now nearly every large village has its zongo where the
stranger population lodges, and the number of these strangers who settle and
become permanent residents has been yearly increasing: for the most part they are
more industrious and enterprising than the indigenous population and when
employment is scarce they find a profitable field of occupation in growing foodstuffs for the markets in the larger towns.[115]

The solid Akan domination of cocoa-broking at this time does little to
confirm the comparative entrepreneurial lethargy of the Ahafos or other
Ashantis; but the availability of large supplies of northern labour for rewards
exiguous in comparison with those which the forest people themselves were
now in a position to require, did certainly mark a decisive *mise en valeur* of
the forest land.

During the 1928/9 cocoa season the newly established Survey Division
of the Department of Agriculture carried out a cocoa survey of the Western
Province of Ashanti which provided the first systematic information available to the government about the structure of cocoa production not merely for
the Western Province itself but for any extensive cocoa-growing area.[116] The
results did not suggest that landholding had yet become at all highly concentrated in Ahafo. No single farm in Ahafo was reported as producing over
100 loads of cocoa, in contrast with the first area of cocoa production to be
extensively developed in the Western Province which showed over 8 per
cent of the farms to be of this scale. Over seven eighths of the Ahafo farms
produced between 20 and 60 loads (= 1,200 to 3,600 lbs), a proportion
of relatively small crops higher than in any of the other forest areas around
Sunyani which were surveyed at the same time. Among the very small
farms, however, those producing less than 20 loads, the position of Ahafo
was less marked, with under 10 per cent of its farms of this scale, as against
a proportion of over 20 per cent in the longest-developed area.[117] The proportion of cocoa farms per 1,000 of the population in Ahafo was the highest
of any area surveyed and the proportion of non-fruiting to fruiting farms
both in the Sunyani and in the Ahafo areas was about 3:1. A total of 1,936
farmers in Ahafo (482 of them women) were recorded as possessing farms
with fruiting trees, out of a total of 3,344 farmers in all (1,215 of whom were
women).[118] The report on the survey expected production in Ahafo to quad-
ruple within a short period, producing a doubling in the mean production

of cocoa per farmer (which was estimated at 36.97 loads in the case of Ahafo).[119] It was also noted (with some dismay owing to the deleterious effects which it was alleged to have produced on the standard of farming care and on the prevalence of disease) that cocoa had become transformed from a form of family production to one in which individual members of a family made their own farms and employed labour.[120]

No equally comprehensive information as a whole is available at any later point.[121] But some insight into the social stratification generated by cocoa-production can be gathered from two studies carried out in the 1950s.[122] Polly Hill's detailed evidence referred to 32 out of the slightly more than 100 members of Hwidiem's co-operative society.[123] The society produced about half of the cocoa marketed in Hwidiem and those interviewed were judged to produce slightly more cocoa on average than those who eluded interview. Twenty-eight of the 32 interviewed were natives of Hwidiem and two of them were immigrants from the Northern Territories. The main interest of these Hwidiem materials is the information which they yield on the quantity of wealth accumulated within families in one of the older cocoa-growing areas of Ahafo and one of the first Ahafo towns to construct a zongo. Twenty-nine of the farmers employed *abusa* (share-cropping) labourers and only one was recorded as plucking his own cocoa.[124] The quantity of loads plucked per labourer in Hwidiem (a direct index of earnings under the share-cropping system) was virtually a third higher than in any of the seven other areas surveyed: it averaged over 40 loads each.[125] Out of the entire force of *abusa* labour identified in Hwidiem at this time (totalling 142), 101 came from the Northern Territories (British or French), 35 from Ashanti, four from the Colony and two from Togoland.[126] In addition to the *abusa* labourers, 28 annual labourers were recorded as working on the Hwidiem farms, for an average wage of £14 (in addition to food and housing).[127] A certain amount of daily labour was also employed in Hwidiem at 2s 6d or 3s a day. Twenty-nine out of thirty farmers had new cocoa farms under cultivation in addition to those already bearing.[128] In comparison with the other areas surveyed Hwidiem stood out as having much the largest average production per farmer (211 loads as against anything from 25 to 116 elsewhere)[129] and as being uniquely free from numerous small farmers producing less than 20 loads per year.[130] It had the lowest proportion of farmers producing 40 loads or less – some 15 per cent as against more than 50 per cent in the majority of other areas[131] – and no less than 89 per cent of its total production was controlled by farmers who produced more than 100 loads.[132] The list of individual farmers included three who produced 500 loads or over, one of whom employed 15 *abusa* labourers and three annual labourers on new farms.[133] Altogether no less than 11 out of the 89 Hwidiem farmers for which information was available were reported as producing over 500 loads, the two largest of them, 1,098 and 1,204 loads respectively,[134] a gross annual yield of £3,500 to £4,000 at the time. Average gross cocoa income of the 30 farmers fully surveyed in Hwidiem was £859 (more than double that of any other place surveyed), while its average *net* cocoa income of £575 was five times the *gross* cocoa income of the least prosperous locality for which the figures were thought trustworthy (unsurprisingly the village of Kokoben near Kumasi, from which half the farmers were currently engaged in establishing new cocoa farms deeper into Ahafo).[135] All the farmers of Hwidiem, unlike any other area surveyed, secured a net cocoa income of over £50 per year and 14 out of 30 secured one of over £500.[136] Most spectacularly of all, 80 per cent of total net cocoa income earned by the Hwidiem group went to farmers earning a net cocoa income of £500 a year or over.[137] If the citizen-farmers of Hwidiem were collectively prosperous in comparison with those of most other parts of the then Gold Coast, the rich citizen-farmers were very much richer. It is not difficult to see why a government which set itself to expropriate much of the surplus which so lavishly accrued to such men in order to spend it on industrial development should have felt considerable assurance over the moral quality of its actions. But equally it is not difficult to see why the political organisation which took the economic interests of cocoa producers for its major rallying cry should have been able to garner energetic and powerful supporters in Ahafo. As an individual any rich Ahafo farmer, like any well-endowed member of any other social group in the Gold Coast at the time, might contrive to maximise the returns on his political energies by aligning himself with the C.P.P. government with the control which this possessed over such unequivocal incentives as the 'loans' disbursed by the Cocoa Purchasing Company. But as a group, with so much money potentially to lose and such solid and available clientages to dispose, the rich farmers of the Ahafo forest combined the maximum of incentive with the maximum of opportunity in their belated political resistance to the clerkly political entre-preneurs of the city and the coast.

The picture of cocoa farm ownership in Ahafo which was presented in the Bray survey for 1956/8 was based on wider geographical coverage and revealed somewhat less concentration of production. But it also confirmed the scale of accumulative opportunities offered by cocoa production. In the survey 103 farmers in six villages (one of which, Gambia I, was rather recently established) possessed 1,003 plots, 609 of which were already bearing cocoa and on average Bray calculated each farmer to produce about 120 loads.[138] Farmers from all of the villages possessed a substantial number of new plots; but Gambia I was the only village in which the majority of plots was not yet in bearing.[139] Total acreages being worked, including newly cleared plots, were estimated at 80 to 100 acres per farmer and the size of plots cleared was thought to have been rising steadily.[140] At the same time, in the older areas of settlement, considerable pressure on land had built up, the size of plots was falling and many farmers had started to move to new areas, in some cases establishing satellite villages.[141] The pattern which emerges is one of much greater concentration in the case of older farms.[142] Only 10 per cent of the farms established for over thirty years were over 50 acres in scale; but they comprised more than 55 per cent of the land area of these older farms. By contrast much the greatest proportion of the acreage of the new farms is made up of farms of between 5 and 50 acres.[143] However over 40 per cent of the plots surveyed overall had been established within the last six years[144] and the pattern of farm development was still firmly expansive, with average holdings still clearly increasing and the frontier of farming continuing to extend into the forest.[145]

The position today is not easy to assess with any confidence. No comparably detailed systematic survey has been undertaken since the enquiries of Polly Hill and F. N. Bray. The gross cocoa production of Ahafo continues to remain high, though the variation from year to year in cocoa yields makes it difficult to say over any short period whether or not the underlying trend is still rising.[146] The frontier of settlement continues to extend in many forest areas. Total acreage of bearing cocoa farms was estimated in 1968 as almost 127,500 acres. But pressure on land around the older communities is now such that outmigration for a substantial proportion of the children in many families who survive into adulthood seems likely soon to become the only alternative to falling incomes. Much capital has entered the area from other parts of Ghana to take up land for civil servants, stranger cocoa-farmers and entrepreneurs from numerous other fields. It is almost certainly harder today than it was twenty years ago for a migrant from the north with no economic resource but his own labour to establish a personal farm and there seems every reason to suppose that it will be decidedly harder still in another twenty years. The beginnings, however informal, of a national capital market and the growing scarcity of cocoa lands (two intimately linked phenomena) are turning land into a factor of production, the cost of which is increasingly out of the reach of those whose only economic asset is their willingness to mix their labour with it. How much longer Ahafo can remain a rural boom area for a majority of its inhabitants depends today largely on factors external to the area itself. Government choices about the proportion of the cocoa surplus to extract through the medium of fixed producer prices will probably remain the most visible lever of external control. But cocoa is in many ways a highly vulnerable crop and technical progress in the control of disease and infestation, matched by the degree of governmental energy in providing or failing to provide such assistance to the farmers might yet prove as important to the securing or imperilling of the long-term economic prospects of Ahafo as the rate of direct taxation on its major product. Beyond the borders of the state of Ghana the establishment of an International Cocoa Agreement might help to guarantee more stable real prices and it is plain that a more redistributive attitude towards international trade on the part of industrial producers might offer better prospects for the integration of the present Ahafo economy into a somewhat more rational structure of local production. But to say this is only to emphasise how far the economy of Ahafo has been rendered dependent on forces at a world level which are as far beyond the imagination of its inhabitants to grasp as they are beyond their power to affect.

b. OTHER PRODUCTS

Cocoa is the only product which has affected, for better or worse, the lives of all who make their homes in Ahafo. The physical conditions in which men live in Ahafo today represent the accommodation of the forest environment for the growing of cocoa. For many of those who now live there their very presence exemplifies the comparative attractions of cocoa-growing in the forest as against subsistence agriculture in the parched savannahs to the north in the Ivory Coast, Upper Volta or Northern Ghana. But the economic activities of Ahafo did not begin with cocoa; they have never been confined to cocoa; and it is not from cocoa that the greatest accumulations of wealth in Ahafo in recent decades have derived. Even the demographic influx so closely tied to the cocoa boom cannot be aptly seen as a simple controlled import of labour (as it might be, *indentured* labour), by cocoa capitalists in search of a cocoa proletariat. Some indication of the complexity of the process of expansion, determined though it plainly was in the last resort by the rhythms of the cocoa boom, can be gathered from the outline of a single economic career, that of the leader in 1969 of the Mossi community from Upper Volta in the town of Goaso.[1] Salamu Mossi came to Ahafo forty years ago from his country, as he put it simply enough himself, 'for money', a commodity not readily to be earned at the time at home. He walked the whole way, carrying *dawa-dawa* and fish to sell during the cocoa season for money which he then proposed to use to buy kola nuts.[2] At Wa in Northern Ghana he was advised that he would be able to sell the goods which he was carrying at Nkasaim, one of the two Ahafo centres for the sale of kola. At Nkasaim he sold on credit the goods which he had carried and waited for the cocoa crop to be sold for his debtors to repay him. But it was a year of extremely low cocoa prices and, in the event, none of the Nkasaim cocoa was bought and none of his debtors was consequently able to repay him. To recover his debts he was obliged to remain in Ahafo until the cocoa trade recovered and in order to do this he took a job in the Public Works Department in Goaso. It was, fortunately from his point of view, a time of considerable government investment in road construction and the Ahafo population showed little inclination even during the cocoa depression to take up the position of government labourers. Five years later he transferred to the Survey Department and worked at cutting lines through the forest. Six years later still he transferred from government employment to work as a labourer in the cocoa-buying department of the United Africa Company. After the Second World War he became a cocoa caretaker for Kofi Owusu, for some years the Chief of Goaso. He had kept this job for twenty years by 1969. Two or three years after becoming a caretaker he also acquired a small farm of his own which produced some 60 or 70 bags of cocoa by the late 1960s. The role of caretaker is a dependent one and it is far from generously rewarded.[3] But it is an important corrective to the impulse to conceive Ahafo society as divided neatly into exploiters and exploited that being the dependent of such a powerful figure in the community as Kofi Owusu should so soon lead to the acquisition of a cocoa farm of Salamu's own and that the role of a caretaker on someone else's farm should not preclude the utilisation and harvesting of a substantial crop on that farm.

The kola which Salamu came to purchase was one Ahafo resource which might well have been marketed long before the British first invaded Ashanti. The nut grows on wild trees in the forest and does not appear ever to have been cultivated there. The export of kola from Ashanti to the dry areas south of the Sahara was one of the best controlled and most remunerative activities of the Ashanti state.[4] If Ahafo produced large quantities of kola in the 1920s (which it did), there is no overriding economic reason why it could not have produced large quantities several decades earlier and have been integrally linked by virtue of doing so to the metropolitan Ashanti economy. But such evidence as there is suggests strongly that the kola of Ahafo was not exploited until well after the British conquest of Ashanti. The main reason for this appears to have been the very lightly populated character of the areas of Ahafo in which kola grows most plentifully. The actual pattern of development of Ahafo's non-cocoa exports seems to have been somewhat more complex. At the time of the British arrival in the area the most valuable local product was clearly rubber, a gathered crop, sold on the world market. Indeed this remained for some time not merely the source of most of Ahafo's export wealth but the key to the economic future of the area in the eyes of the colonial administration. Only the falling world market price of rubber and the failure of experimental plantations led to its decisive supplanting by cocoa. The involvement of Ahafo in the export of kola to the north, a factor of some importance in facilitating the influx of population from the north into the area, appears to have developed in close relation to the expansion of cocoa-growing in north west Asunafo. It also seems to have re-established to some degree a trading route from Ahafo to the north which had flourished in the period between the British invasion of Ashanti in 1874 and the final conquest of 1896. More recently government investment in infrastructure for cocoa production and in a variety of welfare facilities has provided extensive wage employment locally and this has been supplemented by the increasing scale of timber extraction. Throughout these transformations many in Ahafo have also increased their resources by, if seldom relied for their own subsistence on, the sale of food, hunted, gathered or grown, to urban population centres outside the area. Gold was probably dug on a small scale in Asunafo, as in most parts of north west Ashanti, in the nineteenth century;[5] but the only significant deposits in the area to be mined since 1896 lay inside the section of the Bibiani concession located on Sankore stool lands.[6] At one point it was believed briefly that diamonds had been discovered[7] and large deposits of bauxite have in fact been located in the south west of the area, though they have not as yet been in any way exploited. In the early stages of Ashanti expansion Ahafo was said to produce considerable quantities of ivory;[8] but although elephants are still to be found in the western forests of the district today, there does not appear to have been any economically significant attempt to accumulate ivory for the market since 1896.

It is thus a considerable simplification to see the coming of the colonial regime as marking a decisive transfer from an autarkic hunting economy (or an area integrated into a wider economy only through the traditional commercial management of the Ashanti state) into a zone of colonial mono-culture, producing for the world market. Initially Ahafo may well have been an economic dependency of Ashanti, accumulating food, ivory and gold for sale in Kumasi and obtaining the arms and ammunition which it required for efficient hunting upon the Kumasi market. But it is by no means clear that the economic position of the area was ever as neatly encapsulated in metropolitan Ashanti as the political and military features of its constitutional position appeared to demand. There was certainly a traditional trade route from Goaso and Kukuom to the sea at Cape Coast, thirteen days' travel as Davidson Houston was told in 1896[9] or sixteen as Bray's informants reported in the 1950s;[10] and there is no reason to believe that some of the more valuable Ahafo products were not head-loaded by this route to the coast and exchanged there for arms, ammunition and other trade goods. Certainly from 1874 on, following the British invasion of Ashanti, the main trade route from the areas north and west of Odumase to the coast passed not through Kumasi as it had previously done but through Goaso and Denkyira.[11] The extent of individual and group mobility over the two decades before the British conquest of 1896 revealed by administrative documents immediately following the conquest makes it clear that there was considerable trading activity of an irregular character in other directions than along the main trading routes and the speed with which a large volume of gunpowder began

69

to be smuggled into Ashanti via Kukuom from the French territories to the west after 1896 suggests a considerable local sensitivity to market opportunities. The trade flows through Goaso in 1896 were identified as consisting largely of rubber from the area, along with a few monkey skins, in exchange for exports from the coast of gin, salt, gunpowder, brass and copper rods, iron and lead bars, cutlasses and cotton goods,[12] while the bulk of goods traded to Kumasi up to the early 1890s had consisted of forest foodstuffs, dried bushmeat, smoked snails, or smoked fish.[13] By 1896 Davidson Houston reported, 'all connection with Kumasi had been practically at an end for several years past and everywhere the natives seemed delighted at the prospect of being now able to carry on their trade and peaceful occupations unhindered and unmenaced by either Kumasi on the south or Gaman (*sic*) on the north'.[14] It is possible that the coincidence of the relaxation of Kumasi control in Ahafo and the commencement of the relatively large-scale export of rubber from the area indicate an economic motive for Ahafo's efforts towards autonomy, in addition to the military deterioration of Kumasi power which made its seizure possible. If the bulk of Ahafo wealth, such as it was, before the export of rubber came from its capacity to provision a major urban centre, Kumasi as the nearest major urban centre would offer solid reciprocal advantages to the Ahafos by providing a substantial and accessible market for their produce. The demographic decline of Kumasi in the last three decades of the empire[15] must have reduced the purchasing power as well as coercive capability of the metropolis. At the same time the growing world market demand for rubber from 1890 on[16] presented the Ahafos with an economic opportunity which was in no way dependent on facilities provided by Kumasi. The returns on invested labour which derived from gathering rubber and even head-loading it for the fortnight's journey to the coast were clearly superior to those which could be earned from carrying bulky foods to Kumasi. At the same time Kumasi success in imposing central marketing for rubber would place the empire once again in a monopoly position with a good decidedly more valuable than the kola traded to the north and would have enabled Kumasi to extract a large proportion of the profits which an Ahafo who traded his own rubber directly to the coast could hope to retain for himself. In the circumstances a loose political dependency linked to a large measure of economic symbiosis would have been replaced by a form of political dependency in which all the economic advantages could be expropriated by the metropolis. Nor was the rubber trade to the coast one which required for its pursuit the complex combination of military force, diplomatic skill and organisational effectiveness which the kola trade to the north had demanded. In these conditions the local attractions of Ahafo autonomy were evident. It was natural, too, that the first major initiative which concerned Ahafo in Kumasi attempts to reintegrate the empire after the British conquest of 1896 should have been the seizure by his former Kumasi overlord of £160 worth of rubber being marketed by Braimansu, the British-recognised Omanhene of Ahafo.[17] It was equally natural that the British Resident in Kumasi, having once decided to confine the authority of Kumasi chiefs to the town itself, should rule in favour of the Kukuomhene, guaranteeing an economic autonomy to Ahafo in relation to Kumasi to match its now-recognised political autonomy.[18]

For the new colonial administration after 1896 rubber remained for a decade and more the most important product of the Ashanti forests. Considerable administrative effort was consequently devoted for a time to the encouragement of plantations[19] in place of the indiscriminate destruction of the wild rubber trees, as well as to the development of techniques of rubber extraction which produced a less contaminated quality of rubber biscuit for the market.[20] But these were long-term preoccupations and in practice they proved somewhat academic. The depression of the world rubber price meant a sharp fall in rubber exports from the Gold Coast after 1912, checked only by a brief revival in the later years of the First World War and a more impressive one during the Second World War[21] when Ahafo received substantial government investment in road-making into the Mim forests on the expectation, unrealised in the event, that these still contained large quantities of wild rubber trees. In Ahafo itself rubber, kola and cocoa continued for several decades after 1896 to provide economic opportunities for individuals without generating sharp conflicts of political interest. Once the Kumasi attempt to re-establish a monopoly control over Ahafo exports had been frustrated by the decisions of the British administration, none of the three products presented distinctive opportunities for profit from the simple manipulation of political power by communities or their leaders. Rubber trees had not yet become really scarce in the Western Province before the decline of effective demand removed economic pressure on their numbers. Kola was never fully picked,[22] although it was often said that the total quantities sold were never sufficient to meet demands.[23] It was a steady crop, offering less exciting speculative opportunities to local labour than either cocoa or rubber might do at times, but also being far less subject to the huge price fluctuations which often affected world market crops. In the early years of the new century rubber was of great importance in the economic prosperity of Ahafo because of the cash and the trade goods which it brought into the local political and economic arena, both as spoils to be redistributed and as a medium of circulation in the exchange of services. Later it was replaced in this role by cocoa. In due course the increasing scarcity of cocoa land altered this inert relationship, establishing varieties of more or less overt rent and greatly augmenting the political power of those who effectively controlled access to new land. But until this last stage (which cannot have come to any area of Ahafo much before the late 1930s and which did not come to many parts of it until two decades or more later) the main economic components in political conflicts between Ahafo stools (and, where these were involved, stools beyond Ahafo) were either concerned with the economic returns of traditional status as such – the profits of justice and the substantial material tokens of political subordination – or they were concerned with rights to hunt and gather food on lands belonging to the stool. A considerable proportion of colonial administrative energy in the first two or three decades after 1896 was devoted to the attempt to arbitrate boundary disputes. In these disputes the lands claimed by either side were claimed on the basis of prescriptive rights, demonstrated in most cases by reminiscences of past hunting or gathering. In all cases where it was at all clear that there was a motive for the claims besides the simple motive of enhancing communal status, what appears to have been at stake was simply the right to continue to hunt or gather. Fish and snails were the most persistent points of contention, the dispute between Mim and Kukuom over the extent of their rights of snail-gathering still forming the most active field of political rivalry between them for some years in the late 1920s and early 1930s.[24] By this stage the goods which were being competed for were very evidently goods intended for sale on the market as much as they were items of personal subsistence. But this dual character of the goods at stake was in essence nothing new for Ahafo hunters and fishermen who had traded their catches to Kumasi before the world rubber market entered the ken of anyone in the area.[25] It was an important duality, too, because it meant that competition between communities for marketable goods and competition between them for a commodious style of subsistance were not in any way separated in the minds of competitors. Boundary disputes argued out before colonial administrators and eventually litigated over in colonial courts were simply a continuation of communal war by other means. Boundary disputes have not of course ceased today, though now in their public aspect they are pursued exclusively in the courts, whether modern or traditional. Nor have they entirely lost their character as conflicts between communities, in which the loyalties of any citizen of the community are felt to be directly implicated. But what is actually at stake now is increasingly often control over timber rights; and even where cocoa land is also manifestly at issue, the interests of those who will control the disbursement of the licence fees and the charges for access to cocoa land are no longer transparently the same as those of the citizens at large. It is still as much a duty of a chief to litigate on behalf of his community's rights today as it used to be for him to direct the fight on its behalf. But it is a role today in which his services, unless they are supremely successful, are likely to evoke suspicion and resentment much more readily than they do trust and admiration. The gaps between chief and commoner in the economic interests of the community are appreciably wider today than they were half a century ago and now they often resemble the gap between capital accumulation and subsistence. Cocoa and still more timber have altered the balance of political and economic interests within the community between chiefs and commoners, tipping it decisively to the chief's advantage. Men with the capabilities to execute the role of chief effectively are likely in many cases to make use of this advantage for their own profit. Men who lack the will or the ingenuity to make use of it are also unlikely to possess the energy and force of personality to be effective chiefs.

The values involved in timber-extraction are substantial enough to require brief treatment separately, although their impact on the political conscious-ness of most Ahafos remains extremely slight. But a few details of kola and rubber production up to the 1930s will serve to set the erratic progress of cocoa cultivation towards economic dominance and political centrality in the area in some perspective. When Davidson Houston visited Kukuom and Goaso in 1896 the only products which he reported on sale in the towns, apart from abundant rubber at between £1 and £2 a 60 lbs load, were monkey skins priced at between 9d and 2s 6d each.[26] He did, however, note that kola grew prolifically in the area near the Tano river. The efforts of the Com-missioner for the North Western District in 1904 to promote the cultivation of cocoa, kola, rubber and cotton met much initial scepticism in view of the still ample supplies of wild rubber trees for tapping[27] and the fact that a large proportion of the wild kola crop was always in practice left unpicked on the trees. A few chiefs promised to establish small cocoa, rubber or kola plant-ations but it seems evident that their motive in doing so was more the wish to placate their powerful and inscrutable new overlords than it was any rational expectation of profit to be had from the enterprise. Indeed even the colonial officials were obliged to acknowledge the exiguous short-term rationality of such diversification in view of the comparative cost/price ratios of cultivated cotton or cocoa against gathered rubber.[28] The trade of the North Western District was reported as flourishing in 1906, particularly in rubber and kola, although the chiefs persisted in their reluctance to establish plantations.[29] The trade passing through Kukuom alone was estimated to be running at a level at which the toll takings for January and February alone would have amounted to £500.[30] Ashanti as a whole in this year exported 881 tons of rubber at a value of £172,923 compared with 179 tons of cocoa worth a mere £6,701.[31] In 1907, 1,315 tons of rubber were shipped out of Ashanti by rail, compared with 557 tons of cocoa.[32] But rubber-tapping was beginning to run into difficulties in parts of the Western Province because of diminishing supplies of fresh trees and two chiefs asked permission to stop all tapping of trees on their lands for a year. In 1908, 729 tons of rubber were exported at a value of some £90,000, along with 751 tons of cocoa valued at about £50,000, while the value of the kola trade was estimated at £90,000.[33]

Dependence and opportunity

Extensive cocoa planting was reported from the Western Province but rubber was recognised to be likely to retain its greater appeal, being still plentiful and greatly superior 'as a source of wealth to the producer',[34] until cheap transport had altered the structure of marketing costs. In 1909 rubber was still seen as the chief product of the Western Province and local recognition of the need for less drastic techniques of tapping was reported as growing. But the planting of rubber seedlings continued to evoke little enthusiasm even compared with cocoa trees because it was thought that 'those now working will derive no benefit from the present seedlings'.[35] However, when the Provincial Commissioner visited Ahafo in the next year he found that the establishment of a government rubber nursery at Sunyani had in turn produced the establishment of small rubber nurseries at Hwidiem and Noberkaw.[36] In 1911 the total value of rubber and cocoa exported from Ashanti amounted to some £200,000 in the case of each product, while kola exports conveyed by rail[37] amounted to 904 tons at a value of some £100,000.[58] In the same year the Western Provincial Commissioner, indignantly repudiating the notion that his charges were economically backward, claimed that considerably more than half of Ashanti's total rubber exports came from the forests of the Western Province.[39] In 1914 the administrators were still attempting to encourage rubber plantations in Ahafo by distributing seeds[40] and one noted with pleasure on his visit to the district the abundance of both cocoa and kola at Ntotroso and Kenyase.[41] By the last year of the war, despite the huge value of cocoa exports in 1915 and 1916, cocoa prices had fallen[42] and kola which did not depend for its marketing on the availability of international shipping had come back into temporary favour, the trees in many cases, particularly in the Western Province receiving more attention than did the cocoa.[43]

The depression of cocoa prices in later years certainly discouraged farmers in Ahafo, provoking intermittent local attempts to hold up the crop for better prices and a measure of Ahafo participation in the major hold-up of 1937/8,[44] but it did not after 1918 lead to large-scale and complete desertion of farms. The need for diversification of economic outlets for individuals remained a permanent anxiety. It was indeed an anxiety not to be alleviated until the establishment of a government agency for evening out the fluctuations of the world market price. Even then the Ahafos found to their discouragement that the agency in question acted predominantly as an instrument for extracting the cocoa surplus from the area, while in later and less favourable price conditions on the world market it proved a feeble buffer between the malign forces of the market and the real living standards of the Ahafos. The only consistent strategy pursued locally by the administration for the alleviation of this problem was the diversification of economic outlets; but in this case not short-term diversification for individuals but long-term

74

diversification for the Ahafo economy as a whole. Rational enough as a formal solution for the area's problems, it was a singularly ineffective strategy in practice. While cocoa prices were high, the returns on coffee or cotton or food crops tended to be ludicrously low and to encourage their cultivation involved a decisive repudiation of the doctrine of comparative advantage at one of its stronger points. When cocoa prices were low the depressed farmers were at their least able to indulge in new capital investment the returns on which might well be delayed for several years. Not only were most of the products commended as an alternative to the Ahafos economically unattractive at the best of times, they were also in many cases at least as subject to world market price fluctuations and often to fluctuations with much the same rhythms as those which affected cocoa itself. Colonial D.C.s could derive interest and even a sense of adventure from their efforts to extract the oil from a species of local nut, pounding at it with a *fu-fu* stick and mixing the pulp with shreds of plantain before 'expressing' the oil itself, in the hope of disclosing some new local treasure.[45] But local attitudes were less optimistic and inventive. The forms of individual economic diversification in which the Ahafos put their faith remained the old stand-bys: snails,[46] monkey skins, chewsticks.[47] New crops were introduced by the energies of a D.C. or agricultural officer, oranges to make up the deficiencies of local fruit supplies,[48] coconuts,[49] rice and groundnuts. By 1952 sufficient rice and maize was grown in Ahafo for the Area Committee to consider seriously the value of buying rice-hulling and maize-grinding machines for the locality.[50] Small oil palm plantations were tried out on a number of occasions. All cocoa-growing contains a substantial component of subsistence farming and the foodstuffs grown on family farms today are often quite various, though the starchy staples are still usually plantain, cocoyam, cassava or less frequently yam.

The 1920s were a decade in which colonial efforts for diversification were still extensive but they were also the decade in which the overwhelming dominance of cocoa was established over the Ahafo economy. By 1931 the administration had abandoned all hope that coffee might prove an economically viable crop.[51] By 1928 the experiment of growing cotton had proved a decisive economic failure.[52] By 1926 even the high price offered for rubber that year in Kumasi failed to attract the Ahafos to turn their hands to gathering it.[53] Kola, however, remained an Ahafo export of some importance. In a year when the cocoa price was high it hardly formed a very impressive proportion of the total export values of the Western Province: in 1930, for instance, the Provincial Commissioner estimated the total spending power of the province at £325,000 of which cocoa contributed no less than £305,000.[54] But there were many years in which the cocoa price failed to be high. Kola prices did not fluctuate nearly as dramatically, although they were certainly not always satisfactory to producers and there were indeed years in which the latter made efforts to hold up kola from the savannah market just as they did cocoa from the world market. In 1923/4 for example, a year in which there was a lower than average kola crop in Ahafo, the farmers held on to their stocks of the nuts, refusing to sell for less than 20s for a headload of 2,000 nuts, with the result that much of the crop was spoilt.[55] But the next year the same bulk was sold for 10s to 15s and the year after the price climbed again to 25s a load.[56] These figures compared on the whole very favourably with those offered for cocoa at the time in the same villages. Fuller details of kola production were provided by the Agriculture Department's Cocoa Survey of 1928/9.[57] The bulk of the nut grown in the Western Province was found to be inside the area bounded by the 60 inch rainfall line, kola requiring deep retentive soil and at least 50 to 60 inches of annual rainfall. There was only one main area of production inside the Ahafo area, a narrow band running from north of Hwidiem to just south of Atronie, which produced some 3,000 head-loads. Just to the north of Asunafo another band running to the north of Teppa produced a further 2,000 loads.[58] Total average annual sales for the province as a whole were estimated at 28,779 loads (of 80 lbs a load) – some 1,054 tons – and total production was estimated at up to 2,000–2,500 tons. The crop was marketed entirely by Africans and almost all of it was transported north by head-load or donkey, a mere 50 tons passing south by lorry and railway. The Ahafo kola was marketed at Nkasaim and Ntotroso and its total annual sales were estimated at 3,446 loads as against the 18,947 loads from the much larger Sunyani district. The geographical distribution was fairly wide inside Ahafo: Nkasaim 125 loads, Noberkaw 20, Akrodie 7, Mim 12, Ntotroso 1,774, Kenyase 941, Hwidiem 377, Gyedu 99 and Wamahinso 91. In August 1929 the Ahafo D.C. looked forward to an increase in the sales of kola grown in the vicinity of Kukuom, following the opening of the new Goaso–Kukuom road, and emphasised the desirability of encouraging the kola trade.[59] In September 1931 the D.C. noted that kola from the Noberkaw area, close to Kukuom, was transported to the Bibiani mines for sale at 6d per 100 nuts but judged that the trade was diminishing.[60] But in the same year kola still came second only to cocoa in the production of the province as a whole and Ahafo remained one of the three main producing areas for it.[61]

Ahafo involvement in a wider economy following on the events of 1896 was involvement throughout in a wider network than that of the European cocoa buying agencies. Seeing the Ahafo economy from a firmly consequentialist viewpoint, the main economic effect of the provision of colonial and postcolonial civil order to the area has been the development of a large community of farmers growing cocoa for the world market. This was hardly an effect to which the colonial rulers were at any point averse and it is one which may continue to pose grave dilemmas for Ahafos into the foreseeable future. Yet viewing the process more with the eyes of Ahafo agents in 1874 or 1896 or for that matter 1929 or 1931, there were always those to whom the establishment of a superior degree of civil order[62] meant the opportunity to profit from integrating their village into a less global economy. Furthermore even in the case of the world market, as is epitomised however ambivalently by the treaty of 1896 and by the triumph of the National Liberation Movement in Ahafo sixty years later, the direct surplus extracted by the British colonial government itself might well appear to Ahafos decidedly smaller than that elicited for Ahafo rubber by their Ashanti predecessors or for Ahafo cocoa by their Ghanaian national successors. To forget this is always to risk a failure in understanding the politics of Ahafo.

c. TIMBER

Any able-bodied adult (and many older children) can pick cocoa or kola nuts, gather snails or tap rubber after a fashion. But no single able-bodied adult, or even group of adults without powerful mechanical assistance, can transport a giant forest tree to the rail head or dockside from which it can be sold on the world market. There are many Ahafo products for which the provision of rapid and reasonably cheap road transport has altered the price paid to the producer by a dramatic proportion. Before the establishment of an effective public road system in the late 1920s the profitability of cocoa in Ahafo was at best marginal and the prospect of developing large-scale farming of other foodstuffs for export from the area was simply out of the question. But, even with the establishment of a road network which was capable of sustaining (with considerable administrative chivvying and popular labour) the weight of cocoa and provision lorries for most of the year, the large-scale export of timber from Ahafo would scarcely have been feasible. As recently as 1968 the laterite road from Hwidiem to Mim, along which the great bulk of timber traffic out of the area is compelled to pass, was rendered almost impassable to timber trucks for several months by heavy flooding. Only the strenuous use of heavy earth-moving machinery from the Mim sawmills and the availability of large supplies of timber baulks from the same source made it possible to keep the road open at all. The roads so painfully constructed by communal labour forty years earlier were always in danger in the rainy season of being cut to pieces by the passage even of a touring car. To expect them to take the weight of heavy timber traffic would have been absurd. Given the degree of popular labour in their construction, accepted because of their obvious economic value to all cocoa farmers, it would also have been in the highest degree politically provocative to permit the roads to be damaged by timber lorries. The profitability of timber-extraction thus depended directly upon the public provision of a minimal infrastructure, above all of a durable trunk road out of the area. It also required very much larger supplies of initial capital than any other economic activity so far pursued in Ahafo. Machinery for cutting trees, for the clearing and construction of subsidiary roads and heavy transport for moving the logs represent together a quite different form of economic enterprise from any aspect of the production or collection of other forest products.

The economic possibilities of other products also were, of course, first drawn to the attention of the Ahafos by men who came from outside the area. But none of them required much more than a weather eye open to market opportunities for Ahafos themselves to undertake their exploitation in a systematic fashion in due course, if they chose to do so. To anyone fortunate enough to be in possession of considerable initial capital timber-extraction has provided an avenue to rapid capital accumulation unequalled in the recent economic history of Ghana. Indeed, the sheer rapidity of capital formation in the timber industry in the palmy days of the 1940s and 1950s has by now proved so eloquent that many attempt to break into the industry in a specu-lative and sometimes semi-legal fashion, borrowing a little initial capital to acquire a truck and tractor and dispensing with licence fees for the trees which they cut. Among this lower fringe of its practitioners timber-extraction is an anxious and sometimes rather raffish business and certainly one in which it is not beyond the ambitions of an enterprising and prosperous young Ahafo to join. But except as a semi-delinquent example of a career open to talent it is not this lower fringe of timber operators, plentiful enough though it may be simply in terms of numbers, which is important even today. By far the greatest part of the wealth extracted from Ahafo by way of timber, even today when many Ghanaian timber contractors operate in the area, several of them now men of great wealth, has been extracted by two large expatriate com-panies. The larger of these two, Glikstens, were the holders of the first timber concession of which there is now record in Ahafo, taken up in 1947.[1] But it is the second, formerly known as the Victoria Sawmills and today as the Mim Timber Company, which has had the greater and more lasting effect upon the area. The town of Mim was the most populous in Ahafo when Davidson Houston arrived in 1896[2] and it is not clear that it has ever lost this pre-dominance since. But if in 1896 its size reflected above all the intimacy of its links with Kumasi and its standing as a fetish centre, there can be no doubt that its position today, along with a substantial proportion of its population, is a result of the economic importance of the sawmills of the Mim Timber yard. Naturally this political salience has aroused considerable resentment towards the Mim Timber Company (as well as intermittent gratitude among its more direct clients). The company cannot be expected to persist indefinitely. But for as long as it does last it offers the most prominent and concrete testimony to the economic good fortune which Ahafo's integration into the world market has brought to some whose heart (and by now a large part of whose treasure) must be presumed to be firmly elsewhere. It was large expatriate firms which introduced Ahafo to the possibilities of the timber industry and it is they which have so far benefited most handsomely from these possibilities. For most Ahafos the point at which the role of timber contractor might realistically enter their economic calculations is so far beyond their grasp as to be virtually out of sight. But there are enough prosperous and economically sophisticated individuals inside and outside Ahafo who can view the position of the Mim company with an envy reinforced by their own sense of competence for foreign ownership of the Mim works and concessions to be today a rather poor actuarial risk. It is a political as well as an economic achievement for the Charmants to have kept such control over so much of the potential wealth of the area for so long; but in the nature of things it is an achievement which it will require ever greater skill and indeed good fortune to sustain.

The first significant attempt to promote exports of timber from Ahafo came from a government initiative. The Conservator of Forests for Southern Nigeria had reported after a trip in 1907 that he doubted whether the forests of Ahafo and its vicinity were equalled for the value of their timber by any others in tropical Africa.[3] Inspired by this assessment, the Provincial Commissioner for the Western Province, F. E. Fell, began in 1911 to press the government to investigate the possibility of using the Tano river to float logs down to the sea at Half Assini in view of the 'enormous development' in the timber trade which such a use would open up.[4] His plan was to use the tributaries of the Tano during the wet season to float the timber out. Mim forests could be tapped by the Goa river in flood and streams between Hwidiem and Nkasaim and between Hwidiem and the Tano would also be suitable for floating logs in the flood season, while the Aboum river on the left bank of the Tano would open up another wide area. In the second half of 1912 the Conservator of Forests for the Gold Coast travelled through the Western Province and reported that long-term prospects for floating timber according to Fell's schemes were real enough, though he also deplored a short-sighted policy over road construction, a charge which Fell indignantly repudiated.[5] But despite the encouraging tone of the Forestry Department's assessment of technical prospects for using the Tano as a timber route,[6] the difficulties in the event always proved to be too intractable. Similarly, a bold proposal by the Conservator in 1912 to arrest the southward progress of the savannah, protect the swamps, streams and rivers which fed the Offin and the Tano, and to preserve valuable timber supplies, rubber trees and vines by creating a gigantic forest reserve in the triangle Sunyani/Kumasi/Bibiani proved impossible to implement.[7] This proposal would have had the effect of turning the whole of Ahafo into a forest reserve in which all new cutting for cultivation would have been prohibited without the special permission of the Forestry Department and in which no commercial timber cutting would have been allowed at all. Little effort was made for almost two decades after this either to conserve the timber of Ahafo systematically or to exploit it commercially. But neither possibility disappeared completely from the administration's longer-term aspirations. In 1920, for example, when the Chief Commissioner on his tour of north west Ashanti met the Omanhene of Ahafo, the latter reminded him that on the occasion at which the Governor had spoken to him at Tanodumase some years earlier, he had been promised that the motor road from Kumasi would be pushed on into the Ahafo forest. The Chief Commissioner was unable to deny that no such road had yet materialised and he emphasised in his report to Accra the advantages which would flow from its completion: 'In Ahafo are some of the finest forests in the Gold Coast. A motor road will enable these areas to be exploited and its construction can be conditional on the establishment of forest reserves.'[8]

The establishment of forest reserves was always likely to arouse opposition because of the potential constriction of chiefly land revenues and commoner land access. The Forest Ordinance in the Colony itself had aroused fierce controversy from the first and there is some indication that the decision to go on with the attempt to establish the huge triangular West Ashanti forest reserve in 1912 proceeded as much from the difficulty of formulating an acceptable forest ordinance for the Colony as from any opposition current in Ashanti at the time in areas most of which were still very thinly populated.[9] It was in the 1930s that forest reserves first began to be established in Asunafo. The 50 square mile Bonsam Bepo reserve and the 31 square mile Bonkoni reserve were both set up in 1934/5, along with the 104 square mile Asukese reserve, only parts of which were, however, located in Ahafo.[10] In 1937/8 no less than seven new areas, totalling 191 square miles, were established in the Sunyani forestry district and another two areas of 202 square miles were set up as reservations under Native Authority ordinances, several of these areas lying wholly or partially inside Ahafo proper.[11] In the same year Balduzzi, a Kumasi road contractor and sawmill owner began to cut logs for his mill on the Kunso–Wiawso road, north of Ahafo.[12] More graphic evidence of the insidious approach of western capital can be seen in the appearance of a sum of £20 in return for which 'The Mimhene has entered into an agreement with a certain whiteman with regard to certain Forest Reserve', among the list of charges of breach of traditional obligations by Mimhene Kofi Kwarteng, brought before the Asanteman Council by the Akwaboahene in October 1937.[13] The charges were rejected by the Council, the Asantehene warning the Akwaboahene firmly against any similar future attack on Mimhene. But the fact that the Akwaboahene had not only thought it prudent to mention the £20 in his charges but also noted that the money was still held on deposit for

Mimhene at the Asantehene's office makes it virtually certain that, whatever the rights and wrongs of the dispute over allegiance and traditional dues, the £20 from a certain whiteman was no figment of the Akwaboahene's fertile imagination.

In the years immediately following the Second World War the white men began to open up the Ahafo forests for timber extraction at dramatic speed. The Charmant family, Hungarian by origin but employing American capital, began negotiations for concessions on Mim land, paying considerable sums to Asantehene, Akwaboahene and the Mim stool itself. A year or two later, in 1948, they had established a sawmill in Mim and begun their operations.[14] Glikstens's concessions were also registered from 1947 onwards. The land area of Ahafo today is divided up between forest reserves of some 480,000 acres and a residue of some 580,000 acres of waste, water, and actual or potential agricultural land.[15] Timber concessions have been allocated, and are indeed held today, on both forest reserve and other land, though the control of cutting is much tighter on the reserve lands.[16] The Mim Timber Company still possesses huge concessions both inside and outside the reserves, many of them acquired at times when the prices of concessions were drastically lower than they are today. Both Glikstens's working of their concessions in the south of Ahafo and the Mim Timber Company's working of theirs out towards the Bia river and Dormaa Ahenkro have had a profound impact upon the area, opening up the forest to far heavier settlement, providing an outlet for cocoa and foodstuffs along the network of timber roads which the companies were compelled to construct simply in order to get their logs out of Ahafo.[17] Glikstens no longer loom very large in Ahafo life: they have taken their logs and gone. But the Mim company is if anything more elaborately entrenched in the area than it has ever been before. Subject to persistent criticism from political representatives of the area ever since its establishment, though never without vigorous defenders, it has undoubtedly made a visible and practical contribution to the needs of the area and often done more than the government showed itself willing or able to do for the maintenance of communications[18] and the provision of amenities to the area. It was attacked in the Legislature by B. F. Kusi for contaminating the water supplies of Mim and by B. K. Senkyire and again by S. K. Opoku for monopolising timber concessions.[19] It was heavily, if unwillingly, involved in the conflicts between C.P.P. and N.L.M., its workers being assaulted on a number of occasions and its vehicles damaged.[20] Under the Busia government the M.P. for Asutifi, Osei Duah, accused it of numerous delinquencies and caused it to be investigated by a Parliamentary Committee. The military government of the National Redemption Council (N.R.C.) uncovered embarrassing details of loans made to the Progress Party Minister for Lands and Mineral Resources, R. R. Amponsah, by Charmant, while

Amponsah was in office.[21] But it has always so far contrived to keep friends in power to balance the resentment for which it is such a natural target, both members of the C.P.P. business community and United Party politicians. Being in a position to assist in many ways the paths of the local Administrator it has also seldom found it difficult to arrive at a satisfactory understanding with local representatives of the government. Since 1968 it has also made more self-conscious efforts to give the local community of Ahafo a stake in its continued viability.[22] In January 1968 a Mim timber contractor, W. K. Ennin, was appointed a director of the company and in the following year two other Mim citizens became directors. In 1970 they were joined on the board by the Managing Director of Paramount Gin, a large Accra distillers company, and by a Kumasi lawyer. In the summer of 1971 Charmant was said to be making active preparations to offer shares in the company for sale to the Ghanaian general public.

There are, of course, by now many other Ghanaian contractors working in the Ahafo area, including former M.P.s like A. W. Osei (on a rather small scale) and B. F. Kusi, along with major Kumasi operators like F. K. Poku and B. N. Kufuor's Bibiani Logging and Lumber, the largest Ghanaian timber company, begun some decades back with a large concession from his father, the Chief of Nkawie. In 1956 besides the operations of Glikstens and the Mim Timber Company, there was only one contractor working in the Ahafo Local Council area, P. A. Yeboah.[23] But by the end of the 1950s the rush really started. More than twenty contractors were working on lands over which the Council was supposed to exercise control and authority.[24] But the number of timber inspectors whom the Council was able to employ was quite inadequate to keep an effective check on the cutting. There were also frequent disputes over the entitlement of chiefs to allot concessions to contractors.[25] The legal situation was for a time extremely confused[26] and even today there exists no unitary system for the registration of timber concessions and felling agreements. In such a situation neither modern nor traditional authority in the area was likely to prove immune to individual incentives to permit profitable irregularities. By the late 1960s control had become somewhat tighter, although timber remained the most obvious economic field in which considerable sums of money could be made rapidly by those who were either lucky or unscrupulous. But the most important development in Ahafo's timber industry from a political point of view was the emergence of a small group of Ahafo citizens as very wealthy timber entrepreneurs. The wealthiest and most prominent of these men is undoubtedly W. K. Ennin. A brief outline of his biography will thus serve to emphasise the extent to which Ahafo's ties to the world economy have in this instance begun to create foci of highly concentrated economic and political power within the community. Ennin completed standard 7 of his elementary education in Mim in 1930 and passed the entrance examination to Achimota. But since his family did not have the money to pay for a secondary education for him he was obliged instead to take a job as Native Court Registrar, first in the Wenchi district and then in Kumasi in the Kontri clan court. From there he moved to Juaben as Registrar and State Secretary, returning to Kumasi in 1949 as Registrar of the Asantehene's Court 'B'. In 1950 he was promoted to be Registrar of Asantehene's Court 'A';[27] but in 1952 he resigned from this position in the light of prospective changes in Native Administration[28] and the economic responsibility of managing his family cocoa farms after the death of his elder brother. In 1955 he entered the timber business, borrowing £4,000 from the Industrial Development Corporation on the security of his house in Bantama, Kumasi. He had been aware of the entrepreneurial possibilities in timber exploitation many years before when timber extraction was first beginning in Ashanti, having for example advised B. N. Kufuor to enter the industry as long ago as 1941 when the latter was working under him as a bailiff in the court in Bantama. But, unlike Kufuor, Ennin did not come from a wealthy and powerful family and his salary in his most lucrative appointment as Court Registrar from 1950 on was on a scale of £120–£138 per annum.[29] Nevertheless once launched into the business after 1955 he contrived to pay off his initial loan with some rapidity and was able when the Ghanaian government offered extensive loans to timber contractors in the early 1960s to borrow no less than £58,000, a sum sufficient to enable him to buy valuable heavy equipment. Since 1962 he has not merely repaid this loan but built large mansions in Mim and Kumasi and three houses in Accra, as well as putting four of his children through university and maintaining another seven of them as of 1971 in secondary school, including five at the elite Cape Coast school Mfantsipim. At this time he was also maintaining two of his nephews at a secondary school and paying the fees of four students at Mim secondary school whose families were unable to afford to pay for them. The level of economic success implied by this scale of expenditure and the speed with which it has been achieved are plainly sufficient to impress themselves vividly on the Ahafo imagination. It is scarcely remarkable in view of them that Ennin should have been pressed to stand as political representative for Ahafo in legislative elections in the 1950s and in 1969. It is not even remarkable that he should have been approached more recently as a possible occupant of the powerful post of Chairman of the Kumasi City Council. It is even less remarkable, however, that he should regard such approaches with a prudent disdain. In the first generation such drastic economic achievement appears to impress far more than it evokes resentment, creating political power more durable and less invidious than that which can be won by the process of purely political competition. To put it no lower, there is no one in Ahafo, resident or civil servant, whom Ennin is not in a position to patronise. As a patron his style is lavish and in many ways attractive. But it is not difficult to see in such a position the emergence of a degree of purely economic inequality quite unlike any generated by the dynamics of expanding cocoa cultivation and one which can hardly fail in the second and subsequent generations to begin to form a more overt consciousness of class.

CHAPTER 4

THE COLONIAL TRANSFORMATION OF AHAFO

---

a. MILITARY CONTROL AND PUBLIC ORDER

Only once in the history of the British colonial presence in Ahafo and in its postcolonial aftermath did the maintenance of ultimate political control by the central government require the application of substantial military force; and, even then, the required force was in fact applied outside the district. The initial British protectorate over Ahafo had been established by one of the series of local treaties negotiated by the British in the effort to isolate Kumasi in 1896.[1] Although it had been signed by representatives of all the major political units in Ahafo, the treaty did not represent a solid acceptance on the part of all Ahafos of a common political interest, still less of a joint strategy for advancing such an interest. It was simply an index of the temporary dominance of the Kukuom chief Atekyi, based on nothing more enduring than the calculation that in January 1896 more was to be obtained by a collective Ahafo front with the British against the crumbling power of Kumasi. But evanescent though it was as a political commitment, the agreement of 1896 did at least, from the Ahafo viewpoint, have the merit of appearing as a component in the British conquest of somewhere else, rather than a direct experience of undergoing conquest itself.

If Ahafo was ever conquered, it was conquered in 1900 after the failure of the Yaa Asantewa rising. The town of Mim had the distinction of being the last Ashanti outpost to surrender to the British in October of that year.[2] But it seems to have achieved this distinction by purely geographical means, being simply the last place reached by the British forces in their mopping-up operations. It is not clear that when the British detachment eventually arrived there, there was any resistance left for them to encounter.[3] Indeed it is unclear whether there was ever any resistance for them to encounter in Mim itself. Braimansu, Atekyi's successor as chief of Kukuom, who had been recognised by the British as Omanhene of Ahafo, had undoubtedly joined the rebel forces. But his arch rival in Ahafo, the Fetish Chief of

85

Dependence and opportunity

Mim, Beditor, had had either the prudence or the good fortune to be across the Bia river at Wam when the rising began and, since Wam had remained firmly allied with the British, as Wam went, so went Beditor.[4] Even before the Kumasi rising Braimansu had had considerable difficulty in resisting the pressures of his formal Kumasi superiors, acknowledging even in his formal communications with the British that the lands under his own authority did in fact belong to one of the Kumasi clan stools,[5] and being at best intermittently successful in the struggle to restrain his notional Ahafo subordinates from rendering to their former overlords on the new Kumasi Committee of Administration the very concrete embodiments of subjection which the latter persisted vigorously in requiring.[6] Not that Braimansu was altogether without his successes in this war of attrition. He did contrive in 1899, for example, to secure from the Governor of the Gold Coast, through the Resident in Kumasi, a legal judgement that his subordination to Kumasi authority had been permanently and comprehensively terminated. The occasion both of the judgement and of Braimansu's own acknowledgement of the Kumasi ownership of the Ahafo lands was the seizure by his erstwhile Kumasi superior of a substantial quantity of rubber (40 loads, worth £160) which belonged to Braimansu.[7] The fact that the British Governor and his forces could be summoned up on the Kukuom side on such an occasion makes clear that the resources open to Braimansu as a result of the conquest of Kumasi were far from inconsiderable. But perhaps the eventual accession of Kukuom to the rebels at the time of the rising was nevertheless more a reflection of how unequal the tug of war between Kumasi and Kukuom necessarily remained at a time when British control was still so light and still based on such elaborate ignorance of the universe which it hoped to order, than it was a direct token of ideological solidarity with the imposing ethnic empire of which Ahafo had previously been such an unimportant border area. It seems likely that from the Kumasi perspective Braimansu showed himself in 1900 as too weak to be an effective quisling; not as too proud to be a British slave.

The British official who visited Ahafo to reimpose effective political control upon the area suggested that Ahafo's indemnity for the war should be raised above the figure originally fixed and also that Ahafo should be divided in half.[8] One half should be attached to the stool of Wam, to which Beditor had sworn allegiance at the time of the rising.[9] This proposal was, however, rejected by the Governor who considered that it would lead to the remaining half of Ahafo returning under the control of Kumasi and thus to an increase in the power of Kumasi, a consummation devoutly to be deplored.[10] The incorporation of traditional authorities into the machinery of colonial administration was conceived explicitly in later decades as a device for dividing and ruling. Its great merit was, as the Intelligence Report of

1930 put it, that 'as a result of the system of indirect rule in vogue, it is extremely unlikely that any riot or disturbance should be directed against Government authorities. What disturbances occur are invariably in the nature of "faction fights".'[11] From a military point of view the Ashanti empire was a decisively more refractory unit to rule than the rather adventitious union of Ahafo, and one correspondingly much in need of division. The unity of Ahafo – an 'artificial' *oman* in the legitimist terminology which the administration came to favour later under the guidance of their government anthropologist Rattray – was thus preserved simply as an instrumental prerequisite for the altogether more indispensable disunity of Ashanti.

Within the area of Ahafo British ambitions to control developed in substantial harmony with British capacity to do so. Initial efforts to disrupt the military potential for resistance were crude, though no doubt effective enough. The British military officer in charge of the western frontier destroyed 1,200 daneguns in Ahafo, Bechem and Wam in the year after the rising,[12] while when Captain Armitage travelled through these areas with a substantial military force in August 1901, he reported that he had not heard a single gunshot, despite the fact that the inhabitants were essentially hunters by occupation.[13] Physical control of weapons and powder was made extremely difficult, however, by the extent of smuggling across the Ivory Coast border. Armitage on his tour while at Wam came upon an officer of the Colony Preventive Service, F. E. Fell, later to be an energetic Provincial Commissioner in Sunyani, who was engaged in the attempt to establish some effective barrier to the smuggling.[14] In October 1903 it was reported to the Commissioner at Sikassiko by the chief of Diabakrum that lead bars and gunpowder were passing through his village to be sold to Kukuom and Ashanti.[15] A month or two later the Commissioner in Sikassiko reported the establishment of District Reporters throughout the Province, whose function was to be to delate traders in arms, powder, lead and gin to the local chiefs who in turn were to send the smugglers on to Sikassiko. The reporters were to be rewarded in proportion to the total of smuggled goods seized, one of them being posted inside Ahafo at Ntotroso.[16] By February 1904, however, the Commissioner had decided that it was preferable to use women informants, since the men appointed merely took bribes from the gunrunners, sometimes after blackmailing their payers: 'It appeals to their ideas, they having no scruples as to receiving money from both parties.'[17] In November of the same year, the Commissioner of the North Western District urged that it was premature to consider making the sale of powder in Ashanti unrestricted, denying that 'sufficient time has elapsed since the last war, to place much confidence in the Ashantees' and suggesting that D.C.s should continue to distribute the relatively small quantity of powder needed for hunting at a reasonably low cost.[18] Most of the gunpowder smuggled into

Ashanti was still thought to come through Kukuom in December 1904,[19] while in March 1905 the chief of Diabakrum, from whom the Kukuomhene had recently made spirited attempts to exact tributes which properly belonged to the Wam stool,[20] renewed his accusations about the extent of gunrunning through Kukuom.[21] Concern over the extent of arms and ammunition imported into Ashanti persisted for some years after this, it being virtually impossible, as noted in 1907, to prevent Ashantis buying powder from coastal chiefs in the Central Province (who were fully entitled to possess it), without erecting a full-scale customs barrier between the Colony and Ashanti.[22] But by this time the administrative ambition behind the attempts to stop smuggling had become more one of enforcing rules previously made than one of strengthening a still precarious military control. In 1906 one Ahafo hunter had been graciously permitted to acquire an elephant gun;[23] but requests by Braimansu and other Omanhenes of the Western District to obtain double-barrelled guns had been anxiously referred to the Chief Commissioner of Ashanti for a policy decision.[24] In 1909 the Omanhenes of Wam and Ahafo both duly obtained their elephant rifles for £30 each[25] and the Commissioner in Sunyani readily sanctioned the possession by the Mimhene of a double-barrelled gun presented to him by a subject who had acquired it for £10 from a 'scholar' in Kumasi, though the Commissioner also took the precaution of checking with his superior in Kumasi to see whether the 'scholar' had been entitled to have the gun in his possession in the first place.[26] In the next year a full system of gun registration was established in Ahafo, based on the entitlement of each individual who reported his gun to the Commissioner to purchase two pounds of gunpowder and a corresponding quantity of lead. A total of 870 guns were registered and formally stamped in this way by the beginning of September 1909;[27] and more than thirty more were added by the end of the Commissioner's Ahafo tour, despite the fact that many of the inhabitants in Ahafo were at the time out of town in the bush, collecting rubber and snails.[28] By 1914 gunpowder was allocated to the leading chiefs of Ahafo in carefully graded proportions and leading chiefs were given permits to purchase assigned numbers of new daneguns.[29] As early as 1906, a time when there was a full company of soldiers quartered in Sunyani, the Ashantis had been seen by their principal British administrator as a possible bulwark against a large-scale Muslim rising in West Africa.[30] By 1912 he felt able to claim (in the context, admittedly, of an effort to shake off full budgetary responsibility for the troops stationed in Ashanti) that the control of the government was no longer any more dependent on troops in Ashanti than it was anywhere else in the Colony.[31] Even the vigorous gunrunners of Ahafo were by this time no longer quite what they used to be. In the context of the First World War, the administration's anxiety over their activities was transformed from one of preventing potentially insurgent Ashantis from picking up an armoury on the Ivory Coast market to one of preventing the outflow of military materials (powder and lead) in wartime from a British territory to the territory of a foreign state, albeit a military ally.[32] Forceful political resistance might still present itself, at least in prospect, as a military challenge. The proposal to despatch a D.C. to Mim to face down the formidable fetish energies supposed to prevail in that backwoods locality insisted on the need for him to be accompanied on his mission by 25 soldiers.[33] But it was a token of changing British expectations that the D.C. who did eventually establish the administrative headquarters for Ahafo in Goaso in 1914 was in practice, as he plaintively objected, obliged to do so without so much as a single policeman to furnish his immediate *jus gladii*.[34]

The problem of colonial control in Ahafo turned out in fact never to be posed directly after 1901 as one of military force. There were riots in Ahafo, even one riot during the colony-wide political disturbances of 1948 in the notoriously bellicose village of Kenyasi II, in which the District Commissioner and his armed police escort were fired on from the bush and in which a number of villagers were killed. But even in 1948 the Kenyase riot seems to have been less an overt assault on the colonial regime as such than an occasion for the looting of a number of Lagosian stores in the village.[35] (Kenyase II can hardly be said, however, to have been over-provided at the time with what were plausibly unequivocal and substantial tokens of the colonial presence.) Political solidarity between even Kenyase II and its neighbour Kenyase I at the time did not extend far enough for them to be willing to share a single Roman Catholic school between the two communities.[36] In Ahafo as a whole no very militant political solidarity against the colonial regime as such seems ever to have been mustered. By the time that any such degree of political mobilisation might have been readily attained, the old Ahafo traditional polarities between Kukuom and Mim had been transposed, untidily but effectively, onto the divisions of political parties competing on a national scale for electoral allegiance. The vigour of this party competition had the effect, although it was only for the most instrumental of reasons the *intended* effect, of slightly delaying the termination of the colonial regime. In a number of other parts of Ghana – and perhaps even in Kumasi itself – this conflict might in retrospect seem a slightly morally precarious instance of subordinating a persisting political antagonism towards colonialism to the quest of short-run localist advantage. But in Ahafo such a perspective would be simply perverse. The problem of social control in Ahafo since 1901 has always been more one of keeping local factional conflict within bounds sufficiently restrictive to prevent it disrupting production for the world market than it has been one of preserving in the hands of the government, whichever the government happened to be, the possession of a preponderance

Dependence and opportunity

of the instruments of violence. In this sense it would never have been substantially correct to claim that the politics of Ahafo in this period were *about*
colonialism – or indeed about neocolonialism. It would be more accurate
merely to observe that throughout this time the politics of Ahafo have been
situated *within* colonialism or its neocolonial successor.

But the comparative ease with which the British contrived to maintain final
military dominion over Ahafo did not extend to the wider and more delicate
scope of control at which they came increasingly to aim. As their ambitions
expanded to take in more intricate aspects of the formation of a society, the
reassuring immediacy and simplicity of military force was left increasingly
far behind. When it was still a matter of facing a detachment of the
colonial army, Ahafo necessarily lacked the resources to fight back with
much success. But when the conflict of wills became a matter of conducting
their own lives in their own way, instead of comprehensively adopting the
visions of communal development increasingly favoured by colonial administrators, the obstructive resources in the hands of the Ahafos were
handsomely augmented. The expansion of the colonial bureaucracy and
of its postcolonial successor in Ahafo (as elsewhere) is testimony enough
to the expanded scope of the government will to control Ahafo. But it is
at best equivocal testimony of governmental effectiveness in this enterprise.
Given that the bureaucracy did in fact expand, and particularly that its
coercive branch, the police, did so, it would for most of the subsequent period
be accurate to say that no sector of Ahafo society reflected the limitations of
the government's capacity to control it as clearly as did the sector specifically
established to enforce that control. The problem of the impurity of administrative will and purpose faced the British, as they later faced Nkrumah,
with a persistent and ribald commentary on their own conception of the
purpose of their regime. Whether the rule was direct or indirect, the key
problem for the higher echelons of the administrative hierarchy always
became one of who could control the controllers. It began in an acute form
with the military instruments of the conquest itself, the Hausa soldiery.
About these there was, as Armitage judged after his 1901 tour, almost
universal complaint when they passed through the country or were left at a
village 'without the restraining influence exercised over them by a white
officer'. The post, consisting of three Huasas left by Capt. Luckman at Mim,
hired itself out to anyone who wished to extort or recover money from
another native. The chief of the village was powerless and men were tied up
there and not released until they had not only paid the money demanded by
the person employing the Hausas, but had also satisfied their captors.'[37] After
1901 soldiers were not often so much in evidence in Ahafo; but in 1904, for
example, the chief of Aboum complained that six soldiers and a clerk had
descended on his village, taking fowls, mats, sandals, meat (and £2 7s od

90

from the chief himself) and breaking the old gun which he had been permitted to retain 'on account of Loyal Service during the late rising'.[38] Complaints of looting in all the villages along the route from Mim and Kukuom to Sunyani were made in 1906, thirty fowls, an umbrella and a sheep or two being removed from Goaso and local inhabitants being impressed to carry the baggage of the soldiers' wives. The Commissioner instructed the complainants to take their case to the European officer in charge of the detachment from which the soldiers were drawn, a proposal which cannot wholly have reassured the injured parties as to the extent of British commitment to the redress of their wrongs.[39] As late as 1914 the administration was still obliged to despatch six soldiers to help the new District Commissioner in Ahafo to bring in his prisoners, after a brush with the Mim fetish.[40] But it had been implicitly acknowledged the year before by the Provincial Commissioner, in response to the professional complaints of the military commander in Ashanti, that the army should not be expected to carry out normal law enforcement duties. Indeed the Commissioner had pressed actively, if without early success, for the provision in the Western Province of an additional six policemen and one N.C.O. to be stationed at Kukuom.[41] The advent of an ordinary civilian police force permanently stationed in Ahafo in exchange for the intermittent incursions of a no doubt at times brutal and licentious soldiery was a symbolic representation of the will to transform the colonial state at the point of incidence into a civil community instead of what appeared to be simply a continuation of conquest by much the same means as before. But the greater delicacy of control available to a resident authority (and one, moreover, which had been specifically trained in more delicate methods of control) was an ambiguous advance. It proved, predictably enough, to enhance the opportunities available to colonial (or postcolonial) underlings to despoil the local population at least as much as it enhanced the ability of the colonial government to control this population for what were, at least in the government's own view, a purer set of purposes.

The only pure purposes in the colonial situation were white purposes. The key explanation of the impurity of administrative will throughout the colonial period consequently remained for colonial officialdom the inadequate purchase of white purposes on non-white administrative behaviour; and the main cause identified for this inadequate purchase was the lack of a persistent and immediate white presence. Hausa soldiers out of the supervision of white officers, and their successors, government policemen posted in Ahafo during the long periods when no white commissioner was in fact stationed there,[42] were both seen as intrinsically unreliable, as tokens of the extreme frailty of the colonial project. Even the carriers of the more strictly cultural aspects of this project, the Christian communities or those who brought western literacy to Ahafo were, as we shall see,[43] felt to be inherently untrustworthy in the absence of strict European supervision. In its early stages the administration might still be a trifle bemused to find a robust hero of the struggle against fetish cruelty and corruption like Kofi Pong 'transformed' within a few years into a systematic extortioner of whom the local population were 'unaccountably' too terrified for them to dare to denounce him to the British authorities.[44] But later the administration developed a style of vision which was more practised in accounting for the prevalence of such troublesome metamorphoses.

It is probable that the undependability of these putative instruments of the centralist values of the colonial regime caused the Commissioners more exasperation than the sheer recalcitrance of the indigenous Ahafos themselves to many aspects of the colonial project. But, at least until the beginning of party political competition in the area in the mid-1950s, the formal administrative personnel (clerks, police, eventually African D.C.s), however inadequate in British eyes their commitment to the centralist values of the regime might sometimes be, did at least have the major advantage of not being too precisely committed within the peripheral values of Ahafo. In the mid-1950s national party competition came to furnish a forum within which Ahafo factional conflict became in practice a component of a national struggle for political power. But, except in this relatively brief period, the main problem of social control faced by the government in Ahafo did in fact remain, as the 1930 Intelligence Report asserted, the problem of controlling local factional conflicts. Indirect rule was certainly an inexpensive device for maintaining final military control. But the political mechanism which it employed for this purpose had the disadvantage of itself generating intense factional conflict. The more extreme forms of chiefly deviance did not persist overtly for very long. In 1904 a Commissioner in Odumase might still on occasion have to send soldiers to compel an Omanhene to leave his area and come to the district headquarters to resolve some dispute.[45] At other points in the first decade of the century the Omanhene of Ahafo might be found culpably negligent in permitting the regular killing of victims in 'fetish' witch-finding campaigns and might himself be found guilty of ordering the savage torture of a pair of prisoners whom he suspected of having stolen from him. But in later decades holders of chiefly power had learnt considerably greater discretion about the public use of violence. From the time at which an administrative office was established in Goaso, from 1914 onwards, the chiefs contrive to dissociate themselves from such illegal violence as comes to the notice of the administration with much greater success than the colonial police themselves attain in practice.[46] After 1910, except on occasions of intercommunal violence, Ahafo chiefs appear to have found much less difficulty in satisfying the minimal requirements of their British Commissioners than those of their own subjects. In itself this balance of successful attention is a direct measure of the economy of indirect rule as a system of ultimate control. But it is also an indication of why it was likely to be so much less effective as an implement for more active and elaborate social engineering.

While the central government came to will a more elaborate style of control, the initial localised indirect rule in Ahafo also came to be replaced by the re-creation of the centralised Ashanti Confederacy. When the disparity in goals between those who held authority over Ahafo within this new structure and the aspirations for local development now held by the British administrators became more acute, this too came to be replaced by a succession of schemes for local administration and by a national electoral system based on universal adult suffrage. The persistence of chieftaincy as a focus of communal and factional strife is clearly in part a product of the protracted colonial experiment with indirect rule, though this does not in any way imply that chieftaincy ever behaved simply as an instrument in the hands of the colonial rulers nor that it ever drew its political power solely from its capacity ultimately to elicit the support of the colonial regime. In that it has in fact remained such a focus for communal conflict, it would be historically implausible to suppose that chiefly institutions and the behaviour of chiefs were not a necessary condition for much of the more vigorous political conflict which took place. But it would also plainly constitute a rather abject acceptance of the ideology of the colonial and postcolonial state to suppose that such political conflict was in no sense conflict over anything other than chiefly affairs. Indirect rule was a mechanism for generating factional struggle. But much of the factional struggle, which remains such a profound drain on the modernist developmental projects of the state, reflects a perfectly rational deflection of political energy from goals which are well beyond the capacities of the Ahafos to attain to those which, being close to hand, are obviously more within their grasp. It is hard to imagine that either the colonial or the postcolonial state apparatus would have had a very comfortable time if all these surging energies were to be applied in an unmediated form to the conflict for the severely limited assets which were or are currently available for distribution.

There is no simple way of measuring the extent of overt factional conflict within or between communities in Ahafo since 1896, still less of coming to any firm conclusion as to how far such factional conflict as does overstep the threshold of violence can be construed as an index of some deeper experience of political constraint. Destoolment disputes within particular communities, violent brawls between pagans and Christians[47] or between indigenes and Northern immigrants (as far apart as 1916 and 1941),[48] systematic and sometimes brutal clashes between the adherents of rival national political parties, long-drawn-out tussles for the alteration of the 'traditional' chiefly constitution of Ahafo, intermittent clashes between historically counterposed communities like the adjacent villages of Kenyase I and II,[49] protracted battles for dominance of a single town between two or more lineage groups: the political order of Ahafo since 1896 has been shot through with a myriad kaleidoscopic conflicts. There have been a considerable number of occasions over the decades when these conflicts have been felt to threaten a violent disruption of public order. But the two major peaks of potential for protracted violence came in fact some forty years apart: at the end of the first major tussle for the 'traditional' dominion over colonial Ahafo and during the height of the contest between the National Liberation Movement (N.L.M.) and the Convention People's Party (C.P.P.). The first resulted in the short run in the imprisonment and later the exile of Beditor and its only permanent result perhaps was to preclude the possibility of Mim replacing Kukuom as suzerain of an independent Ahafo. The second resulted in an initial N.L.M. victory in Ahafo, but a victory which was eventually reversed by the application of the power of the general government.[50] There have been a number of other incidents of violence focussed exclusively on the modernist face of Ahafo in the last quarter of a century – notably the riot at Kenyase II and a series of labour disputes in the Mim timber yard in 1968/9 in which armed police were called in by the District Administrative Officer to control the timber workers. But it was to some degree a mark of the continued efficacy of indirect rule that the major clashes of 1956/8 were still fought out in Ahafo in terms of the control of traditional office and of the amendment of the traditional constitution. From the perspective of C.P.P. national policy the resuscitation of Kukuom's claims to paramountcy wore a crisp instrumental air:[51] merely a means, as it had been for the British in 1896 or 1901, of pruning the political power of metropolitan Ashanti. But within Ahafo its meaning could not remain so inertly instrumental. As far as Ahafo was concerned, it was not important whether the continued significance of Kukuom claims was a causal product of indirect rule as such or merely of the unsuitability of the restored Confederacy as a system for administering Ahafo in particular.[52] It has been a mark of how far the politics of Ahafo remain local to this day that it can hardly be denied that the Ahafo chiefly contest from 1956 until the present time has been a political problem of Ahafo, while it has been as much a political resource as a problem *for* the successive central governments which have possessed the power to decide it, for as long as they had the power to decide anything, in one direction or another.

The full arbitrariness of this external discretion in determining the political destinies of Ahafo can be seen clearly in the occasion which in the eyes of the administration constituted the most drastic rejection of the authority of the modern state in deciding Ahafo's disputes between 1901 and the present day, the occasion when Beditor of Mim summoned his warbands to arms and trapped the Omanhene in the town of Goaso late in March 1915. Open military confrontation between Beditor and Braimansu, the then Omanhene of Kukuom, had been narrowly averted on a number of previous occasions: the time in September 1905 when Beditor claimed that the Kukuomhene had put him 'in fetish',[53] the time seven years later when Beditor's men marched on Kukuom in the belief (said by a British Commissioner to have been universal in Ahafo at the time) that Braimansu had stolen the Obo fetish from Mim.[54] In these contests the considered British judgement a mere two years before Beditor's final downfall had been that Kukuom had been decidedly more at fault than Beditor.[55] It had been a lengthy and bitter war of attrition, even if it had never quite reached the point of a pitched battle. But in March 1915, as a result of a land dispute, Beditor, finding himself goaded beyond endurance, determined on a pre-emptive strike. Calling together his men from throughout the Mim division, from Mim Mohu, Bediakokrom and Kenyase as well as from the town of Mim itself, he led them, accoutred for war and heavily armed, on Goaso where he was due to meet the Omanhene.[56] At his first meeting with the Omanhene, the arms and many of the men were left outside the town but threats and insults were exchanged and war songs sung by Beditor's men. At this point Beditor's plans were thrown into disarray by the hasty arrival of a British Commissioner with a small force of police. The arms understandably remained outside the town after this arrival and it is not at all clear that Beditor had intended in persisting in his challenge, once the Kukuom party had had the good fortune to pick up such powerful assistance. But shortly after this, the Commissioner was informed of the discovery of a number of loaded guns hidden in the bush near one of the paths into the town and further searches on a more systematic basis at either points of exit or entry to the town uncovered several other caches of arms. Subsequent investigations did not establish any comprehensive and lucid picture of what had actually happened, let alone of what would have happened, had the British Commissioner never put in an appearance. But they did serve to identify Beditor in the administration's eyes as an active criminal, 'a dangerous Fetishman', as well as a dedicated Mim imperialist. ('We call Beditor the Omanhin in Mim,' one witness helpfully explained.)

Braimansu of Kukuom had risen with the Kumasi forces in 1900. He had frequently and determinedly disobeyed the orders of the British administrators. He had even, indeed, been involved in the protracted and revolting torture of two men whom he suspected of having stolen money from him.[57] Beditor by contrast had contrived, possibly more by luck than good judgement, to remain neutral in 1900. He had restrained his people under conditions of great provocation, while Braimansu built up his local power with methods which aroused intense local hostility and suspicion. Unlike Braimansu, Beditor had never previously been discovered to have perpetrated actions which the British considered outstandingly barbarous. But behaviour which might have been in no way unusual for Braimansu five years earlier, constituted by 1915 too great an infraction of the colonial regime's key value: the duty at all costs not to challenge (or even appear to challenge) the military control of the government. Considerations of the political advantage of Ahafo itself weighed as nothing in the scale against the axiom of maintaining absolute military submission to the government of the Gold Coast. It is hard to believe that they have come to weigh much more heavily[58] with the post-colonial successors of the British.

b. HYGIENE AND RESPECTABILITY

Over the sixty years for which it existed the colonial order aspired to bring to Ahafo in addition to forms of wealth aptly adjusted to the requirements of the metropolitan economy, some advances in both health and material civilisation. Different members of the colonial administration attached different values to these various goals. But once an administrator was permanently resident in a particular area it was difficult for him to avoid a measure of commitment to all three. It was certainly facilities for the engendering of wealth which were the first of these colonial offerings to be received with much enthusiasm in Ahafo itself. Even in 1915, at a time when the administration had set itself more exacting targets in Ahafo than the fostering of production for the market, the main evidence of local enthusiasm for civilisation, an enthusiasm which the new District Commissioner found to be reminiscent in its intensity of the frontier in Canada or the United States,[1] was the eagerness of the Ahafos to construct roads. Roads were the form in which the colonial dispensation was welcomed in Ahafo with most alacrity – in the light of their evident prospective contribution to economic growth. But the D.C., Cardinall, was plainly correct by 1915 to see Ahafo responses to colonial opportunity as more complex in ideological commitment than a simple urge to utilise to the full the position on the world market destined for them by the doctrine of comparative advantage. For one thing, western medicine had begun to make its first inroads on the steady domination of disease over the local population. For another – and certainly a visually more dominant one – the shape of traditional Ashanti settlements and the design of the houses which went with them had begun to be replaced by more regular town and village layouts and more enclosed and solid dwellings. Residential reorganisation and the imposition of elaborate rituals of cleanliness were common colonial undertakings. As projects neither was devoid of a core of rational altruism. But in execution and in the pattern of psychological commitment which they aroused in individual D.C.s, their meaning spread out a long way from the core of rational hygiene into a comprehensive confrontation with the dangers of 'matter in the wrong place'. While it is scarcely surprising that it should have been the more demonstrably beneficial components (at least at the level of individual experience) of the civilising enterprise which have entered lastingly into the cultural values of Ahafo today, it is clear also that the initial ventures in 'civilising' Ahafo in this fashion had as much to do with the exorcism of colonial anxieties as with the fostering of local goals.

A certain paranoid tinge to the colonial vision of Ashanti as a whole persisted for more than two decades after the conquest. The relationship which from below necessarily fostered both dependency and resentment, developed from above an uneasy compound of arrogance and suspicion. As late as 1922 the intelligence-gathering activities of the Gold Coast Regiment could be summed up in a startling depiction of the population whom they were supposedly maintained to defend:

Character. The perpetuation through generations of the enervating influences of the forest's miasma, a soil satisfying primitive wants in lavish profusion, religious customs which enforced idleness on two days in every seven and were often accompanied by prolonged debauch, a system of succession and of family ownership of land which deprived the individual of the greatest stimulus to personal effort – such are the factors which have combined to evolve in the Gold Coast native a mental and physical inertness, a deficiency of will-power, a contempt for work and a childish desire to assert his independence, wholly incompatible with prolonged effort or honest labour. The frequent feuds which have led to the disintegration of the Agni-Ashanti people, and the form of fighting imposed by the forest and bush have made the individual cruel, vindictive, treacherous and selfish.[2]

Cultivating a measure of paranoia in their conception of those against whom they might have to fight would be the occupational disease of military intelligence officers, were it not in fact largely their occupation. No political officer – in the words of the official guide to new incumbents, 'the officer responsible for the maintenance of satisfactory relations between the natives and the central administration'[3] – would have cared to put his signature to such a portrait even in a file firmly marked as 'Secret'. It was hardly a tone which Captain Rattray would have approved and it is notably in conflict with the patience and sympathy informing the fieldwork on which he was engaged at the time. But it does serve to highlight, however luridly, the inverse ratio between security and distrust. There were many different objects for eminently plausible distrust when the British first arrived in Ahafo and correspondingly many fears to be exorcised.

Physical sickness had been central to the image of the west coast of Africa, the fever coast, ever since extensive European trading contact with the area had been established.[4] Elaborate theories about the causation of different types of disease, especially malaria and yellow fever, were developed and refined.

97

Dependence and opportunity

The forest miasma which reappears in the 'rational' foundations of colonial military planning in 1922 was a typical category of this nervous intellectual exploration. Medically more than a little archaic in 1922, its survival indicates an instructive continuity in sentiment. The fear of disease is naturally not a feeling to which many D.C.s would care to testify in their official files. But when Cardinall, arriving in Goaso in 1915 to take up control of his first district, noted that he was four days away from the nearest white man[5] or when the Provincial Commissioner in December 1930 complained that the Goaso D.C. had once again gone sick and had to be removed to Kumasi hospital,[6] the physical exposure of the early D.C.s is made evident enough. Goaso was, even by the standards of the Gold Coast, an unhealthy station for its administrators; and the mortality rates for whites in the Gold Coast, though favourable enough for strictly economic reasons when compared to those for the local population, continued to seem very high when compared to those for middle-class Englishmen in their own country. Much of the more elaborate sanitary work prescribed for Goaso at some of the points where there was a resident D.C. in the town can only be adequately understood if it is seen in this light. The marginal utility of much work in clearing the bush and cleaning the town might not be very great; but any enhancement of the medical prospects for residents in such a disease-ridden environment was desired with urgency. Nor was it desired solely on behalf of the British D.C. who did happen to reside there temporarily. The fear of physical illness could and did serve as a powerful stimulus to sympathy with the dismal medical condition of many of the local population. But the balance of public concern over health between local population and colonial official was hardly an even one; and it would be over-generous to interpret the amount of attention (and indeed of money) devoted to the conditions of the D.C.'s existence strictly in terms of their instrumental necessity for the continuity of civil government in the area. The insistence by medical officials on the D.C. living a minimum distance apart from the rest of the community may have been designed in part as an affirmation of social distance (to be of potential value in the practice of social control). But the elaboration of criteria by which the amenities of the D.C. must be separate from those of everyone else was too profuse to have been determined solely by the requirements of keeping mere people in their place.[7] Dirty water, flies, insects in general, above all germs did plausibly represent a much more intimate threat to colonial officials for most of their time in Ahafo than the insubordination of those whom they were attempting to rule. There simply was more anxiety that needed to be allayed by symbolic enactment of the ritual of keeping matter in the right place, than did so in that of keeping men in the right place. At the time when Cardinall took over the Ahafo district, he had to march for five days from Sunyani before reaching Goaso, along a track which was 'just like a tunnel, so thick was the overgrowth of the tree tops'.[8] The sense of enclosure within the largely virgin forest was plainly more than a little oppressive. At Goaso itself the physical conditions of existence were hardly relaxing. His bungalow was invaded by armies of soldier ants on five days within a single week and he was obliged to abandon it for the time being. However imperturbable any individual D.C. would be careful always to appear (not least in his official account of the manner in which he carried out his duties), it is easy to see how much greater the pressures to reorganise and to tidy up the communities of Ahafo were certain to become as soon as there were British administrators resident in that 'most buried spot'.[9]

Reorganisation of towns and villages and modification of the characteristic housing constructed in the district had begun in a desultory way rather earlier, some of it plainly a product of emulation of the development of other more prosperous areas rather than a response to the initiatives of the visiting administrators. The fact that the Omanhene Braimansu had succeeded by 1914, in addition to largely depopulating the area round Kukuom, in erecting the first iron-roofed two-storey house seen in the district, was an indication of the cultural appeal of the growing 'civilisation' of Kumasi as well as a measure of the short-term effectiveness of his monopolisation of the profits of 'justice'.[10] Certainly no index of the cultural triumph of the colonial regime as such, it would have required a more than slightly optimistic eye to see it even, as the Commissioner for the North Western District had seen the fact that many chiefs were building up their towns and erecting good houses for themselves in his report for 1905, as an indication of 'settled times' and general acceptance of the colonial order.[11] But there were other indices of advancing 'civilisation' in Ahafo by the time of Braimansu's architectural investment which did constitute either direct or indirect responses to the consolidation of the colonial regime. During his first extended trek in Ahafo Cardinall found in the still today somewhat remote village of Pomakrom which he was only the second Englishman to visit, a village which 'was like one of those described by former visitors to Ashanti of a type now almost unknown. There was no main street. All the huts were massed together, with only the narrowest of passages between. Completely round the village was a cleared space, serving as the principal meeting-place, scrupulously clean and studded with great shade-giving trees.' Even the houses themselves were unfamiliar: 'Ashanti huts of the old pattern had no rooms. They consisted usually of four or more shelters raised on mud plinths which were kept scrupulously clean and shining by constant renewal of a red wash. All these shelters were enclosed on only three sides, the fourth opening on to a yard.'[12] The population of Pomakrom was for historical reasons predominantly female and Cardinall found the lack of privacy in these open huts most dismaying when he came to take his bath. The difference between the type of house still to be found at Pomakrom and that found in most Ahafo villages by 1915 was clearly not a result of direct governmental suggestion, although it may have had something to do with the greater security produced by the Pax Britannica in comparison with the concluding stages of the disintegration of the Ashanti state. But the drastic differences in town settlement patterns, while their rationality also hinged on the comparative physical security of a township under the new regime, did reflect more direct colonial efforts too. General instructions on clearing the bush around villages had been issued for the Western Province as a whole by 1910.[13] In August and September of that year the Provincial Commissioner toured Ahafo with a doctor and noted that 'some attempts at clearing had, in compliance with orders, been undertaken at all the Ahafo villages visited'. But 'in other respects, the Ahafo towns are undrained, the houses closely packed together, and insanitary'. Only in Mim had the chief, acting on the advice of the Commissioner, opened up a main street through the town and improved the layout correspondingly.[14] Villages outside Ahafo in which a sanitary inspector had been working had been greatly improved and even villages closer to Sunyani which had not received this direct attention, were better built, ditched and drained than those in Ahafo. Stimulated by the visit the Commissioner proposed the appointment of six Native Sanitary Officers for the province, one for each division at a salary of £24–£30 per annum and the Chief Commissioner ensured that the Principal Medical Officer for Ashanti duly applied for another six sanitary inspectors in his annual estimates.[15] Late in the following year the Provincial Commissioner reported strongly in favour of the establishment of a representative Provincial Council in the Western Province, to include the chiefs of Mim, Kukuom and Noberkaw, as well as a delegate chosen from the young-men of Ahafo. The function of this council was to be the drawing up of byelaws for enforcement by a hierarchical series of native tribunals. The subjects covered in these bylaws were to be extremely extensive: the regulation of hunting and fishing, the storage of powder, marriage, adultery and divorce, 'fetish and generally all native customs not repugnant to humanity and natural justice', oath and court fees, rubber-tapping, property-disposal, gambling and minor criminal offences like petty thefts or trivial assaults. But it was a mark of the expanding ambitions for colonial control that the first subject which came to the Commissioner's mind in drawing up his letter should have been – as it surely could not have been even five years earlier – the subject of sanitation.[16]

In some respects it seems likely that the extension of colonial structures of control may have weakened rather than strengthened the capacity of communities to protect themselves against identified threats. It is hard, for instance, to imagine that a chief of Kukuom before 1896 would have hesitated to ban the sale of bad or rotten meat in his town, while in 1912 the

Omanhene apparently felt it more prudent to send an enquiry to the Commissioner as to whether his authority extended to the right to issue such a ban, a course of action which for purely geographical reasons must have involved a delay of about ten days.[17] But if the internal capacity of the communities to act effectively may have been somewhat enfeebled, they did now begin to receive some measure of external assistance. In the same month in which the Omanhene wrote to ask for his sanction, the Ahafo chiefs received instructions from the Commissioner to co-operate with the doctor who was travelling in the area in the attempt to extirpate trypanosomiasis ('sleeping sickness'), the disease carried by the tsetse fly, an insect which was then, as it is now, common in the forest.[18] The instructions envisaged that the chiefs would ensure that those who were found to be suffering from the disease would take the medicines prescribed by the doctor and that the chiefs would duly execute the doctor's recommendations on cleaning bush around the towns and any other sanitary instructions which he might give. In practice, however, while 14 out of the 5,290 individuals examined for the disease in the Sunyani district proved to be infected with it, not a single one of the 2,926 examined in Ahafo was found to be so.[19] Two years later a more grandiose venture into social medicine, the Yellow Fever Commission, in its enquiry concerning the main trading routes into Ashanti, again displayed Ahafo as a relatively medically privileged environment, traversed only by one major traffic route, from Pulliano through Wam Pamu and Kukuom to Bibiani, along which cattle and other trade used to pass at the time when the Bibiani mines were in operation and which would be revived in the event of the mines reopening.[20]

From the establishment of the district headquarters at Goaso, sanitary work and town improvement became relatively persistent preoccupations. But strictly medical attention remained decidedly intermittent. The main health problem of Ahafo in local eyes continued to be not the more spectacular epidemic tropical diseases on which the government medical department's attention seems initially to have been predominantly focussed, but the more familiar hazard of influenza. Early in December 1918 both of the leading candidates for the vacant stool of Kukuom died of the disease near the Bia river and six other victims died in Kukuom itself.[21] At the end of the month the weekly death toll from the epidemic was estimated at 170, most of whom came from Ahafo.[22] Six years later, in August and September 1924, there was another epidemic in the district from which at least 15 died at Sankore, 8 at Nkasaim and 2 at Hwidiem.[23] There was not at this time much that the government's medical services were in a position to do to check a 'flu' epidemic. But when it came to the eradication of smallpox, western medical skills were more effective and Ashanti culture proved extremely hospitable to their exercise. Ashanti religious culture being happily pluralist, there were no theological obstacles, as there had been at earlier stages in Christian Europe or America[24] or indeed in Islamic Turkey[25] to the utilisation of whatever novel invisible forces the whites might care to offer. Vaccination was merely a particularly reliable fetish power. By 1926 the Provincial Commissioner could write with confidence that the Ashanti population had been largely immunised against smallpox and suggest that only economic considerations precluded the virtual elimination of the disease.

If vaccination could be made permanently compulsory and a regular system established of vaccination and revaccination as suggested, it is probable that this disease could be practically eliminated, since unlike some of our own country-men, the people are aware of the efficiency of vaccination as a preventive measure and conscientious objectors do not appear to exist. Smallpox is a very real entity to the populace and they are entirely willing to be vaccinated.[26]

This level of organisation was at the time beyond the powers of the colonial government and minor outbreaks did continue to occur in Ahafo after this point. There was one at Kenyase I for example in December 1928;[27] but immediate preventive measures were taken, an isolation camp built and a dispenser sent to take precautions. No deaths occurred.[28] Smallpox appeared in Goaso in 1946[29] and an outbreak was reported in Mim in 1950, but it turned out in fact to be only chicken pox.[30]

By the mid-1920s the colonial commitment to improving the health of the population had become (at least at the level of administrative intention) a more integrated project. In 1918 a new native hospital was being erected in Sunyani at a cost of £7,000. When it was proposed to cut this figure by £1,000 by omitting a ward for women, the Provincial Commissioner argued strongly against the proposal, pointing out 'how very necessary it is to have Female Accommodation in a Province like this, where development is taking place at a greater rate than almost any other part of the Colony, and how essential it is to be able to obtain the trust of the women and prove to them the advantages of skilled medical treatment'.[31] When the hospital was opened in May 1929 by the Chief Commissioner of Ashanti, the chiefs of the Goaso district were duly in attendance to be presented to him. As a medical specific, vaccination stands in a notably simple causal relationship to the possibility of contracting smallpox. But the further acceptance of western medical beliefs and of the practical strategies which followed from them was a slower process for the Ahafos and one which it required the nagging presence of the colonial administrator greatly to expedite. During the year 1926/7 the medical officer for the Western Province paid four visits to Ahafo, largely in order to urge on the cleaning up of the villages which had lapsed altogether while the district was without a commissioner in 1925.[32] The diseases which came most prominently to his attention on these occasions were yaws (widespread among the children of Goaso), guinea worm which attacked a few people in Hwidiem in July and August, and whooping cough of which there was an outbreak in Kenyase in November.[33] In 1929 all these diseases recur as a focus of concern, with the addition of chicken pox.[34] The whooping cough epidemic in Kukuom in October began with the deaths of two children and the D.C. was sufficiently alarmed to send for the Medical Officer from Sunyani. By the time that the latter arrived in his touring car, six days later, inflicting appalling damage on the newly repaired road, no sick children were to be found in the village (the Omanhene alleging that they were with their mothers who were working on the road) and the isolation hut which the Omanhene had been instructed to erect was still not properly finished.[35] When the sanitary overseer reported two days afterwards that the Omanhene had still made no effort to get further work done on the hut, the D.C. threatened to summon him to explain his 'slackness' to the Provincial Commissioner and also to confiscate his powder and guns for six months.[36] The Omanhene's relative lack of interest may have been influenced in part by the fact that the outbreak had turned out to be so much less severe than it had been the preceding year. But the disease was endemic in the district through-out the wet season and tended to reach epidemic proportions once a year. The D.C. indeed judged that this annual epidemic was the main cause of infantile mortality in the district.[37] Hence it seems more plausible that the scepticism of the Omanhene and the delinquent 'slackness' which logically followed from it was less a product of the relative valuation of infant as against adult lives than it was a rational response to the evidence available to him for the efficacy of the isolation of infectious diseases (as against for example vaccination for smallpox) as a method for the control of disease. Within modern western culture the authority of a doctor inheres in the role, at best probabilistically related to causal efficacy in the arrest of disease. But in the 1920s in the Ashanti tropical rain forest, the authority of a doctor was a compound of in the first place (as can be seen from the instructions to the trypanosomiasis mission in 1914) the authority of a white colonial bureaucrat with a more contingently demonstrated array of unintelligible (and hence magical) powers. Vaccination appeared to be a powerful fetish against smallpox; but epidemics of whooping cough had always come to an end without white fetish intervention in the past and the mode of white fetish intervention in the case of whooping cough, behaviourally indirect and even evasive (go build a hut) as it appeared, was not made more convincing by any apparent decisive acceleration of the termination of the outbreak. How, after all, could an isolation hut serve any very effective medical purpose when its destined occupants were strapped to the backs of their mothers, toiling away at another obsessional requirement of the colonial inspiration, the maintenance of the road? If life is often too short for an unflinching observance of the germ theory of diseases in all the nursing routines of Korle Bu hospital in Accra today – or perhaps even in Guy's Hospital in London – it is hardly a matter for great surprise that the Omanhene, whose instruction in the ideology of western medicine was of a more random and indeed arbitrary character should fail to demonstrate any great fanaticism in the execution of this aspect of the reception of 'civilisation'.

A similar obstacle to the cultural hegemony of western medicine arose in the case of another outbreak of disease in 1929, and even more in 1930, the guinea worm of Kenyase I. The disease reached the proportions of a serious epidemic by July 1929 and was still continuing in October.[38] In March of the following year the chief himself was suffering from it.[39] In June 1930 the D.C. visited Kenyase and reported that the village's very bad guinea worm had lasted for two years. The water tank for the town had dried up in the dry season and the infection was carried by a small neighbouring stream, although the chief had now forbidden its use.[40] The village's condition was unenviable:

In every compound there are many cases and the village as a unit is incapable of doing anything. Though told that it is due to their water that they are ill and though they politely agree, they all believe their misfortune due to a curse. Certain people whom they badly treated and drove into the bush apparently cursed them. For that very year they got guinea worm. The very funny thing about this is that no strangers have been affected, though using the same water. The road contractor and his boys have been there six months using the same water and have had not a case.[41]

However the D.C. discovered within a few days that a number of people in Ntotroso had contracted the disease, all of them while they were living at Kenyase. 'This seems to negative the curse idea.'[42] The remedy adopted was to cut a path to another stream, some considerable distance further away from the village, which flowed directly into the river Tano itself (and so could not contaminate any other villages) and to construct a dam in it so that the infected could dip their buckets upstream in it without contaminating it by paddling in it. The sanction to use this supply was to be the chief's swearing his oath that this water only was to be used.[43] Indirect rule and the 'civilising' mission were in evident tension here. The rationale of the water-use regulation was of little cultural plausibility to those who were obliged to walk the extra miles, carrying their heavy supplies of water. But the sanction which was to drive them to do so was altogether ideologically more in harmony with the local explanation of the misfortune which had befallen them than it was with the alien explanation which alone made their additional effort rational.

Abject credulity in the efficacy of western medicine is certainly not, even today, a predominant attitude in Ahafo. But it is not clear that scepticism towards the powers of doctors is any more acute than scepticism, for example, towards the dependability of modern mechanical transport. In the form in which either of these dispensations reach Ahafo, they do not furnish rational grounds for anyone to put their trust at all comprehensively in the reliability of their powers. There are many in Ahafo who are too poor to be able to take advantage of either facility on particular occasions when it would be convenient for them to do so. Indeed, there are few in Ahafo who have access to either facility at the peak of expense at which it does become rational to feel confident about its safety and efficacy. Both the level of sickness and the danger – and still more the irregularity – of transport arrangements are sobering in comparison with those of an industrial society. But it probably is correct by now to say[44] that it would be being as socially eccentric, even faddish, for anyone in Ahafo today to refuse under any circumstances, if costs were omitted from the consideration, to have recourse to western medicine as it would be for them to refuse under any circumstances to ride in a motor vehicle. This does not necessarily mean that the inhabitants of Mim today would feel any more authentically committed to constructing an isolation hut, if there were an epidemic of measles and whooping cough in the town today, than they were when they refused to build one as recently as 1939 (despite the fact that nineteen victims had died within a fortnight on that occasion[45]). However the sheer weight of the bureaucratic presence being what it now is, they would today be much less likely to succeed in evading such an instruction and even if they were in fact successful in remaining inactive in despite of it, there would today certainly be some among their number who would be prepared to admit that their doing so betrayed a measure of social irresponsibility. The relationship between western medicine and Ahafo was no longer a wholly external one by 1939. By 1930 A. W. Osei of Goaso, a school fellow of Dr Busia in Kumasi and later to become M.P. for Ahafo in 1956, had begun his twenty-four year period of service as a nurse in the Department of Health. On his retirement from the government service, he opened a private clinic in Goaso to which Dr Hastings Banda, the present President of Malawi, came once a week from Kumasi to attend to the patients.[46]

By 1937 western medicine had become enough of a natural recourse for such a relatively poor individual as a Grumah labourer who had signed on as a caretaker for £2 10s 0d for a year to purchase medical attention for him out of his salary to cure him of yaws. But natural though it may have become as a recourse by this time, it was decidedly not cheap. Two lots of pills from a 'native doctor' were alleged to have cost his employer 16s and injections from Dr Asafu Adjaye and Dr Dove (for which the Grumah labourer denied having undertaken to pay) were assessed at 15s. The Goaso court upheld the labourer's claim for the payment of his wages, but accepted the propriety of the deductions for the 'native medicine', the pills. The verdict was an index of the Commissioner's judgement of what medical beliefs it was plausible for a migrant Grumah labourer to hold, not an assessment of the medical skills of Drs Asafu Adjaye and Dove. But the fact that the employer of the Grumahs should have thought it worth enlisting the skills of the two Kumasi doctors and the fact that these should have begun to draw income from Ahafo by 1937 shows that the profitability of medicine as a career (like that of law in which both the Asafu Adjaye and Dove families had also been prudent enough to invest heavily by this time) was based on extensive cultural change which now reached out even to an area like Ahafo.[47] No evidence survives of the relative effectiveness of the 'native pills' and the two Kumasi doctors' injections in the relief of the yaws. But it may certainly be taken as evidence of growing belief in the efficacy of the latter agency, that the Goaso magistrate's court list for the last quarter of 1937 should include two convictions for practising medicine (by giving injections) without licence or qualifications and one for aiding and abetting the giving of unauthorised injections.[48] It is not clear whether these cases represented a novel form of confidence trick or merely a technically illegal entrepreneurial effort to provide scarce goods. Even today Ahafo has scarcely reached a level of medical rationalism sufficient to threaten members of the modern medical profession with being held legally accountable for the damage caused by their more negligent actions. At one very early point in the colonial regime, an aspiring Ahafo traditional practitioner, accused by a patient of having caused him permanent deafness by providing him with a medicine which he had applied in his nose, was threatened darkly by the Commissioner with gaol unless he paid his victim heavy compensation.[49] But more recently the administration could hardly be accused of excessive interventionism in its handling of the 'traditional' sector of Ahafo medicine. Disease is too rife in the area and modern medical resources at the disposal of the state are too scarce for it to have either the will or the ability to prevent much of the distribution of medical provision, whether modern or 'traditional', being left to the market to allocate. Unauthorised injections and irrevelant pills and potions are still the main medical stand-bys for many in Ahafo. The public bureaucracy is on the whole happy to leave it to the best pills to win.

When Ahafo first acquired a modernist representative agency of its own, medical facilities vied with roads and schools in the forefront of its attention. Among the applications for scholarships received by the Ahafo Area Committee in November 1949 was one from an Akrodie boy at St Augustine's school at Cape Coast, requesting support for the completion of his secondary education and his taking of the government training course for dispensers so that he might become the first qualified dispenser in the Ahafo area.[50] In December of the same year the Area Committee drew up its full five-year

Scholarship Programme.[51] The total sum allocated for the full five years was £3,140, of which £2,650 was taken up by scholarships for secondary school for five years at £50 per student per annum and for teacher training for two or four years at £20 or £30 per student per year. The remaining £490 was reserved for midwifery training (an area in which western techniques had little difficulty in demonstrating their edge over prevailing practices) – three three-year courses at £10 per student per year – and for dispensary dressers – five two-year courses at £40 per student per year. In order to make the competition as widely and fairly open as possible, the scholarships were to be advertised in the local newspapers, the *Ashanti Times* and the *Ashanti Pioneer*, copies of which were to be bought for the Committee members to take to their communities, and the competition was to be announced by beating the gong-gong in every village. As an indication of recognition of public and private goods, while the secondary students were to be left free to make careers wherever these might lie open to their talents, the midwives, teachers and dispensers were to be bonded to put their acquired skills to use in the public service. The secondary schoolboys represented progress for the area as a whole, collective (if vicarious) upward social mobility for the individual Ahafo citizen. But the teachers, midwives and dispensers were not a good which had to be consumed vicariously; they were themselves decidedly a social investment. In the following year the Committee began also to invest in the construction of permanent buildings for the provision of modern medical services. The establishment of a maternity clinic was one of the main items of projected expenditure in the second quarter of 1950[52] and by September of that year the midwife's building was nearing completion in Goaso and a Health Centre was operating in the town.[53]

When the first elected legislature of the Gold Coast came into operation in 1951 medical facilities were defined from the beginning as one of the main development goods which it was the primary function of the member to attract to his constituency. The Member for Kumasi West, B. F. Kusi, pressed for the establishment of a full hospital in Ahafo on many occasions in the legislature: in February and November of 1953 and in February of 1954 for example.[54] He also made strenuous efforts inside the legislature and by direct approaches to the Ministry of Health to remedy the water supply in Kenyase, Akrodie and above all Mim in which bilharzia had been spreading rapidly in 1952 and in which in March 1953 Kusi alleged that four people were dying every day from the pollution of the water by the Victoria Sawmills Company (now, the Mim Timber Company).[55] He also attempted without success in November of 1953 to elicit a promise of government support for the Health Centre and Maternity Clinic which the local authority had begun to construct in Hwidiem.[56] Kusi's loyalist C.P.P. successor as M.P. for Ahafo, B.K. Senkyire, continued to press the claims of Ahafo for a hospital on the grounds of the scale of the constituency's population – almost 50,000 in his estimate – and the extent of its contribution to national cocoa production, allied to the distance, some 75 miles in each case, from the nearest hospitals in Sunyani and Kumasi.[57] In January 1956 when the Ahafo Local Council met again after a suspension of three months caused by the political tensions, the medical officer's bungalow and the clinic at Hwidiem had been completed, although construction of the wards had not yet been started, since the Ministry of Health had rejected the plans which had been submitted for them.[58] A maternity clinic at Kukuom had its foundation stone laid in March of this year by no less a dignitary than Dr Belshaw, leader of a UNESCO delegation inspecting the progress of community development in the Gold Coast.[59] In June 1956 the chief of Hwidiem in an anxious plea for the provision of a police post in his town in order to restrain the prevalent political violence laid great emphasis on the fact that Hwidiem's Roman Catholic doctor provided the only fully qualified medical services within Ahafo and that the existing level of social conflict might soon preclude his remaining in the town.[60] The condition of the Hwidiem hospital was considered to be highly unsatisfactory by the local administrative officer. The wards were inadequate and neither the people of Hwidiem nor the Ahafo Local Council showed any readiness to provide further funds to add to those which had built the hospital building itself (from the Kumasi West District Council and the people of Hwidiem) and the medical officer's bungalow (from Hwidiem special rates).[61] The government representative seemed eager to leave 'absolute control of the hospital' to the mission. In June the next year A. W. Osei, Senkyire's United Party victor in the parliamentary election, resumed the pressure for opening a health centre in Goaso, while adding a complaint of his own about the degree to which the government's medical restrictions obstructed trained nurses (like himself) in opening and operating effective private nursing homes in the rural areas with visiting doctors.[62] During the following year the public dressing station at Goaso was visited once a week by the Medical Officer from Sunyani, though it was left for weeks at a time in the day-to-day charge of un-licensed dispensers who were suspected of giving unlicensed injections.[63] When Osei had originally raised the possibility of providing a hospital for Ahafo in the House in January 1957, a Northern M.P., Adama, went so far as to claim that the absence of a local hospital in Ahafo had produced conditions in which many quacks could maintain thriving practices in the area.[64]

It is, thus, perhaps legitimate to take 1957, the year in which the Gold Coast was transformed into the independent nation of Ghana, as a convenient, if arbitrary, boundary in the definition of the political meaning of modern medicine in Ahafo. Neither Osei, himself a former career nurse, nor his party colleague Adama, in that the latter was also a Member of Parliament, could be taken as culturally representative of their areas. But if it had come to the attention of a Northern M.P., defending the interests of his potentially migrant constituents, that the prosperous cocoa forest of Ahafo was a hazardous zone in which to attempt to make one's fortune, because the government's provision of modern medicine was still so distinctly offhand, any suggestion that the continued prominence of health facilities among public goods demanded for Ahafo was culturally alien to the majority of its population becomes grossly implausible. There is, to be sure, some element of ideological circularity in determining what issues are extensively canvassed in public representative institutions: not every political value which the Ahafos might have felt would have quite done for ventilation on such an intractably public occasion, while, conversely, some of the more persistent bees in Osei's own bonnet, the urge for example for Christian dialogue with the Union of South Africa, must have been decidedly idiosyncratic even as foci of interest, let alone as moral tastes, among the Ahafo population at large. But it would be an error to lay great emphasis on the self-defining character of modern political goods in the debates of Parliament. Nkrumah's rule may at times have been somewhat tyrannical; but Ghanaian public discourse under his sway never attained the predictability of that of a true totalitarian state. In a legislature in which an M.P. could define a capitalist as someone who 'has got a bad aim of production'[65] and in which it never did quite happen, as Kofi Baako wearily proposed on that occasion, that all M.P.s duly did go off to the Winneba Ideological Institute to get their terminology straight, it makes little sense to suppose that the public language of commendation exercised much control over what items came publicly to be commended. The regularity of political pressure by Ahafo M.P.s of either political party from 1951 to 1966 for hospitals and clean water supplies, even if it may initially have been, as perhaps even the Area Committee and the Local Council's early health investments may have been, an articulation of what the more educated and prosperous conceived to be good for Ahafo, had clearly become by 1966, what was judged by most Ahafos to be good for Ahafo. (One major cause for the political currency of western medicine was the plain fact that it *was* good for Ahafo.) Even today what is good for the Ahafo educated is thought to be good for Ahafo. Whatever the writings of Frantz Fanon may have come to mean for a few isolated students at Legon, there is certainly as yet no counter-elite ideology available to the Ahafos. Accordingly, between 1959 and 1966 medical facilities – and above all a proper hospital – came to be seen as a key example of the public goods which were being denied to Ahafo by the C.P.P. government for purely political reasons.

It is not at all easy, either in the case of the promised hospital or of the provision of piped water, to be certain how far the interpretation of the fortunes of Ahafo in this competition for public health goods did represent conscious discrimination by the C.P.P. government against an area which had displayed such vigorous N.L.M. loyalties in 1956/7 and how far it was simply a consequence of the general depletion from 1959 onwards of the government's financial capability to provide development resources for any project which did not directly involve the interests of the President himself. When Osei once again advanced the health claims of Ahafo as a ground for providing government health clinics in Teppa and Goaso and for subsidising the mission clinic at Hwidiem,[66] he had clearly not come to expect, despite the government's promises in the year of independence to deluge the country with clinics and health centres, that Ahafo should acquire anything so grandiose as its own hospital. The following month, when a memorandum came to the Cabinet of Ghana, proposing the establishment of Health Centres out of Cocoa Marketing Board grants, the Regional Commissioner for Brong–Ahafo suggested siting one at both Anwiam and Goaso.[67] By June 1959 it was agreed that the Goaso Health Centre should be transformed into a hospital in the second phase of the Seven Year Development Plan and provision was to be made in its siting for this proposed extension. Tenders were requested for the centre in April 1960 but any decision on them was deferred by the Prime Minister's personal order until his return from London at the end of May. At the first meeting of the Standing Finance and Development Committee after his return, in mid-June 1960, the contract for building the Centre was awarded to Osei Bonsu Ltd for £G 20,000, the work to be completed within six months.

As late as December 1958 A. W. Osei was merely enquiring hopefully whether the government proposed to establish a central hospital for the Ahafo area.[68] By June 1959, when the Kukuomhene (whose contacts with the central government must be presumed to have been rather good by the unexacting standards of Ahafo) offered to the Medical Officer in Sunyani to present as a free gift to the government the 'hospital building' which he and his people had just erected at a cost of £6,000, he did so on the presumption that the government intended at the time to build a 'hospital' in Ahafo.[69] In itself the willingness of Kukuom to invest £6,000 in a building to be used for this purpose is eloquent testimony of the fact that the possession of a 'hospital' in one's own town had come to represent a public good of sufficiently uncontroversial character for it to serve as a major item of communal aggrandisement. Too much weight should probably not be placed on the title of the building; but there is no reason to doubt that the Kukuomhene's application betokened firm Ahafo expectations of the arrival of governmental investment in medical services. In November of the following year Osei raised the question of the fate of Ahafo's hospital in a debate on a Development Loans Bill, complaining that, although there had been provision for a proper hospital for Goaso in the Development Estimates, when he visited the town a fortnight earlier he had discovered that what was being built was a health centre, 'something which is very different from the original plan. This shows that the original estimate of £G 200,000 has been reduced to a very low figure.' No information had been provided, he complained, about the cost of the health centre. It was not even clear who had reduced the original figure and no explanation had been provided of why the government had decided to ignore the medical needs of Ahafo which remained as pressing as ever.[70] No public explanation does in fact ever seem to have been offered[71] and Ahafo is not obviously any closer today to having a proper government hospital than it was in 1960. Osei continued to press the government, as late as March 1964, to upgrade the Goaso Health Centre into a proper hospital.[72] But by this time the second phase of the Seven Year Development Plan was regressing rapidly in the light of the government's increasingly alarming fiscal situation and the meagre £G 2,000 a year subsidy to the 34-bed mission hospital at Hwidiem was a fair indication of the extent of the economic resources at its disposal for attending to the hospital needs of Ahafo.[73] Governmental opulence has not increased greatly in recent years. The only period since 1960 in which Ahafo's prospects for acquiring a decisive increment in its medical resources have been at all rosy was the span between 1970 and the demise of the Busia government in which the energetic M.P. for Asunafo, Alfred Badu Nkansah, whose overall record for extracting development resources for Ahafo from the admittedly regionally sympathetic Progress Party administration was eminently successful, was serving as Ministerial Secretary in the Ministry of Health.

In addition to the saga of Goaso Hospital and to Osei's continuing concern with the general quality of medical services in the rural areas, there was one major theme in the health requirements of Ahafo and in the political activities undertaken to attend to these requirements which came to the fore in the later years of the C.P.P. regime. Osei's parliamentary attempts to elicit piped water for the area went back to April 1961 and were resumed in February 1962.[74] The inhabitants of Hwidiem and Kenyase I and II were alleged by him to have to pay 1s 6d for a kerosene tin of water in April and those of Kenyase were claimed to have to travel seven miles to buy water for 1s for 4 gallons and to have suffered severely from bilharzia, guinea worm, hookworm and a variety of other water-borne diseases. On this second occasion Osei broadened his argument into a comprehensive attack on the immobilism of the Department of Rural Water Development. In February 1962 the Brong–Ahafo Local Council was in fact forced to hire a water tanker to alleviate the worst effects of an exceptionally severe drought which had been causing great distress in Goaso, Hwidiem, Mim and Acherensua and which led to the almost complete evacuation of a number of the villages on the road from Mim to the Bia river, including Biaso and Gambia I.[75] In June 1963, in answer to an enquiry from the Regional Commissioner, the D.C. in Goaso despatched a list of twenty villages in whch it was necessary to dig wells in order to avoid drought in the future, a list which still took in major centres like Goaso, Mim and Kukuom, as well as little villages like Dechem. In November 1963 the head of the Water Supplies Division of the Ministry of Communications in Accra wrote informing the D.C. in Goaso that it was proposed to supply Goaso with pipe-borne water in 1963/4, warning of the imminent arrival of a survey team and seeking an assurance that the inhabitants would undertake communal labour for the digging and trenching. In the event, the supply proved slow in coming. The D.C. in Goaso had enquired optimistically in May 1964 as to when the work was due to begin. Three and a quarter years later a newly arrived District Administrative Officer in Goaso began his contribution to the district file with a brisk note to the Regional Engineer of the Water and Sewerage Corporation in Sunyani:

As you are aware, there is not a single town in Ahafo area which is served by water supply by your corporation . . . The main towns in this district which should be given immediate attention in order of priority are Goaso, Acherensua, Hwidiem, Mim, Kukuom and Kenyase. I shall be grateful if you will let me know as early as possible whether you have any immediate plans for water supply in this district and, if so, when you hope to implement them.

Fourteen harrying letters followed over the next two years, in addition to many others pressing the claims of Wamahinso, Ntotroso, Kenyase and others. In September 1969 the water began to flow in the Goaso pipes.

Numerous other Ahafo communities were due to receive piped water supplies over the subsequent two years, a mark of the politically favoured status of the region under the Progress government. It is not easy to identify with certainty all the causes of Ahafo's long neglect and its belated good fortune. Difficulties over the acquisition of foreign supplies appear to have delayed the arrival of the necessary pipes in the country in the early stages. Fairly self-conscious political choices seem to have been taken by the economic advisers of the N.L.C. government and reaffirmed by those (to a considerable extent the same persons) of the Progress government to redistribute public expenditure as far as possible from urban to rural development. The Water and Sewerage Corporation under the former U.P. politico Modesto Apaloo was able to make a rapid, reasonably cheap and incontrovertibly useful contribution to these aims with its rural water development schemes. Having government political backing, it was well-placed to secure such foreign supplies as it required. The comparative inanition of the department under the last years of the C.P.P. regime does also appear to have been a fairly direct political product of the low priority allotted by the C.P.P. even in its closing stages to the provision of development resources to rural areas, particularly when the latter had a lengthy record of political antipathy towards the governing party. But although the enviable, if brief, experience of Ahafo between 1969 and 1972 was clearly a reward for the political membership of its leaders in the équipe which had taken control of the government in the elections of August 1969, Brong–Ahafo enjoyed no comparable privilege during the N.L.C. regime. There seems, in consequence, to be no pressing reason to doubt that the success of Goaso, as opposed to a very large number of other communities, in securing a healthier and more convenient water supply in the summer of 1969, was largely a product of the turbulent enthusiasm released on its behalf by its local civil administrator over the preceding two years. In a government of officials, a type of government which returned once more in 1972, the tireless voice of a particularly energetic official was as effective a political resource as a district could readily acquire.

In contrast with the more strictly medical and utilitarian components of this effort to make Ahafo clean and safe, the less directly rewarding and more aesthetic aspects of residential organisation have failed to establish themselves in the Ahafo mind as instances of incontestable progress. Not that other facets of the colonial presence have left the public appearance of Ahafo communities unaffected. Motor roads and even timber tracks passing through the smaller settlements impose their own minimal spatial control on the disposition of houses, which in a shut-away and somewhat inaccessible hamlet like Asuadei still form a rather higgledy-piggledy cluster even today. Some effort is made in the case of the larger towns like Mim, Kukuom or Goaso to fit new houses into the existing grid designs. But the extent of public commitment to keep towns neat and town developments regular in layout and 'civilised' in construction tends to seem deplorably relaxed to the eyes of stranger ideologues of modern development like Community Development Officers or even perhaps to returned secondary schoolboys from the community itself. In its own eyes Ahafo's failure to 'progress' today is largely a matter of the inadequate level of government investment in public facilities in the area. But to the mildly colonial eyes of the welfare bureaucrat, the disarray of Ahafo townships appears more as a reflection of the lack of local commitment to the values of order and progress, the increasing tendency to regard communal labour as a chore fit only for the female sex or the northerner and the persistence among even the relatively wealthy of patterns of expenditure which seem distinctly regressive. One paradoxical consequence of these differing fates of the colonial venture in medicine and public amenity has been that, while it is today virtually certain that infant mortality is drastically lower and the expectation of life at most ages somewhat higher today than it was in for example 1950, the actual physical appearance of Ahafo townships (with the exception of one part of Mim) has probably changed very little. A fair number of two-storeyed houses were erected out of cocoa profits in the 1950s, in Hwidiem,[76] Kukuom, Goaso and elsewhere and a number of local and public buildings set up, particularly in Goaso, while in Mim the large quantities of wealth generated in the timber industry, both from the Mim Timber Company itself and from leading independent operators from the town like W. K. Ennin has led to the construction of several impressive mansions and of a veritable stockade for the company itself. The speed at which capital can be accumulated in the timber industry by the talented entrepreneur has undoubtedly had a major impact on the economic attitudes of a small number of wealthy Ahafos and the extent of conspicuous consumption which it has opened up to them and to the European timber men working in their midst has certainly reinforced tastes for individual expenditure. But, outside Mim at least, expenditure on storey-houses of the type which is constructed is scarcely a reflection of novelty in Ahafo tastes. A store of wealth, an investment which yields a reliable and substantial rate of return, an asset which if parts of it are allocated judiciously to the more pressing exponents of familial obligation can admirably confirm the householder's ethical responsiveness, above all a massive representation of an achieved economic stake in the community, a storey-house had been a token of satisfied individual ambition in Ahafo since the days of Braimansu himself.[77] Yet the individual disposition to raise such massive monuments was no index of any communal will to adorn the town at large, let alone to keep its public spaces as clean, neat and deodorised as the D.C.s had striven to make them.

The grid plans on which the larger Ahafo towns are constructed appear to date back to the 1920s, a time at which Ahafo's relations with the outside world were beginning to be transformed by the steady advance of the roads and the consequent metamorphosis in the profitability – at least in the long term – of cocoa-growing. But the first major impetus to the reorganisation of Ahafo settlements came earlier, with the establishment of what was intended to be a permanent district headquarters at Goaso. Such a reformation was seen as being part of the project of bringing 'civilisation' to Ahafo from the beginning. One of the main reasons in the Provincial Commissioner's arguments for the indispensability of police and of a detachment of three or four prison warders, as well as a proper prison for the new district[78] was that it would be essential for the new D.C.s to have prison labour at their disposal to carry out sanitary work.[79] The site for the Goaso headquarters was chosen in August 1913 by an administrative officer and a doctor from Sunyani.[80]

The work of clearing it began the same month.[81] By March of the following year it was virtually complete, despite the absence of the D.C. for all but fourteen days out of the period of construction. The extent of clearing and the large amount of communal labour contributed by the inhabitants of Goaso on behalf of a largely absent prospective administrator and one with no immediate coercive resources open to him suggested at least some local conviction that advantages might in due course follow from doing the now rather more obtrusive whites a favour. The Provincial Commissioner, anxious to augment his administrative forces, was quick to interpret it in a note to his superiors as a testimony to the strength of local enthusiasm for a permanent British presence and as an act of trust predicated on the assurance of this presence which it would be a gross breach of faith not to satisfy.[82]

Not only did the Omanhene and his chiefs present themselves to the Commissioner as 'keen on development';[83] but the latter also found several of the Ahafo villages on his route much improved. In one of them, Hwidiem, a whole new village was in the course of construction.[84] In Goaso itself the new D.C. not only embellished the new bungalow with grass and rose bushes,[85] but also marked out a new and better site for the upper and lower towns, with streets and avenues and town plots.[86] When the Provincial Commissioner revisited Ahafo in October 1914, he reported Hwidiem new town as being 'quite good', Kukuom and Ntotroso as improved and a certain amount of progress with the Mim roads. But his real enthusiasm was reserved for Goaso itself, in which the administrative station was greatly improved and the rebuilding of the town in compounds of seventy feet square (which he judged 'too big') appeared to him as an example of excellent town planning, prospectively a 'model village'.[87] When Cardinall took over as D.C. in 1915 the town was still in the process of moving to the new site and he found that the local population as a whole still displayed 'an intense keenness to progress'.[88] In February and March 1915, however, the Provincial Commissioner's verdict was less enthusiastic. The work in Goaso itself he found disappointing and, although a number of streets had been knocked through in Kukuom, little progress was detectable even there since the previous October. Cardinall, he complained on several occasions, 'does not do enough tail-twisting anywhere'.[89] When the Provincial Commissioner next visited Ahafo in October 1915, in company with the Chief Commissioner of Ashanti and his wife, he found Kukuom being laid out and partially moved a short distance to high ground, while the Chief Commissioner himself, inspecting Goaso, noted its large streets and the many houses in building.[90] In 1916 the sanitary condition of Goaso, as well as of Sunyani and Wenchi, was reported as 'fairly good' and the rebuilding of Goaso was judged complete.[91] But in February 1917, shortly before Goaso station was closed down because of wartime lack of administrative staff, the D.C.'s energies were still being applied to complete the removal of all trees from the Goaso streets and the government surveyor was moving on to Kukuom for a fortnight to complete marking out the new town there.[92] Colonial efforts to clean up Ahafo went substantially into eclipse for several years after this temporary abandonment of the administrative headquarters in Goaso. A Provincial Commissioner visiting Ahafo in May 1926 remarked balefully that Goaso was still at that time the same dilapidated place it had been when he visited it six years earlier.[93] In the absence of a British administrator Ahafo enthusiasm for 'progress' was left to find its own outlets, undirected by the 'tail-twisting' which had accompanied their earlier efforts at reconstruction. Even with a D.C. like Cardinall who 'didn't give them enough to do', it no doubt seemed only prudent to manifest some enthusiasm for whatever the colonial powers-that-were seemed to consider the desirable future. Perhaps, too, the enthusiasm for the prescribed future could be a trifle more heartfelt when the present fell below the highest standards of strenuousness.

In any case, the modulation of the colonial presence to a more intermittent and less intimate encounter made it possible to proceed towards the future at a less alien and frenetic pace. Between 1920 and the Commissioner's return in 1926 to find Goaso 'still the same dilapidated place' there had been another major flurry of rebuilding in 1922/3, when the colonial administrative grip began to tighten once again. The number of compound houses had nevertheless fallen slightly from the 53 recorded in the census of 1921 to the 48 counted in the Agriculture Department's cocoa survey of 1927/8. Only towards the end of the decade, as Ahafo's cocoa production climbed steeply with the progress of the motor roads, did the total of houses rise to the 87 counted in the Sanitary Census of December 1929.[94] The tendency for the old Ashanti house to disappear and be replaced by the square compound houses of the coast was noted in the census report for 1921,[95] confirming the rapidity with which the Ahafos like the Ashanti as a whole adopted such innovations as were evidently to their individual advantage. But the activity of rebuilding towns to meet colonial specifications was less evidently beneficial to particular rebuilders; and the D.C.s who set themselves to 'ginger things up' found it a 'terribly slow' and disappointing business. The absence of water (an indispensable component of the swish construction) served as a sufficient ground for inactivity in the last few months of 1922, while most of the adult males were employed for the first three months of the next year in carting cocoa. In April (and very belatedly) the snails arrived.[96] In December 1923, however, these Sisyphaean efforts of the D.C.s received an enthusiastic tribute from a Roman Catholic priest, the only 'non-official' European who knew the district at all well[97] and who had accordingly been asked by the Provincial Commissioner for his comments on the progress of Ahafo.

Colonial transformation: Hygiene and respectability

I was often perfectly amazed when a village was in sight, and more than once I lingered about in the wide mainstreet – a boulevard – to wonder at the cleanness, the order and the uniformity and spaces that are the chief factors in making those villages 'Model Villages'. Nkasaim especially struck me. I had seen there half a dozen ruined compounds, and I found a large street with two double rows of large and well-finished compounds.[98]

Altogether, the Ahafo villages were outstandingly the showpieces of all the villages he had seen in his travels throughout Ashanti. This lyrical appreciation of cleanliness, neatness and order in residential settlements, a common theme of colonial taste,[99] though one which was often unleashed elsewhere in a sharply more obtrusive and insensitive way than it ever was upon Ahafo, seems never to have evoked a very deep allegiance from the Ahafos.

The main theme of governmental activity in the towns in the 1920s was not, however, the enactment of this aesthetic of order, but the extension of sanitation. Provincial expenditure on sanitary labour and refuse disposal which had represented a little over 10 per cent of total provincial expenditure in 1923/4 had climbed to over 30 per cent by 1928/9.[100] When it came to achievement, however, progress was not as steady as it was simply in expenditure. Ahafo's sanitary condition was described as continuing good in 1923/4;[101] but two years later, after the station had again been closed temporarily in 1925, the general level of cleanliness once more 'left much to be desired' and the particularly filthy state of Goaso was 'affecting the Government area to a marked degree'.[102] In 1926 and 1927 a great deal of administrative energy was unleashed on the accumulated filth and its feared encroachment on the 'Government area'. Repeated efforts were made to improve the water supplies in Goaso, both for the administration and for the village, an objective which had been picked out as an urgent health need by the Provincial Commissioner as early as 1923.[103] Lack of success in remedying the deficiencies of the water supply led to serious contemplation of the possibility that the district headquarters might have to be moved elsewhere and to a visit of the Chief Commissioner himself late in 1927 to inspect the situation and take a final decision.[104] Vigorous administrative squabbles between the Engineer's Department in Kumasi and the political administration broke out on several occasions over the difficulties of co-ordinating town planning between transient D.C.s who did not always understand the instructions or survey plans left by their predecessors and engineers who could not always time their arrival as far afield as Goaso to coincide with the airy promises of their superiors.[105] Despite these contretemps the extent of administrative co-operation between Kumasi, Sunyani and Ahafo over sanitary matters in these years was as broad as it was over the construction of roads. The five years between 1926 and 1931 probably did more to change the appearance and the life patterns of the Ahafo settlements than any previous or subsequent period of the same length. It was a period, too, in which administrative preoccupation over development priorities was more morally concerned than it had often been in the past. In the formal report on sanitary conditions in Ahafo in 1926/7 the Commissioner had pointed to the anomaly of administrative regulations which made it possible for the government to fine chiefs for failing to do road work but gave it no coercive recourse against chiefs whose violation of sanitary regulations might entail 'loss of life, maiming or disease'. 'In other words, the condition of roads is of more importance than the sanitary conditions of a town.' He did, however, claim that the attitudes of Ashanti as a whole had changed over the preceding three years from the view that sanitation was 'a nuisance rather than a necessity' to the view that 'sanitation was a necessity though somewhat of a nuisance', a view confirmed by the number of recent applications from chiefs to have their villages laid out and sanitated.[106] By July 1930 the increased sensitisation of the administration to the significance of sanitary work was indicated by the urgency with which the D.C. in Goaso repudiated the visiting Medical Officer's charge that sanitation was being sacrificed to road work in his district.[107]

Under these impulses sustained progress was made in establishing a new sanitary regime in Ahafo. By 1931, Goaso was no longer the same dilapidated place it had been six years earlier, as the Commissioner had harshly judged in 1926, nor was it still as 'simply filthy' as it had been found that year. The Provincial Commissioner in 1931, looking back at the development in the light of the census returns, noted a vast improvement in the preceding ten years in housing, particularly in the Sunyani, Wenchi and Goaso districts. The Goaso district itself had the highest average number of inhabitants per house in the province, a difference which directly reflected the type of building.[108] 'In the large towns and villages along the motor roads the old Ashanti compound, a rough quadrilateral built of swish or stick and roofed with thatch or leaves is gradually disappearing and being replaced by well constructed compounds 60 to 80 feet square with verandahs, corrugated iron roofs and swish walls covered in cement plaster with plenty of air space between the houses.' Despite the heavy debts incurred by communities in producing this transformation, the inhabitants 'fully appreciated', according to the Commissioner, the considerable benefits from a health point of view which the changes provided. Indeed, even chiefs 'residing in remote villages far from the motor roads are repeatedly asking the District Commissioner for the services of village overseers to lay out their villages for them'. Among the miscellaneous objectives of the administration the goal of road improvement was not the only one to come into conflict with this wave of enthusiasm for village embellishment. It was impossible even for the most agile D.C. to combine a dedication to the speedy completion of the new housing schemes with the full customary hostility towards the Ashanti propensity for getting into debt. Corrugated iron was a particularly costly and technically advantageous component of the new building style. A rash of applications from the major Ashanti chiefs (including the Kukuomhene) to be permitted to borrow large sums of money for the purchase of these sheets from the United Africa Company in Kumasi in return for mortgages on the cocoa crops brought a personal and absolute prohibition from the Chief Commissioner of Ashanti himself. But only a few months later the exiguous manipulative skills of the Goasohene were bent to the goal of acquiring just such a loan for no less than £975, a sum which was bound to leave the town in debt for some years to come; and the D.C. in Goaso was unable to deny the reality of the need, even in the teeth of his superior's explicit prohibition.[109] As he wrote nervously to point out, if the inhabitants of Goaso did not receive the loans so that they could purchase the iron sheets before the rains began, the laboriously constructed walls of their new houses would simply be washed away.

Besides the replanning of the towns and the general effort to clean and tidy the new residential spaces, more specific efforts were made to mark off and set limits to some of the more highly cathected forms of potentially contaminating matter. Even the dead were given a less socially fluid resting place in the new public cemeteries. Official sites were allocated for the dumping of refuse and incinerators planned and built for its more permanent dispersal.[110] Above all the public latrine made its appearance as a focus of administrative concern. Latrines were under construction in Goaso, Hwidiem and Nkasaim by the middle of 1926.[111] Covered latrines were planned later in the year in addition for Kukuom and Acherensua.[112] By November 1929 the administration's toilet-training activities extended as far as the D.C. haranguing the women of Kenyase II for their 'filthy habits' in not employing the public latrine in the town and ordering the chief to punish them if they failed to do so in the future.[113] When he visited the town in August of the following year he was outraged to find the compounds still filthy[114] and proceeded to take his revenge on the resolute disorder of the village (so unlike the prim virtues of its neighbour Hwidiem)[115] by knocking down eighteen houses, including that of the chief himself. By July of the same year the cleansing activities of the administration had reached out far enough into the recesses of the forest for three latrines to have been constructed and the bush duly cleared even in Aboum.[116] When the chief Commissioner of Ashanti visited Ahafo in February 1931, largely to reassure the disconsolate farmers about the plummeting price of cocoa, he indubitably testified to the aesthetic impact of these sanitary activities, but he did so with a singular lack of enthusiasm.

The landscape along my route, apart from forest, consisted principally of large square unfinished houses of a standard type which most of the people are too poor to complete. Teppa especially has two long rows of perfectly aligned mud walls. I doubt if they will ever turn into houses. A most dismal sight. The other principal feature is of course the public latrine. In seven months in the N.T.s I never remember seeing one except those made by whitemen in Tamale etc. Here in Ashanti the people seem to take trouble to draw attention to them.[117]

(The Commissioner's economic pessimism was a simple reflex, as so often, of the price of cocoa on the world market at the time.) The Provincial Commissioner visiting Ahafo in May 1931 also commented with horror on the three latrines 'bang on the main road and in the centre of town in full view of the householders on the opposite side of the road' and vowed darkly that something must be done to abolish 'the beastly practice of building latrines at the approaches to the village', a view with which the Chief Commissioner predictably enough concurred.[118]

In the end Ahafo matter proved far too refractory for colonial energies ever to succeed for long in restricting it to approved places. Devices for reducing it to order were apt in Ahafo to take a form which caricatured mercilessly the tastes of those who had originally advocated them. But the energies devoted to the cleansing enterprise were not wholly without their reward. New, if not always very durable, institutions were devised to superintend the operation. A Provincial Sanitary Committee for the Western Province was established in July 1926 and in the following year Goaso district acquired its own District Sanitary Committee.[119] Monthly progress reports on sanitary work were demanded from December 1926.[120] New government employees were drafted into the district to help with the cleansing, increased supplies of sanitary labour to keep the town of Goaso in fit condition for a European to reside in its vicinity and to prevent its dirt – or indeed its productive activities –[121] from insinuating themselves too close to where he did in fact reside, and, of more general utility, village overseers to superintend the layout of the new sites. In Goaso itself the new plans provided for a proper market place and a butcher's slab for the more hygienic slaughter of cattle or sheep for fresh meat. The relationship between the administration and the local population remained throughout marked by a highly ambivalent blend of conflict and co-operation, not unlike that which characterised the efforts to complete the construction of the new roads. As perhaps in the latter case, most Ahafos may well have conceived the end state desired by the administration as a genuine public good; but their eminently egoistic conception of the rationality of work made them nonetheless eager to escape contributing their own labour to its promotion. They were also unable to reproduce in their approach the evanescent single-mindedness which the administration from time to time displayed. Seldom able to give the project their undivided attention, whether or not it evoked their unambivalent enthusiasm, and increasingly economically unequipped to provide the heavy capital cost of the iron sheeting needed for the roofs of their new houses, they must often have resented keenly the tendency of the D.C.s to construe the speed of reconstruction as a simple index of moral virtue and to take a certain spiteful pleasure in requiting the less speedy (and thus more indolent) by pulling down their old and dilapidated houses before they had completed their new ones. There is a classic colonial symmetry to the occasion when the D.C. determined to stop the inhabitants of Goaso from dancing until they had cleaned the town up.[122] The compound of paternalism and anality was hardly likely to establish a commanding sway over the allegiance of the Ahafo population. But the Ahafos have in the event taken from the experience of this five-year colonial sanitary crusade what it was in due course instrumentally convenient for them to have taken. Ahafo today does not exhibit a Scandinavian obsession with the domination of dirt. But in a tropical forest environment which remains recalcitrant to cleanliness, and in the light of the very much larger numbers of people who now inhabit it, the Ahafos have kept their environment within levels of pollution which their indigenous culture would scarcely have insisted on but which have in fact made possible a healthier and a more agreeable life.

c. GODLINESS AND GOOD LEARNING

i. Godliness

Amongst his other attributes, the God of the whites at the time when they came to Ahafo was a jealous God. One of the prime requirements which he exacted from his worshippers was an exclusive claim on their loyalties: 'Thou shalt have none other gods but me.' Since the Ahafos at the time were amply furnished with deities of their own, the jealousy of the white god was not calculated to endear him on arrival to the majority of any Ahafo community. For the new godliness to advance, it was necessary for a multiplicity of diffuse and intricate godly allegiances to be compelled to retreat. At first, too, the existing repertoire of divine meaning and concomitant practical power was naturally largely in the possession of the holders of local authority in the community. Becoming a Christian was thus an inescapably political act, an act in fact of subversion. It was also paradoxically one towards which the whites themselves were necessarily and not merely by accidental individual disposition deeply ambivalent. It was agreeable for a colonial administrator to be able to advance civilisation; but it was essential for him to be able to maintain control. Within a system of indirect rule the dependence of even the most devoutly Christian D.C. upon a range of comfortably pagan chiefs for ensuring social control precluded him from sanctioning a crusading Christianity.

Dependence and opportunity

Whatever his personal sense of the relationship between Christianity and civilisation, the D.C. was forced by the exigencies of his public role into a strenuous and taxing neutrality. It can hardly be an accident that in the huge bulk of detailed daily description of the lives of the Commissioners in Ahafo from the conquest up to the early 1930s[1] there appears to be not a single recorded example of their participation whilst in the district in public Christian worship. Christian prayers might be said on formal occasions – British Empire Day for example – but so equally might libations be poured to fetishes in the D.C.'s presence. The colonial order in Ahafo embraced a relaxed syncretism in religious observance. Christianity consequently was much more of a diplomatic problem for the administration than a cultural triumph.

The date at which the colonial regime appeared in Ahafo made it substantially easier to adopt this vigilant administrative neutrality than it would have been for the exponents of Christian imperialism in earlier centuries. By 1896 Britain was essentially a secular state in which religious denominations were regarded as a form of voluntary association entitled to the widest degree of toleration compatible with observance of the secular law of the land. The spiritual conquest of Ahafo could be left in consequence to be conducted, as that of New Spain plainly could not,[2] on an authentically entrepreneurial basis by a variety of mutually hostile bodies, the missions, which were organisationally independent of the public authority. Their independence gave the missionaries the opportunity to operate with a measure of public irresponsibility which may have been much to their advantage; but it obliged them to undertake the Christianisation of the area as a process of conversion instead of one of simple subjugation. Even in this process there was abundant Christian provocation in the face of local susceptibilities. But the only instance of frontal ideological assault upon Ahafo spiritual values came in fact from a representative of a different universalist religion, a Hausa hearing a call from Allah in February 1915 to burn the Mim fetish house, the abode of Ahafo's premier fetish, and ending up with a pathos apparent even to the Provincial Commissioner in the colonial gaol at Goaso.[3]

A more theologically committed colonising power would have cast the political embodiments of Ahafo religious ideas as leaders of communal resistance to external aggression and the Christian converts as spiritual collaborators with the occupying power. The political motive for becoming a Christian would have been seen by the menaced community as a quisling motive. An institutionally agnostic colonial power by contrast was willing, other things being equal, to leave the missionary entrepreneurs to what they could get out of the spiritual market. Other things, of course, were seldom precisely equal. But since Ahafo was at least not an Islamic area and was indeed soon seen, as a part of Ashanti, as a potential bastion of resistance to the universalist challenge of an Islamic rising throughout West Africa,[4] the implication of the colonial government did not extend in the shoring up of the religious values of the 'natural' rulers, as it did in northern Nigeria and at times also in northern Ghana,[5] as far as excluding missionaries from the area. Islamic political authority might be largely solidary in its resistance to Christian incursions, since Allah also was a jealous God and Mahomet his jealous prophet. But Ashanti deities were more accommodating and had nothing against new gods as such. Hence the missions had little initial difficulty in getting a foothold in Ahafo and, by the time that local resistance had become more vigorous, the administration was no longer in a position to buy administrative peace and quiet by closing the door in their face. The pattern of Christian incursion into Ahafo reflected the district's integration into the cultural nexus of metropolitan Ashanti. Writing may first have arrived in Ahafo direct from the coast and been used at once on its arrival in the Ahafo drive for political independence from the metropolis.[6] But there is no evidence that Christianity had entered the district before 1896 and when traces of it do first appear in Ahafo nearly a decade after the conquest they plainly emanate from Kumasi. There had been Christian missionaries and schools in Kumasi itself at intervals throughout the nineteenth century, their presence accepted by the Ashanti court as part of its gingerly exploration of the facilities possessed by the increasingly intrusive West.[7] The centralisation of the Ashanti empire made the prospect of converting the court, of bringing off a Christian revolution in Ashanti like that achieved in Buganda, an extremely seductive one to European missionaries and one which was made both more alarming in the attempt and more alluring if achieved by the spectacular reputation of Ashanti barbarism. As long as the empire maintained its political independence, however, the Christian missionaries were in practice tolerated simply because of their possible utility, as the Muslims had been for many decades before them.[8] Like the Muslims, too, their prospects for eventual conversion of the empire were poor. With the British conquest, however, Christian incursions on Ashanti society were no longer subject to the strategic control of a dominant court. In these new conditions the structures of Ashanti society proved to be readily permeable by the appeals of Christianity. The lower orders in Kumasi had been regarded with some contempt by its political leaders as far back as the visits of Bowdich and Dupuis in the early nineteenth century.[9] The position of domestic slaves was particularly unenticing. The Basel missionary Ramseyer set himself up in the face of the British administration as the authentic representative of the slave population against chiefly oppression.[10] The stratification of Ashanti society and its propensity for factional strife within each local community provided a variety of occasions for the initial investment in Christian allegiance as a political tactic. It was easy for the missions, lacking as they did a dominating preoccupation with the maintenance of social control, to serve as energetic defenders of social groups which were undoubtedly genuinely oppressed. Once the initial investment in Christian allegiance had been undertaken in particular communities, the motor of factional conflict within the community, reinforced shortly by the advantages for social mobility furnished by the Christian provision of education, served to augment the denominational clienteles in a fairly steady fashion. As a political instrument Christian allegiance offered substantial advantages in the form of external political assistance and long-run economic aid to factions whose political resources within the community might well be initially exiguous and which, however much the political administration might sympathise with them, were too impotent against local holders of power to serve as a possible alternative instrument of political control. The political detachment of the missions left it open to them to accumulate adherents very much from the bottom upwards, commencing usually with quite tiny minorities. The administration by contrast, being anxious above all to cut its costs, was obliged to proceed firmly from the top down and nothing less substantial than the immediate control of large majorities could suffice for it.

This perspective on the advances and retreats of different godly allegiances is rather crudely demographic. At the level of moral perception the issues are less simple. Not that the strictly political constraints ceased to carry weight in this sphere also: the market needs of missionaries and administrators duly bred highly selective traditions of historical perception. Comprehensive and mutually incompatible interpretations of the factional history of communities were developed. The moral character of the Christian histories was comparatively linear. They recorded the steady triumph of universalist and rationalist religious values (not perhaps the most obvious characterisation of Christianity from the perspective of Europe itself) over the particularist and barbarous superstitions of Ahafo. It is important to emphasise the partial historical contingency of this perspective in order to avoid seeing it as an inevitable stage in Parsonian modernisation. Many of the aspects of Ahafo godliness to which the Christians took vigorous exception do wear an exceedingly superstitious air to the secular western eye: witch-finding to take an obvious example. But in this case the intimate link between the civilising rationalism of European Christian universalism and the date of its arrival is easy to indicate. When the sophisticated Jesuit missionaries entered Ethiopia early in the seventeenth century, one of the local doctrinal heterodoxies which shocked them most profoundly was the fact that the Ethiopians did not believe in witchcraft. (A Portuguese priest who preceded the Jesuits in the sixteenth century had also been rather startled that the Ethiopians were faddish enough to object to spitting in church.[11]) The scope of the Christian ideological triumph in Ahafo, now a much more predominantly and vigorously Christian area than, for example, the United Kingdom, has meant that the presentation of the coming of Christianity to the area as a simple victory for modern civilisation over indigenous barbarism has come to be pervasively accepted in Ahafo itself. It is thus essential to emphasise the historical con-tingency of the Christian interpretation of this history and to insist that, whatever judgement is passed on the felicity of the transformation, it was not the felicity which caused it to occur. The historical triumph of an ideology equating Christianity and modernity must not be permitted to prejudge the explanation of why this particular ideology did triumph.

One ready way of avoiding this historicist misconception is simply to con-sider the administration's rival moral history of the advent of Christianity in Ahafo, concentrating as it did on a rather extended vision of what comprised the rituals and judiciously ignoring the supposed theology. The fact that Christianity did not make its appearance in Ahafo as the spiritual arm of the colonial power protected it from being seen as a religion fit only for quislings. This has clearly contributed substantially to the emotional ease and the absence of introverted bitterness which mark the present-day Christian identity of Ahafo. But it also meant that the only motive which a man could well have for becoming a Christian, except at the most severely transcendental level, was one which explicitly placed him not only in opposition to the values of the community to which he belonged (which was perhaps in some measure intrinsic to the process of conversion) but also in opposition to its political superiors. Those to whom it was at first appealing to become Christian were by and large those to whom it was not appealing to remain what they already were: neither particularly prosperous nor particularly free subjects of existing religious and political power. It is difficult to disentangle the causality of the process of incipient Christianisation with any precision. Doubts remain as to how far the aggressive separatism of the convert communities was a product of the intractable rigorism of the missionaries themselves and of their earliest and most severely tried followers and how far it was a product rather of the extent to which it was only to the outstandingly alienated and aggressive that Christianity had any strong appeal to make. But, whatever the precise causation of the initial definition of the role of Christian in Ahafo, it was soon quite clear what the social definition of this role was to be. Becoming a Christian in Ahafo was a local version of the delinquent solution. It was seen overwhelmingly as such, naturally, by the non-Christian residues of Ahafo communities; but this was also substantially the way it was seen by the colonial administrators. To become a Christian was to adopt an entire con-testant way of life, a pugilistic posture in defiance of the respectable and the powerful, which gave endless opportunity for the gleeful offending of the sentiments of the majority and which was able to call on a variety of external assistance to protect its exponents from the righteous vengeance of the community. What most inflamed the moral resentment of the administrators and led them to develop the rich vein of moral abuse which they directed at the authenticity of the delinquents' spiritual convictions, was their inability to extricate themselves from commitments to both offenders and offended.

The example of northern Nigeria and of northern Ghana make it plain that it was not simply the non-Christian character of Ashanti religion which generated this uncomfortable posture. In part, no doubt, it may be attributed directly to the different military situations in the aftermath of the conquests of northern Nigeria and of Ashanti. The dependence of the British for the maintenance of political and military control upon the existing political structures was far more abject in the case of the Hausa-Fulani emirates at the outset[12] than it was in Ashanti and it always remained so throughout the colonial period. Initial military dependence and long-run political dependence made it difficult for the British administrators to enforce educational and religious penetration of the north by the missions and on the whole they made little effort to do anything of the sort. But there was another reason besides the more comprehensive political subjection of Ashanti which explained the degree to which the administration was implicated in the Christian penetration of Ashanti. Islamic godliness had been defined necessarily as infidel by the Christian West ever since it first entered the ken of the Christian world.[13] But it was a monotheist faith, explicitly and very recognisably within the Judaic tradition and few of its articles could be judged to be 'repugnant to morality' as such with any plausibility. It was a very different – and no doubt from a colonial point of view a manifestly inferior – civilisation; but it did not require the researches of a government anthropologist to make plain the fact that it *was* a civilisation. By contrast its own distinctive form of godliness was intimately implicated in the exceedingly lurid reputation of Ashanti as a whole. The 'land of fetish' was the epitome of savage superstition. The many features of the society which they had conquered which continued inter-mittently to unnerve the colonial administrators were for long represented for them by the idea of fetish-worship. Within Ashanti religious culture access to spiritual power was both the main sanction of normative social control and a potential instrument of amoral personal power. The guarantee of the public order of each local community, from the colonial viewpoint not merely a desirable power but an indispensable one, was as much premised on belief in the power of 'fetish' as was the power to perpetrate nameless evil. Christians – even 'alleged Christians' – who took their stand upon their religious duty to reject all demands to recognise fetish authority were not merely proclaiming themselves unruly subjects, self-righteous delinquents; they were also pro-claiming themselves dedicated foes of a pattern of beliefs which often figures in colonial records as a synonym for the savage and dreadful.

Accusations of cruelty and even of murder in witch-finding campaigns were always set out in the early years of colonial rule in Ahafo as indictments of the barabaric influence of fetish belief. In April 1906 in Dadiesoaba 'a travelling fetishman' was alleged to have accused a woman of witchcraft and to have killed her when she refused to pay his purgation fee.[14] In June of the same year a complaint was brought to the Provincial Commissioner in Sunyani that a woman in Dantano had been charged with witchcraft by her own son before the court of the Omanhene at Kukuom and driven from her village upon conviction.[15] Two years later, in 1908, a series of instances of torture and murder in cases of witch-finding by the 'Bungulu fetish' came to light in Dadiesoaba, Mehame and Akrodie. Women were alleged to have had ground chilis rubbed into their genitals and to have been savagely beaten for denying their witchcraft. But they were too frightened to testify to their mal-treatment and on examination steadfastly proclaimed that they were guilty of witchcraft. The leading prosecution witness, a man called Kofi Pong, himself largely responsible for bringing the crimes to the notice of the administration, was approached by one of the fetishmen concerned with a substantial bribe to suppress his testimony.[16] When in the following year the Western Provincial Commissioner proposed to the Chief Commissioner of Ashanti the establish-ment of a new district in Ahafo and Wam with its headquarters at Mim, the list of motives which he gave for his proposal began with the claim that the long-term economic development of the area would justify it and that the short-term improvement in the prevention of smuggling to and from the French territories and in the efficient collection of spirit licence revenue would make it acceptably cheap in the meantime. But they culminated in the proposal to establish colonial hegemony over the Mim fetish. The assurance that much crime, 'particularly crime connected with extortion', currently went undetected in 'the remoter parts of Wam and Ahafo', a natural in-ference from the cases in 1908, was linked directly with the great strength of fetish, particularly in Ahafo. The District Commissioner who was to be established at Mim, 'a great hotbed of fetish and superstition', would require in order to establish his dominance a permanent detachment of twenty-five soldiers. The ringing conclusion of the proposal makes plain how much the administration saw its secular and *political* task in Ahafo as a spiritual con-quest of fetish.

I do not say that at the initial inauguration of a station at Mim, the Fetish would not be in active opposition. It probably would, but its active opposition with a sensible district commissioner would take little time to overcome. A district com-missioner would soon be able without force to put Fetish opposition or opposition inaugurated by Fetish into the background. It is easily done, in time, by judicious ridicule and an attitude of superiority; after that, I will not say fetish opposition will not continue but it works in the background.[17]

The key problem posed by the adoption of this strategy for subduing the powers of the fetish was the ambiguity as to just what was being shown as superior. Christianity at least did proffer an alternative metaphysical and normative view of the world as a substitute for the familiar 'superstitions' which it strove to supplant. But it was too total a substitute to be other than politically disruptive in the short run. The secular 'superiority' of the pretensions of the administration need not have been weakened – might indeed have been strengthened – by their gingerly handling of encroaching Christianity. But it could hardly be exemplified by their anxious efforts to regulate and render respectable the exercise of fetish powers. To labour away at the project of systematising fetish oath fees for example was not a plausible way of demonstrating the administration's assurance that the sanctions of fetish oaths were wholly illusory.[18] Both the maintenance of social control within communities and the prevention of communal violence between them required the conduct of very elaborate diplomatic relations with fetish power.

A measure of such political recognition must have been exacted from the administration in any area of Ashanti. But two characteristics of the Ahafo division made it certain that in this case the measure would have to be a larger one. For Ahafo was not merely geographically peripheral from the viewpoint both of metropolitan Kumasi and of the new administrative capital of the Western Province at Sunyani – and thus for several decades much less subject to effective administration than most areas of Ashanti; it was also as an 'artificial division' of Ashanti, peculiarly devoid of any established pattern of local political integration. The major split within it came between the new political centre, Kukuom, the seat of the Omanhene, and the larger and more prosperous town of Mim which had much stronger links with metropolitan Ashanti, in particular with the Akwaboa stool in Kumasi, because of the notorious fetish sited at the 'Obo' rock near Mim Mohu. The initial British commitment to the Kukuom stool in this polar opposition may have been in part fortuitous. It is clear, too, that it might easily have been reversed by the perhaps not altogether deliberate 'loyalty' of Beditor, the fetish chief of Mim, during the Yaa Asantewa rising, in which Kukuom itself had had the bad taste to join the rebels. But once the British administrators had become thoroughly committed to Kukuom, they found themselves faced with an excessively complex assignment when it came to combining internal social order within the Mim community with the preservation of inter-communal peace in the Ahafo division as a whole. From 1901 up to the exile of Beditor, which was precipitated by the narrow averting of a major confrontation between Mim and Kukuom, and in some small measure even after this and up to 1928 when Beditor's successor Yaw Bofa was banished in his turn and when the District Commissioner claimed finally to have 'broken the temporal power of the Mim fetish',[19] the administration felt compelled to treat the Obo fetish not only as an important item of real property, producing substantial revenues as they had treated other fetishes in the past, but also as a major focus of political power.[20] When the first hapless English D.C. arrived at his headquarters in Goaso in 1914 he was not in fact endowed with even a handful of police with which to enforce his will – let alone with the twenty-five soldiers which his superior had judged essential a few years earlier. In these circumstances the apprehensive references to the 'turbulent Ahafo factions' of Mim and Kukuom and the unruly disposition of the Ahafos, not to mention the urgent need for police because of the 'considerable Fetish worship' in the district or the fact that 'the enforcement of authority may at any time become necessary' show an entirely realistic sense of administrative impotence in the face of local power.[21] It was no easy matter for a D.C. without obvious coercive capacity of his own on which to call to demonstrate the appropriate superiority in his 'palavers with the Mim Fetish', when he was in fact dependent for such effective control of the district as he could muster on instruments which were wholly culturally homogeneous with those of the Obo fetish itself and when, indeed, he was necessarily largely dependent for his control within the Mim community upon the power of those who controlled the fetish. In the end a direct confrontation between the fetish and the colonial power could only end in one way, as the fate of first Beditor and then Yaw Bofa showed plainly enough. But it was a protracted struggle and one in which, as the fetish and its custodians gradually learnt to pick as opponents only those who were more their own size than was the colonial government, the local variety of godliness came to show impressive doctrinal flexibility and political dexterity. In 1914 it had been alleged that the Mim chief objected to a European visiting the Obo rock because Europeans destroyed the power of fetishes and because the latter was a substantial source of revenue.[22] Even in 1924, ten years later, the Obo rock had never been visited by a European, though Cardinall had observed it from Mim Mohu.[23] But when, a year or two later, the government Survey Department wished to survey the area of the rock, the fetish chief consented to the procedure for an honorarium of £9 6s od and a guarantee that the man who did survey the area *should* indeed be a European.[24] By becoming the backer of the Kukuom interest in Ahafo the administration had cast itself in the first decade of the century as the dedicated opponent of the more overweening claims of Mim fetish power. According to one of its own representatives it had not on the whole increased its political appeal to the Ahafos by doing so.[25] But it had never been in a position to cast itself as an outright foe of all fetishes as such. In due course the Obo fetish learnt how to accommodate itself to colonial norms and the spiritual apparatus of that 'dangerous fetishman' Beditor[26] came to enjoy administrative protection and even sympathy against the exorbitant claims of the missions to remove the final fetish taboo from the town, prohibition of dogs.[27]

Dependence and opportunity

In this case too, as we shall see in the field of education, the process of mutual accommodation of indigenous culture and colonial requirements must be understood as an activity of mutual socialisation by the two initially opposed interests. Its product is a comfortable syncretism in which traditional public ceremonies of a fetish character continue to represent the social identities of a resident population, the substantial majority of which is now formally Christian or Muslim. In the last phase of rampant and self-confident traditionalism, that which followed the restoration of the Ashanti Confederacy in 1935, the taking of fetish oaths in Kumasi remained on occasion the focus of political struggles within individual Ahafo communities.[28] But the cost of access to these political services which the vigour of Kumasi exploitation imposed helped over time to spoil the Ahafo market for the commodity. In the meantime the colonial government had developed a system of fetish-licensing on a more local basis, as a complement to its list of prescribed fetishes. It was never as important, even at a purely cultural level, as the list of colonially recognised chiefs, a permanent index of modernist claims to maintain political domination. There still continued to be intermittent clashes between colonial respectability or convenience and the demands of fetish power in the decades after the D.C. broke the temporal power of the Obo fetish – to say nothing of purely traditional survivals such as the attribution of the Omanhene's death in 1930 to his having stolen from Kukuom's Abese fetish.[29] The process of road construction, for example, was slowed at intervals in 1929 when some untoward occurrence reminded the Mim labourers that their fetish tabooed work on Fridays.[30] The inhabitants of Goaso appealed to the requirements of the fetish in 1930 in justifying their reluctance to move from their old village to the carefully planned new town. 'The fetish has been respected long enough', commented the harassed D.C.[31] In 1931 in the course of a dispute between Akrodie and Fawohoyeden the playing of an accordion on the Abese fetish day in Kukuom provoked the Omanhene into striking the offending musician and nearly started a riot.[32] It was the suicide of a Fawohoyeden woman in 1934 which led the Chief Commissioner of Ashanti to ban all witch and wizard-finding throughout Ashanti. The prompting to do so came from the appearance of a new fetish – a tortoise found by a little boy under a bush in a small village near Wenchi which had established such a spectacular reputation as far afield as southern Ahafo that the Wenchi stool had drawn £330 in revenue from the first year of its operation and lorry loads of women had been transported to the fetish site for screening. The Fawohoyeden suicide had been instructed to visit the fetish by the chief of her town.[33] The means of transport adopted for the movement of such numbers and the quantities of money accruing to the Wenchi stool (possibly designated in part to such a worthy modernist purpose as the education of the future Dr Busia) show the clear capacity of fetish

130

energy to adapt itself to the opportunities of colonial 'modernisation'. Not that such a scale of influence would have been in any way remarkable in a thoroughly archaic fetish. The renown of the Mim fetish stretched as far as Keta at a time when the Gold Coast as a whole was devoid of modern roads, let alone railways;[34] and it certainly was no closer to being a charitable institution than was the Delphic oracle. But the speed at which the Wenchi tortoise expanded its clientele in 1934 and the distances over which they came plainly did reflect the impact of the colonial Public Works Department and indeed of the cheaper lorries produced by the Ford Motor Company. In this instance, other aspects of the colonial presence prevented the fetish from consolidating its position. But three years later in 1937, it still made sense for the District Commissioner to explain competition between the Akwaboa and Hia stools of Kumasi for the overlordship of the Ahafo village of Ayumso by the large prospective revenues of its fetish.[35] The latter stages of the accommodation between fetishes and colonial authority were on the whole less dramatic, though there was one lurid story of a fetish murder as late as 1944 in which an Akrodie man was alleged to have paid £30 to get a human corpse for his fetish[36] and successful prosecutions for fraud by witch-finding were still taking place in 1942.[37] In 1937 the D.C. in Ahafo received four applications for a licence from fetishes, only two of which he granted.[38] In 1941 the Goasohene applied successfully for a renewal of his licence for Goaso's Bonsam. The Ahafo fetish file concludes with a note by the D.C. that in this district no licences were granted for herbalists.

Eventually the Fetish Militant was bludgeoned into a coexistence so peaceful that it no longer made sense to see the residuary powers of surviving fetishes, even in the background to which they had undoubtedly been consigned, as in opposition to modern authorities, whether public or private. It is a sufficient boast for Goaso's Bonsam today to be able to echo the Abbé Siéyès's reply, when asked what he had done during the French Revolution: 'J'ai vécu.' For while it is clear today that the Fetish Militant has indeed been supplanted and while Ahafo is not plausibly any longer a place of nameless buried villainies, it is also clear that it is not the Church Triumphant which has caused its supplanting. The Church has certainly expanded demographically in a most convincing fashion. Against the seven Christians in Ahafo according to the 1911 census (very possibly the only category in Ahafo not under-recorded on that occasion) or the 360 Christians for the Western Province as a whole, indeed even against the 314 Ahafo Christians recorded in 1921,[40] might be set the total church attendance at morning services of 670 adolescents or adults noted one July Sunday in 1971 in the town of Goaso alone. On this occasion the figures were probably slightly inflated by out-of-town Catholics appearing for a special visit from their priest who resided outside the district. (There had been a resident European Catholic priest in Goaso in 1943; but by 1949 Catholic congregations in Ahafo were once again being ministered to from as far away as Bechem.⁴¹) But the scale of regular worship is undoubtedly very considerable by present American standards, let alone those of Great Britain. One reason why this broad stream of religious observance should not be interpreted too readily as an index of the mastery of the Church Triumphant is the simple fact that this total of worshippers was split up among ten denominations. Fetish power was inherently pluralist, at least geographically. Most communities could in due course get their hands on a fetish of sorts and, while it was certainly not true that one fetish was as good as another, at least the loyalty of a fetish to the community in which it was located was more or less above suspicion. But the form in which Christianity had come to Ahafo was severely post-Reformation and, while it lacked the easy accommodation to local particularism which was the essence of the fetish faith and while it proffered as any virtuous modernising institution should appropriately have done a form of authority and thus of participation overarching the boundaries of individual communities, it opened up new divisions of its own within these communities. Most institutional embodiments of modernity which have arrived in Ahafo have presented themselves as unitary and rational in character: the colonial government, the school, the church, the market. The Church in particular was especially bound to set out its merits and its claims in a universal mode. The victory of the universal over fetish localism might easily have been a stern conquest, felt (and resented) as much as a suppression of existing identities as a synthesis of fresh ones. If today the Ahafos wear their Christianity for the most part casually, though not exactly lightly, if the Christianity of Ahafo lacks all trace of a messianic tinge or any suggestion of fanaticism, this is an index not merely of the comparative delicacy of the colonial hand in Ahafo as against other parts of Africa or indeed of present-day Ghana. It is also a consequence of the relaxed pluralism of religious institutions which makes it as easy for ten different Christian denominations to live side by side in the little town of Goaso, as it would be for the same number of denominations to coexist in a great western city. By the time that they had reached out to Goaso even genuinely ecumenical denominations like the Roman Catholics had learnt some of the spiritual complaisance from which the new African churches had sprung so vigorously. All of these denominations were a very long way from the Molochs of the Council of Trent or Calvinist Geneva. Once both churches and fetishes had learnt a measure of mutual good manners, they had little spiritual difficulty in coexisting in peace. Less than a month after the Commissioner's settlement of the bitter recriminations in September 1918 between the Wesleyan missionary and Yaw Bofa, the fetish chief of Mim, the local Wesleyan catechist whose deportation Yaw Bofa had been demanding with vigour for months was fully reconciled with him. Indeed the two men were soon on the best of terms.[42]

The possibility of such tranquil cohabitation, which is very much the dominant mode of today, was not an illusionist trick of the colonial government, any more that it was a result of the disciplined sensitivity throughout of the convert communities. Rather, it derived from the long-drawn-out collision between the political requirements of the administration and the competitive incarnations of the delinquent solution which the offshoots of the various missions represented, the constellation of Christian gangs by which the chiefs of Ahafo found themselves harried in the first three decades of the century. The sharply political character of these conflicts should not be concealed by their eventual resolution in an accommodation which seems decisively instrumental rather than ideological. If to the administration the Christians long appeared as inauthentic exponents of the creed, it was equally plausible for the Christians to portray their traditionalist opponents as fundamentally inauthentic and manipulative in their allegiance to fetish authority. Had Christianity not been so strongly linked with access to literacy it seems entirely plausible that it would never have come to gain even titular hegemony over the majority of the population of Ahafo. As it was, the capacity for interim conflict and the capacity for ultimate reconciliation between Christian and pagan both stemmed from a certain metaphysical disengagement which seems to have characterised Ahafo religious sentiment throughout, a product perhaps in part of the carefully fictive but necessarily hasty ideological creation of communities in Ahafo.

The reality of this disengagement is evidenced neatly in what ought by rights to have been a stark confrontation of spiritual authorities, the prosecution of the Christian 'elders' of Noberkaw before the D.C.'s court in 1922 for fishing in the sacred Tano river.[43] The case presented two drastically separate aspects. One of these was a matter of undisputed public political conflict between identified groups of antagonists, each of which was manoeuvring with energy to call in the support of overwhelming power from outside the communities of Ahafo. The second, a matter of ideological presentation, concerned the identification of the causes and meaning of the acknowledged public conflict. Because the only evidence of the confrontation which survives is the records of a colonial court proceeding, there is no independent means of gauging whether the decision of the D.C.'s court that the Christian version was simply a series of lies was objectively correct. But within the adversary context of the court's procedure the selecting and marketing of the two competing plausibilities is revealing quite apart from the relation of either to what contingently was in fact the case.

The recently established Roman Catholic community in Noberkaw, initially manned largely by men converted in Kumasi in the course of trading activities or of schooling, had, it was acknowledged by both sides, been granted permission to preach their religion in the town in return for a strict undertaking not to fish in the Tano.[44] The penalty in the event of default was to be the penalty prescribed by the Omanhene: £16 plus £4 for a sacrificial sheep. In return for this undertaking and the commitment to respect the laws of the town generally, they enjoyed not merely the right to minimal toleration but also the privilege of such comparatively ostentatious forms of communal self-advertisement as summoning the congregation to service with a handbell imported from Kumasi. The case arose from the discovery by the chief and a number of other denizens of Noberkaw that the Christians were indeed engaged in fishing in the Tano and that they had set up a fence in the river and gathered at least one large basket of fish. After a certain initial shiftiness about the source of the fish in question, the Christians as a whole took full communal responsibility for the operation. They also claimed the sanction of the D.C., through their European priest, for their fishing, and threatened the chief, if he made any effort to interfere with their fishing with physical violence: 'If you are a brave man you can follow us and stop us from fishing.' They then returned to the river to continue their illicit labours. It was a direct political challenge, delicately poised between the threats of immediate assault and the invoking of powerful external patrons. In response the Noberkaw chief reported the dereliction to the Kukuom elders, had the drums beaten in Noberkaw itself and took the additional precaution of sacrificing a sheep. A major riot was averted by the hasty arrival of the Catholic priest who 'happened' to be in Kukuom at the time. On the following day the priest discussed the matter with the chief and attempted to persuade him in the light of the recent outgoings of the Catholic community on the acquisition of a teacher from Kumasi to reduce the fine from the full £16 plus £4 costs. Since the chief had already informed the Kukuom council, however, he was in no position to reduce a tariff for the offence which had been set by the Omanhene himself. Accordingly the Noberkaw-hene and Asafohene of Noberkaw appeared before the Kukuom council, along with the priest's clerk and the offending Noberkaw Christians. The clerk had been entrusted by the priest with the task of settling the dispute and, if possible, of reducing the fine. His conduct of this operation was represented by the Krontihene of Kukuom and the Noberkawhene as an admission of guilt combined with the rendering of a public apology on behalf of the offenders – 'begging' the Krontihene on their account. The Krontihene in practice diminished the fine to £12 and waived the sheep costs, a degree of leniency which suggests that the priest's clerk had made some effort to be propitiatory. But one of the Christian witnesses[45] alleged that the priest was incensed at what he considered to be an insulting response to his request and decided accordingly to abandon the effort to settle the dispute, while the Noberkaw Christians themselves repudiated any suggestion that they had accepted the authority of the Kukuom elders to ban them from the Tano or to punish them for their supposed offence and they continued resolutely with their fishing. Accordingly the Noberkaw-hene applied to the D.C. in Goaso for a summons against the five Christian 'elders'.

The Christian account of these events, apart from a discreet avoidance of the issue of their own threats to the chief of Noberkaw before the providential arrival of their priest, differs mainly in adding to the narrative a secret prelude which altered the apparent meaning of most of what ensued in a decisive fashion. It was the rejection of this prelude as pure fabrication which enabled the D.C.'s court to bring in a verdict which simply upheld the sentence of the Noberkaw and Kukuom stools and in addition bound over the five Christian 'elders' accused for £10 each to refrain in the future from fishing in the Tano or from inciting anyone else to fish there. It was perhaps less the intrinsic implausibility of this belated story which governed the D.C.'s judgement than it was the identities of the men who advanced it. In at least three cases these could be readily represented as striking examples of Christian allegiance as a continuation of factional politics by other means. The leading spokesman of the Christians was himself a former chief of Noberkaw. He had not, it is true, been formally destooled for dereliction of duty or ritual mishap but had surrendered the stool voluntarily to the current chief when the latter returned from the Ivory Coast, since he was the elder of the brothers. For a former chief, even one who had supposedly abdicated voluntarily, the new religious organisations provided extensive opportunities for the accumulation of political clients and emotionally committed personal adherents by activities which enjoyed distinctly better prospects for external protection than intrigues within a home community in a more austerely traditional vein now could. Neither of the other two witnesses who propagated the Christian version of the events was actually a denizen of Noberkaw. One was the leader of the Christian community in the village of Siena. The other, a Christian convert of only fifteen days' standing, hailed from Mim. Both had records of previous conflicts with the Noberkawhene. The Siena 'elder' indeed had even been forced to pay a fine on behalf of his nephew for the very offence of fishing in the Tano and had been sentenced to expiate the offence by carrying a sheep on his head from Siena to Noberkaw. (It emerged, though, that the assign-ment of actually carrying it had been passed on to another man.) In the case of the Mim convert colonial identification of Christianity as a delin-quent solution was powerfully reinforced by the fact that the witness had been gaoled in Sunyani for six months for illegitimate resistance to the Noberkawhene and for disturbing the peace and had only escaped being forced to enter into a bond for his future good behaviour on his release by the good offices of the chief.

The story advanced by these men displayed ingenuity and malice in about equal measure. They began with an occasion when the Noberkawhene, in Kukuom at the time for the resolution of a boundary dispute between Ahafo and Sefwi Wiawso, was alleged to have learnt that the people of Wiawso were permitted by their chief to fish in the Tano and also that chief Kobina Kufuor of Nkawie had permitted the people of Tanodumase and other villages to fish in it and they had made a great profit from doing so. Attracted by the prospect of these gains, the Noberkawhene had discussed the issue with the Krontihene of Kukuom and they had agreed that the Christians should 'fish in the river first and if there was nothing wrong' the rest of the population should then be permitted to do so also. A variant of the account, better calculated to explain the secrecy with which the Noberkawhene had gone about his plans, was that he had already fined many pagans for fishing in the river and if he did not permit the Christians to fish first, thereby emphasising the risks of a frontal assault on the religious powers of the Tano, those who had been fined in the past would want their money back. This crude shift in the interpretation of the religious obligations of the chief himself was accompanied by a neat theological modification, disclosing that the previous economically wasteful dispensation had been based upon an obvious doctrinal error. 'We serve the River itself and not the fish in it and we are not going to only look at the fish and get no profit from it.' Fired by this exhilarating scheme, the chief returned to Noberkaw, and went unattended late one night to the house of the leading Christian in the town. There he and a number of Christians, including the witnesses who testified in court, made an elaborate (and naturally rigorously secret) agreement to execute the scheme but under no circumstance, even if challenged, to make the agreement public. The secret complicity of the Kukuom Krontihene and the Noberkawhene was thus to protect the Christians in their fishing. It was also to explain why in the course of the wholly public dispute at Noberkaw and Kukuom after their 'discovery', no mention could be made of their having been in fact specifically permitted by the chief himself to act as they had done. The Noberkawhene attempted (successfully as far as the D.C.'s court was concerned) to discredit this story by the argument that any such permission given in secret by a chief as an individual, would have been wholly *ultra vires* and consequently devoid of authority. He supplemented this contention with great success by a more crudely *ad homines* set of arguments. The Christian tale as set out was indisputably ragged. The Christians do not seem to have decided with any clarity whether they were accusing the chief of having double-crossed them because of an intrinsic animosity towards their faith or merely of not having had the courage to acknowledge his own devious and irregular actions when the matter was forced against his will into the light of day.

But, whether or not the scruffiness of the Christian rendition of these events did, as the D.C. unhesitatingly assumed, reflect its comprehensively fictional character, what the conflict of versions does disclose very clearly is the unexotic character of Christianity in the form in which it did make itself at home in Ahafo. Given a Christianity which was organisationally plural at the time of its arrival, and given an acute reluctance of the colonial administration to ride roughshod over local susceptibilities on its behalf, there hardly existed the structural basis for any lasting *odium theologicum* between fetish and Christian God or even between their respective adherents. As in the later case of the C.P.P. the sheer ebullience of faction and the resolutely tactical eye of its practitioners effortlessly swamped the prospects for lasting domination by any crusading ideology.

ii. *Good learning*

No aspect of social action brings out the intrinsic difficulty of giving a clear and neutral outline of the changes which have taken place in Ahafo between 1896 and the present day as sharply as does education. The difficulty arises mainly from the fact that these changes are not only changes in social experience but also changes necessarily in its political meaning. At a purely sociological level education is one of the most salient examples of structural differentiation. In 1890 there were no extrafamilial institutions of education in Ahafo. Today a large proportion of the population under the age of sixteen spends many hours a week in special buildings constructed out of public contributions. Within these buildings the children are under the charge of public officials, many of whom are recruited from other parts of the country and in the case of secondary schools even from other countries and who are paid out of the national revenues. The withdrawal of the greater part of these age groups from the labour force for large parts of most working days and the additional local expenditure both individual and communal which their attendance at these institutions imposes on adult members of their families is for the most part accepted in Ahafo today, as it is still not accepted today by many in certain parts of northern Ghana, as being a form of socially rational investment. In part this acceptance is simply a product of the comparative wealth of Ahafo. Residents with children of school age complain persistently about the burden of primary and middle school fees; but for those with access to land in the cocoa-producing zones the economic burden is usually not impossibly high. In the case of secondary schools, however, costs are decidedly higher, since in these schools, being, as patterns of settlement in a rural area like Ahafo in fact require, predominantly boarding schools, their fees represent a substantial monetised subsistence cost. A fifteen year old boy in Ahafo in 1890 would have been a net contributor of food to his family. In a middle school in the town near his family food or cocoa farm his work contribution in out-of-school hours would probably be sufficient at least to provide for his subsistence. But for a fifteen year old boy at a secondary boarding school some forty miles or more away the position is very different. Even if the family's landholding is sufficiently small in relation to its labour force for it to be able to farm it out of its own resources in his absence, it will now have to provide out of its marketed surplus for food costs for him which at home would have come out of the food crops of the farm itself. Even if the real producer price of cocoa is high, the terms of trade for the family cocoa farmer are only likely to be favourable insofar as food costs for the family labour force can be kept low by food production on the farm itself. Where the real producer price of cocoa is low and above all where a farm family is transformed from a condition of labour surplus to one of labour deficit by the removal of an adolescent son (and thus obliged to make up the deficit by purchasing on the market), the economics of invest-ment in secondary education become simply prohibitive for the majority of families. There is a small number of scholarships for secondary school students provided by local taxation or occasional wealthy philanthropists but access even to these opportunities is not unaffected by existing patterns of social stratification. There are many children even from quite poor homes who continue to attend middle schools until late on in their adolescence. But for the great majority of households the break between supportable and in-supportable expenditures on education comes precisely at the transition from middle school to secondary school. Unfortunately this break is also the lowest point in the educational hierarchy at which there is now good reason to sup-pose that family investment in education is clearly economically rational. The instrumental meaning of education in Ahafo over the last few decades has plainly been its promise of access to careers open to talent and industry rather than to inherited wealth. The prestige of these careers came from their pro-viding rewards no less reliable and often no less lavish than those which were handed on to the heirs of the rich. But if modern education has been above all, at least in retrospect, a means of social mobility, the frontier of social op-portunity to which given levels of educational advancement has given access has recently become a rapidly receding one. Investment in an education at Achimota is probably even today, as Governor Guggisberg might have wished it to be, investment in a security every bit as safe as the Bank of Scotland (and certainly, world commodity prices being what they are, one decidedly safer than the Bank of Ghana). But whereas the costs of buying secondary edu-cation are rising steadily, at least in nominal terms, and the proportion of the gross national product spent upon secondary education has also greatly increased, the rate of return on family investment in education has fallen drastically at all levels. In the case of university education (largely free inside Ghana) and probably of most secondary education, the margin of return was previously so wide that investment remains rational even at the present diminished rate of return. But there can today hardly be doubt that the average rate of return on investment for families in pre-secondary education is predominantly negative in strictly economic terms. In its earlier and historically more arbitrary incidence modern education not merely opened up avenues of dramatic upward social mobility but did so in a way which reflected to a considerable extent the initial openness of socal stratification in Ahafo. But in this aspect the colonial era was an age of innocence. There can be no doubt that by now the system of modern education has become instead the most powerful agent of class formation in Ghana and one which is already imposing extremely rigid restrictions on the prospects of intergenerational social mobility. If the politics of Ahafo is still today very much a politics of faction rather than one of class it is the schools of Ahafo which above all ensure that this pattern cannot endure indefinitely.

Until, however, the process of class formation does become clearly reflected in the consciousness of local communities, it will not be the purely economic aspects of education which have the greatest impact upon political structures and political consciousness. A purely economic view of the meaning of education requires a decisive abstraction from all its cultural characteristics. In Ahafo today, instrumental though the orientation towards education of most of its inhabitants undoubtedly remains, the advent of commodity production for the world market and of political independence as a modern nation state have constituted too dramatic a process for most of them to remain altogether unmoved by the cultural forms in which these instrumentalities have been made available. Not that the economic aspect of education lacks political salience: indeed the public provision of local secondary education is a form of national investment for which the political demand is as active as it is for any other local development resource. But its provision by the national government means something much more dynamic than the furnishing of a socially inert increment of welfare like a supply of piped water.

When the instrumental possibilities of western literacy first came to the attention of Ashanti in the nineteenth century, their significance was represented mythically as a symbol of virtuous white superiority over ignoble black savagery, an index of cosmological felicity as much as a technique of environmental control.[1] The barrier between literacy and illiteracy remains at an individual level one of powerful and readily intelligible projective hostility. But the external world has by now marked Ahafo far too deeply and pervasively for such individual distaste and distrust to be easily transposed at a communal level into a form of morally assured political primitivism. Like it or not Ahafo is now obliged to live with both national economy and national polity. In order to do so with any confidence and facility it is compelled tacitly to accept the compatibility (if not necessarily the equation) of social virtue with modern cultural proficiency. An effective political protagonist for Ahafo today must necessarily be judged a competent technician of modern cultural apparatus. Every Ahafo M.P. from 1951 till today has enjoyed such accreditation: B. F. Kusi, whose schooling was largely financed by the sophisticated Kumasi District Commissioner Peter Canham,[2] B. K. Senkyire who attended secondary school in the south,[3] A. W. Osei, a schoolfellow of Dr Busia in Kumasi,[4] S. K. Opoku, Osei-Duah and Alfred Badu Nkansah all of whom were themselves schoolmasters and the last of whom was not only a university honours graduate but also a master in the first secondary school ever to be established in Ahafo. Pragmatically the arrival of this and other secondary schools in the area may have been conceived predominantly (and quite correctly) as an enhancement of local competitive opportunities for modern economic roles and the substantial rewards which they carry. But the import of this particular form of educational plant affected local social identities as well as competitive positions. If access to economic power required the import of foreign plant, so too over time did access to cultural status. Ahafo's supreme provinciality, only mildly mitigated by its mounting wealth, could be subjectively transcended in the end only at a cultural level. The advent of modern institutions of secondary education is thus seen as a form of cultural public good, an instance of collective cultural upward mobility. Following in the footsteps of metropolitan Ashanti, as usual some distance behind, Ahafo has accepted at last the logic of white economic power and the military subjugation which preceded it. Having proved culturally as well as militarily or economically unable to defeat the hegemonic structures of European power, the Ahafos are being forced in part, even today in the aftermath of the colonial regime, instead to join them.

The rate at which modern education did in fact come to Ahafo was largely a product of the protracted and uneasy encroachment of Christianity upon the district. The intimacy of this link was not relaxed institutionally until after the Second World War, though the offence which it evoked was diminishing appreciably some time before. An understanding of the advantages of literacy in Ahafo, however, clearly predated the British conquest of 1896. Literate Fantis had acted as intermediaries between the British on the coast and the chief of Kukuom as early as 1889-90 in a determined diplomatic initiative designed to muster external military support for the Ahafos' efforts to throw off the suzerainty of Kumasi.[5] The Kukuomhene at one time had retained one of these, a man called Fletcher, as a permanent clerk before the conquest: he was still, indeed, the only chief in what is now southern Brong–Ahafo who did employ a clerk as late as 1901.[6] The position of clerk was potentially one of considerable power in the early development of indirect rule. The capacity to interpret one party to the other was a ready source of initial privilege; the Kukuomhene's clerk was the only man in Ahafo entitled to possess a fire-arm in August 1901.[7] But it was also an easy position to exploit for personal advantage and in consequence rapidly became and long remained a focus of vivid projective hostility for both administrators and administered. A chief might hope that his clerk would be simply an effective diplomatic instrument for the protection of the interests of his people against those of the British administration. But the same access to modern cultural facilities which enabled the clerk to deal effectively with the colonial administrators (allied to the privileged proximity to his employer which this effectiveness earned for him) meant that the clerk was equally well placed to manipulate both chief and administrators to his own advantage. The dependence of chief upon clerk was often edgy and resentful. It was marred by intermittent but acute distrust, epitomised by the suspicion, reminiscent of the fears of the peasantry of the *ancien régime* in the face of their priesthood, that cultural advantage might also represent a form of sexual advantage.[8] But the proximity of clerk to chief meant in practice that such suspicions were substantially restrained by real understanding, while at worst they could always readily be dissipated by the chief's dismissal of a man who in legal terms was simply his employee.

But for the British administrators the role of clerk to the chief was more pervasively suspect. Sensing, accurately enough, the margin of irresponsible freedom which was intrinsic to the clerk's role and struggling to establish and sustain a morally plausible conception of their own role, they came with increasing frequency to blame the more disquieting aspects of indirect rule upon the malice or chicanery of the chiefs' clerks, along at least one occasion with the more specific identified delinquencies of their own clerks. Controlling the conquered for (a British conception of) their own good was a project the moral ambiguity of which never lay far below the surface. After the first few years of British rule, it was more comfortable to conceive administration as no longer being deployed upon the axiomatic hostility of the conquered. But a sense of effortless moulding of the subject population to their destined goals continued to prove little, if any, easier to capture and preserve than it had been at the time of the conquest itself. Recalcitrance might not be firmly patterned and ideologically overt but it was certainly omnipresent. Such indocility made it essential in the hot, exhausting and feverish conduct of an administrator's duty for him to retain a clear sense of whom to blame for the frequently abortive outcomes of so much painfully expended energy. At the height of a colonial administrator's fantasy he might aspire to establish a relationship with his subject population which was not only direct and authentic but also intimate and mutually enthusiastic. But in any relationship of political control authenticity and mutual enthusiasm are always likely to militate against one another. Hence it was of especial importance in the colonial relationship that particular recalcitrance could be identified as being a more complex phenomenon than a simple gain in authenticity.

The moralisation of indirect rule relied upon a measure of ideological acceptance of chiefs (as a group) as the 'natural rulers' of their people. Accepting them as such precluded the identification of all individual chiefs as simply amoral and manipulative egoists. Most chiefs certainly were seen by particular administrators in these reductive terms on occasion and some few were seen thus for most of the time (Chief Beditor of Mim would be a notable example). But the socialisation of British administrators being what it was, it would not have been structurally tolerable for all chiefs to be seen this way all the time. No such ideological imperatives, however, protected the role of chief's clerk from the most clinical understanding. The administration's definition of his role as that of an alien cultural broker between a natural community (an odd identification in any case in what was recognised to be the 'artificial' division of Ahafo) and its morally designated colonial overlords was hardly a neutral one on its own. But it naturally differed from that of either the clerks or their employers. The clerks were paid to represent the interests of their masters with all the diplomatic deftness at their command. Their vocation was to enact the will of their masters with all the resources of their intelligence. But their avocation from the viewpoint of the administration was to preserve, through the malice imputed to their will, their chiefly masters from the taint of blank hostility to the conquerers. Chicanery in a clerk was a far more acceptable explanation of environmental recalcitrance than deliberate obstruction in a chief. The former was clearly criminal, the latter at least potentially political. Individual 'natural' rulers might well be simply criminals too. But if all 'natural' rulers were evidently engaged in obstruction, it would have been hard to avoid the suspicion that the obstruction represented the resistance of communities and not merely the delinquencies of individuals. Such considerations freed the imaginations of the Commissioners for a very full exploration of the manipulative resources of the clerk's role and a correspondingly sardonic evaluation of it. It would not however be a realistic assumption[9] to suppose that that role was in fact as morally footloose as the administration judged it to be. As in the case of the administration's grounds for keeping lawyers out of Ashanti in the early decades of its rule,[10] while the reasons for the disquiet may have been based on an accurate enough assessment of the manipulative opportunities of the roles, it would be naive to take the reasons given for the attitude as an adequate representation of the causes of it.

Literacy was seen in the first instance as much more than a set of cultural techniques, as indeed above all a form of power. From the viewpoint of powerholders within the local Ahafo community, the natural ambition was to gain more reliable access to the power, while undergoing the minimum of cultural contamination from their utilisation of the techniques. For the colonial administration in its early stages, the ideal balance might well appear to be precisely the reverse. The English presence in Ashanti might be conceived less self-righteously as a *mission civilisatrice* than that of the French just across the border (though this difference was certainly not reflected in the relative advancement of education in the two forest districts by 1950);[11] but any long-term account of what the British supposed themselves to be doing in Ahafo could not afford to neglect the theme of cultural benefaction. Education scarcely emerges from the mass of personal documentation of the District Commissioners' daily activities as a powerful focus of emotional commitment. Nor was it a matter in which external administrative pressures seem to have been particularly insistent until the coming of the first C.P.P. government. But if the hungry sheep were to look up and request such cultural fodder, it was inherently difficult at an ideological level not to consent to feed them. The balance of advantage and risk was struck neatly enough both for colonial power and for chiefly authority by an agreement to accept and to foster education as a process provided that it was not directly linked to adult political agency. Adult possessors of the power of literacy were intrinsically suspicious to both chief and commissioner. Adults within the community who were committed to the aggressive cultural transformation of the community were clearly a political threat to the chiefs and to the established definition of the community. Indeed it seems apparent that the appeals of this aggressive cultural transformation, the prospective Christianisation of Ahafo, to those to whom it did appeal, were strongly linked to the opportunities which it furnished for individual escape from the prevailing structure of social control in some of its more irksome aspects. 'Alleged Christians' as the administration preferred to put it[12] were to be defined as essentially political malcontents and as such were to be subjected to strict and not over-sympathetic supervision. Since the mechanism of indirect rule did plainly require the maintenance of a political authority the legitimacy of which depended upon suppositions of traditional continuity, social change linked too directly to assault on the cultural basis of this continuity was a blatant political threat. Yet it was not a simple matter for an administrator to disengage himself from those who were attempting, not altogether without success, to bring the most obtrusive cultural values of the administrators themselves to those whom a Provincial Commissioner described on one sultry occasion as 'savages'.[13] Christians in Ahafo certainly provoked communal strife. Their very presence was potentially provocative and some of them clearly felt no great anxiety to minimise the provocation. But it was important for the administration, as well-armed prophets of western civilisation, to be able to assess them as something more dubious than prophets who happened not to be armed. Authentic exponents of the spiritual values in conflict with chiefly ruffians bore some prospective resemblance to martyrs: hence the alacrity with which the administration cast slurs upon the authenticity of the 'alleged Christians' commitment to Christian values and the tendency to see them instead as pseudo-Christian ruffians in conflict with authentic chiefs.

Within this structural political frame the contingencies of geography contributed greatly to the actual pattern of educational penetration in Ahafo. Thinly populated and culturally on the outer periphery of Ashanti as it was, it was natural for Christianity to come later to Ahafo than to many other parts even of the Western Province. The first indigenous Christians reported in Ahafo were the 'alleged Christians' of Teppa in 1908 who had derived their instructions from the Wesleyan mission in Kumasi.[14] In 1911 the census recorded only 360 Christians for the whole of the Western Province of Ashanti.[15] But by 1914 the Wesleyan mission had established a church with a native pastor and a school in Kukuom, causing considerable friction in the town, and had made clear its intention to extend its activities by setting up schools in Mim and Goaso in addition.[16] The opening of what was envisaged as a permanent district administrative headquarters for the area in Goaso early in 1914 had brought the colonial administration into a more protracted and intimate contact with the problems raised by this cultural clash. In September 1914 the acting District Commissioner Johnstone put forward a proposal, based explicitly on his recognition of local hostility to the expansion of Christianity and consequent resentment at the link between schooling and proselytising, to establish in Goaso a government school on the model of that in Sunyani, the provincial capital.[17] Johnstone had in fact been asked repeatedly in Ahafo why the government did not set up such an establishment and had been assured that there was widespread local willingness to allow children to attend school provided that it was a government and not a mission institution. He felt able to guarantee a minimum attendance of thirty boys and the provision out of local labour, should funds for a permanent building not be immediately available, of an 'ordinary swish, grass-roofed building' for the purpose. Both the Provincial Commissioner and the Chief Commissioner of Ashanti supported the project without hesitation, though the latter acknowledged with regret that it was not the best of times at which to be proposing an increase in government expenditure.[18] He noted, however, in his communication to the Colonial Secretary in Accra that he would like the Governor to know that 'even the unenlightened Ahafos are beginning to realize the advantages of education'.[19] Two and a half years later the Director of Education in Accra raised the matter again, proposing, if the Chief Commissioner thought that a school could get local support in Goaso, to open one in 1918.[20] But the Chief Commissioner recommended postponing its establishment once again since the district administrative office would be unlikely, even when it did reopen, to remain open for long until the war was over.[21] In the event Goaso never acquired its government school and the expansion of education in Ahafo remained until the Second World War exclusively dependent upon the entrepreneurial energies of the missions, above all of the Wesleyans, the Scots Presbyterians and the Roman Catholics.

Local representatives of the administration continued, in consequence, to have good reasons for ambivalence towards the progress of education in the district. The Wesleyans in Mim were compelled in September 1918 after sharp conflict with the chief and with pagan members of the community to draw up an agreement which recognised among other matters the right of parents or guardians to decide if their children were to attend school.[22] The Provincial Commissioner blamed the Wesleyan mission superintendent, a European, for the conflict and fully endorsed the settlement. But six days later in Goaso he was to be found holding forth to the population on 'the usual topics' – among them the merits of sending their children to the school in Mim.[23] The Commissioner might well find himself committed to the defence of Mim chiefly authority against the tactless assault of the missions with their overt threats to call in the assistance of higher powers over the heads of the administration.[24] But he could hardly maintain such a commitment at the cultural level to the preservation of Mim as an inviolate centre of 'fetish worship'. Nor, even from the viewpoint of the Ahafos themselves could the theme of cultural preservation comfortably continue to dominate the issue of modern education to the exclusion of other more vulgarly economic matters. The absence of educated Ashantis meant the employment of 'foreign natives' in skilled occupations in Ahafo,[25] as it did elsewhere in Ashanti. When the demand for a government school was renewed in Ahafo in 1921, this time for one to be sited at the seat of the Omanhene at Kukuom, it came from a new Omanhene who, like his stool clerk, had established his modernist efficacy in the economy as a cocoa broker before his installation.[26] At the time the administration saw the fact that the demand emanated from such an economically sophisticated pair as a reason for treating it as unrepresentative of current Ahafo attitudes and, possibly emboldened by this insight, made no effort to comply with the suggestion. Unfortunately the same privileged insights which may conceivably have made the opinion of the Omanhene an unreliable index of existing Ahafo sentiment at that time also made his opinion a better guide to the future requirements of the area and indeed to those of the colonial administration in the area than that provided by those delicate barometers of communal sentiment, the British administrators themselves.

Education provision did expand in the next few years but always in the divisive and educationally jejune form of mission schools, most of which were run by men who were catechists first and educators very much second. The rate of their arrival can be traced largely by their involvement in communal fracas of a scale sufficiently dramatic to find their way into the courts. The Catholics of Noberkaw in 1922 pleaded as a reason for lowering the fine inflicted upon them for fishing in the sacred Tano river that they had just laid out £12 in Kumasi on a teacher.[27] In 1923 the Catholic teacher and catechist at Akrodie appeared as the natural authority to whom to appeal in a case of conscience which turned upon a Catholic woman's refusal to swear a chief's oath and her attempt to execute her divorce in what she took to be the approved Christian style. The catechist very prudently proclaimed his inexperience, as a mere 'boy', in the technology of Christian divorce and insisted in seeking advice from his superiors in Kumasi on this part of the dispute.[28] By 1924 there were mission schools at Kukuom, Mim Akrodie and Kwapong but the Noberkaw teacher had disappeared from view.[29] The standard of these schools was low, the teachers semi-literate and incompetent. None was on the government list of assisted schools. The District Commissioner, Judd, drew repeated attention to these deficiencies, bringing up the issue at the Ashanti Political Conference and eliciting an expression of his partial agreement in the Western Provincial Commissioner's report for the year.[30] In 1926 another four villages – Hwidiem, Noberkaw, Acherensua and Dadiesoaba – established small mission schools and the Scots Mission school at Kukuom was picked out of the eight Ahafo schools as 'the best of a bad lot'.[31] Early in 1927 four out of eight had once again closed down, three of them as early as September 1926, leaving operative the Scottish Mission school at Kukuom (32 pupils), the Wesleyan school at Mim (34), the Wesleyan school at Hwidiem (32) and the Wesleyan school at Akrodie (for which the number of pupils was unknown to the administration).[32] Only the Scottish Mission teacher held a government certificate of teaching competence and he was anxious to improve his school. Significantly a senior representative of his mission had recently visited Kukuom and extracted from the Omanhene an undertaking to build a new school large enough to house two teachers and their appropriate components of pupils. Kukuom was in fact the only school in the district to comply with the new Education Ordinance in May of the same year. The four Wesleyan schools were duly closed down in June, though they were shortly reopened, with the exception of Hwidiem for which no teacher was now available, pending inspection by the Inspector of Schools.[33] Even at Kukuom the D.C. complained in June that the Oman- hene was taking insufficient interest in his new school and that there was a strong case for setting up a government school. By October 1927, however, administrative anxiety had shifted from the lethargy of the Omanhene to the Wesleyan mission's demand from him of £1,000 for the rebuilding of the school, a figure which was regarded as absurdly high.[34]

In the following year, 1928, government commitment to non-disruptive educational advance appeared to be bearing fruit at last. At the beginning of the year the Kukuomhene was taken as one of a trio of Ashanti chiefs to inspect the new elite educational establishment at Achimota[35] and in June the construction of his new school in Kukuom for 40 pupils began at the cost (judged respectable by the administration) of £350.[36] At the same time government recognition of the indispensability of some form of effective and responsible modernist education began to appear more frequently. One Com- missioner noted the pointlessness of voluntary representative agencies without literate members who could dare to disagree with the opinions of white officials.[37] Another attributed the failure of the Native Jurisdiction Ordinance, the fulcrum of the whole system of indirect rule in Ashanti, to the unavaila- bility under prevailing market conditions of well-educated and efficient stool clerks.[38] A purely individualist conception of educational advantage which was what the administration had permitted to be marketed in Ahafo provided no incentive to the literate for taking communal administrative responsi- bility instead of fleecing their fellows in the role of cocoa broker. The suggestion of the acting Provincial Commissioner that the 'natural com- munity' could be reintegrated by the inculcation of a certain 'Pride of Race' by making it part of the curriculum of all government-assisted schools was a little naive; but the difficulty of putting a good face on the actual products of the government's educational policy (or absence of such) in Ahafo was increasingly apparent. In March 1929 the D.C. was still receiving applications for the establishment of a government school in the district, a demand which he felt to be eminently justified, especially in view of the deplorable behaviour of the local Christian communities which he attributed firmly to their lack of European supervision.[39]

But once again governmental indecision over the future of Goaso as an administrative headquarters, allied with economic stringencies resulting from the end of the cocoa boom, prevented the establishment of a government school, while locally by 1930 it had become clear that the new Kukuom school was never going to materialise[40] and the scarcity of teachers produced by implementation of the Education Ordinance had left only a single school – the Wesleyan school at Mim – in which only standard 1 was taught.[41] It had a total of 15 infant pupils in July 1930 and had only increased this to 22 (all boys) in 1932.[42] At this point as the Commissioner ruefully noted less than ½ per cent of the local children under the age of fifteen were undergoing education in Ahafo. The 1931 census recorded the presence of 65 persons in Ahafo educated up to standard 4 or beyond.[43] Since, however, no mission school in the whole of western Ashanti as late as 1928 offered education beyond the third standard[44] and since there was no record of any school in Ahafo actually attaining even this level, the 65 must have been made up almost entirely of 'foreign natives' and of the small number of Ahafos who had received education in Kumasi and in the government school at Sunyani.

Even this meagre level of educational progress had begun to generate a fresh range of problems, some of which were to become very much more acute by the early 1930s. In June 1930 a District Commissioner noted for the first time that he was being approached repeatedly by a young sixth standard leaver (accompanied by his mother) who had been unable to find employment commensurate with his new status and who rejected the proposal that he should return to farming because it would make him a laughing stock among his companions. The D.C. saw it as a gloomy portent of a future in which 'there will be many more of his type'.[45] Slightly later the Omanhene's dismissed stool clerk found it natural to base his claim for damages against his former employer on the grounds that he had been treated as a 'mere labourer' and not as the 'civilised person' that he was.[46] Not only was modern education beginning to be a source of high status (and thus necessarily of the restrictions upon possible occupation which the risk of derogating from such status imposed); it was also seen explicitly as the basis of entitlement to fairly specific economic rights. The provision of a school within a community might already be seen as a cultural public good, a sort of modernist stool ornament which it behoved a chief to provide for the embellishment of his community. Indeed it would soon come aptly to figure side by side with more archaic costs in the indignant claims of destooled chiefs for the recovery of stool debts which they had been unwise enough to pay out of their own pockets.[47] At an individual level educational investment might come to be seen as a simple investment in upward social mobility, an available avenue to consumption the returns of which did not fluctuate as drastically as did the world market price of cocoa. The provision of school teachers by missions might continue to seem an effective mode of denominational expansion. But as early as the 1930s, even at times when the total educational provision in Ahafo had shrunk to a dozen or two infants, the first signs had appeared of the close links between modern education and some of the most intractable problems of contemporary Ghanaian social and economic structures. It might still for a time be true that the rate of educational wastage was lower in Ahafo than it was further south – simply because the base of the educational pyramid was so narrow that there was little difficulty in providing access within western Ashanti up to the seventh standard for all who had reached the third standard and who wished to continue with their education.[48] But given the rate of expansion in the modern sector of the economy outside agriculture, it was necessarily only a matter of time before 'the curse of the coast', the school leaver unemployable at the level of remuneration to which he judged his education to entitle him, became the curse of the forest too. The severely unvocational character of the education actually available meant, also, that the economic gain from education as such was largely confined to that which derived directly from the dissemination of a measure of literacy. During the colonial period the promotion of literacy, even on this restricted scale, did to some degree assist governmental communication with the population at large. It was an appropriate symbol that as early as 1924 when the D.C. was distributing posters identifying cocoa pests around the district in order to instruct the farmers on crop-protection that schoolmasters should be paired with chiefs as agencies for disseminating the information and that the three sets of posters supplied for Goaso district should find themselves consigned, one to the D.C.'s office in Goaso, one to the Omanhene's *ahenfie* ('palace') at Kukuom and one to the Wesleyan school at Mim.[49] Over the years this instrumental convenience, while it certainly did not realise the colonial ambition of creating comprehensive ideological subservience on the part of the local population,[50] did appreciably alter the terms on which local administrative cooperation could be transacted. In 1928 the absence of prospective literate members had been judged sufficient grounds for abandoning the idea of an agricultural advisory committee in the rather more metropolitan venue of Sunyani. By 1950 the major problem identified by the D.C. in the operation of the Ahafo Area Committee, the active representative of Ahafo development aspirations in the face of Kumasi neglect, was the difficulty of stopping the only local literate member from talking all the time.[51] The transfer of literate skills was an ambiguous provision, facilitating administrative and economic efficiency as long as the colonial regime remained unchallenged and enabling the continuation of an effective administration in the aftermath of its departure, but leaving behind it a complex pattern of inequality the propriety of which was substantially acknowledged even by those who did not benefit from it. The self-righteous maintenance of colonial economic privileges by an entrenched *bourgeoisie de la fonction publique*, protected by its own praetorian guard (the officer corps of the armed services being increasingly clearly identifiable as simply the *bourgeoisie de la fonction publique* in arms) is a direct product at a normative level[52] of a pattern of colonial educational development which established education as a criterion of 'civilisation' and 'enlightenment' and which attributed to the 'civilised' man, as the Omanhene's dismissed stool clerk suggested, a quite different set of economic rights to those of a 'mere labourer'. Ordinary citizens of Goaso

Dependence and opportunity

today may construe the point of education bleakly as protection against being cheated by literates.[53] But as yet the literates whose chicanery is clearly identified enough to be resented are not mostly located very far up the ladder of status stratification. It will probably be some little time before mere labourers in general come to construe as their most inveterate cheats, the well-defended successors of the 'civilised men'.

It is not surprising that the place of education in sharpening class stratification should still be unclear to many in the forest. As late as 1933 there was still only a single school in Ahafo: the Wesleyan school at Mim. By contrast in 1971 in the town of Goaso alone there was a total of five primary and five middle schools with a total enrolment of 1,716 pupils (936 boys and 780 girls).[54] Virtually every little village in Ahafo now boasts its own school. When this growth did come it was an extremely rapid one. Its rhythms were tied in part to those of the world cocoa market. The recovery of cocoa prices in 1936 and 1937 produced Wesleyan schools with large new buildings in Hwidiem, Goaso and Mim by December 1937 and the English Church Mission opened schools at Kukuom and Kenyase, though the Kukuom one promptly closed again.[55] A small school was also opened by the Roman Catholic Mission at Sankore. In April 1939 a comprehensive list of schools in Ahafo was compiled by the Provincial Inspector of Schools.[56] Thirteen schools were listed with a total of seventeen teachers and enrolment of 499 pupils. Of these schools nine were considered by the Inspector to serve some useful educational purpose. But several had been created as a result of 'rampant sectarian bickering' to provide 'cut-price education' as a means of denominational expansion. The uncontrolled pattern of development of the infant schools was producing great wastage at standard 3 and the total absence of government economic support and the consequent involvement of stool finances in school building and in the provision of teachers' salaries caused chiefly authority to be elaborately implicated in the denominational competition. Roman Catholics in particular were extremely reluctant to contribute to the payment of stool debts contracted for the provision of non-Catholic mission schools, even where as in Goaso they were prepared, *faute de mieux*, to send their children to the schools so provided.[57]

The development of representative institutions for Ahafo as a whole seems to have been initially less damaged by this denominational competition in the educational field than individual communities had been. The Ahafo Area Committee, established to disburse the local entitlement from the Ashanti National Fund, spent two thirds of its first revenues in September 1944 on schools, preserving a measure of denominational balance overall in the allocation which the contingencies of history would have prevented inside a single community.[58] When a District Education Committee was formed in 1947 in the midst of the postwar cocoa boom, a time when local investment

in education was rising rapidly, elaborate efforts were made by the administration to preserve denominational balance in its membership.[59] From 1949
onwards scholarships were distributed for secondary education and for a
range of vocational training, particularly in midwifery, dispensing and
teaching, both by the Area Committee and the Native Authority.[60] The total
number of schools in operation increased rapidly. Goaso, for example, had
two schools with 333 pupils in 1950 (129 of them in classes beyond the sixth
year), while Ahafo as a whole in that year possessed four senior schools
offering ten years of schooling and twenty others providing six years, a
striking contrast with the Agni *cercle* of Abengourou across the border.[61]
By 1956 Ahafo maintained nine middle schools and 28 primary schools.[62]
Denominational conflict, even over questions of financing, became progressively less important in the course of this dramatic educational boom.
But the very high cocoa prices and the influx of cocoa farmers from outside
Ahafo into the virgin forest which these prices had promoted produced in due
course novel strains of their own.

The use of voluntary cocoa levies to raise revenue for the provision of
schools within a community met increasing opposition in 1957 and 1958.[63]
Such levies could only be raised with the consent of a majority of the community. They do not seem to have inflamed denominational sensitivities particularly and were resisted not on grounds of conscience but on those of
equity. Stranger-farmers, settlers from outside Ahafo itself, complained that
many of them had children of their own in their own home towns for whose
schools they were already having to pay and they objected vigorously to the
imposition, in addition to the traditional stool payments, of what they saw
as a form of double taxation. From the viewpoint of Ahafo, land for cocoa-
planting was an economic resource, the returns on which were clearly a
proper basis of communal investment in public goods. From the viewpoint of
the stranger-farmers the economic returns on their labour in Ahafo were
equally clearly a proper basis for taxation for the provision of public goods. The
disagreement lay in the identification of the public for which the goods were
properly to be supplied. Ahafo economic nationalism saw the law of Ahafo
as the economic base of Ahafo society. It was happy on the whole to accept
permanent increments of any factor of production, labour naturally included.
But in the case of those who had been granted permanent title to land the
export of returns on their invested labour was construed as a form of internal
colonialist economic exploitation, a discreet pillage of the forest. Education
was a sensitive index of this contest over communal identities. Where a man
was happy to invest for the future of his children was not only a fair indicator
of where part at least of his treasure was likely to remain, it was a partial token
too of where his heart would be also. For a man to insist on the right to export his entire accumulated earnings was to define himself as an alien exploiter.

Dependence and opportunity

Educational provision was the most expensive form of public investment undertaken by Ahafo communities. It was undertaken with increasing frequency as it came to seem rational to progressively larger sections of local communities; culturally rational to the Christians whom the American anthropologist Lystad estimated in 1950 to make up about 50 per cent of the population,[64] and economically rational to others because of the dramatic economic opportunities which educational advantage had already furnished to the few. It came belatedly, too, to receive considerable government commitment. As late as the beginning of the Second World War, as the Inspector of Schools noted in his gloomy survey of Ahafo education, no government money at all had yet been spent on schools in the district. By 1953, when Kojo Botsio, the Minister of Education and protagonist of the Accelerated Education Plan, visited Goaso,[65] a very different governmental attitude was in evidence. The development of primary and middle schools which ensued was extremely rapid, slightly too rapid indeed for the supply of competent teachers. But any decline in average educational standards which was plausibly associated in some areas with the C.P.P.'s impressive attempts to create universal primary education, was no great threat in Ahafo where standards of teaching had never risen much above the provision of basic literacy. It is natural today for even such a stalwart and militant opponent of the C.P.P. as the restored chief of Mim to see as the one undeniable basis of C.P.P. achievement this vast expansion of primary education. It was only in the provision of secondary education that the role of the C.P.P. government in Ahafo was more equivocal.

Every Ahafo Member of Parliament, those of C.P.P. as much as those of U.P. allegiance, from B. F. Kusi onwards, felt it their duty to ask repeatedly in the legislature for the provision of secondary schools in Ahafo. As late as 1964 A. W. Osei, the United Party member, could still complain bitterly that there was no secondary school in his district.[66] Because Ahafo had been unwise enough to align itself with the N.L.M. cause in the confrontations of 1956–7 it was not for several years a favoured recipient for development resources. It did eventually acquire a Ghana Educational Trust Secondary School and, in the last rush of C.P.P. political initiative in 1965, three Teacher Training Colleges at Teppa, Hwidiem and Mim, the last of which has recently been converted into a secondary school. This last addition was a response to the severe shortage of teachers which resulted from the rate at which the primary sector of education was expanding. It was an impressive sequence of organisational improvisation in which a civil servant toured the country distributing guarantees of teaching staff to any local communities able and willing to provide the necessary buildings.[67] Considerations of political bias hardly entered into the selection in this case and none of the towns chosen had in fact been exactly a dependable bastion of C.P.P. support. Acherensua which was eventually picked as the site of the secondary school had on the other hand played a very prominent part in the competitive violence of the 1956 election campaign and in the subsequent establishment of effective C.P.P. control over Ahafo. The scars of those conflicts were no longer particularly fresh by the time that the school arrived; but the siting of it at Acherensua was explicitly intended by party officials at the time,[68] and was universally interpreted locally, as a direct reward for political services rendered.

d. POLITICAL CONTROL AND POLITICAL ADMINISTRATION

The story was told in Accra recently of a Ghanaian District Administrator[1] who remarked to the inhabitants of his new district, shortly after his arrival, that huts just like their own could be found among his people also – only to be more than a little mortified by the response that they had not known that such buildings could still be found in England. Almost certainly apocryphal, the story is nonetheless *ben trovato*. Nothing establishes the continuity between colonial and postcolonial state structures in Ghana as evidently as the lack of modification in the role of district administrator over the last three quarters of a century. It is true that at one point during the C.P.P. government, the formal status of the local representative of the government and the scope of his effective powers were markedly restricted and the colonial title of District Commissioner and a corresponding degree of administrative licence conferred instead upon the official local representative of the governing party. But the experience of this phase was sufficiently disagreeable for its termination to be welcomed by the great majority – perhaps indeed by almost all who were not direct dependents of the party bureaucracy – and its duration was not in the event protracted enough to necessitate drastic innovation when the colonial administrative structure was duly restored by the military action of members of the public service in February 1966. Former officials of the C.P.P. naturally tended to regret the disappearance of a more effective and delicate agency of control and current members of the public service to commend the restoration of administrative regularity; but for the majority of Ahafo citizens, the C.P.P. District Commissioner seems to have epitomised the major vices of the government which he represented – above all its bullying qualities[2] – while apparently failing to secure any share in the credit for its more popular achievements, above all those in the educational field. One claim which no one in Ahafo troubled to advance about the demise of the Party District Commissioner was that it represented any loss in local popular opportunity to control the representative of the central government. A C.P.P. District Commissioner was hardly a colonial figure but his conception of the prerogatives inherent in his office and his assurance of the availability of externally supplied military power with which, if necessary, to enforce these commands, scarcely fell short of those of his colonial predecessors. Only in its sanctioning ideology and in the relationship which it established with existing foci of social and economic power in the locality did the C.P.P. role differ from its colonial model.[3] In other respects the symbolic action of the Party in appropriating for its own local officials the authentic colonial title may be read correctly very much as it appears: as an expression of the insistence that the Party government and not the public services were the heirs to the legitimacy claimed by the colonial government – but thus also as a tacit admission that the legitimacy of the state apparatus of independent Ghana was institutionally continuous with the illegitimacy of the colonial state apparatus of the Gold Coast.

But, if the C.P.P. regime, however wryly and temporarily, did modify the D.C.'s role considerably, no other developments since the conquest of Ashanti appear to have done so at all drastically. Major shifts in the organisation of local authority like the restoration of the Ashanti Confederacy in 1935 or the creation of the Brong–Ahafo Region in April 1959 certainly affected the shape of the network of political pressures of a more or less discreet nature to which the District Administrator's will was subjected in the course of his duties. The advent of an elected Ghanaian government in 1951 and the re-appearance of an elected one in 1969 in both cases somewhat restricted the scope within which the Administrator had previously been free to choose to act. The first appearance of a Ghanaian in place of a European as D.C. in Ahafo, the future Commonwealth Secretary A. L. Adu in 1946, was recognised by both Commissioner and people as presenting novel opportunities (and perhaps also novel perils). But its main effect probably was to make it easier for an energetic Commissioner to acquire a clear understanding of what was going on in the district at large. The social distance between a Ghanaian D.C. and the population of his district was considerably narrower than it was in the case of white personnel. The ethnic solidarity displayed by the chief who urged his people to help Adu because the status of all Ghanaians – and the prospects for their grandchildren – were at stake in the effectiveness with which he discharged his duties was an evanescent privilege of novelty; but the narrowing of social distance was permanent. It has had its disadvantages as well as its advantages. D.C.s in recent years have been accused of taking up land in Ahafo in return for services rendered (and of using government labour to farm it), as well as of deriving improper advantages from the closeness of their relationship with local timber contractors. Whatever the truth about these particular allegations, they indicate clearly enough the watershed for projective suspicions. The problem of gifts in fact was one which the colonial D.C.s also encountered.[4] It is hard to draw the line in principle between friendship, politeness, faintly dubious speculative investment and specific corruption in such exchanges and even harder to determine which side of the lines particular alleged transactions have fallen in practice. But it seems unlikely that the unofficial costs of the narrowing social distance between a D.C. and the population of his locality approach those imposed in the colonial period (and still more in the postcolonial period) by the police force in exchange for the manner in which they discharge their duties.

One other aspect of the narrowing social distance was potentially even more problematic. A Ghanaian D.C. was not a white man. But he was also not necessarily a man at all close in culture and language to the people whom he was despatched to administer. The administrative language of Ghana remains the colonial language: English. The language of all post-primary education and consequently the language of much private conversation among the best educated of Ghanaians remains the colonial language. One outstandingly effective and charming recent Ahafo Administrator was a Ga who refused to address his predominantly Akan charges in Twi (despite his adequate command of the language). In a sense he used his tribal origins and the carefully preserved linguistic gap as instruments for accentuating the social distance between himself and the people of the district. By contrast one of his successors, an Ashanti and a slightly younger man (who was culturally easily approachable for an Ahafo) found his more local identity a considerable disability in one important context. After two years of Progress Party rule the protracted struggle over Ahafo's traditional constitution was temporarily focussed, at least in Ahafo itself, upon an Ashanti-sponsored attempt to destool the Hwidiemhene, an adherent of the Kukuom faction.[5] The Progress Party regional boss for Brong–Ahafo and powerful Ministers in the central government were strongly committed to preserving the real economic independence of Ahafo from Kumasi. But they had not at that time succeeded – and were in the event because of the Party's imminent removal from power never to succeed – in establishing an official settlement of the constitutional dispute on these terms. The District Administrator was an official under the orders of the government. He was also an Ashanti. Since his official instructions were to stall the dispute for as long as he conceivably could (even to a Kukuom partisan, the constitutional position of the Hwidiemhene in this particular dispute was relatively weak), both sides were certain to regard the Administrator as improperly biased in his actions, very probably, in their view, because of his complicity having been bought by their opponents. To the advocates of Ahafo localism, the mere fact that he was an Ashanti was eloquent testimony of the grounds of his shameful bias, while to the supporters of the Kumasi interest, it served to aggravate his offence in failing to discharge his duties in the ways that the law plainly required. In those aspects of his role in which a District Administrator necessarily serves as the arbiter of local 'traditional' conflict, the lessening of social distance beyond a certain point is always liable to appear as the removal of all pretence to the sole, if frail, normative asset available to him in the management of such conflicts: the claim to impartiality. To be ideologically uncommitted in local factional conflict, rule must be essentially alien rule: perhaps the sole functional aspect of the colonial order. But even to eschew completely the least trace of ideological commitment in local factional conflict could never extricate the rulers of an area like Ahafo today from the necessity of practical commitment in local conflict of this sort. The impartiality of disinterest may have made colonial rule ideologically tidier than its postcolonial successor, but there is no reason to believe that the latter has not been substantially more agreeable as a form of government for the Ahafos themselves.

But more agreeable though it has plausibly been, it has nevertheless remained with some clarity an exercise in the maintenance of political control. The government of men has been little, if at all, modified even in overt performance in the direction of the administration of things. Things do of course get administered after a fashion in Ahafo. Modern transport, modern distributive networks for marketing, modern health and educational facilities have all been in some measure adapted to the cultural rhythms of Ahafo, but even with due cultural adaptation their mere presence requires a substantial degree of modern organisation. It is also eminently a part of the District Administrator's role to keep such organisation from foundering completely in the face of the natural and cultural obstacles of the Ahafo environment. Neither at all 'red' nor particularly 'expert', he remains the focus of an enormously wide nexus of responsibilities,[6] which it would be as impossible for the most energetic to discharge exhaustively as it is simple for the more indolent predominantly to ignore. The core of the role, the range of responsibilities beyond which it cannot be narrowed by the least vigorous, is the retention of minimal political control, the maintenance of public order and of a preparedness to execute simple direct commands. The main facility available to the Administrator in securing this level of compliance is his ability to summon to his aid a weight of direct coercion – whether by army or civil police – greatly in excess of that which can be mustered by any group of those under his authority. The Ahafo population has never been comprehensively disarmed, though attempts of a sort were made to make it so early in the colonial regime and echoed by the C.P.P. government during the 1956/7 struggles. The terrain of Ahafo is singularly favourable even today for guerrilla activity and it must have been even more so three quarters of a century ago at the time of the British conquest before the forest began to be thinned out for cocoa cultivation and timber production. Yet at no time since 1896 has any effort apparently been made to maintain armed resistance to the government over any extended period of time in Ahafo itself. A preponderance of accessible firepower has not always been enough to maintain docility or to contain local faction fighting within the bounds of respectability. But it does appear to have been quite adequate to the task of deterring the Ahafos from any sustained frontal challenge to governmental authority as such. Ahafo has shown little proclivity for armed struggle or violent resistance and public order in the district since 1900, while in no way Utopian in its placidity, has long compared favourably with that prevalent in major American cities. But, while the role of the Administrator in maintaining control is seldom rendered a nervous one by the weight of direct and violent challenge to his authority, it is not for that reason an unexacting role. Organised and violent confrontation has indeed been a very intermittent affair in Ahafo, despite the cherished traditions of military heroism which the older communities enjoy. Passive obstruction, however, is a much less fugitive performance. Except perhaps briefly during the C.P.P. drive for dominance, the Administrator has never had to live in perpetual fear of being assaulted; but he has always had to live with the experience of being more or less blandly ignored.

Overt disobedience to the command of an Administrator, particularly a direct refusal to his face to do what he had ordered, was never a prudent course for an ordinary citizen. Indeed it was never less than rash for even the most elevated of Ahafo citizens, combining as it did the repudiation of political subservience which was involved in open military resistance with the avoidance of any trace of physical protection which such resistance might, however temporarily, have provided. But between a direct refusal to do what he had been told and a simple failure to carry out an instruction, a gulf was fixed great enough to afford an infinite range of opportunities for evasion and self-exculpation. To identify the precise blend of incomprehension, strategic manoeuvre and sheer inertia in such 'passive' derelictions would only be possible on the basis of the most detailed observation, observation which the reluctance of governments to be studied at being seen to be disobeyed and that of most citizens to be studied at being seen to disobey their government may well preclude in principle. It would certainly be impossible in principle to reconstruct such obstruction with fidelity from the resources of governmental archives. What can, however, be reconstructed is the pattern of attitudes fostered in the administration by the experience of such covert or inadvertent obstruction. The centralism of colonial administration was not blurred until its concluding decade by any great anxiety to incorporate the volatile additive of democracy. The image of governmental processes favoured by the administration until this last decade was that of a hierarchy of obedience and one in which the fact that the lower echelons of the hierarchy were governed indirectly was in no way intended to imply that the obedience was expected to be any less direct. The government of the Gold Coast always expected that every Ahafo would do his duty and his duty was to do what he was told –

to obey a 'lawful order'. The policies of those towards the peak of this pyramid, being based upon beliefs as to what was the case, were in theory entirely open to information from below. But since there was sometimes some moral unease among the administrators about the propriety of 'spying on the people',[7] and since the intelligence derived from such espionage activities as were conducted was decidedly spasmodic in its availability and capricious in its coverage, they were never able to rely upon the possession of much even of the information which they would have required in order to pursue their policies with efficiency. At the same time a certain auditory insensitivity in the colonial structure as such guaranteed that they should not be swamped with unwanted and unacceptable information from those whom they were assigned to control. It is an innocent superstition to assume that it is always to the advantage of a government to know exactly what it is doing. The damped-down quality of the communication between the colonial population and their rulers may have been predominantly functional for the rather exiguous administrative resources and the distant and generalised control to which alone the latter aspired. But whatever its felicity or otherwise as a system of colonial control, it had obvious disadvantages as a preparation for a more ostensibly democratic system of political organisation. If in the colonial administrative structure the role of information about the attitudes of the administered population to the policies being carried out by the government was severely instrumental (the right to determine the *goals* of policy remaining in their own eyes firmly with the colonial authorities) it is hardly surprising if the same structure continued to serve a rather similar function at a point at which the people were notionally governing themselves.

In attempting to grasp the character of this approved hierarchy of obedience when in operation, it may be illuminating to separate the depiction of the project in which the Administrators considered themselves to be engaging from an analysis of the more active obstructions which met them in the course of their duties. The conception of administrative action revolved around the confident issuing and the ready receipt of 'lawful orders'. From time to time Administrators would give what turned out to have been unlawful orders; punishments in court cases which were beyond their powers to award, commands to engage in communal labour for purposes unsanctioned by the administrative regulations of the Gold Coast. But except in the case of court verdicts or sentences (which were subject to reversal or modification by the stricter application of the law by superior officers or in higher tribunals) the degree of control of administrators' actions attempted by the regulations was extremely loose and the scope of administrative discretion correspondingly generous. Where the orders of an Administrator were considered by his superiors to have been unlawful – *ultra vires* – they were categorised as technical errors, as the product of mistaken beliefs about what was legally the

158

case, what the regulations prescribed. Higher officials of the colonial administration were in no way chary of passing heavily moralistic judgements
on the performance of their subordinates. But it was their infirmity of
purpose, not their flouting of authority which evoked by far the greater part
of the scorn. The cardinal defect in the colonial conception of morality was
not *akrasia* so much as it was inertia. Inertia was an outward and visible sign
of weakness – an inward and spiritual disgrace which afflicted from time to
time all but the very highest ranks in the colonial authority[8] and to which
young white D.C.s were every bit as subject as mature black chiefs. Their
inability to execute the tasks assigned to its local Administrators might
eventually lead the colonial government to the insight that a given policy was
politically mistaken. But Ahafo was too peripheral a location for such a
realisation ever to have stemmed from the incapacity of its Administrator
alone to enact the fantasies of the central government. The failures of the
Ahafo D.C.s were thus never valuable gains in information for the central
government but always merely demonstrations of the lack of effective energy
– and thus the lack of moral force – on the part of the D.C.s in question.
D.C.s, like chiefs, are repeatedly indicted for 'slackness', for not making
their charges 'do enough', for not 'twisting their tails'. But unlike the chiefs,
while the D.C.s do undeniably sometimes commit errors, they are never
judged to have *committed* sins. Their sins are always sins of omission.

This appears to have been a simple product of the colonial situation. As
against the administered (though hardly against one another) the administrators were solidary. A body of men recruited at something less than random
from their own society,[9] they faced the Ahafos, as they faced the rest of
Ghanaians, as an ideologically blithe corporate interest group. They may have
suffered persistently from a shortage of personnel[10] – Goaso in particular was
often abandoned for long periods of time simply because of the lack of an
available officer to post there. But they had no qualms about their social
identity and little uncertainty as to whom they wished to recruit: as the Chief
Commissioner noted happily in 1919 of the arrival of three new D.C.s, one of
whom was to spend a considerable time at Goaso, 'all three charming men of
the right class'.[11] The rightness of the class was not so much a matter of pure
ascription as it was a guarantee of the appropriateness of the conditioning.
The mark of the public school lay heavy on all British colonial administration in the first half of the twentieth century. The best type of colonial
administrator was the public school hero: as the Chief Commissioner of
Ashanti said in 1916 of Ross, the founder of the Goaso station, 'clear, straight
and fearless'.[12] 'No man will ever succeed with Eastern rulers or with their
subjects,' as Stratford de Redcliffe warned a novice in the Stamboul Embassy
some decades earlier, 'unless he is as firm as a rock and as *just* and honest as
a God.'[13] The conception lost a little of its sense of intricacy in the transition

from diplomat accredited to an independent state to colonial official, but the main outlines are preserved with fidelity. The chiefs, however, not being of the right class and lacking the incomparable advantage of a public school education, were still to be assessed fundamentally by the same criteria. When Braimansu, the Omanhene of Kukuom was implicated in 1907 in a particularly repulsive torture case, Commissioner Fell pleaded for him that 'though uncouth, he is a strong chief' and that he had been 'nothing if not straightforward in the matter . . . After all we are dealing with savages who a few years ago did what they liked.'[14] When all due allowance had been made for uncouthness, the ideal chief appears – despite the singularly unpropitious context – as recognisably clear, straight and fearless too. The Queen Mother was the best 'man' in Mim in 1931 because of the sheer stubbornness with which she stood up to the pressures of the remaining local political interests.[15] When the Omanhene of Kukuom was considering coming to live at Goaso for a time in September 1930 because his people were trying to destool him, an eminently Akan fashion of exploring the political intimations of the situation, the D.C. commented sharply that it seemed to him 'a poor way to meet a crisis' and advised him not to run away from his troubles.[16] All in all the colonial culture of indirect rule demanded a more robust style of confrontation by chief of his refractory people than the more flexible and diplomatic tactics of Akan tradition would have required. Both the hierarchy of authority and the techniques of discipline of the colonial regime recapitulated many aspects of the public school. 'If I have any more complaints about you in this matter, I will send you to Kumasi,'[17] (*sc*. to the Headmaster), the Commissioner warned the Kukuomhene early in 1905. And in March of the same year, when the warning had clearly not taken effect, his tone was even more minatory: 'I am told that you say you will not bring or send cases to the Commissioner here, and that your clerk is talking in the same way. If I hear any more of this sort of thing I shall send soldiers to Kukuom and arrest both you and your clerk and send you in to Kumasi.'[18] Less draconic sanctions which were often invoked included the withdrawal of valued privileges, carried over from the days when the chiefs could still 'do what they liked', such as their gunpowder allowances and the award or retraction of (in themselves meaningless) insignia of colonial preference: chiefs' medals or government message sticks.[19] It is not difficult to grasp that the type of petty harassment involved in restricting customary privileges might be effective. But it is a more striking testimony to the viability in at least one dimension of the colonial project that colonial medals or tokens of authority could come to enter into the factional competition between stools as real values and their withdrawal consequently to constitute a real threat.[20] It did not take the Administrators long to realise how very far from solidary their charges were in relation to the new rulers. As early as 1906 Chief Commissioner Fuller wrote to the Colonial Secretary in Accra suggesting a halving of the Ashanti garrison:

It must be remembered that it is daily becoming more difficult for the Ashantis to combine. By a fortunate coincidence it appears to be part of an Ashanti Chief's duties to dislike all other Chiefs. The result is that every important Chief and would-be leader is surrounded by jealous enemies whose suspicion and fear of his self aggrandisement could be fanned into a stronger flame than patriotism or mere hatred of our rule.[21]

The convenience of this dependable political dispersion did not go un-appreciated. Where the summit of the indirect component of the colonial hierarchy met the base of its direct component – and where for the most part in the first half of the twentieth century its least elevated white members con-fronted its most elevated black members – the formal tone of the encounters was expected to be studiedly gracious. To a Commissioner addressing him by letter every Omanhene, except in the event of some monumental and recent delinquency, was 'My Good Friend'. Dissident mutterings or – almost un-thinkably – direct defiance naturally removed the velvet from such phrasing at once. Even a failure to maintain his standards of ceremonial politeness, a value notionally as much sanctioned by Akan culture as it then was by the culture of the colonists might well imperil it. The fact that an Omanhene had displayed no manners towards a subordinate would be noted and deplored,[22] while a Chief of Goaso in 1918 whose demeanour towards a Commissioner was less than punctilious was judged to be 'too casual to be even a headman of carriers'.[23] The amity of the ideal relationship was certainly in no way a qualification of its resolutely hierarchical nature. The best that an Omanhene could aspire to in the way of a colonial epitaph was the comment by the Chief Commissioner in a telegram that the government had lost 'a loyal and true friend'.[24] But the loyalty was as asymmetrical as the friendship. It was the successor to the 'rebel' Braimansu, not the 'loyalist' Beditor, to whom the colonial administration showed itself loyal in the crucial encounter of the protracted civil war between Mim and Kukuom. It was as politically desirable for the colonial government as it is for the government of modern Ghana to maintain an atmosphere of good feeling between chief and administrator. But while the present government of Ghana is as eager as was the colonial government to moralise the link between chief and Administrator as one of loyalty of the former to the latter, it is just as reluctant as was its colonial predecessor to discern a moral content in the same link in the opposite direction. The Administrator is paid by the state of Ghana and where his treasure is, his heart is expected to be also. Indeed in the event of an Administrator who was devoid of any local political commitment by a prior local identity and who did define his duties in terms of obligation to those whom he administered instead of merely to the central government, the only explanation of such conduct which would be likely to carry plausibility to most Ghanaians would be one which suggested the existence of supplementary sources of treasure. (The British penchant for economically gratuitous ideological partisanship in local factional struggle – Rattray fostering the restoration of the Ashanti Confederacy or Meyerowitz helping to hack it to pieces again – lacks so far any latter-day equivalent.) This mandatory loyalty of localism to centralism and lack of an equivalent moral commitment of centralism to localism indicates one key paradox of the modern Ghanaian state, even in its intermittent passages of elective democracy. Formal citizen equality and an ascending conception of legitimacy are certainly part of the official rhetoric of the society today. But in the organisation of the administrative structure itself, the moral vocabulary recapitulates with some precision the moral vocabulary of the colonial order. And with that vocabulary goes what is quite unmistakably a descending conception of legitimacy.[25]

Where the Administrator confronted those who were several rungs below him in the hierarchy, young men – or for that matter old women – colonial standards of politeness were substantially relaxed. A chief might be a good friend – or at least a *loyal* one – but commoners were hardly treated (or perhaps even seen) as being capable of such elevated emotions. In this respect the present-day Administrator is certainly a less forbidding figure. Although he is not for most citizens approachable in the way that a chief is[26] and although indeed he takes some pains to maintain this distance except among the members of the modern bureaucratic personnel in the district, the implicit paternalism of his role is not made as effusively apparent today as it often was under the colonial regime. It is still very much part of his duties to harry people into doing things which the government feels it desirable that they should do but for which they themselves display little enthusiasm. But it is impossible to imagine an Administrator today writing of his exploits in quite the tone adopted by the colonial D.C. in March 1930 – and in a diary designed to be read by his superiors.[27]

Gong gong beaten early but the people did not turn out till I went from compound to compound. This was amusing as the mammies were hiding behind doors and locking themselves in rooms. After some quite cheery hide and seek they turned out and work went on from about 9.30 to 3 p.m. during which time the people were not slacking.

The assurance of this extraordinary performance and its ostensibly pre-pubertal jollity is redolent of the assumption of total administrative solidarity in the face of the administered. The frank acknowledgement of juvenile pleasures (though, naturally, not the least trace of any admission of more adult pleasures) was one of the privileges of complicity. An Administrator was expected to record with complete openness the joys and miseries of his efforts to keep his charges in order. For a number of years he was even expected to make a daily record of his progress for regular presentation to his superiors who would duly annotate it and pass it back again. It was supposed to be a secret record: showing it to anyone but his superiors elicited sharp rebukes.[28] Unlike the spiritual diary of the Puritan the D.C.'s diary was an instrument of external, not of internal discipline, part of a continuing process of self-examination and self-criticism but conducted in the face of the community to which he was fully responsible, the community of the Administrators. Thought reform for the Administrators was to be a continuous process but it was a Maoist technique for the engineering of guilt and the fostering of courage which operated exclusively within the ranks of the literati. The metaphor, if somewhat fanciful, does draw attention to one major consequence of the extent to which the white bureaucracy was truly solidary. Each Administrator did have to execute his role within a severely constraining normative framework. One apprentice Commissioner summed up the inadequacy of his handling of an intricate aggressive ploy of the Omanhene of Kukuom with proper humility: 'I was not properly prepared for this.'[29] The apprentice posture is of course to some degree maintained today among new recruits to the political administration, as it necessarily must be among those entering any novel and complex social role. But no one today is expected to serve their apprenticeship in such glaringly public conditions. The rituals of intimacy within the white bureaucracy and the experience of cultural distance between it and those whom it ruled caused the process of administration itself to foster the most active dynamics of solidarity within the white bureaucracy. The fault line in the colonial hierarchy of obedience in Ahafo ran up to 1946, sharply and wide, between black and white, leaving the white roles heavily and effectively controlled, even if it did not always mean that the actions of the Ahafos themselves were at all as successfully organised. Today the fault line between Administrators and administered is hazier and less regular and the dynamics of solidarity among the Administrators themselves are correspondingly weaker. This at least, in the fullness of time, may prove to represent an opportunity for the democratisation of the postcolonial administration. But it is also important to note that if such democratisation does not eventually materialise, the confrontation between a less solidary (if slightly less privileged) administration and a somewhat more solidary grouping of the administered might also in due course make for singularly violent and economically regressive social and political conflict. One of these days the natives might easily get restless.

The fact that the role of British Administrator was exercised in so much more conspicuous a situation and that it was thus much more heavily and effectively sanctioned within the solidary values of the white administration itself than for example the role of the C.P.P. District Commissioner should not, however, be interpreted as implying that the higher echelons of the colonial bureaucracy had a very precise idea of what was being administered.[30] It was the aesthetics of the D.C.'s performance of his ritual obligations on which information travelled plenteously and regularly upwards, not the causal impact which his performance had upon the lives of those whom he was administering. The Colonial Secretary in October 1913 was unable to cast any light for the benefit of the Governor on a reference to one of the major clashes in the Mim/Kukuom struggle – one which had nearly led to the murder of the Kukuom *okyeame* in Mim:

I cannot trace, nor does the C.C. refer me to, any report on the 'trouble' last July. Mr Fell alludes to the episode as a 'victory' of the Omanhin over Mim, writing, I assume, of a diplomatic or other success. Mr Ross describes the occurrence as a riot. With regard to the Kumasi influence at Mim, it is, to me, a matter of surprise that the C.C., as it would appear, was ignorant of the fact that the linguist of one of the Kumasi chiefs had held 'Full Court' and tried cases at Mim. If the practice was not previously known to Mr Fuller, it does not argue well for the efficiency of his intelligence bureau at Headquarters. The C.C. does not say whether he was cognizant of the practice. But I gather he was not: or he would have stopped it.[31]

On this occasion the Governor, Sir Hugh Clifford, took the trouble to rebuke the Chief Commissioner for his unimpressive showing and to emphasise to him that major political incidents in Ashanti should be reported in future to Accra. But three years later when Clifford was informed of the suicide of Braimansu's successor, Braimansu II, his response, after expressing appropriate regret, was to ask, without success, if the Secretary for Native Affairs knew anything about this particular Omanhene and to enquire rather flatly, 'Where is Ahafo?'[32] The fact that the Secretary for Native Affairs knew virtually nothing about the Omanhene and that Clifford in the fourth year of his Governorship did not know where Ahafo was were embarrassing enough together to provide grounds for some effort to excuse their ignorance. The apologetic tone of the Secretary's insistence that Ahafo was 'a *very small Division*' is easy to catch. But it certainly was true that Ahafo, whatever could be said as to its size was at the time, comparatively speaking, a division of no importance. It has indeed never been exactly a cynosure for the more metropolitan of Ghanaians. A considerable amount of high level political energy has been devoted recently, particularly under the Progress Party government, to the effort of resolving its traditional constitutional disputes. In addition to these individual attentions, it is no doubt true that substantially more information about all areas of Ghana percolates through to branches of the central government in Accra today than did at any point during the colonial period – the sheer increase in the scale of the national bureaucracy would alone serve to ensure that. Some of this information, too, is certainly of a kind such that it could facilitate political control. The motley forces of public order in Ahafo before 1951 certainly never included such a specialist informant on the scope of political control as the resident Special Branch official in the late 1960s. But, although very many more facts about Ahafo are now located somewhere in Accra than ever were in the colonial days, there is some doubt at a purely mechanical level as to how accessible most of them are even to the higher levels of governmental authority, while the somewhat reduced solidarity of the civil bureaucracy as such and the potential conflicts between civil and military interests or, when a party regime is in power, between civil bureaucrats and party politicians, may well mean that such information as is mechanically accessible cannot be relied upon to be available to the government as a unitary political interest.

One further aspect of the British administration in action, in itself one of no great causal significance, serves conveniently to define how far its solidarity was a product of its membership in a society situated firmly beyond the borders of the Gold Coast. Much of what the colonial administrators spent their time in doing can be presented by the sympathetic as functional to the project of subjugating the Ahafos to the demands and the prizes of the world economy. In Ahafo this proved to be a project which required organisation far more pervasively than it required coercion. It is also a project to which virtually all of its inhabitants today are too firmly committed, many of them having in fact made their way to the area specifically in order to consummate the bargain, for past efforts devoted to it to evoke much in the way of present-day resentment. This being modernity, the corresponding aspects of the colonial enterprise, the bringing of roads, health and wealth, can be seen as instances of modernisation (progress, *nkoso*) and their more culturally displeasing concomitants can be excused by Ahafos, at least at this distance, since the departure of the colonialists has served in large part to purge them. (It is easier in Ahafo, as it certainly is not on the campus of the University at Legon, to find those who sentimentalise the colonial regime than it is to find those who still feel a burning sense of oppression and resentment towards it.) But however evanescent the more blatant cultural concomitants of British rule have proved to be – and some have proved decidedly less evanescent than others – it is clear that it would be misleading to ignore them completely when what is at issue is the mechanics of solidarity among the Administrators themselves. Many ceremonial aspects of the colonial order could be understood by the Ahafos simply as ciphers for expressing the establishment by the British of an empire substantially wider than that of Ashanti. The insistence on high standards of ceremonial politeness (chiefs being reprimanded for example for smoking a pipe near where the D.C.'s court was sitting[33]) and on a dutiful standard of practical helpfulness[34] did not tax the social imaginations of the Ahafos. More abstract and purer items of colonial ceremonial were accepted with equanimity: flagpoles and Union Jacks, decorative arches, as well as carefully cleaned roads, for the visit of dignitaries like the Chief Commissioner of Ashanti,[35] the sending of representatives to Kumasi to greet the new Chief Commissioner[36] or trips to Sunyani or Kumasi to greet still grander visitors,[37] colonial medals and message sticks for chiefs,[38] the celebration of British Empire Day,[39] might all be innovations in Akan culture but they were not in any way antipathetic to its style. Some of them even evoked a measure of nostalgia after their cessation. The Ahafo M.P., A. W. Osei, even had the temerity to ask Kofi Baako in Parliament in 1958 why the government had abolished British Empire awards, without substituting any of its own.[40] Some of the public representations of deference to authority proved excessive in the eyes of the Administrators themselves, though not always to their post-colonial successors. Instructions were issued in 1929, for example, that motor roads were not to be closed in future for Governors or Chief Commissioners to pass down them.[41] In general it seems to have been true that the maintenance of such formal ceremonials as were exacted was not resented and the idiom of deference was one which chiefs in particular showed themselves in no way reluctant to adopt – especially when they had recently been rewarded for more exacting and practical co-operation. In return for the £120 government 'dash' passed on to them for their services in clearing the main Kumasi–Sunyani road of the hundreds of trees blown across it by a whirlwind in May 1925, the chiefs of the Western Province asked the Commissioner to convey 'their deepest gratitude to His Excellency and to assure him that at any time and on any occasion they will do all that in them lies to assist Government and prove their loyalty to the British flag'.[42] Indeed the only significant problems which appear to have arisen over the required public ceremonials came with the beginnings of the transfer of power, when the location of authority was genuinely somewhat ambiguous. Had Nkrumah had the nerve to visit Ahafo in 1949 the idea that a chief might have had a duty to turn his subjects out to greet him formally on his arrival would have seemed merely comical. Had Osagyefo the President honoured the area with a visit twelve years later any chief who failed to turn out his subjects in some quantity would have been a poor actuarial risk. But in 1952 the question of whether a chief, in effect an indirect official of the colonial regime, had to turn his people out to greet the Prime Minister of the Colony on a party political tour proved to be a very nice point indeed.[42]

The colonial Administrators in Ahafo had little difficulty as a body in eliciting deference – at least at the level of overt behaviour – to whatever they chose to construe as symbols to which deference was obligatory. At the time when an *odikro* (headman) could ask in genuine puzzlement whether deference was in fact obligatory towards the Prime Minister of the Gold Coast, no one was in any doubt as to whether it was in fact mandatory to prepare for the celebration of the Coronation of the new Queen of the United Kingdom.[43] It was not, however, those symbols to which the Administrators were entitled to exact a compulsory deference which best symbolised the solidarity among them. Symbolically the Political Service was never permitted, despite considerable enthusiasm among its members for the idea, to acquire a uniform of its own. Unconventionality in dress, of course, was not encouraged – standard civil service wear of khaki serge or white drill were favoured – but in the way of distinctive accoutrements for their forest duties, the special tie and blazer badges (to be obtained from Hawkes) which they had acquired a right to by 1924 were hardly the glowing insignia of rank which they coveted.[44] It was projects less clearly related to the local duties of their role – the functional requirements for maintaining British control over Ahafo – but which were nevertheless strongly related to the identities which they necessarily maintained while at these local duties, which best epitomised their solidarity. On the occasions when these projects forced themselves on the attentions of the Ahafos they did so as opportunities for the prudent, not as direct commands. The opportunity for the Ahafos to contribute to the Edward VII Memorial Fund (the Omanhene gave £30[45]) or to funds for the war effort in 1914 ('I do not care for the govt mixing themselves in it as it is difficult for the natives to dissociate subscriptions from govt orders'[46]) or in a slightly different tone in 1918 ('Told the Ahafohene and representative about the Aeroplane Contribution suggested and spoke to them about the war'[47]) were hardly requirements of the civilising mission. But the insistence that they were *not* commands and the purposes for which they were assigned exemplify the corporate optimism that the civilised might come authentically to love their civilisers. Appropriately the most emotive and organisationally elaborate project for eliciting expressions of gratitude from the administered (and one of the clearest ritual expressions of the sense of identity among the Administrators) was the expression of solidarity with the heroic dead. The Flanders poppies vended in the Ahafo forest on Armistice Day from 1925 to 1930 – and no doubt long afterwards – did not realise immense sums for the war victims: somewhat over £1,000 a year in these years for Ashanti as a whole and some £20 to £40 from Ahafo.[48] As usual, the concept of the voluntary gift became a little blurred as it passed into the less direct echelons of the colonial hierarchy, the Mimhene for example charging a number of his subjects in 1929 for 'failing to obey the lawful order of a chief: viz to buy a Flanders poppy'.[49] But it would be the naiveté of the cynical to see this ritual simply as a hypocritical and inefficient taxing device. The point of the ritual was precisely that the Ahafos should express themselves voluntarily as beholden to the dead of their masters. To recognise the sanctions which made such expenditure rational for the Ahafos was to obviate the point of the ritual. What was Ahafo to those who had died in Flanders fields where the poppies now blew – and what were the dead in Flanders fields to those who now lived in Ahafo? It was a key to both the solidarity of the Administrators and to the logical incoherence of the colonial project that there had to be and yet could not be an answer to this question. At the heart of the solidarity of the Administrators there was both pride and insecurity: the pride that they would feel when the administered themselves appealed for tactical advantage to the colonial ideology ('We have heard a white man lie today', as the Mims murmured at the hapless Wesleyan missionary[50]) and the insecurity of the knowledge that fundamentally the search for authentic and dependable appreciation was hopeless ('European grave all bushed up', the Sunyani D.C. noted resentfully in 1931. 'They don't care', assented the Provincial Commissioner[51]).

Many of the more active obstructions which the Administrators encountered in the course of this eventually forlorn enterprise were common to other areas of the Gold Coast in which it was undertaken. The axiomatic moral unreliability of all African instruments of colonial rule was a complex consequence of the disparity between the social moralities of the colonising and colonised communities, accentuated no doubt by the structural changes in roles belonging to the colonised community produced by their incorporation into the colonial hierarchy of authority. It was no part of the explicit purposes of the colonial administrators to make chiefly roles more irresponsible and autocratic than they had been under the looser authority of the old Ashanti Confederacy. Nor is it really clear that the net effect of colonial control was to provide an opportunity for wider and more irresponsible exercise of authority by the holders of chiefly office. The sanctioning of Native Authority police forces and of the building of chief's prisons, to say nothing of the provision to chiefs of such facilities as handcuffs, certainly implicated the colonial power in the exercise of a good deal of highly arbitrary authority, a consequence of which the administration could in the nature of things hardly remain unaware for any great length of time and about which it fussed anxiously and ineffectually at regular intervals. But an examination of the record of chiefly authority in Ahafo in the first few years of colonial rule, a period in which the administrative hand lay so lightly upon the area that such violence as was deployed by chiefs could not plausibly be attributed to their authority having been augmented by the colonial regime, does nothing to establish any greater delicacy or responsibility in the exercise of chiefly authority before the corruptions of colonialism really got at it. Nor indeed is the historical record of metropolitan Ashanti in the century before the conquest exactly unmarked by traces of arbitrary power. It is certainly not clear that the attempt to destool a vigorous chief who was abusing his office was a more hazardous project under the colonial regime than it had been before the British conquest. But whether or not the conduct of the Akan chief was really less likely to appear to the British as that of an officer and a gentleman, simply because of the incorporation of his office into the colonial hierarchy, there is no doubt that some of his conduct did appear to them as falling well below this dizzy standard. The more lurid exploits of chiefs themselves tended to disappear from the colonial record as the decades passed, whether because of an increase in their discretion or a modification in their susceptibility to the morals of the colonisers. In the last two decades of colonial rule, chiefs in Ahafo are not found any longer actively condoning the rubbing of ground chilis into the eyes or genitals of subjects with whom they are engaged in dispute. But if the public behaviour of chiefs themselves does from the colonial viewpoint improve drastically, that of their immediate entourage lagged appreciably behind. Offenders charged before native tribunals continued to get beaten up in the vicinity of the chief's *ahenfie* ('palace') until extremely late.[52] Clerks, those spearheads of the colonial educational venture and exemplars of the spiritual advantages of literacy, were less likely by 1945 to turn out to have spent five years in a gaol in the Colony, as the Omanhene found one of his less satisfactory incumbents to have done some years earlier.[53]

Apart from the Augustinian assumption of the intrinsic sinfulness of all non-Administrators – 'they listen and do nothing'[54] – the main explanation adopted by the administration of the problems which it faced in Ahafo was the elaborately anomalous character of the division as a political unit (up to the restoration of the Ashanti Confederacy in 1935) or the equally anomalous character of its relationship to Kumasi after it had ceased to be treated as an independent political unit. It was the conventional wisdom of the administration, apt to be produced without noticeable irony after the recital of the most baroque confusions, that in unravelling disputes about traditional issues, one must 'always be governed by well-established Akan custom'.[55] As the respect for traditional legitimacy among the administration rose, with the establishment of the Anthropological Department and the researches of the indefatigable Rattray, the administration became increasingly morally (ideologically) discomfited by its own makeshift expedients in the 'traditional' field[56] and attempted to resuscitate a more authentic tradition, an enterprise constructed solidly around a category mistake. There is a certain undeniable if abstract charm to the contrast between the solemn and nervous colonial espousal of Ashanti legitimacy after 1935 and the inventive fluidity of the conception of traditional legitimacy prevalent in Kumasi itself, which made it easy for a Wing-Chief to identify the land rental for a commercial plot for Cadburys or the U.A.C. in Goaso as 'something found on the land' and thus due to the Kumasi stool by analogy with ivory, game or a share in the snail harvest.[57] Except in the eyes of conservative ideologues a flexible and inventive view of tradition is not necessarily an unmixed blessing. It was hard for the Ahafos not to view the re-creation of the Confederacy as a massive refeudalisation, a purposeful exploitation, like that of the eighteenth-century French nobility, of rights which were now utterly unrelated to any function previously discharged by their possessors and which in conditions of capitalist agriculture and commerce were grossly and ostentatiously exploitative.

The account favoured by the administration of the peculiar technical difficulties of administering Ahafo altered with the shifts in the administration's conception of Ahafo legitimacy. In the early days after the conquest it was illegal Kumasi interference which made Ahafo difficult to govern and once the restored Confederacy was firmly in operation once again, it was the sheer vigour of Kumasi exploitation of Ahafo which most perturbed the British officials. But in the decade or so before the Confederacy was restored, a political process helpfully studied by Tordoff,[58] the administration's moral sensitivity to traditional legitimacy was in a particularly inflamed condition. In this period the lack of legitimate structure and stability in Ahafo history evoked growing embarrassment and may well have led Ahafo's Administrators to have a more accurate awareness of the arbitrariness of colonial rule in action there, than was at all common in political formations in which traditions of legitimacy were less volatile and structures of political control correspondingly firmer. The blend of apology and insight can be picked up in a set of supplementary handing-over notes left by an experienced D.C. to his novice successor.[59]

With the administration of the Goaso district it is possible that you will not be able to apply the exact maxims with which you have been inculcated during your period of instruction and that at first you may be a bit at sea; the salient points, however will be the same – it is the way in which they have to be applied which you will perhaps find a little hard at first. The reason for this warning is the fact that the Ahafo Division is not a natural tribal unit of its own, it is an arbitrary Government made unit. You will find the History in the District Record Book, and you'll note from that that some 30 years ago the present Goaso district was a sort of 'New Forest' under the Asantehene and his personal property, the people being his hunters and being looked after by various Kumasi chiefs. They had a row with the Kumasis and in 1900[60] they were made a separate unit and the Ohene of Kukuom was made the Head Chief. You will understand therefore that we are not dealing with a division which has an old and united history to hold it together, and that 2 or 3 of the 'stools' now under Kukuom consider themselves to be his equal if not his superior from the native point of view. One has to be on the look out the whole time that the Omanhene does not abuse his power and be 'down' on the others; at the same time we have to be careful and sometimes stretch a point in his favour, if any of the sub-stools try and be insolent or flout him in any way. You will find that most of the points regarding the service and the exact status of the various stools have been laid down from time to time, as disputes come to light but there must be hundreds which have not been selected and still have been gone into with great care; you will also find that some of the chiefs will play the old trick and bring up to you as a new head matters which have been already laid down.

The proportion of overt to covert manoeuvre in this ceaseless mutual competition to erode existing power and to develop new power has varied from time to time, following the shifting sense of tactical advantage. Formal boundary disputes, frequently involving the control of major economic resources[61] and *ad hominem* prosecutions for the abuse of public roles run alongside more inventive and secret intrigues and the attempt to enlist the aid of supernatural agencies. One Omanhene was in fact destooled for having failed to dispose of his fetish paraphernalia, as he had promised to do on taking up his office.[62]

The government may have capitulated briefly in 1935 to the Kumasi view of political legitimacy. But there is no reason to regard its acceptance of any local version of legitimacy as exhibiting the vice of sentimentality. The mechanisms of stool succession were seen as being pervasively economic – the stool going to the highest briber[63] – and the psychological links between ruler and ruled were identified with parallel cynicism. The charge that 'to the native' respect and fear meant the same thing[64] was certainly an example of cultural absolutism; but as an expectation it must have given a certain edge to the most relaxed sense of paternalism. However, except for a brief period in the immediate vicinity of the 1935 restoration, it was not these axiomatic irritants of the process of indirect rule which most worried the conscientious Ahafo D.C. so much as the sense of being at the distant periphery of a very active centre. Until shortly before 1935 it was seen as a centre whose activity was specifically illegal. Not long after that year it came to be recognised with at least equal definition as a centre whose activity, even if it was now technically legal, was malign in its motivation and politically and economically regressive in its impact. In many parts of Ashanti the restoration of the Confederacy may have been an unmitigated advantage from the viewpoint of the Administrators. But in Ahafo any increment in the political docility of the population was more than counterbalanced by the costs to colonial conceptions of equity and progressive administration imposed by the greater indirection of the rule. If there was a hint of paranoia in the judgement of a D.C. in July 1928 that, 'there is always a suspicion of Kumasi intrigue behind anything that happens in Ahafo',[65] it remained a persisting political consideration in Ahafo that Kumasi *was* a notably active centre on the periphery of which to be.

The Kumasi *reconquista* of Ahafo appears in fact to have been assisted by the restoration of civil order and peace produced by the initial British conquest of Ashanti. When Davidson Houston visited Ahafo in 1896 to sign the

Treaty of Protection, he found a people who 'had thrown off the Kumasi yoke', who had had virtually no contact with Kumasi for several years and 'were much pleased to sign a treaty'.[66] The only blemish in their eagerness to enter the British protectorate was identified (if not altogether understood) in the position of Mim. Before signing the treaty Davidson Houston

made them all acknowledge Atetchi as their King publicly before me, as I found that Chief Beditor of Mem, apparently taking advantage of Atetchi's advanced age, had been getting somewhat out of hand. I myself had at first some difficulty in getting him to come to Kukuom for palaver. I warned him to be careful not to give any trouble, and he promised not to do so now that they were under British Protection – Mem being the largest and most important town of the country. Beditor evidently for some time past has been trying to separate himself from Atetchi's rule.

A year later, whether because of Beditor's political energies, a dislike of the colonial presence once it was firmly established or simply the improved opportunity for the exercise of Kumasi influence presented by the return of peace, the Committee of Kumasi Chiefs established by the government had had considerable success in its attempts to recover this influence. Commissioner Vroom, after touring the outlying districts, saw it as being a conscious aim of this committee to reclaim prestige long lost to the King of Kumasi in districts which had revolted against Kumasi and he regarded their prospects of success as reasonably strong because the idea was 'generally entertained that all their actions have received the sanction of the government'.[67] Under these pressures Ahafo, like Tekyiman, Wam and Berekum 'already recognize the Kumasi Chiefs as their head-Chiefs and prefer perhaps to refer their differences to the Native Committee rather than the Resident'. This development no doubt made it even more important to insist that the Kumasi Chiefs' request for a compulsory repatriation of Kumasi refugees in Ahafo could be 'entertained only on condition that the Ahafo country itself is not interfered with by them'.[68] The massive tug-of-war foreshadowed in these first two years of the British presence in Ahafo has never entirely ceased ever since, though Ahafo localism and Kumasi imperialism have at different times each made gains massive enough to give them the fleeting appearance of a final decision. By now indeed there is some little doubt whether the tug-of-war has not become principally an internal struggle fought within the minds of individual Ahafos. The political field is too uneven and too heavily shadowed for it to be at all easy to preserve much purity of political commitment within it. Even such a doughty protagonist of Ahafo autonomy as Braimansu I can be found in April 1906 remitting the fees for a forbidden Ashanti Great Oath sworn in his territory to the Chief of Mampong;[69] while even the latter-day Chief of Mim who heads the Kumasi party among the present Ahafo chiefs would hesitate in public to espouse a rate of economic expropriation from Ahafo stool lands to the stool revenues of their traditional masters in Kumasi which at all approached the latters' 'traditional' entitlements. Complaints of Kumasi interference in the area never died away for long between 1896 and 1935: 1897, 1906, 1909,[70] 1911,[71] 1913,[72] 1919,[73] a strong revival between 1924 and 1927 with the return of Prempeh from exile,[74] and a steady increase from this time onwards until the triumph of the campaign in 1935. It is hard in principle to see how such pressures should have been prevented, with the continued existence of the Kumasi chiefs, the growing mobility of population and the increasing involvement with commerce centred on Kumasi. The Provincial Commissioner's notes in 1916 on the Akwaboa stool bring out both the closeness of the relationship and the fluidity of legitimate authority within it: 'a Coomassie stool taken to Ahafo after the 1900 rising, the Chief of which has been oscillating between Mim and Coomassie since 1907. He recently laid a claim for subjects before C.C.A. In 1914 he professed to be permanently settled as one of Beditor's captains.'[75] It has never in the past been an easy business to impose stability on a universe of political claims in which all legitimacy is prescriptive and in which any actor with a public role – any incumbent of a stool in particular – can rationally aspire to modify an existing arrangement and establish a fresh set of prescriptive rights. Nor is there any reason to expect it to become an easy business in the near future.[76]

CHAPTER 5

CHIEFSHIP AND THE COMMUNITY

Ghana became independent in 1957 and as a former British Colony she adopted a constitution in line with that of Britain. Administration of the country now came to depend on the might of our educated men. Powers of Chiefs started to diminish and in 1960, a chief became just a ceremonial head. Councils of Elders were abolished and Town Development Committees emerged. Every town and village had one and they were responsible (to) the various Local Councils. Chieftaincy under Nkrumah became a political tool. Those chiefs who opposed the government of the Convention Peoples' Party were destooled. The chiefs of Ghana owes gratitude to the Army and the Police who restored freedom to them on Thursday 24th February 1966.

Many people argue that chiefs would not command respect and dignity if they participated in politics. But in my humble opinion, it is through politics that chiefs will mean something to their people in future; therefore they should be allowed to take part in politics actively on local and district levels. They should not be left to play their role behind the scenes as some people has suggested. Arbitration Courts of chiefs should be recognised in a way that all civil cases should be routed through the Chiefs' Arbitration Courts before it enters the Magistrate Grade two Courts.

Chieftaincy is a very complicated matter which the government should consider very carefully. There is one thing we must bear in mind when we talk of preservation of chieftaincy, we must bear in mind that chiefs are human beings and not objects which could be 'preserved' in an archive just for cultural display. If we are going to preserve chieftaincy, there must be a definite purpose, meaningful and well planned one so that chiefs should not become ridiculed objects before their subjects.[1]

This extract from a school essay on 'The Role of Traditional Authorities in the Government of Ghana' is a clearer statement on the 'Problem of Chiefship' than most of the educated men, on whose might the administration of the country did in fact depend in the late 1960s, could offer. For many decades the literati of Ghana have alternatively extolled the vigour of chiefship and rung its death knell. Perhaps the intensity of debate is as good an indication as any of the vitality of chiefship. The extraneous ideologies to which western education has exposed Ghana's ruling elites have convinced many of the incompatibility of chiefship and modern government. The most ardent reformers have discovered, however, that is it neither practical nor expedient to extirpate it. Legislators in Accra have pruned it to some semblance of national symmetry but the manner in which it is rooted in the local communities remains inscrutable to them, perhaps even more so than the processes of modern government appear from the perspective of the towns and villages of Ahafo. In transit from Accra to Goaso, from textbook and archive to discussion in the palmwine booths, the investigator can collect a range of dissimilar interpretations of chiefship which appear to defy analytical synthesis. Not only do the views of administrators, villagers and the chiefs themselves vary, there are inconsistencies and outright contradictions within the expressed view of each individual – particularly if he is educated. The chaos into which chiefs and administrators have from time to time found themselves plunged is undoubtedly a consequence of this welter of interpretation and misinterpretation. The engagement of chiefs in widening fields of political interaction has produced consequences beyond the expectation of all parties involved. Chiefship is indeed 'a very complicated matter'; in its involvement in contemporary government it has suffered most by being aggregated conceptually as 'a national institution', in spite of its intense local variation of form and function. As the Ahafo school essayist suggests, two typical government solutions to the 'problem of chiefship' have been to define its purpose and meaning unilaterally in universally acceptable terms, or to turn it into museum stock. Meanwhile, the political uses to which chiefship in its present multivalent form may be put proliferate, opening arenas where party, chiefs, subjects and even the perplexed administrators themselves, may score gains and losses out of the unpredictability of relationships.

In the following two chapters we shall examine the roles of chiefs and elders in Ahafo from various perspectives, building up in a very tentative way a picture of the contemporary institutions of traditional leadership. First, we shall confine ourselves to the realm of the stool community, examining the politics of inter-stool relationships in the next chapter. The main questions directing the discussion which follows are how chiefly office is acquired and maintained, the political uses to which it may be put, the nature of chiefly authority within and beyond the community, and the interpretation and management of roles.

It is important to take the historical circumstances under which our study was carried out into account. The effect of these should become apparent in our discussion of particular issues. The most important single event has been the promulgation of the Chieftaincy (Amendment) Decree by the National Liberation Council in December 1966. This ruled that all chiefs who were ' . . . contrary to customary law at various times before the commencement of this Decree elevated or treated as elevated to the status of Paramount Chiefs by the Government of Kwame Nkrumah, shall, notwithstanding anything to the contrary, be deemed to have reverted to the status enjoyed respectively by chiefs of those stools immediately before the said elevation'.[2] The Decree also removed from office all chiefs enstooled in similar circumstances and, where an incumbent could be traced, restored the previous chief. In cases where Paramounts were reduced they and their subject chiefs were required to revert to the pattern of allegiances obtaining before the intervention of the Nkrumah government. In Ahafo this had the sweeping effect of abrogating Kukuomhene's Paramountcy, transferring the allegiance of the 27 other Ahafo chiefs from him to the Kumasi State Council, and reinstating twelve deposed chiefs. These changes radically affected chiefly politics in Ahafo during the period in which our study was conducted, insofar as they have focussed public attention on chiefly affairs, have put in question constitutional arrangements throughout the district, and have confronted many chiefs with an unsympathetic public and the problems of re-establishing a stool council. It could be argued that a period in which political structures, motives and methods were being re-evaluated and scrutinised locally and nationally with much candour, was an appropriate time to enquire into the meaning of chiefship in Ahafo. It might also be said, however, that this 'abnormal' situation confuses interpretation. In practical terms there was some risk that a government commission of enquiry into lands and chiefship in Ahafo may have over-rehearsed chiefs in their political attitudes and confused them with regard to our own research role.[3]

a. THE STOOL COUNCIL

In chapter 1 we noted the importance of regarding the community in Ahafo as politically dynamic. The hierarchy of realms and allegiances typical of the Akan area provides a framework for the political advancement which is every community's ambition. An examination of the 28 stools in Ahafo (see map B) cannot allow one to identify the clear expression of a structural norm, the constitutional arrangements and stages of growth being so variable. However, one can say that the basic organisational formula is a settlement nucleus consisting of several segments, each delegating an elder to the stool council and one of them providing the chief. The wider realm of the stool consists of subsidiary communities recognising the authority of a stool elder in the first instance, and the chief and his council ultimately. We have noted that the stool itself forms part of a wider realm – a political level which we shall discuss in the next chapter.

A council of elders is a *sine qua non* of chiefship at any level in the Akan area. The principal segments of most Ahafo towns consist of people who are reckoned to have migrated over the years from the same Akan community. The eldership of this segment is generally vested in its longest-established, 'royal' family; it seems that the segment is rarely in itself a matrikin unit but that it gains political coherence from its matrifamily nucleus and its recruitment from a particular Akan locality. There is some tendency – not absolute, by any means – for the homesteads constituting the segment to be grouped together territorially, either within the stool town or as a dependent village elsewhere in the realm. Recognition of a new segment is not automatic, it depends on formal acknowledgement and incorporation by the stool council and the establishment of an official eldership. Here we may see the politics of communal aggrandisement at work within the community, a restless confrontation of political interests involving the award, and occasionally the withdrawal of recognition to particular groups, contests about which 'royal family' should hold office, and disputes about which eldership rightfully belongs to which segment.

The number of recognised segments does not necessarily correlate with population size; a small stool like Kwakunyuma has four principal segments, while a larger stool like Goaso may have only two. Rattray, Busia and others have made us well aware of the representative functions of these segments. Ideally, all recognised members of the community have access to the stool council through their respective segment elders. The argument here is somewhat circuitous in the case of Ahafo, for citizenship itself is mainly contingent upon access to the representative functions of an elder, which in turn depends on shared local origins rather than on common lineage membership. At any rate, representation is perpetuated and given added legitimacy by the process of succession within the dominant matrifamily. This is supervised and sanctioned by the stool council and the overlord to whom the chief is himself subject. An elder who dies in office is allowed by superior authority to have his stool ritually blackened and placed in his family's stool house. As the family's stock of black stools grows over time so too does the legitimacy of its claims to the office. The basic organisation of the stool is thus an economic and political association of co-resident segments expressed primarily in terms of common recognition of the chief's authority. The coherence of each segment is in turn dependent on the recognition of the authority of an elder, and segment membership is primarily dependent on an association with a community of origin over a period of time or, in a few cases, on common matriclanship.

Although citizens themselves may not be subject to status differentiation within the community, there is some ranking of the segments to which they belong in terms of their representation on the stool council. There is no consistent formula for stool offices throughout Ahafo, but a broadly familiar Akan pattern expresses relative seniority, primarily on the basis of the

TABLE 2. *Composition of stool councils in Ahafo, 1968–9*

Categories of elder	Aboum	Acherensua	Akrodie	Anwiam	Asufufuo	Ayumso	Dadiesoaba	Dantano	Etwineto	Fawohoyeden	Goaso
(1) From chief's segment											
Queen mother	●	●	●	●	●	●	●	○	●	●	○
Adehye panin						●	●	●			
Abusua panin											
Gyasehene	●			●	○	●	●	●		●	
Gyasewahene											
(2) Matriclan titles		1						1			
(3) Military titles											
Krontihene			●	●	○	●	●			●	
Akwamuhene	●	●				●	●	●		●	
Nifahene	●	●	●			●	●			●	
Benkumhene	●	●			○	●				●	
Twafohene					●						
Adontenhene	●	●					●	●		●	
Ankobeahene							●	●	●		
Kyidomhene	●						●	●		●	
(4) Other segment elders											
Abakomahene	●		●	●							
Abontendonhene											
Mamahene				●			●				
(other)											
(5) Stool officials											
Akyeamehene											
Okyeame				●			2	2	●	●	
Sanaahene	●		●			●				●	
(other)						●					
(6) Officials included as elders											
Asafohene		●	○			●			●		
Okomfo						●		●			
Untitled											

NOTE. This table records information given by the Ahafo chiefs in interviews during 1968 and 1969. Pomakrom and Siena, whose chiefs were not interviewed, are not included.

Gyedu	Hwidiem	Kenyase I	Kenyase II	Kukuom	Kwakunyuma	Kwapong	Mehame	Mim	Nkasaim	Noberkaw	Ntotroso	Sankore	Sienchem	Wamahinso	Total
●	●	●	●	●	○	●	●	●	●	●	●	●	●	●	26
															3
			●												1
		●				●	●	●		●	●	●	●	●	16
											●		●		2
						1		1							4
●	●	●		●	●	●		●		●	●	●	●	●	18
							●			●		●	○		9
●							●			●		●	●		11
							●	●				●	●		9
												●			1
											●	●			7
						●					●				5
●						●					●		●		9
						●						●			5
						●	●								2
													●		3
●						●									2
							●	●		●					3
	●	●				3	●	●			2	●		2	19
				●	●					●					7
															1
													●	●	5
	●			●				●			●				6
	8		7					10							25

Key: ● eldership established and with present incumbent;
○ eldership established, but with no present incumbent.
Otherwise, figures indicate the number of established elderships with present incumbents. Totals express all established elderships.

priority of settlement of each segment's core. Rank is expressed in particular functions, notably the right to deputise for the chief, and in seating and speaking protocol on official occasions. It is clear that stool council composition is nowhere fixed and immutable in Ahafo, it is a facet of the continuing political process within every community. For example, the installation or deposition of a chief may involve not only changes of personnel but also changes in the component offices of the council. On such occasions a group may press for independent representation and recognition of their own elder. However, the council does not consist exclusively of segment elders; a few members are appointed from among locally prominent men without regard to group affiliation within the community. These are often elderships 'without portfolio', or the important, largely executive positions of *okyeame* (stool spokesman) and *sanaahene* (stool treasurer). In Ahafo it is not uncommon for an eminent 'stranger' to be appointed to such an office.

The 28 Ahafo stools are obliged to register their elders at the district office, a statutory control over those who may concern themselves with accessions, depositions and other important changes. These lists approximate to Table 2, which records stool council membership detailed by the chiefs interviewed during 1968 and 1969. The same figure distinguishes between offices with and without current incumbents. Acherensua, Asufufuo and Goaso stools were experiencing constitutional problems as a result of N.L.C. Decree 112 and could offer no complete list of elders. Acherensua, a former Convention People's Party stronghold where 'modernist' ideals held sway, had been without a stool council for several years until its present chief was reinstated. No single explanation can adequately account for the variation in the sizes of the stool councils, but the most significant factors appear to be the extent of population and territory (i.e. the size of the realm), the political rank of the stool in the wider state organisation and – very important – the stability of membership over the last hectic twenty years. Kukuom, the former paramount stool, has had no significant changes in personnel over the last ten or fifteen years, and with 11 elders has one of the largest councils. Mehame, a smaller realm which has seen extensive changes in personnel, now has only five elders. On the other hand, when we asked the chief of Etwineto, a relatively stable stool, why he had only four elders, he quite reasonably observed that were he to establish many more, every Tom, Dick and Harry in town would be on the stool council.

All stool councils have, or reckon they should have, a queen mother (*ohemaa*). She is in fact more likely to be a sister or other close matrilateral kinswoman of the chief, rather than his mother. This office implies some precedence over chiefship itself, for the queen mother plays a key role in accession and deposition. A school essayist described her as 'the most distinguished figure in the Akan society . . . as she is the person who gave birth to the clan or state at its very beginning'. Ever since she 'began to share her rule with Kings' she has come to act 'as an adviser to the Chief dealing mainly with matters connected with womenhood of the royal house and the state'.[4] Although her participation on such formal occasions as stool council meetings may be quite passive, it is clear that she may play a highly influential role behind the scenes.[5]

There is much about the titles and functions of stool offices in Ahafo which seems anomalous in terms of accounts of constitutional arrangements in other Akan areas. One might, for example, expect ranks of the kind described here at the level of an Ashanti Division, a unit with something like the territorial extent of the whole of Ahafo, and not at the level of the small stool communities. The adoption of ranks appropriate to a higher political level may be regarded as a symptom of community aggrandisement and as an aspect of the long period of dispute and competition about the establishment of an Ahafo state. In many cases it is impossible to establish precisely when a particular eldership was established and under what circumstances; in smaller stools it seems that many elders 'grow into' office, recognition of their status being a somewhat *ex post facto* affair. It would be difficult and misleading to present a stereotype of stool council composition in Ahafo; however, an examination of the 28 Ahafo stools suggests the following six categories of elder, some or all of which may be present in each stool (see Table 2):

1. Elders representing the chief's own household, matrifamily or community segment.

2. Elders representing community segments, titled on a matriclan basis.

3. Elders representing community segments, titled according to the traditional military formation.

4. Elders representing community segments, titled according to the names of these segments or some other special designation.

5. Elders appointed on personal merit to perform special functions; these elderships are not formally vested in a particular family nor do they carry representative responsibilities.

6. Community officials whose status as elders is equivocal but who may be included in the stool council.

Because the chief is the moderator rather than a representative of intra-community interests, and because the queen mother also plays a special role in the continuity of stool affairs, a small group of other elders is responsible for the affairs of the chief's family and the segment to which he belongs. According to our interviews three stools have *adehye panin* or senior elder of the 'royal family'. Only Kenyase II hene reported having an *abusua panin*, the elder responsible for the whole clan segment from which the chief was appointed. Sixteen, however, said they had a *gyasehene*, and it is apparent that this is an important and high-ranking office. According to Rattray, the gyasehene is the head of a divisional chief's household in Ashanti, a very old office which is often 'male' in that succession is patrilateral.[6] Rattray also notes that the post may be filled on the chief's nomination, a pattern which seems quite common in Ahafo. Ahafo chiefs sometimes describe the gyasehene as the 'palace head' or as the 'chief's son', but he seems to function primarily as a spokesman for the interests of the wider community segment to which the chief belongs. Two chiefs said they had a *gyasewahene*, or deputy to the gyase.

Stool elders in Ahafo are rarely identified by matriclan titles – e.g., Akoanahene, Agonahene. It is even rare for the *abusua panin* or the *adehye panin* to be identified – as he might well be elsewhere in the Akan area – by the appropriate clan name.[7] Although matrilineal succession implies that an eldership is associated with a particular clan, stool offices are primarily identified in the well-known idiom of the Akan military formation. Seventeen of the 28 Ahafo stools have an established *krontihene*, formerly the war leader but now described as the chief counsellor of the chief, 'just like in England, a Prime Minister' according to Mimhene. He is generally regarded as the most senior of the elders, the chief's deputy, and usually represents the second most important segment of the community. The *akwamuhene* (nine stools) is second-in-command of the army, and is followed by the *nifahene* (eleven stools) or right-wing chief, and the *benkumhene* (nine stools) who leads the left-wing. Following in formation are the *twafohene* (one stool) or advance guard, the *adontenhene* (seven stools) or leader of the main body, the *ankobeahene* (seven stools) or chief's bodyguard and the *kyidomhene* (nine stools) leader of the rear guard. It is difficult to establish the terms in which these titles denote rank differentiation and, where precedence was explained to me, the order apparently changes from stool to stool. Fawohoyedenhene ranked the *adontenhene* the third-senior elder, Mimhene gave priority to the *nifahene*.

As Table 2 should suggest, the *okyeame* or stool spokesman is regarded as an indispensable official throughout Ahafo. He is the most important of the elders appointed by the chief for the duration of his reign (category 5 above). In an essay on chiefship an Ahafo schoolboy wrote:

No body is entitled to speak directly to the chief but through the Okyeame. He is the person who directly receives the praises and abuses of the chief. Okyeame always pronounces judgement after a trial . . . Being the confidential officer to the chief and the state he has to be able to keep secrets if required . . . he has to be eloquent in speech, represent a high level of morals, have a good memory as an adviser on traditional law and custom, have an impressive appearance considering the duties he has to perform as an ambassador to other states, and so on.[8]

Although the chief may not in fact always communicate by way of the okyeame, he may never transact official business in the okyeame's absense. His spokesman is his witness and invigilator, a personification of the public eye which is continually upon him. So close is the relationship that 'sometimes the Okyeame is called the wife of the chief' (Dadiesoabahene). In several stools this very active role is subdivided, the leading spokesman sometimes being designated the *akyeamehene*. Although the okyeame is regarded essentially as an officer of the chief, his appointment is apparently subject to stool council approval and may even become vested in particular families, sons or nephews being schooled in the necessary skills.

The *sanaahene* or stool treasurer is an office which, chiefs claim, is becoming more common throughout the Akan area. In smaller stools his functions are obscure; he seems to operate more as an auditor of the chief's spending than as an accountant or banker.[9] It was considered an appropriate post for a wealthy and respected citizen, doubtless in expectation of his financial patronage.

The *asafohene* (sometimes *asafoakye*), the leader of the common people, is the most prominent of the sixth category of officials – those whose status as elders is equivocal. Responsibility for choosing the asafohene rests primarily with the common citizens of the community, although the appointment may be given official approval by the stool council. It is clear that in larger and longer-established stools the inclusion of the asafohene among the stool elders would be regarded as a contradiction in terms, even if the 'headman', as the office is now commonly translated, were only occasionally admitted to council meetings. Six Ahafo stools ranked as an elder the *okomfo*, the priest of the community's principal fetish or god. These were conspicuously the stools renowned for the potency of their local deity. There are many references in Akan lore to original transfers of power from gods to stool chiefs, and histories refer frequently to uneasy relationships between priest and chief in traditional government. In the first two decades of this century Mim was divided in this way, Bofa, priest of the god Obo, vying for power against Ntokor, the civil chief. Currently the principal deity of Ntotroso is Apomasu, celebrated annually at a colourful ceremony. It seems significant that although the chief did not include its young and influential priest in his main list of elders he subsequently explained: 'He is an elder of the stool [but] he has no official position (*dibre*) – he just looks after the god.'

Three other titles occur quite frequently in Ahafo: the *abakomahene*, the *abontendonhene* and the *mamahene*. Although clear interpretation is not easy, all appear to denote pre-eminence among the various segment elders of the community. It is striking that they refer to qualities of citizenship or the physical segments of the town rather than to kinship or the military formation. In the new, immigrant society of Ahafo these offices are allocated typically to prominent established townsmen on the strength of their personal qualities. Their family claims to the position, or even the clear definition of a community segment for which they are responsible, seem to be secondary considerations. *Mbakoma* are people of high rank, *omanma* are distinguished citizens, the suffix-*hene* indicating chiefship of these categories. *Mbonten* are the streets or segments of the community, *don* apparently referring to the *other* parts of town not clearly represented by other established elders. In some cases these ranks seem to be co-ordinate with the *krontihene*.

If stool council organisation in Ahafo seems chaotic it is largely because so many offices are in the process of establishment or are, like the three described above, inherently negotiable. Certainly, it seems important to dispel any notion that there is a rigorously observed formula for eldership in Ahafo or that claims to the office are deeply rooted. We may see this more clearly, and come to understand something of the dynamics of stool council membership, if we consider some of the criteria on which elders are appointed and the functions which they are expected to perform.

The responsibility for appointing stool elders in Ahafo is, like most other aspects of public decision making, diffused throughout the community. If a chief says that he has the authority to seek out and appoint new elders, he would not normally mean that the choice is his alone but that, as in other decisions, his is the final sanction. A few of the chiefs currently attempting to re-establish stool councils are susceptible to accusations on unilateral action; chiefs such as Acherensuahene feel keenly the vicious circle in which they are caught: to appoint elders they depend upon the counsel of elders. They are exhorted by the District and Regional Officers to establish elderships, official-dom being apparently as anxious as any party to see stools 'properly constituted'. Otherwise, pressure to establish a new office comes primarily from within the community itself, and is a product of its own internal growth. Fawohoyedenhene described the process thus: 'when you are put on the stool you go about from house to house to choose the elders. The choice depends on how many people there are in the house, a large household has a leader who may become one of your elders.' Although an oversimplification, this expresses the importance attached to particular family groups which have become subsidiary nuclei of population growth within the community. By natural increase and by immigration from a common place of origin, such a segment is likely to have achieved a corporate identity already as, for example, 'the Bepasi family'. Wamahinsohene explained: 'someone may be chosen to represent a large number of people, say from Kumasi, so that these people may acknowledge [literally 'see'] the chief . . . This man here [pointing] is representing the Berekum people.' The total number of elderships is thus seen as a reflection of the overall growth of the community: 'seven [elders] were with my predecessor ... because the town has grown there are now eleven' (Hwidiemhene). Segment growth can also justify the promotion of an elder: 'formerly there was no Adontenhene; the man was Akaasehene [leader of the Akaase people] but he has a huge family [*na busuafuo dooso*] so I made him Adontenhene after discussing it with the elders' (Akrodiehene). Growth within the community can thus be seen to affect council composition with regard to the disposition of offices, as well as size.

Although elderships are most commonly discussed in terms of the representation of the segments and houses comprising the community, matrifamily interrelationships remain an important idiom for describing the development of a stool council. A chief may refer to some of his elders as 'sons of the stool', implying that their offices are in some sense regarded as a product of the association of other lineages to the 'royal family' by marriage and patrifiliation. As we have seen in chapter 1, community growth is seen to stem from a man and his wife, the original settlers. The two matrilineages implied in this association are consolidated locally by the birth of a son to the couple and the provision of a royal heir by the sister of the founder. The problems of securing the latter from a home community far away are clearly recognised, and are reckoned as the basis for the distinctive patrilateral succession to chiefly office characteristic of the two important stools of Mim and Sienchem. With each marriage, successive chiefs are seen to introduce to the royal household representatives of other matrifamilies, sometimes from the locality but frequently from the community of origin. In the past, strategic marriages within and between communities seem to have enhanced the claims of particular groups to stool council representation. Whether by kinship and affinity, or simply by local association, relationships deriving from the various communities of origin are considered very important. An example of this is Ntotrosohene's assertion that an immigrant who has been an elder in the parent community has a sound claim to office in Ahafo: 'Some [elders] bring their own stools with them from home and I make them elders again here.'

The assumption that the proliferation of elderships may be traced, in many cases, to the association of other matrifamilies with the royal household, may underlie the common assertion in Ahafo that it is the task of the gyasehene, the 'palace head', to superintend the accession and deposition of other elders. It is said that provided an elder appointed to a newly created office serves the chief and his successors loyally until his death, the office becomes vested within his own matrifamily. To this extent the perpetuation of his office depends on his own statesmanship. Dadiesoabahene explained: 'My predecessor had few elders and therefore I have created some. If he can stay with me until his death, then his successor will be chosen from the same house – if he can perform the customs by giving a sheep and paying *aseda* [thank-offering]. The stool passes to his family.' In due course the stool council will sanction the ritual blackening of his stool, affirming the family's right to the office. It is important to note, however, that very few Ahafo stools have more than two or three elderships instituted in this way, and that most councils consist mainly of relatively new offices. Fawohoyedenhene asserted: 'It is customary for a chief when he comes to the stool to create some new elders.' The historical antecedents of this 'custom' would be difficult to establish, and it may be in part a rationalisation for the difficult task of rebuilding a stool council which confronted Fawohoyedenhene and other chiefs at the time of our meetings. It should be emphasised that given the contemporary demographic and economic growth of the District many offices lack the heritage which formalises their place in stool constitution. The perpetuation of the office itself is almost as closely dependent on the personal political performance of the individual incumbent as is his own hold on his position. However important birthright and corporate claims to representation may be, it is clear that the establishment of new elderships depends very largely on the personal qualities of particular prominent citizens. As is typical of the Akan area, succession to elderships and chiefships in Ahafo ordinarily takes account of the suitability of individual candidates to perform each role. The potential incumbent of a new office is characteristically 'someone in the town who loves all the people (*odo obiara*), who knows how to address the elders, one who does not wish the town any harm' [Nkasaimhene]. 'If someone comes and stays here for a long time and I find he has a good mind and knows the customs, then I can make him my stool elder' [Ntotrosohene]. In more figurative terms, Noberkawhene explained: 'If there is someone in this town who has served me well and, in the old days, would carry my stool to war for me, I would say – 'he has become tired serving the stool, so he must be given an office (*dibre*). He may be told to become the Adontenhene or the Akyeamehene. This is how an elder is created. Anyone who works hard for the stool can be made an elder.' A qualification for eldership which seems to be increasingly important is wealth, although not many successful businessmen seem anxious to expose themselves to the demands for financial patronage which involvement in stool affairs would undoubtedly imply.

Our interviews with the Ahafo chiefs suggested that the extent to which organisational and operational norms were formalised varied according to the size, political importance and length of establishment of the stool, as well as the extent to which it had been affected by recent constitutional upheavals. Kukuom, the erstwhile paramount stool, has the best record for continuity and duration of incumbents in office; its chief gave by far the most detailed and orthodox statements of traditional norms, including those concerning appointments to elderships:

'The office of elder dates from the very beginning so if, say, the Gyasehene dies, the office must go to someone from his own family. The stool is the property of the people who set up the town, they created it and so it would be wrong to give the office to someone who comes from another family. If someone like Gyasehene dies, the office must go to one of his family. When there is no elder in a particular house the chief and his elders meet and decide to create an elder from that particular house. They consult the family, and they consider among themselves and put forward one person. The head of the family chooses the candidate. If the Gyasehene finds someone in the town who has a good mind he can recommend him as an elder.'

[Kukuomhene]

Other smaller, recently established stools have fewer elders, whose titles and functions are often unclearly defined. Protocol and procedures appear to be known only vaguely and to be observed without rigour. Gyedu is a stool small in both population and territory which does not appear in official lists earlier this century. Its present chief acknowledges political dependence on nearby Ntotroso, an extraordinary admission, particularly as the stool is statutorily regarded as independent. According to him, the appointment of new elders was an almost casual affair: 'When you have a village and someone comes to settle, if you find him sound you can make him one of your elders. The same with the next man who comes along. You, the chief, choose the elders.' Other chiefs, faced with the problems of re-establishing stool councils as a consequence of the recent N.L.C. decree, were continually confronted with the problem of what could be considered 'traditional' and what could not. Many stood accused of handing elderships out not only to families which had no established rights to them but even to those lacking the fundamental qualification of citizenship. Their attempts to keep up appearances of constitutional accord to outsiders such as ourselves were inclined to fall foul of outspoken dissent. During an interview the chief of one of the smaller Ahafo stools pointed out to us his 'gyasehene', but the latter expostulated: 'I don't want him to call me his gyasehene, for he has made the people who came here to dig [i.e. the 'stranger-farmers'] his elders.' The exchange continued: 'Yes, you are my gyasehene' . . . 'I'm no gyasehene of yours.'

What constitutes tradition can clearly be as vexed a question for the Ahafo chief or elder as it is for the sociologist. Chiefs and stool councils interpret and make tradition, and at the same time they are judged by those to whom they are politically responsible in terms of what is regarded as traditionally proper. These problems have been compounded by the rapid development of Ahafo and also by the confusion about the superior political authority to which the stools are subject. Normally it would be a function of a divisional or state council to 'stabilise' tradition, to sanction the creation of new

187

elderships and succession to office, and to control procedures affecting the realm at large. The concern of superior authority for constitutional propriety in subject realms is well illustrated by Acherensuahene's report of his recent declaration of allegiance to the Asantehene:

'When I went to Kumasi to swear before the Asantehene, he asked me to introduce my elders in rank to him. I replied that there were elders but that I had not appointed them to offices. He asked me where was my gyasehene, krontihene, akwamuhene, and when I said I had none he told me to come here and appoint them . . . I was to create the elders and send them at once to him. When I came from Kumasi I decided I should create a queen mother before I created any of the other elders, because it is the queen mother who will help me create the other offices.'

The sanction of prior authority raises one further point about stool council growth. It is recognised that there are some offices which are proper to some levels of political authority and not to others. It was sometimes asserted that only the major Ashanti Divisions (Mampong, Kokofu, etc.) should have an Asafohene, leader of the youngmen. At the other extreme, it would be politically pretentious for the headman of a subject village to give his senior men the stool ranks of nifahene, benkumhene, and so on. At this level, however, a queen mother and a gyasehene or krontihene seems permissible in Ahafo. The headman of Dechem, one of the important Goaso subject villages, explained: 'I have created three elders – but this is not a very important matter. They are strangers, but I have appointed them in the village so that they can help me whenever there is any trouble.' Such moves are significant in the aggrandisement of the community, for the village of today with its small group of senior men advising the chief may be the stool with a formalised council of its own tomorrow.

The corporate functions of the stool council in Ahafo were usually described in terms of shared responsibilities of two kinds: to resolve conflicts of interest within the stool community and to pursue communal interests with regard to the world at large. These tasks were often described in simple terms as dealing with 'trouble in the town' and 'trouble for the town'.[10] Although the magistrate's court and other new institutions have obviously taken over many of the peace-keeping and juridical functions of the stool council, elders still regard the settlement of disputes as one of their principal obligations. In their representative capacity they may be the advocates of interested parties, otherwise they are an elite body set apart from the ordinary townsfolk and collectively responsible for the welfare and progress of the community. This is commonly expressed in material terms; an elder is expected to shoulder community debts, just as he may expect to benefit from profits. Describing the stool council as a political cadre responsible for external affairs, Sankorehene drew attention to the military offices held by elders:

'We have krontihene and adontenhene; if Kwaponghene says he is coming to wage war on us the nifahene will lead the army with benkumhene following and the adontenhene next . . . If there is a war you need to have elders.'

Diplomacy is at least as important as warfare, indeed elders were expected to assure a courteous and hospitable reception for visitors and emissaries to the stool.

Taking a normative and summary view, I would describe Ahafo Stool Council procedure as follows. Meetings are convened on the chief's direction in a special chamber of the Stool 'palace', several times a month in the larger stools. They are occasioned by some routine business such as recurrent festivals, but are usually called *ad hoc* when a particular issue is presented to the chief: a quarrel in the town, a breach of custom or a letter about sanitation from the District Office. Sessions are exclusive and privileged, although in reality open doors and windows make it difficult to prevent an audience gathering. Punctuality is not stressed, although at an early stage in proceedings an inaugural libation of gin is poured, which marks the commencement of business in earnest. When the issue has been explained, by the okyeame or a petitioner, the opinion of each elder, seated in rank-order around the chief, is sought, usually but not necessarily starting with the most junior. Ideally the last opinion to be expressed is that of the chief. Coming *ex cathedra* it constitutes the final decision and marks the conclusion of discussion. After the first telling-off of opinions, a pattern of freer discussion, addressed to the chief, establishes itself. The treatment of the issue is cyclic and repetitive, involving summaries for the benefit of the frequent latecomers. Great importance is attached to good rhetoric, temperate behaviour and respect to other elders, above all to the chief. Abusiveness in this context is a *sin*, in that it must be expiated by the ritual sacrifice of a sheep. Nevertheless, everyone must have the fullest opportunity to speak, and members are more piqued if they are denied this than if their point of view does not win through. Tangential issues and matters of personal character are explored at will and, very important, elders and others in attendance are entitled to excuse themselves to consolidate opinions or clarify particular points in small groups outside. Business is transacted essentially on a face-to-face basis, with witnesses being summoned from the town and written communication kept to the barest minimum. Solutions are almost invariably sought in terms of elaborated verbal formulae, decisions to which no one objects being pursued by continual restatement and rephrasing. Fawohoyedenhene described the decision taking in his Council thus:

'If they [the elders] all agree I shall confirm their decision. If they say something I disagree with I shall ask them to explain again. They say "I have taken this or that stand for this or that reason." I tell them if I find their explanations unclear and we consider the whole issue again. Then, when I am satisfied, the matter is decided.'

This suggests the subtle influence of the chief's authority as well as the influence of his counsellors; the predominant tactic of 'talking it out' often makes meetings very lengthy, and it is by no means clear whether the passing-around of gin expedites or protracts matters.

When the chief has pronounced the decision it may be announced in the streets by the town crier or otherwise made public by the okyeame. If the issue is not within the stool council's competence it is duly referred to the town development committee or another appropriate body.

In summary, it could be said that the stool councils depend on a broad framework of formal procedural rules, within which there is, nevertheless, much tactical freedom and *ad hoc* control. This informal management of transactions is closely dependent on the distribution of authority among the participants, and may be observed most clearly in the protracted and circuitous discussion which precedes the taking of decisions. As members of academic committees might agree, the virtue of such procedure is that it is *not* constricted by rules and that men who are of venerable status within the community can depend on their respect for each other and deference to the chair to expedite matters.

b. THE AUTHORITY OF THE CHIEF

The position of the chief in Ahafo, his succession to and maintenance of office, the current bases of his authority and his rights and duties, may be taken to apply to a large extent to the stool elder who is, in effect, the 'chief' of a community segment.

Kukuomhene gave by far the fullest account of the norms governing the selection and installation of a chief in his community. He was rightly cautious about the general applicability of these norms throughout Ahafo, observing: 'I know little of other towns, I know only of my own.' However, the less generous accounts given by other chiefs contain in outline most of the features he mentions:

KUKUOMHENE: 'When the stool is vacant or a chief dies, the elders of the town ask the queen mother to give them someone to be enstooled as a chief. The queen mother will select someone from the royal family. If she makes a choice and they like the man they enstool him as chief. If not they tell her so. If the second and third persons she proposes are rejected, the elders have to make their own choice. They make him a chief. When the queen mother has made her choice he is brought to the okyeame, who introduces him to the townspeople. If they approve they claim *apatom nsa* [about £4 13s 0d]. That is the first thing he has to pay. Then one case of gin. They then tell him they are going to make him a chief. We then pass him on to the gyasehene and we fix a date about 40 days away – or any time we think fit. We summon all the people and tell them we have a candidate for the chiefship. In due course the krontihene, gyasehene and all the people will meet, and the okyeame is asked to show the man to the townspeople. First he must have his share of the money, then he makes the announcement. When he has been shown to the people the stool is fetched. Ours is a big stool (*akonnua kese*) on which no one is allowed to sit. When there is a ceremony it is carried there but no one is allowed to sit on it. When there is a new chief we set him down on the stool three times.

'When you have been put to the stool three times you have to swear an oath before the elders. You say *Yawada* [Thursday], and say that the ancestral stool which was vacant has been taken over by you. You swear not to lead the people astray, to be faithful to the people, and just. When you have sworn all the people shout *"ose!"* [hurrah!]. They then ask you to sit and all the elders come and swear allegiance to you. They swear that they will serve you and will not lead you astray. They say that if they bring a case before you and settle it, they will not complain. They swear before you one by one. Then they put you in a palanquin and carry you to the palace. They send you to the gyasehene and hand over to you all the property and regalia of the stool – that is on another day, it is the chief who fixes the date when he goes to the palace. The ceremonies are held outside until they take you to the palace. On the day you go to the palace you have to kill a sheep to appease the spirits.'

This account expresses quite clearly the 'say' which the various parties to accession may expect to have: the queen mother and the royal family, the elders of the stool, the townspeople, and the population of the realm at large.[11] As the 'pretending' paramount chief of Ahafo, Kukuomhene makes no reference to the sanction of superior authority normally required in accession. In Ashanti, a new chief would be introduced to the divisional or paramount chief to whom his stool was responsible and, if so entitled, would be installed formally as a member of the Divisional or State Council. It is certain that the criteria on which the candidate is assessed changes subtly as this widening range of political interests is brought to bear. The royal family may propose a candidate most likely to look after its own interests in the community at large. From the community's point of view, however, a chief should have no such sectional interests at heart, but should be the impartial moderator of the stool as a whole and the advocate of its corporate interests. For this reason it is asserted that a chief may not take up office if he is party to any litigation or unresolved disputes within the community. *Adwene pa*, good character or attitudes, is the most common expression used to summarise these very relative attributes of public officeholders. Otherwise, the physical health and material wealth of the candidate are qualities sought by virtually all parties to the selection process.

Dependence and opportunity

Kukuomhene's account emphasises the sanctioning role of the stool elders, enacted in the rites of succession by their lifting the chief (almost) onto the stool three times. Later they in turn acknowledge his new status as moderator of community interests by swearing allegiance to him and agreeing to accept his final word in communal decision making. The accession ceremonies are punctuated by formal payments from the chief which serve to endorse the changes in his status. Finally he is entrusted with the paraphernalia of office, the ornaments, umbrellas and other accessories which are the important material expressions of his authority. His move to the 'palace' (*ahenfie*) symbolises his dissociation from the house and community segment in which he has lived hitherto. He may not necessarily live in the palace full-time, and in Ahafo it is commonly put in the queen mother's charge, but for all official purposes it is his home, the political centre and gathering point of the stool community. To complete his transition from the private citizen to the moderator and representative of his people the new chief acquires the name of an illustrious predecessor; thus Yaw Brayie became, on accession to the Aboum stool, Nana Atechie Mensa.

In all but two of the Ahafo stools, Mim and Sienchem, succession to chiefly office is matrilineal. This is normally expressed in the rule that a candidate's maternal grandfather must have been a chief. Although this pattern is general in the Akan area, there are important cases where paternal succession is either permitted or is the rule. They raise interesting structural questions, notably how ruling groups are perpetuated where matrilineal idioms otherwise prevail. Sienchemhene acknowledged: 'Our stool is different . . . we have no special royal family. We succeed paternally (*ye di agya dee*).' Asked whether Sienchem had a queen mother and on what terms she was appointed, the chief explained: 'When the first ancestor came here he brought his wife and he was told that when she bore a child that would provide the heir. Since we do not marry from our own family when we take someone to sit [on the queen mother's stool] then she *becomes* my sister . . . she is from my family but it is because she is queen mother that she becomes my sister. But her daughter can never become queen mother.' The chief noted that his predecessor had in fact been the queen mother's son, but that 'it was wrong to make that man a chief; because he can not perform the customs it would be detrimental to the community if he remained long in office'. In his opinion, such an infringement of tradition was typical of the era of C.P.P. rule in Ghana. Succession to the chiefship of Mim, according to the present Mimhene, may be either matrilineal or paternal. Asked whether this was 'uncustomary' by Ashanti standards, Mimhene replied: 'it is Ashanti custom. Even in Bantama, the nearest place to Kumasi, who is supposed to be the prime minister of Kumasi, he is paternally inherited.' The principle on which paternal succession in Mim is apparently based is the ruling segment's bond with Akwaboa, its community of origin in Ashanti. Akwaboa is the Kumasi stool to which Mim is reckoned to be subject and through which its allegiance to the Asantehene is expressed. Mimhene explained that a son of a chief is eligible for the stool so long as he can trace a direct maternal link to the Akwaboa community:

'Our stool takes both (matrilineal and paternal) because all we who are in this town hall from a place called Akwaboa, and those Akwaboa peoples are the royals of this place. And when a man is elected as a chief in this place and he does well, after his death he can either choose his nephew, his maternal nephew, to succeed him, or his paternal son. My own son can succeed me . . . If they find that the maternal sons are not good they can take one of my sons. But it is a taboo if you don't take one who hails from Akwaboa, our place. Otherwise he can't succeed our stool. If your son hails from Akwaboa, he can succeed you. His mother must come from Akwaboa.'

This rule is perhaps the most salient expression of the importance of the community of origin in stool organisation in Ahafo. Mimhene was emphatic that the relationship with Akwaboa had nothing whatever to do with matrilinearity or clanship; from the chief's point of view the bond was perpetuated by marriage: 'If you have married from abroad, any sister village, then your son can never be a chief'.

An examination of the reported relationships among successive incumbents of each Ahafo stool over the last twenty years or so indicates that although a norm of unilineal succession may be strongly asserted, in reality the orthodox line has been interrupted or even changed in all but a few cases. The most common explanations of such deviation are the need to enstool one who is technically ineligible to act as regent, and the constitutional vagaries brought by political party competition in the 1950s. Chiefs accounted for deviation from the unilineal norm in these terms:

KENYASE I HENE: 'My predecessor was a son of the stool of Kenyase. Formerly my mother was the queen mother and my father the okyeame of Kenyase, and at that time the royals were too young, so my mother borrowed someone from outside to be a chief. When I grew up, my mother destooled that person and put me on. He was one of my uncle's sons, a close relation of my mother's but not a proper royal of the stool.'
NOBERKAWHENE: 'Kwaku Nsiah was no relation of mine at all, he was by no means supposed to accede to the stool. It was through the C.P.P. government that he got it. He has nothing at all to do with the stool.'

More detailed enquiries usually suggested competition for office among individuals and groups in the ruling segment or within the community at large. There are several notable cases where a tenuous claim to office has clearly been offset by the strong personal qualities of an individual. There are enough examples of this kind of accession to oblige one to take account of criteria of eligibility other than strict matrilinearity. The competition for chiefship, often strenuous, suggests that there are interests involved in the acquisition and maintenance of office which are unlikely to appear in the normative accounts given by the chiefs themselves. The perquisites of chiefship include fees, the usufruct of stool farms, buildings and other property, and opportunities to collect 'thank offerings' (*aseda*) from supplicants or to cream-off revenue accruing to the stool. In fact, chiefs are inclined to complain of the heavy material demands made on their private resources by their public responsibilities, but the distinction between the chief's personal and his stool property is quite strongly asserted, and there cannot be many chiefs who relinquish office much worse off than when they acceded.

Apart from these material advantages, chiefship has other attractions; it bestows honour and authority on the individual and, if he survives well enough to die in office, the prospect of a kind of immortality, the ceremonial blackening of his personal stool and promotion to the venerated ranks of his ancestors. Chiefs speak altruistically of the sense of responsibility which prompts them to accept office, in terms of serving both their lineage and their community. Local leaders generally, whether chiefs, local councillors or Members of Parliament, like to explain how they were talked into accepting office – particularly by one in a position of high authority or respect. For example, Mimhene explained:

'I was appealed by the elders to succeed [my predecessor]. I said I can continue my work as a clerk. At that time I was secretary attached to Goaso District Committee. I objected to being a chief because of my duties, but they pressed me. Even the Akwaboahene in Kumasi asked me. Because of this constant pressing, I have to take it. I was not candidated, I was nominated.'

If there is a stereotype of the Akan chief in the contemporary Ghanaian press or literature it is of an aging man of family and property, a dignified figure in his ornate *kente* cloth and sandals, uneducated but wise without being over-serious, a man with time on his hands to enjoy his political craft and the gin with which his supplicants are expected to ply him. The *curriculum vitae* of the Ahafo chiefs indicates that they are predominantly men in their fifties and sixties, although at one extreme Nkasaimhene is probably a centenarian and at the other, Anwiamhene is a young man in his late twenties. They had lived all their lives in Ahafo, with the exception of five of them who had spent periods working outside the district. Table 3 records approximately how long each chief had held office – not necessarily at one stretch, for many have had two terms, having been reinstated after the 1966 coup d'état. All the chiefs had their own substantial cocoa farms, but were understandably more reluctant to give details of their private income than their private expenditure. Many complained of the expense of running a large household; all had wives, 16 were polygynous and several had more children than they could enumerate in the immediate interview situation. It is interesting that more chiefs felt that feeding and clothing dependants was the greater financial drain than the demands of education.

Only five chiefs had any kind of education in the formal sense, three of these being literate in English (Table 3). The Commissioners reporting on a new constitution for Ghana in 1968 lamented the lack of education among

TABLE 3. *Age, periods in office and education of the 28 Ahafo chiefs* (Age reckoned from interviews and enstoolment registration)

	Approximate age of chief (to Dec. 1968)	Years absent from Ahafo	Years in office (to Dec. 1968)	Number of times in office	With some education
Aboum	36	26	3	1	Technical training
Acherensua	60	—	2	1	—
Akrodie	60	—	9	1	—
Anwiam	28	?	10	1	Primary
Asufufuo	55?	—	12?	2	—
Ayumso	66	—	21	1	—
Dadiesoaba	40+	—	12	1	—
Dantano	64	—	13?	1	—
Etwineto	70?	—	4	2	—
Fawohoyeden	38	—	4	1	—
Goaso	50+	—	7	2	—
Gyedu	70	—	17	1	—
Hwidiem	56	8?	8	2	'a little'
Kenyase I	40+	—	6	2	—
Kenyase II	38?	?	10?	1	Standard 7
Kukuom	60	—	23?	1	—
Kwakunyuma	60	—	12	2	—
Kwapong	48	—	2	1	—
Mehame	55?	—	7	2	—
Mim	65	12?	15	2	Literate in English
Nkasaim	100?	—	22?	2	—
Noberkaw	56?	—	16	2	—
Ntotroso	34	—	2	1	—
Pomakrom	87	?	?	2	—
Sankore	65	6?	16?	2	—
Siena	?	?	?	1	—
Sienchem	60	—	6?	2	—
Wamahinso	38	?	3	1	—

Ghanaian chiefs: 'the failure of the chiefs to adapt the institution (of chief-ship) to bring it in line with the modern democratic process may be attributed, except in a few instances, to the half hearted attempt and, in other cases, complete neglect to educate stool or skin occupants.' The Commissioners went on to recommend compulsory education for all stool heirs, optimistically feeling that this 'would be the surest means of rationalising the institution to bring it in tune with the processes of modern government'.[12] Certainly, not many of the Ahafo chiefs could boast of much modern, worldly experience. Five had been engaged, before accession, in small-scale commercial enterprises in Kumasi, selling roofing sheets or cloth, or working as carpenters and tailors. Five other chiefs had been engaged locally in non-farming activities, cocoa-broking, timber-dealing, shopkeeping, weaving and stonemasonry, but it was generally felt that such activities were not compatible with the tenure of chiefly office. Only three chiefs were in any sense active businessmen. Kenyase II hene was a successful timber contractor, Wamahinsohene the owner of a small fleet of transport vehicles, and Aboumhene, a former Department of Agriculture technical officer, was engaged in trading oper-ations in Kumasi. It was apparent that these enterprises could be reconciled with chiefly status because they were conducted outside the stool community and because of their scale and the relative wealth they assured. Local and lucrative occupations would have been regarded as mercenary and demeaning. Nevertheless, it was clear that chiefs could, and did, invest private wealth in shops, public transport vehicles and other enterprises in which their active involvement was minimal.

The chiefs of the C.P.P. era, many of whom were enstooled quite candidly without any orthodox claims to office, and were duly ousted after the 1966 coup, were generally younger, better educated and more urbane than their predecessors and successors. We shall refer to them again in the context of the Kukuom–Ahafo State Council. One cannot concisely assess the effect of this brief shift towards openly competitive terms for the succession to chiefship in Ahafo, but certainly a precedent of a kind has been set which neither the people nor the chiefs themselves can readily ignore and which may, eventu-ally, be expressed in some change in the personal qualifications expected of officeholders.

Taking a quite different perspective, let us examine chiefship briefly in the context of national legislation, considering the interests and intentions which appear to underlie statutory change and the way this has been interpreted locally in Ahafo.

As we noted in chapter 1, government (*aban*) is seen somewhat ambigu-ously as being second only to God in its power but as being, at the same time, a force quite distinct from traditional authority. Thus a chief may say that 'nothing is impossible to the government', and announce a few minutes later that 'government has no say in chieftaincy affairs'. Underlying this is an apparent distinction between the ability of government to regulate the organisation and competence of chiefship, and a denial of its right to interfere in the politics of chiefship. Other chapters of this book deal more fully with changes in chiefly authority earlier this century and in the context of local government development. In summary, the circumscription of chiefly authority over the last twenty years has been directed towards limiting the judicial and executive competence of the chiefs, establishing economic controls and stabilising processes of accession and deposition. A major trend has been the central government's attempts to define the structures and functions of chiefs throughout Ghana in nationally uniform terms, and to standardise for administrative convenience such terms as 'chief', and 'stool'. Although such changes have certainly implied an overall reduction of chiefly authority, repeated guarantees have been given for the 'survival' of traditional political institutions for the sake of their practical governmental value. The Commission enquiring into a new constitution for the Second Republic of Ghana reasserted: 'we disagree with that school of thought which holds that chieftaincy occupies merely an ornamental or honorific status in our society', but pointed out that the value of the institution was essentially local.[13] This re-emphasises the discontinuity which still exists between the central and the local political institutions in Ghana, and the misinterpretation prevalent on both sides. The tendency in Accra to view chiefship in abstract 'cultural' terms – manifest in traditional robes, first-fruit ceremonies illustrated in daily newspapers, and so on – seems to reflect an imperfect understanding of the essentially local bases of chiefly authority which, as we shall see in due course, have remained substantially beyond the scope of central government legislation. The circumscription of chiefship has tended to follow in the wake of local government reform, and has rarely been tackled as an end in itself.

If the central authorities' main worry in implementing the Local Government Ordinance of 1951 was the involvement of the chiefs in democratic processes, the latter appear to have been more immediately concerned about the erosion of their economic privileges. Over the next two years the Ministry of Local Government was obliged to issue a series of circulars explaining the terms in which responsibility for the collection of stool land revenues had been transferred to the new Local Councils. One of these interpreted the relevant sections of the Ordinance (71–76) in detail, emphasising that it did not affect the basic ownership and allocation principles of stool land.[14] Ever since, the issue of revenues has remained central to the Ahafo chiefs' suspicion of the central authorities' interference with their privileges. The 1952 State Councils (Ashanti) Ordinance, part and parcel of the local government reform of the early 1950s, sought to protect stool property both from outsiders and from abuse by the officeholders themselves, in addition to attempting to regularise matters of membership and procedure. Section 44 of the Ordinance demanded that all subjects should assist and respect a State Council or chief, on payment of a maximum fine of £5 – something short of the capital penalty of bygone days. Some attention was also given to matters of definition, notably of 'customary law': '. . . a rule or a body of rules regulating rights and imposing correlative duties being a rule or body of rules which obtains and is fortified by established usage and which is appropriate and applicable to any particular cause, action, suit, matter, dispute, issue or question . . .'[15] It is clear that this legislation was more for the guidance of administrators and the senior councils of Ashanti than for the information of chiefs in the rural communities.

The first constitution of Ghana in 1957 undertook to 'guarantee and preserve' chiefship, but the most serious reassessment of chiefly authority came four years later with the Chieftaincy Act (no. 81) of 1961. Many Ahafo chiefs who were not of the C.P.P. pursuasion recalled with indignation Dr Nkrumah's purported assertion that he would 'set the chiefs running without their sandals', but the 1961 Act does not reflect a particularly harsh attitude to traditional authority. Its main intention seems to have been to put chiefly institutions on a nationally uniform, bureaucratic footing. Chiefs were categorised in four grades as follows:

(*a*) The Asantehene and Paramount Chiefs who are not subordinate to the Asantehene;
(*b*) Paramount Chiefs who are subordinate to the Asantehene;
(*c*) Divisional Chiefs;
(*d*) Adikrofo [headmen] and other Chiefs not falling within the preceding categories.[16]

The competence of chiefs in matters of jurisdiction and stool property was quite rigorously defined, and such bureaucratic procedures as minuting, accounting and auditing were demanded of state councils. National control of chiefship was vested in the Minister of Local Government, who had the final sanction in matters of accession and deposition and who could 'at any time withdraw recognition from a chief if . . . (he) considers it to be in the public interest'.[17] However, a section labelled 'undermining power of a chief' read as follows:

3. (1) Subject to the provision of this Act, a person shall be guilty of an offence if he
(a) commits any act with intent to undermine the lawful power, and authority of a Chief; or
(b) fails or refuses to recognise a Chief.

(2) Nothing in this section shall prevent any person from bringing a claim or complaint against, or instituting proceedings for the destoolment of, a Chief in accordance with the procedure sanctioned by customary law.

For those chiefs who knew and could cite it, this section was a strong supplement to their authority, and could be evoked by the C.P.P. in its dealing with unwanted elements. It also reflected a government intention to slow down the rapid turnover in chiefs which had resulted from their involvement in party politics. A ministerial circular addressed to regional and district officers observed:

The cabinet was informed at a meeting held on the 27th October by Osagyefo the President that the practice of preferring charges against Chiefs and attempting by subversive means to effect their destoolment was becoming rather prevalent throughout the country. Apart from the heavy expenditure such disputes involve, they tend to undermine the institution of chieftaincy.

(2) My Minister would be grateful therefore if you would ensure that section 3 of the Chieftaincy Act, 1961 (Act 81), which makes it an offence to undermine the authority of a Chief, is adequately enforced in your Region in order to reduce such practices to a minimum.[18]

The C.P.P. government's concern is further indicated in a Legislative Instrument entitled 'Chieftaincy (Destoolment Proceedings) Regulations 1963'.[19] This obliged all traditional councils to 'make and forward to the Minister a list of the names and any customary posts or titles of all persons who are entitled by custom to give final approval to the destoolment of a chief'. For official purposes, an 'elder' was by definition a person appearing on such a list. The Instrument further defined the circumstances in which a meeting of these elders to consider the deposition of a chief should be convened and conducted, and the way in which the issue should be referred to a superior traditional council. An appendix included a specimen form and questionnaire which was then required for transmission to the Minister.

A further ministerial circular interpreting the 1961 Chieftaincy Act drew attention to the terms in which the chief's judicial authority over his subjects should be exercised. Although his right to arbitrate was recognised, it was pointed out that a subject was not obliged to accept a settlement and could appeal to the civil authorities to hear his case or override a judgement. It is unlikely that many Ahafo citizens were aware of this provision, and it is of interest primarily as an indication of the ambivalent official view of traditional authority – that it was to a large extent supplementary to civil processes and dependent on popular acceptance.

In the early 1960s the confused view of 'tradition' as retrograde in a socialist state and at the same time as a valuable part of the national heritage continued to prevail in central government circles. In August 1960 a letter from the Principal Secretary to the Ministry of Justice filtered through the Regional and District Commissioners to the Kukuom-Ahafo State Council. This letter pointed out that

certain traditional and constitutional set-ups or stools have been enshrouded with archaic and obsolete procedures . . . these out-of-date procedures have almost always been a source of great inconvenience when traditional and constitutional matters came up for attention . . . The time has come for these cankers to be examined and uprooted from the fabric of our society. It is therefore [the Ministry's] wish that you impress on all State Councils the need to revise or modify the procedures. This is a national crusade in which you are expected to take an active part.[20]

Having been thoroughly confused by this circular, the Ahafo State Council was visited two years later by the regional organiser of the Brong–Ahafo Arts Committee who

in his address dwelt at length on the importance and necessity of discovering most of our traditions, customs and festivals which had died down or [were] lost from the face of Ghana through the British colonial mis-rule. He therefore appealed to the Chiefs to co-operate and help the Government to bring to light our Traditions, customs and festivals which were buried by the Colonialists . . . [21]

The C.P.P.'s reputation for eroding chiefly authority disposed the police–military National Liberation Council benevolently towards the chiefs in the years following the 1966 coup d'état. Several N.L.C. decrees sought to redress some of the malpractices alleged to have occurred during the C.P.P. era, notably in matters of accession and deposition. A Chieftaincy Secretariat was established, but soon had more business to deal with than it could reasonably tackle. The Commissioners under the chairmanship of Mr Justice Akufo-Addo responsible for proposing a new constitution for Ghana felt obliged 'to put the whole problem of the place and status of chiefs in the government and administration of this country in the proper perspective', describing this as 'a most important and vexed question' and as a 'controversy which has raged over the years'. They recalled the 1949 Coussey Commission's observation that 'no African of the Gold Coast is without some admiration for the best aspects of chieftaincy' and recommended a thorough integration of the chiefs into the processes of local government – the level at which the essentially local virtues of their authority could be put to the best advantage nationally. At the same time, however, the Commissioners complained of 'the failure of the chiefs to adapt the institution (chieftaincy) to bring it in line with the modern democratic process'. They felt that the formal gazetting of accessions and depositions was the surest way to stem the flow of incumbents in and out of office: 'In this way the chiefs will be saved from becoming pawns in the game of politics.'[22]

When it was promulgated in 1969 the new Ghanaian constitution once again asserted: 'The institution of chieftaincy together with its Traditional Councils as established by customary law and usage is hereby guaranteed.'[23] A national, and regional Houses of Chiefs were set up to administer traditional affairs but at the lower level the integrated traditional/secular Local Councils for which the constitution made provision were not established before the Progress Party government of Dr Busia was overthrown by the second military coup d'état of 1972.

When we look at the individual stool communities in Ahafo the 'homogenised' chiefship for which the central authorities have legislated over the last two decades is not much in evidence. It is rather the organisational variation, the reflection of relative political growth, which is apparent. Undoubtedly legislation has been directed most explicitly towards the higher levels of chiefly authority, the State and Divisional Councils of Ghana. For the lower levels there is an apparent concern, inevitably delegated to the District Officer, that whatever is beyond the reach of the statutes with regard to stool organisation should be 'traditionally proper'. However arbitrary his judgement of this may be the District Officer, even if he has not been reared in Akan society, is aware of certain basic principles which he may be concerned to see applied. Foremost of these is the well-known tenet that a chief must take counsel; several of the recently reinstated chiefs in Ahafo reported that they had been chivvied by the District Administrative Officer to establish new elderships. This officer could speak in detail about 'Ashanti stool constitution' and implied that the application of his model was in some sense consonant with efficiency and good government. Although he would certainly see the chiefs as principal generators of political trouble, he would probably agree with the secondary school essayist who wrote that where they are properly constituted traditional authorities 'are almost indispensable ... in that they help to release the Central Government from some minor numerous tasks; and also help the people to know how to go about their own matters without any helping hand from the Central Government'.[24]

Several interview questions were directed towards discovering how the chiefs construed their relationship with central government and their political dependence upon it. A direct question 'does the government (at that time the National Liberation Council) help and support you' invariably elicited a positive response, hardly surprising if our status as investigators was at all equivocal. Responses to the follow-up question, however, indicated the prevailing interest in aggrandisement; asked: 'how could the government help and support you *more*', many chiefs said it should authorise their elevation to paramount status or, in more general terms, solve the vexed question of the Ahafo State Council. Thereafter, reference was usually made to the need for improved local amenities, schools, clinics, and roads. Dadiesoabahene expressed the patronage of the government thus: 'Everyone who is doing his duty likes to get promotion. Were the government to offer me the paramountcy I should be happy. Then everyone here would be able to say that since I have become a chief I have been able to raise up the stool.' It could do this because 'government has the power as it has the soldiers and police . . . nothing is impossible to the government – they have created many district paramount chiefs'.

Most of the Ahafo chiefs and elders have a broad, critical awareness of the transformations in traditional authority during this century, and the transference of many of their functions to national, central agencies. After some experimentation, questions on this subject were phrased in terms of four historical periods: the traditional precolonial era; British overrule; the years of C.P.P. rule from Independence in 1957 to the 1966 coup d'état; and the 'present' government of the National Liberation Council. The transition from traditional to British rule was usually described in terms of the replacement of power based essentially on physical coercion by the civil processes resulting from the introduction of '*aban*' – government. Noberkawhene explained:

'They [the British] came and changed some of our rules. In the early days when someone had committed an offence his head was cut off. When they came they told the Asantehene that this practice was bad. We were happy to see that rule cancelled. Then when you offended you were sent to court for sentence.'

Mimhene took quite a scholarly view of the slow but hopefully persistent development of good government:

'Before, this Ghana was a very fearful place. Even our own place like Kumasi, when a royal dies they execute some people. About 100 people should be executed. But when the colonial government came and the churches were introduced, gradually we did abolish this. I compare this to bribery and corruption. Now that slavery and execution of people are done away, when a good government comes in a few years we shall also do away with bribery and corruption.'

Several chiefs observed that the decentralised pattern of the precolonial Ashanti political organisation allowed the chiefs and elders considerable freedom of action in their own communities.

In those days Osagyefo Asantehene was our ruler, and when someone gave me offence I went and reported him through the [Kumasi] Okyeame . . . If there is something to discuss and we find [the Asantehene's] decision unsatisfactory, we can meet and then go and tell him – "well, you are our chief, but we are not happy about your decision" – and he would listen to us. He would say – "you are my servants, I withdraw it as you do not understand it". The way we served him was not by carrying him food and firewood. We simply went there to pay our respects and then came back' (Gyeduhene).

Some felt that this freedom bordered on anarchy: 'in those days everyone relied on himself; if I thought your town bigger than mine I could come and fight you, and if I won I took your town ... We were governing ourselves, but because it was no good the whites came and showed us how to govern' (Hwidiemhene). Although they attached much importance to political changes wrought by the arrival of 'government' with its courts, police and white officials, the Ahafo chiefs also emphasised the effect of Christianity, education and 'civilisation'. These were usually characterised as the blessings of colonial expansion; specific accounts of its disadvantages dwelt on the licensing of guns and ammunition, the need to transport the bodies of those who had been killed long distances for autopsy, and other relatively minor inconveniences. A few felt that the economic strength of chieftaincy had been undermined, but this was a criticism more commonly levelled against the C.P.P. government. It was interesting to hear the British praised, in not altogether complimentary terms, for their political acumen in dealing with the chiefs. 'I can think of no bad point about them,' Sienchemhene confessed, 'but then if a white man was putting pepper in your eyes you would never guess'.

Asked in which period they felt they or their predecessors enjoyed the most authority (*tumi*), the Ahafo chiefs tended to favour the years of British overrule. Their main index of relative authority was the extent to which the 'youngmen' showed them respect and obedience. Other criteria were the extent of their judicial competence, access to lands revenues and – significantly – whether or not they were united in a State Council organisation. Nkasaimhene was one of twelve chiefs favouring the colonial period: 'During that time the government made me a big chief, so that when I talked people trembled. You say something and I challenge you, I send you to the government – then you will not get off lightly. That is why we liked that government.' Akrodiehene took the same view: 'In those days, when someone wanted to do something on your land he had to come and see you personally. Nowadays if someone wants to cut timber, a man sitting in Accra issues the authority ... There are many differences between those days and now. Even in those days, it was the chiefs who sent their own clerks to collect the land revenues, but nowadays we don't get as much as a sniff at it.' Goasohene recalled: 'We were sitting on the local court in those days. We had our own policemen, and if you spoke against any chief an order would be given to come and arrest you. All these were taken away when Kwame Nkrumah came . . . We were very happy indeed during the Gold Coast days.' Mimhene saw the colonial government's relationship with the chiefs in much broader terms: 'This place was termed a Commonwealth Nation – one part of it. The English people have a very recognition [*sic*] towards their king in England, so when they came they also met our natural rulers so they showed the same recognition towards our chiefs here. Our chiefs were having dignity here. Then Kwame Nkrumah came to reduce it.' Kwaponghene felt that good communications was the virtue of this relationship: 'The British did not trifle with the chiefs at all. If they wanted to tell the chief anything they would go to the chief's house. Kwame Nkrumah would sit far away and say "this shall be done".'

Most of the seven chiefs who regarded the precolonial era as their political heyday mentioned the essentially physical expression of power. 'In those days people respected their neighbours,' Dadiesoabahene explained; the authority of the chiefs was not questioned, and civic achievements were considerable: 'In those days we worked well, but nowadays if we beat the gong for communal labour, you find the people slipping away after a couple of hours.'

The comparisons between these periods and the years of C.P.P. rule were usually pernicious. Many chiefs felt, in the words of Kenyase I hene, that the C.P.P. had 'cut back all our power', but that since the 1966 coup it was 'reviving a little bit, but not in full measure' (Mimhene). With good reason, the chiefs reinstated by the N.L.C. spoke warmly of the police–military government, but only Sankorehene regarded the present regime as the acme of chiefly authority. The three who favoured the C.P.P. era spoke realistically of the physical sanctions which might be deployed through the party: 'If, as a C.P.P. man, I said that you should be removed now,' Wamahinsohene recalled darkly, 'they would remove you.' Ayumsohene and Etwinetohene pointed out that the short-lived Kukuom–Ahafo State Council was contemporaneous with the years of C.P.P. rule: 'the chiefs had the most power after Independence, for then they had a State Council to discuss their affairs. When a youngman stood in front of a chief and abused him the government would fine him £10 or £20. At the moment there is nothing like that' (Ayumsohene).

A few chiefs – all of whom had been reinstated by the N.L.C. Decree in 1966 – felt insecure among their people and doubtful of public support for their role: 'The chiefs cannot walk in the main streets,' one of them observed, 'but rather go by the side streets so that people cannot pester them.' These chiefs put a high value on central government backing:

'It would be good to have chiefs in the National Assembly because when the elders are there the young men will not have the opportunity to play the fool.

You can see how there are some people in the town here making nonsense against me. The chiefs would be able to speak up and get back some of their former power. The youngmen do not like the chiefs just now. They do not respect chiefs' (Goasohene).

It was clear to Goasohene that no body politic (*oman*), whether Goaso or Ghana, could survive without the chief's essential and exclusive functions:

'If we just send the young men to the assembly they will not know the customary rites to perform. A place without a chief becomes a public (*sic*) place; as there is no respect, everyone speaks as he likes. Where there is a chief, an offender can be threatened to stop. A chief has to perform the customary rites to bring progress. Where there are no chiefs people will just carry on in the community as they please.'

It is apparent, however, that both the central government and the chiefs themselves regard chiefly authority as something which is essentially local in derivation, and which can be guaranteed and modulated but not transformed by statute. Let us therefore continue our examination of chiefly authority in the local functions it performs and in the communal political uses to which it may be put.

The value of a chief as a communal symbol remains great. The office is the kernel of community growth, and is expressive of historical continuity – in the popular phrase – 'from time immemorial'. The chief's rank, headman or wing-chief, expounds the community's position in the wider political structure of the state. The chief epitomises the principle of citizenship against all outsiders, whether they be stranger-farmers or the officers of the Ghana government. As we have seen, the office is set apart in many ways. The chief is *primus inter pares* among a category of elders marked out as a broad stratum from the commoners, the 'youngmen'. Today the elders reinforce this distinction in their dress and in their bearing among their people. The chief is also set apart from the segments which comprise the community, and is the moderator of their interests and symbol of their conjunction. He is the controller of spiritual affairs, the communal relationships with stool ancestors and local gods and fetishes. Through them he is custodian of the health and prosperity of his people, a bridge between the physical and metaphysical welfare of his realm. All these may be onerous responsibilities, and the distinction which is constantly sustained between incumbent and office makes the citizens attentive that the man is up to the job. Today the chief is subject to this scrutiny particularly in his role as manager of the material resources of the stool and of public decision making.

The political importance of chiefly office, the popular respect it is accorded, and the legitimacy of an individual's claim to it are justified in its heritage, expressed in historical narrative. In a discussion of this elsewhere[25] we have noted that a history is in a very real sense the property of an individual or group. As custodian of his community's interests it is the chief's right, and also his duty, to tell history in such formal contexts as litigation. Accounts of the past are continually discussed and reshaped by those in whose hands the political initiative rests – typically the stool council. A stool history thus draws together past events, present political interests and future communal aspirations; the stool regalia and paraphernalia of office, the official oath and the libations poured to the spirits and the ancestors all serve as mnemonics for this otherwise dynamic, oral tradition. The chief is the living representative of a line of predecessors of whose doings the histories tell, and whose importance to him rests not only in the fact that they are the previous incumbents of the stool but also in that they are his own immediate lineage forebears. As people of the spirit world (*asamanfo*) their powers are more diffuse and metaphysical than his, but in the realm of political action he is their agent and is as responsible to them as to the corporate interests of the stool community at large. They will expect to be shown respect on all formal occasions and to be given their 'share' in the form of a libation whenever there is drink about. They have the habits and whims of old men, and often the chief must adopt a tone of cajolery to ensure that they apply their spiritual attentions to the corporate growth and welfare of the stool.

The stool holy days, which demand the participation of the whole community, are occasions for the pouring of libations. Thursday, the oath-day of the former Ahafo State Council and the day of the Ashanti Earth Goddess Asase Yaa, is the most generally observed holy day. It is considered polluting to work in one's farm on this day, and although it is difficult to assess the extent to which the rule is ignored or circumvented it is still unquestionably the day on which one is best assured of finding the master of the house at home.

The spiritual bases of chiefly authority certainly warrant close attention in Ahafo. The district's reputation for its dense population of gods and fetishes (see chapter 4) is largely attributable to the orientation of settlement around the Tano river, sacred throughout much of the Akan area. Innumerable fetishes (*abosom*) have been fished out of the Tano and carried into communities all over the area.[26] Most commonly they are given a Twi day-name referring to when they were discovered, and Tano (or Tei), the name of their 'father': e.g., Tano Kofi, Tei Kwadwo. Interpretation of the plurality of 'Tei Kofis' in Ahafo presents no problem to an Ahafo chief, although assessments of their relative virtue are inevitably subjective:

'The Tei Kofi here in Ahafo is one Tei Kofi from the Tano. The Tano gave us Tei Kofi. All the Tei Kofis, Siena's, Anwiam's, Asufufuo's, Kwapong's,

Noberkaw's, all these came from the Tano...If someone puts up a shed and say he has Tei Kofi there and calls the people to worship, that may be a different kind of Tei Kofi, not the one we have here in Ahafo...If someone goes to the North [of Ghana] and gets a fetish and brings it here and calls it Tei Kofi that is not the real *Tano* Tei Kofi' (Asufufuohene).

The higher, more abstract deity Nyame, regarded as cognate with the God of Christianity and Islam, does not receive much direct attention from the people of Ahafo, but ceremonies for the best-reputed fetishes still draw large crowds. Even the educated and literate chiefs are convincing in their assurances that their respect for these spiritual forces in their communities is genuine.

In Ahafo, there is a distinction, which certainly warrants closer investigation, between the fetishes and the fewer, loftier entities we might call gods. Although they may be categorised as *abosom*, the latter are named geographical features such as the Tano and the Mim rock (*Mim buo*). They are immovable and pre-date settlement; as Aboumhene explained (in English): 'A fetish is one which can be taken away from somewhere, or brought from somewhere, but a god is the one we come to meet. A fetish may tell you "there is a god here" – that is, immovable property.' The distinction also appears in such comments as 'There is no fetish at Kenyase, Kenyase has a rock (*obuo*)' (Hwidiemhene). Unlike the territorial gods, the fetishes are mobile, have special efficacies, depend on people to look after them and give expression to their powers, and are more ephemeral in that they tend to rely on the good will of satisfied customers in a quite keen market. The importance of many of them rests in their association with a group or segment within the community, or with the community as a whole. Some are reckoned to have been carried into Ahafo by original settlers and, like others adopted locally, have propitiated the establishment and growth of stool and their component segments. 'The duty of the Fetish', Kukuomhene explained, 'is to encourage people to settle here.'

Some fetishes are very active in that their oracular, healing and other powers are regularly tapped through the agency of a special priest. Occasionally a priest may take responsibility for two or more fetishes but the choice is held to rest with the latter. A fetish may thrive on a particular aptitude, curing impotence or ascertaining marital fidelity, and some, moving with the times, have acquired skills in bringing success to commercial ventures and promotion to those involved in modern bureaucracies. They demand heavy fees and some humouring, but although their clientele may come from far and wide they are reckoned to have a primary obligation to the immediate community in which they are housed. Most chiefs list three or four fetishes which have this kind of responsibility, but some of these are 'quiescent', being seldom consulted and unattended by a priest. A chief and his elders may have little to do with the discovery of a fetish, but they may certainly sanction its entry to the town. In this respect it has the attributes of a quasi-citizen, including a house of its own in town and an interest in communal aggrandisement. The fetish may also, like a citizen, support or challenge a chief, mainly through the agency of its priest; Akan history, ancient and modern, makes frequent reference to trials of strength between these spiritual and temporal authorities, and the long-standing dispute between the Beditor and Ntokor stools of Mim is a case in point (see chapter 4). On the other hand, a chief may use his patronage of a fetish to considerable effect. In February 1969 Ntotrosohene mounted a quite lavish ceremony for his stool's premier fetish Apomasu, using this as an opportunity to display his own civil pomp and pageantry. Where they are without priests a chief is expected to continue caring for stool fetishes, including them in libations and making occasional sacrifices for them. Several chiefs reported that their queen mothers had been entrusted with this task.

Bonsam, currently the most active of the Goaso fetishes, is celebrated every forty days before a crowd of as many as 200. The priest, 'ridden' by Bonsam, sits on a dais surrounded by his elders in an arrangement strongly evocative of a stool council. His 'queen mother' sits to one side among a group of female acolytes, and two bands, one of men, the other of women, provide the strongly rythmic music to which the priest dances. Bonsam's 'court' had an orthodoxy which Goasohene's own stool council at the time lacked, and indeed a criticism commonly levelled against the chief was that he had neglected both the premier fetish Nantia, and Bonsam. He felt obliged to put in an appearance at one celebration of Bonsam attended by the District Administrative Officer and ourselves, and showed as much courtesy in greeting and taking leave of the priest as he might expect one of his own subjects to show him. He was cautious enough, however, to obscure himself from the crowd with his umbrella. Bonsam's priest (*Bonsam okomfo*), an affable man who discussed his role with candour, was in everyday terms a successful cocoa-farmer, distinguished mainly by his long ringlets. His father's brother discovered a pot while walking one day through the forest, and the pot possessed him and 'rode' him deep into the wilderness. In due course he recovered and reported his find to Goasohene who told him to bring the pot to Goaso. When he had built a hut for it in town the pot explained that it was called Bonsam, and thereafter the fetish acquired a reputation for curing sterility, leprosy and sleeping-sickness. After his father's brother's death the present priest was possessed and, on the diagnosis of a priest in the small town of Atronie, became Bonsam okomfo. He explained that he was personally subject to Goasohene and that the fetish also respected the chief's authority; whatever the present Goasohene's attitude, it was the responsibility of fetish and priest to conduce his welfare and the growth of the community. The priest was emphatic about his reluctance to become involved in political affairs. He had never been a party member, had never registered as a voter, and even felt it would be improper to look in on local court proceedings. However, he was proud of his membership of the Ghana Association of Fetish Priests and several years previously had danced at an exhibition in Sunyani. He reported that there was mutual respect but little freemasonry among fetish priests in Ahafo, and he rated their relationships with other religious bodies and with the government as good or indifferent.

Chiefs with territorial gods described them as the 'owners' of the stool community while, conversely, stools were usually regarded as the proprietors of the fetishes. The senior fetish of a stool was described as the 'elder' (*opanin*), usually by virtue of precedence and its constructive role in the establishment of the community, as well as its association with the ruling group: 'Tei Kofi was brought by my ancestor who established Acherensua. He held ceremonies for it and got money, and soon the town began to grow. Tei Kofi is the chief of Acherensua . . . no one trifles with Tei Kofi as he is the one who established Acherensua' (Acherensuahene). Like the stool elders, a conscientious stool fetish keeps a close check on the words and actions of the chief: 'When I go to the fetish it will ask me who came here and what he did. If I don't tell the truth it will tell me I am lying and remind me what the truth is. It is just like this machine [pointing to the tape-recorder] – when you go home it will tell you all we have discussed' (Nkasaimhene). The fetish advises the chief in his dreams about present and future political events and – if their relationship is sufficiently intimate – tutors him in the strategies of aggrandisement. However, it is recognised that this counsel is not necessarily infallible; a fetish need not be impeccable and its altruism is as much tempered by material interests as any citizen's. Relationships with fetishes have decidedly commercial undertones: 'When my ancestress Twiwaa came here the powers of the fetish overcame her . . . she made money out of the fetish [and] used the money to improve the town' (Asufufuohene).

Insofar as it is associated with a particular group, the fetish may serve as a political symbol within and between communities. The reputations of Ahafo fetishes may be expressive of the expansion of settlement and political priority among Ahafo stools (see chapter 1):

'When my ancestors were coming from Kumasi and reached Sienchem, there was a fetish called Tei Kwadwo there, the most senior of all, and they discovered our own Tei Kwadwo there. When it got here it went and picked up Asubonten [another fetish] from the Fawohoyeden river. They come from the water, they are related to one another. They look after the stool and if something happens to them the community will be ruined. They are the souls of the town whereby my ancestors established this place' (Fawohoyedenhene).

Although the role of the fetish has undoubtedly diminished in significance, it is clear that it has not been supplanted by any new church or cult. As we, have seen in chapter 4, lenient heterodoxy in Ahafo has given new belief and practice opportunities as good as, but not necessarily better than, those con-fronting a fetish making its way from the banks of the Tano to a house of its own in town. Unquestionably, the fetishes remain pre-eminent in their associ-ation with Ahafo chiefship over all other spiritual resources. No chief, however well-educated, denied their continued validity, and although nine-teen claimed nominal or active membership of a modern church or sect[27] – some listing up to five different churches to which they had belonged over the years – all were agreed that such loyalties were incompatible with the ideal of a chief as moderator of community interests. Six chiefs explicitly stated that on accession they had allowed their commitment to a church to lapse: 'I am a Christian, but because of the stool I am a semi-Christian. I belonged to the Methodist Church. I go seldomly. As a chief I am expected to perform traditional rites' (Mimhene). Anwiamhene explained: 'I was a church member, but when you come to the stool you have to pick up a glass and pour libations for the stool, and this does not allow you to go to church . . . I am a Christian, but because of the stool I cannot really say that I am.' True to the ideals of chiefly impartiality several chiefs said they made a point of attending the major functions of all religious groups to which they were invited, a patronage which could prove expensive as these were usually fund-raising 'harvests'. Kenyase I hene felt that sectarianism should not be taken too seriously, and saw all groups as reconciled in the prevalent belief in one High God: 'I know that God created everything.'

In the past, a chief's oath was an important expression of his authority. By declaring it a subject could – and may still – bring a private dispute to the juridical attention of the chief. The oath is a word or phrase, commonly a Twi weekday, which refers to a dreadful event or fortunate escape in the history of the stool. Although the judicial competence of the chief and the forfeits he may exact for improper or unsuccessful evocation of the oath have been severely diminished, it is still applied to bring a public grievance to the attention of the chiefly hierarchy. On risk of progressively graver penalties and the incurrence of heavier expense a citizen might swear the oath of his divisional chief or paramount, and such appeals to higher authority are an essential feature of deposition charges today. An oath is still not mentioned lightly: 'When I came to the school I found that Wukuada [Wednesday] was the stool oath. I think there was a big battle here long ago and after that we chose the day as an oath . . . It is something we don't like to talk about; it was a big, big battle' (Akrodiehene). A short extract from an interview with the literate chief of Aboum may indicate the onerous nature of the oath:

[Question: What is your stool oath?]
[Pause]

[Question: Is it incorrect to ask someone his oath?]
No.
[Can you tell me your stool oath?]
[Aside in Twi to our assistant:] How can he know all these things?
Koguina Efiada Amanehun ('The tribulation of *Kogyina*'s Friday')
[Question: What does this mean?]
This will need more drink
[Laughter. More drink is brought]
[Aside in Twi:] After all, you are from the government and I don't know what benefit...
I remember so many things, how Aboum suffered, how we lost our grand-mothers, so many other people...

Aboumhene then continued to give a lengthy and doubtless confidential account of the events which inspired this oath. Understandably, a subject is even more reluctant than the chief himself to talk about such matters.

The oath often bears in an interesting way on the growth of the community. The Hwidiem oath is *panini afutuom* (grievous eldership): 'When my ancestor first came here he was living alone and people spoke of his house as a place where no people lived. He was sorry he was living alone and so this became his oath' (Hwidiemhene). Oaths also reflect wider political incorporation, both as a hierarchy of appeal and because subject stools may adopt the oath of an overlord. For many Ahafo chiefs today this is one of a number of ways of expressing their political orientations in the pro-Ashanti/pro-Kukuom allegiance dispute. Thus Asufufuohene currently uses the oath of his supposed Ashanti overload Nkawiehene – 'I swear by Nana Kwow of Nkawie.' Kenyase I hene explained: 'Because we owe allegiance to the Asantehene he has given us an elder who must lead us to him. For us this is Hiawuhene, and so we use his oath ... we say *Baffuor Wukuada* [Baffuor's Wednesday].' Most of the chiefs advocating Kukuomhene's paramountcy use the former Ahafo State Oath *Yawada*, or *Braimansu Yawada* (Braimansu's Thursday) – a reference to the decisive encounter with the Ashantis which preceded the 1896 Treaty of Friendship and Protection with the British.

C. MAINTAINING OFFICE

The chiefs' own view of their functions places emphasis on their responsibility to the groups comprising the stool community and assuring their unity (*kroye*), on which corporate welfare and growth depend. No chief implied that the job was an easy one: 'In my opinion, chiefship is an onerous heritage (*asodie*). We get nothing whatsoever from chieftaincy, just debt and heavy expenses. A chief has to sit there and solve people's problems, and that makes for expense. But as we have been put here to serve and develop the town we have to accept it for what it is. Good or bad you have to do it, it is your obligation' (Kenyase I hene). Responsibility to one's lineage is the pre-eminent reason for undertaking office: 'Because it is the property of our ancestors we just have to be chiefs. It is a sin if the ancestors' property is put before you and you refuse it' (Fawohoyedenhene).

The chiefs took their role as moderator of intra-community affairs very seriously; it was essential to be continually watchful for issues in the making, and to press for their speedy solution. It was also considered imperative to take counsel at all times: 'For example, if I said that the town was mine alone and went off privately into a room with you, without summoning my elders; or if someone brings a drink for the stool and I don't call the elders but just swig it myself; or if I get a message from the D.C. or am called by the European, and don't tell anyone and go off alone instead of going with the elders, I would not find favour as a chief' (Fawohoyedenhene). In Mehame-hene's opinion, Kwame Nkrumah's greatest failing was his reluctance to take counsel. Several chiefs observed wryly, however, that 'taking advice' now-adays seemed to imply bending to every public whim. A taker of counsel within his own community, the chief was also a giver of counsel to others on the community's behalf: 'It is we chiefs who have to put matters before the Local Councillors and Members of Parliament, we are most important because we were here long before they came along' (Ayumsohene). The chiefs emphasised the need for integrity in handling the stool finances, and utter impartiality in moderating community interests. Patience, clemency, equanimity and composure were all indispensable to the role, the effective management of which was held to depend on scrupulous decorum and reserve in all day-to-day public conduct. A chief ought not eat and drink in public, should avoid casual arguments with ordinary people and should above all avoid sexual intrigues. The chief's preoccupation with communal growth was asserted in these terms by Fawohoyedenhene:

'I have to bring all the townspeople together and I have to see that everyone works well when there is a project in hand. You remember I told you last time that we have a piece of land stretching from here to Biamu, and that I have been fighting to reclaim it so that the townspeople can get part of it to make their farms? This is a chiefly duty. I have to pursue the welfare of the town. Even if the people of Kumasi make a certain law which seems to go against the interests of the town, I must speak out.'

For Hwidiemhene, a successful chief was one who could 'talk well enough to bring projects to his town'. This was held to depend on the extent to which the chief could count on the respect and support of his people: 'If there is a meeting and the chief can speak well enough for the people to follow clearly, they will say "Hwidiemhene is a good chief." [A chief] should be wise. Being a good chief', Hwidiemhene concluded, 'takes a lot of doing.'

In our meetings, the Ahafo chiefs were much exercised by the problems of maintaining office, and spoke with almost as much candour about political strategy as about political norms. Securing the goodwill of fickle subjects demanded a persuasive tongue, a clear and unbiased mind, close attention to changing attitudes within and beyond the community, personal wealth, and a great deal of time and patience: 'When you are made a chief, so many troubles can come your way . . . when you become a chief people regard you as their servant. Chieftaincy is for old men for when you are a young man you have no time for the job' (Fawohoyedenhene). Although normally reticent about discussing each other's affairs, chiefs readily listed the Ahafo stools which had a reputation as 'hot seats'. The turnover in officeholders in such stools is regarded with somewhat morbid pleasure elsewhere, and there is candid admiration for even a rival who manages to hold down opposition for a number of years. Some chiefs find it impossible to believe that there are other stools more plagued than theirs: 'Mim stool has always been the most troublesome,' averred Mimhene. 'That's why many destooled chiefs are inserted in your paper there. I was able to succeed for 15 years until the old regime removed me from my stool, but look at the others – six months . . . three . . . ' There is a shrewd awareness that stools are usually 'bedevilled' by nothing more mysterious than human fallibility: one is repeatedly assured that it is people, not stools, who make trouble.

Although in ideal aloof from the gossip of his people, the percipient chief keeps his ear to the ground and seeks to ensure that he has preferably first-hand knowledge of issues as they arise. His personal security may depend on this and so many chiefs assert the importance of maintaining participation in all public decision-making processes within the community – including the new Town Committees (see chapter 7). This vigilance demands that he should not absent himself for long periods. Maintenance of office may thus have to be reconciled with the way the chief makes his personal living: 'As the chief cannot go away and work, he must make a farm of his own. If the chief is educated he can work, otherwise he must make a shop, so that he need not go far from the town' (Ayumsohene). It was well recognised that private wealth greatly enhanced a chief's staying-power even if, like Kenyase II hene, his interests as a timber contractor meant extensive commuting throughout the region. The political deficiencies of a munificent chief may readily be forgiven. Many chiefs dwelt on the problems of finding ready cash, as access to land revenues is currently blocked, particularly for the entertainment of visitors. A chief must keep up appearances to justify his own claims and to make the office worthy of the community: 'if you have no decent cloth, no nice house, it is a disgrace. When I was putting up this house I sought the people's help, but they gave me none. I used my own money to build it. Now, if I had not been working where would I have got the money to build, and get a nice cloth? No nice house, no decent cloth – that is a disgrace to the chief of a town. A chief must work and get plenty of money for his own benefit' (Dadiesoabahene). Every chief should add to the regalia and property of his stool; it is well known that appearing in full panoply on public occasions greatly enhances the prestige of incumbent and office.

Although preoccupied with maintaining office in the context of the immediate, face-to-face relationships of his own community, the chief is also aware, as we shall see in the following chapter, of the extent to which he is dependent on the wider chiefly hierarchy and other external authorities. A chief like Akrodiehene, threatened with deposition charges by his towns-people, may place a high value on these outside sanctions: 'before you are recognised as a good chief you must obey your senior. It is no compliment for a common man to call you a good chief, only if the (chief) you are serving calls you a good chief is it worth anything. The people will only say you are a good chief after your death.' Most chiefs today very clearly regard the favour of the District Officer as a great political asset; nevertheless, as those reinstated after the 1966 coup are keenly aware, a government guarantee of rights to office is no substitute for the goodwill of one's own subjects.

For 'a few hectic years' (in the words of one Ahafo citizen) tenure of chiefly office was undoubtedly dependent on political party affiliation. Chiefs were not, on the whole, apologetic about their party involvement in the decade prior to 1966, which they tended to see as a reasonable response to the fervid political climate of the nation. Given that this was the prevailing mode for the expression of political relationships, a refusal to participate would have been tantamount to abdication. What was perplexing, and has made many chiefs wary of future engagements in party politics, was the way party identities subsumed virtually all contraposed interest groups without discrimination, one party colour eventually implying commitment to what has been hitherto a spectrum of discrete, contingent identities. The chiefs thus found themselves involved in conflicts of interest within their own realms which were not congruent with the normative view of the chiefly role discussed above.

The vigour of party politics in Ahafo in the late 1950s and the extent of the chiefs' involvement are remembered vividly today:

The various Ahafo chiefs took sides with the existing political parties. The chiefs acted as political agents. In the hurly-burly of political propaganda wavering in the atmosphere, some villages became at loggerheads.

Even after Ghana's independence there were many reported cases of rivalry among the Ahafo leaders. Some groups of people were moving to and fro, beating up other people, ransacking houses attempting life and some to the extent of assassinating some politicians. Power-drunk and die-hard party fanaticals would come all the way long in their wheezing land-rovers, peugeots, etc., from the other regions particularly Asante, to indulge in fierce political campaigns in a very rowdy atmosphere. There was a period of unrest among the people of Ahafo.[28]

Although no community in Ahafo seems to have been committed exclusively to one party, most could be identified as either 'strong United Party' or 'strong Convention People's Party'. It is interesting that such identities are reckoned to be attributable to and expressive of the party commitment of the chief. Mr S. K. Opoku, former C.P.P. Member of Parliament for one of the Ahafo constituencies, recalled: 'Akrodie . . . that was a U.P. town – dominated by the U.P.' (What about Hwidiem?) 'It was C.P.P.' (Dantano?) 'That was another C.P.P. stronghold.' (Sankore?) 'Oh, oh, U.P.! These dominations came from the chiefs, you see. You see they took a very great interest in the whole issue. You see, the propaganda was that the C.P.P. wanted to take the Golden Stool away, so any chief who was close to the Asantehene – at that time they were using the Asantehene as the head of the party – and so all typical Ashantis wanted to back the U.P.' Later this engagement of the chiefs in party politics was regarded as disreputable, mainly because of the sharp conflict of chiefly roles it involved. On the one hand, party commitment could be justified by the norm that a chief must be resolute in all his public actions; the indecisive chief is not simply weak, he is politically suspect. A rather obscure moral fable about 'Nkonko's hand' was evoked by the Ahafo chiefs to stress the impropriety of irresolution and fence-sitting. A chief's public commitment must, of course, be expressive of consensus within the community, seldom if ever achieved in the name of one political party. With the insistence of nation-wide propaganda and the incorporation of interests with which they could readily identify, the chiefs' emergence as party zealots is understandable. However, because he could not carry with him the entire community nor anticipate the ways in which party membership could resolve with stark simplicity hitherto complex local political oppositions, the chief's performance of his role as the moderator of competing interests was severely impaired. Retrospectively, this readiness of the chiefs to declare publicly their partiality was considered both disruptive and ignominious.

The intensity of these sentiments prompted twenty of the Ahafo chiefs in 1968 to declare that they would avoid any future involvement with a political party. Three chiefs could offer no decisive opinion and only five felt that, on balance, it would be wise to commit themselves as they had in the past. It would be tempting to argue – but impossible to substantiate – that these attitudes depended on what the chiefs had managed to get out of party involvement previously. Mimhene, who had lost a great deal since 1957 and owed nothing to the C.P.P., felt somewhat predictably that such involvement was 'a filthy thing'. However, Kukuomhene's blunt opinion 'I do not like parties' is difficult to reconcile with the Ahafo Paramountcy and other prizes which C.P.P. patronage had assured him. Ayumsohene explained: 'It was not good for a chief to join a party, but they did so out of fear.' Now, he felt convinced of the inherent incompatibility: 'The party has one mind and chieftaincy has another mind. If you mix the two together you are lost . . . if you are a party member you will not have the right mind to rule the town.' Other chiefs were clearly aware of the contradictory values of political norm and political strategy, setting the possible gains of party commitment against the rule that a chief should be the moderator of, not partisan to, competing community interests. Kenyase I hene considered the party's strategic snags: 'At first the chief should sit back and watch the youngmen. When one party comes to power they will not be able to abuse him if he has not joined. Because we joined one of the parties last time, when the other came to power it was disposed to remove us. We should just watch, to see whether it goes to right or left. At first we never knew, we joined one party and then were destooled.' Acherensuahene advocated an impartial role for the chief: 'As the townspeople all belong to the chief it is not good for him to side with some of the people and abandon the others. You have to make sure that all the people in the town stay united, you must not divide them.' This reflects a view of parties as essentially 'for the youngmen' and not 'for the elders'. However, a number of chiefs expressed the contrary view that to appear non-committal amid ardent partisanship could be construed as a declaration of disinterest in the political advancement of the community. It was part of a chief's public responsibility, Hwiediemhene noted, for a chief to ensure that the most suitable Local Council or Parliamentary representative was elected. Complete disengagement from party politics in the community could deprive the chief of strategic intelligence, Sienchemhene explained: '(a chief) should only go to meetings . . . some parties are formed for the detriment of the community or the country. If you join you have to abide by their good and bad rules. But if you do not attend their meetings and they are plotting against the town, you cannot tell them to stop. If you are present you can advise them to do the right thing, and tell them how to develop the town.'

The Ahafo chiefs seemed to feel that the parties were a political resource whose uses they had been unable to master. This is not to say that the parties operated against chiefship or that the chiefs are likely to participate skilfully in the future. It does, however, indicate how the chief's role as politician has become more exacting and ambiguous; on this question, Aboumhene made his feelings of perplexity explicit: 'I for one don't like [party membership]. Well, no one can hardly cease to be a politician in this world . . . for me, you can hardly cease me from making politics. Hardly. I am a politician. I want to know my rights, I mean you can not hide it. So, to your question,

I apologise and say that a chief cannot be a politician, yet he must be a politician.'

All Ahafo chiefs are exercised by the persistent threat of deposition which has, by all accounts, intensified in recent years. The concern of the government is reflected in legislation over the last few decades, the endorsement of accessions and depositions ultimately being vested in the highest levels of authority. Much of the confusion has been about the kinds of charge which are admissible, who has the right to press them and with whom the final sanction for destoolment rests.[29] The general Ashanti principle that only those involved in the enstoolment of a chief may concern themselves with his deposition is echoed in Ahafo, but the wide range of political levels and persons engaged in the process, from the government Minister and the State Council to the citizens themselves, can make it very difficult to interpret today. If the principal responsibility for pressing charges rests with the stool elders, the initiative for raising them may come from any citizen. Some doubt has been cast on the government's role, hitherto assumed to be a rubber-stamping of the appropriate State Council's decision, by its indirect influence in the C.P.P. era and its direct initiative in the months after the 1966 coup.

It is in matters of accession and deposition that the public are most actively engaged in the politics of chiefship. Just as popular assent is required at the installation of a new chief, so deposition charges cannot be pressed successfully without public support, although the initiative may be taken by a single individual: 'Only one man need to do this; everyone has his enemy. You may do something which you think is secret and someone has seen you. Perhaps others have seen what you were up to and did not tell you. The first person will go and say to someone else, "look, this chief of ours is misbehaving". The other will say, "in fact I saw him, but I could not speak out". Then all three will mention the matter to the Krontihene who will say, "yes, that is the truth" . . .' (Gyeduhene) – and so the pressure against the chief mounts. 'The town divides in two, half for the chief and half on the other side. The division comes when there are two people contesting for the stool, and this brings about the fighting' (Wamahinsohene). The persistence and coherence of the factions involved in these manoeuvres is clearly recognised: 'Every chief has got some people with whom he is especially cordial, and for whom he buys drinks. These people stay by him and the others go to the other side. When the others overcome your people, you are destooled' (Wamahinsohene). For the chiefs themselves 'proper' destoolment procedure repudiated factionalism. An aggrieved citizen should take his complaint to his segment elder who would then put the matter to the chief – if necessary before the stool council – avoiding throughout any public confrontation. Akrodiehene, at a time when he was being plagued by deposition charges complained: 'In my case, things were not done that way. The youngmen plotted, and they even threw stones and damaged the roof here while I was away. They damaged the houses of my supporters too . . . In times other than now, youngmen had no say in destoolment.'

Ahafo chiefs tended to complain that their subjects took a cynical and materialistic view of stool politics. The chiefs feared conspiracies and particularly the modern menace of 'stool contractors', individuals supposed to engineer accessions and depositions for financial gain. Fawohoyedenhene commented: 'There are some people around here who do not care about the welfare of the community. They are only out to upset the town. We have one of these in our town here. When a new chief is enstooled this fellow always finds trouble with him. He starts innuendoes against the chief, he will disagree with you even if you have not offended him. This poisonous man may go to a chief's friend and say that the chief was speaking evil against him . . . he will go from person to person until he has suborned them all. Eventually, even your elders will dissent against you and will, even within a month, have drawn away from you.' An elder took up the tale, explaining how the 'contractor' would collect money to bribe the State Council and other officials, leaving the elders to press the case: 'By the time we have finished it will have drained as much as £3,000 from the stool funds. The bad man will in fact have used all this money to buy nice furniture for his house. So thereafter this man will be interested in destoolment and make trouble for anyone who comes along.' The chief continued: 'He has a bigger farm than anyone else's in town, no one can better him. Because he is rich he has gathered about 100 of the youngmen around him . . . When he tells them to go and make trouble they will not refuse.' The chiefs' sensitivity to such conspiracy kept them continually on their guard. 'It is envy that causes destoolments', Sankorehene declared, envy which may have its origins very close to home: 'I may be envied by my maternal uncles and brothers when I am carried in my palaquin at ceremonies. One of them may bribe the others and say that since I have become chief I have not done anything good for them. They may put up charges against you without your being able to find a witness. They may bribe the Gyasehene, Krontihene and Akwamuhene, and they will turn on you say "you have offended us". The chiefs are destooled for no reason at all.' If such fears are justified in reality, one must ask again what it is about chiefship which continues to make the expenditure of time and money by rivals worthwhile.

Some chiefs did not care to dwell at length on the sensitive subject of deposition. 'My elders are around me now, tomorrow they may say "you said so-and-so yesterday – do you realise that by your own mouth you are guilty?"' (Dadiesoabahene). It is notable that a chief against whom deposition charges are being pressed is rendered virtually incapable of public action. He will avoid attendance at public meetings and deal only with the most essential business in the seclusion of his palace.[30] The focal point of destoolment proceedings is the list of charges, usually eight or nine in all, but sometimes as many as twenty, which are presented to the chief and ultimately to the State Council. Although stylised, these charges offer some insight into the changing public view of chiefly authority and functions. An examination of the constitutional cases heard by the Kukuom–Ahafo State Council (1958–66) indicates the prevalence of two types of charge: using stool money and property to personal advantage and failing to 'bring developments' to the community. A common prelude to the serving of charges is the demand that the chief should make a public statement of his accounts. As it is unlikely that even the most honest chief could do this plausibly this invariably lends immediacy to the complainants' case. Nearly all lists of charges include a reference to the chief's failure in community aggrandisement, for example:

Charge 1: That since he was enstooled as Sienchemhene, there has not been any improvement in the town, with the exception of debts. And this shows that he is not eligible person to be a chief in the town.

In his reply to this, the first of 18 charges, the then Sienchemhene replied:

Charge 1: That during my enstoolment as the Odikro of Sienchem the school was up to Primary 3 but now is up to Primary 6 and with my help there is a motor road to Sienchem for easy travelling and transportation of foodstuffs from Sienchem to other big towns in the Country.[31]

Prominent among the more material complaints against the chief are accusations of misplacing, pawning or selling stool property without the stool council's sanction, or of failing to enhance the regalia, palace and farms. A group of charges is usually levelled against the chief's failings as a moderator of community affairs. He has proved slow to prevent disputes, weak in judgement, or reluctant to summon his elders or his people when an issue arises. Particular events are cited: an argument in the streets, an incident in a local bar. Some spiritual omissions or misdemeanours are invariably included, such as failing to perform the rituals which assure communal welfare, or laxity in observing prohibitions. The norms invoked are, according to Kenyase I hene, 'just like government laws', and are certainly assessed as such in State Council sessions.

Charges are not confined to traditional formulae but also challenge the chief in contemporary political idioms. This syncretism may best be conveyed by reproducing a list of charges prepared by the 'Hwidiem Youth Association' and served on Hwidiemhene by the stool Krontihene in September 1958, when C.P.P. fervour in Ahafo was reaching a peak. Copies of the list were sent to the Kukuom–Ahafo State Council, the District Officer, the Regional Commissioner and the Clerk of the Local Council:

Dear Nana,

Charges against you

For your information and necessary action, you are hereby requested to answer or to comply with the undermentioning charges so far preferred against you by the Krontihene, Opanin … and the above Organisation Executive Committee members. The members are expecting to meet you on Monday, the 6th of October, 1958.

Charges: 1. That you as an Odikro of the town have entirely discarded our god by name (Tano-Kofi) the property of the royal family, and

2. That you have failed to secure the god with a fetish priest after an amount of (£70) Seventy pounds and (£50) Fifty pounds respectively had been borrowed and given to you by the Oman to do so, and

3. That you have failed to quit from your present premises to the Royal house since you were enstooled, according to your own promise made before the Oman, and

4. That you have ceased the rights of the Krontihene Opanin . . . to enter into the premises of the god (Tano-Kofi) which is entirely against custom, and

5. That you have appointed your own regent to represent you at all times during your absence from the town, whereas the Krontihene is present, and

6. That you are not loyal to your subjects, and

7. That you are under the Kukuom State Council, and you have failed to negotiate with the Omanhene to restore your clan position as the Akyiamehene (Chief Linguist) of the State Council and had protested against the wishes of your subjects, and

8. That you had strongly rebelled or had stood as an opponent to the Ghana Government during the struggle for the Country's Independence in 1956, and as such you have diminished the popularity of Hwidiem, and

9. That you have failed to attend a meeting of your subjects after you had been instructed by the Regional Commissioner, Brong–Ahafo, to do so during your last meeting held at Goaso with the Commissioner, and

10. That you have shown a disrespect to the Ghana Government as well as to the Omanhene of the Ahafo State Council, and

11. That you on the 14th day of May, 1956, as an Odikro of Hwidiem declared your policy as a superlative member of the defunct National Liberation Movement, and that you on that day in question swore the great oath of Ashanti to abdicate your stool if the Convention People's Government went into power, and

12. That you have failed to prepare the Royal house, and to remove the God (Tano-Kofi) to the said house after you had been instructed by Nana Bantamahene to do so about (3) three years ago, and

13. That you as an Odikro of Hwidiem acquired land at the

Hwidiem junction with the intention of building an Ahenfie [palace] for the town, now the building plot has been disposed to a certain european for petrol selling purposes, and

14. That you have not been able to make any additional stool properties to the old ones now in your possession.

Your earliest attention, coupled with goodwill and cooperation will be esteemed by,

Your faithful servants,

XX [32]

Although chiefship acquired many secular features in the early 1960s, charges of 'Ignoring the Government of the day' or 'Denigrating Osagyefo, Dr Kwame Nkrumah' were always salted with charges of a more conventional, traditional kind.

The destoolment charges indicate some congruence between the public view of chiefly roles, and the opinions of the chiefs themselves. Enquiries among the Goaso citizens suggested a general respect for the office, if not always for the incumbent himself. Non-citizens would explain: 'I am only under him because it is his town.' Education seemed to be the principal influence on the individual's view of chiefly authority, producing a familiar, somewhat doctrinaire attitude characterised by ambivalence and contradiction. A Goaso schoolteacher announced: 'the chief is only ceremonial', but his subsequent account of the many functions of the chief today would lead one to doubt this. Mr T. N. Baidoo, former C.P.P. District Commissioner, declared roundly: 'It is only in matters of tradition that the chiefs come in, but generally speaking, in matter of general administration, the chiefs have no say at all.' Moments later, Mr Baidoo was outlining the contemporary role of the chiefs as follows:

'He is solely responsible to see to the welfare of the town. He should see that if a money is collected to development it is well used or spent. And then he is to be more or less a liaison officer between his people and the representative of the government. He should also be at one with his subjects so that he is more or less a mouthpiece in certain matters... He is the Chairman of the Development Committee, and so when members meet and discuss anything about the development of the area, of the town, he will have to translate, to communicate, has to see the representative of the government and put before him the views of his people here, because as the Town Committee represents the town in matters of development and he, being the Chairman of the Committee, he should let the government know what are the needs.'

If these are 'strictly matters of tradition', we must be sure that our interpretation of the term is correspondingly broad.

Less-educated people do not take such an analytical view of chiefly roles, expressing straightforward qualitative opinions: 'there are more bad chiefs than good chiefs', but few feel that the chief's authority over them is without limits: 'he can not ask me to pound his fufu for him'. Taking the most obvious point at which the chief's functions impinged on them personally, nearly everyone said that his main right was to demand their participation in communal labour. It is significant that very many also said that the chief's main duty was to pass on to them information from the government. Reference was also made to the chief's constructive role in community welfare and development, seen as closely dependent on his expertise in 'uniting the people' and mustering communal resources: 'If you are a chief, if any progress comes to the town during the tenure of your office it is a credit to you. So, people opposing the chief will always try to hamper progress so that they can cite it as an instance when they want to destool you' (Goaso Town Committee Secretary). Conversations with townsfolk did not leave one with a very clear idea of what they reckoned were the attractions of chiefly office to its incumbents. One young man felt that to be conciliatory, tactful and impartial all the time must be extremely tedious. Estimates of Goasohene's normal annual income, averaging around £500, suggested that people did not have a grossly inflated view of the material benefits of chiefship. It was generally agreed that a chief who indulged in extortion would not be tolerated for long. A wealthy candidate for chiefly office would be assured greater public support than a poor one: 'If you are a teacher with no money you cannot be a chief. When the rich man becomes a chief that is fine. When there is a debt the rich man can settle it himself. If there is a dispute for the stool between a rich royal and a poor one, the former will always win through.' If a chiefly candidate is calculating what he might get out of office, one may be assured that his people are calculating what they might get out of him.

One must conclude, however, that chiefship is not ordinarily uppermost in the citizen's mind, that his interest in it and knowledge of particular issues is contingent and selective. It is apparent nevertheless that the office remains, for stranger and citizen alike, the clearest expression of the corporate political identity of the community. The basis of such authority as the chief enjoys is undoubtedly still embedded in the intricate multiplex relationships within the community and is therefore as difficult for the citizen to explain as for the sociologist. 'The chief may argue,' one Goaso resident observed sceptically, 'but his voice will not carry across the Goa river.' Perhaps one may conclude that within the confines of the town at least his voice has not yet been deprived of its persuasive power.

CHAPTER 6

THE POLITICS OF THE AHAFO STATE

According to Hwidiemhene, the most significant change brought to Ahafo by the establishment of British overrule was the suppression of the chief's role as military leader and the new demands made on his political and diplomatic skills. Pax Britannica, 'civilisation' and government reduced the opportunity for pursuing political ends by physical force but at the same time greatly extended and diversified the range of other political opportunities. Today a community judges the success or failure of its chief in terms of his advocacy of its interests in the widening field of political interaction and his acumen in pursuing all available opportunities. However, the interests of aggrandisement (*nkoso*) can never be furthered without regard to the wider interest in political unity (*kroye*), for it is pre-eminently within the context of a State or Divisional structure that political growth is expressed. The central problem in Ahafo today is the specification of this unity; the interests in communal aggrandisement are frustrated in that they can not find coherent expression in the form of competition within an accepted framework. Inter-community politics is not simply a matter of playing games according to agreed rules, it is a matter of negotiating the rules themselves. Although interpretatively the situation is doubtless as taxing for the actors as for the analyst, it would plainly be wrong to suppose that it is novel. Nevertheless, in this complex exercise the identification and exploitation of opportunities demands all the political skill and subtlety for which the Akan people are justly celebrated.

Aggrandisement, or more politely 'progress', is the chief's watchword, and as this implies besting political rivals competition and confrontation have the appearance of being endemic in Ahafo. This is not to argue that negotiation is always relished, on the contrary it may bring great tension and reduce other public processes within the community to a standstill.[1] It is felt that the consolidation of constitutional gains depends on a period of relative peace for it is only then that a chief can direct time, money and public goodwill to such tasks as the ceremonial blackening of stools by which political growth is measured. This in turn depends upon the persistence of the wider political unity, and a recognition of the dignity of rivals. It is significant that in speaking of Ahafo

223

as a whole, chiefs do not care to dwell on past conflicts which have been resolved, or to recall victories gained over their neighbours.

It is possible to detect three intertwined strands of meaning in the idea of aggrandisement in Ahafo today. It is taken to apply to the acquisition of public amenities, economic resources and enhanced political status. The competition for public amenities falls more directly within the purview of chapter 7; the chiefs spoke about this at length, relating the physical growth of the community to the need for school buildings, a post office, road improvements and so on. Such gains at the expense of one's neighbours (in terms of Local Council budgeting) could be enhanced if they involved amenities on which other communities were obliged to depend: a hospital, a secondary school, a Local Council headquarters. Economic competition centres primarily on land, which is itself closely related to competition for enhanced political status. As Ntotrosohene put it: 'He with the most land becomes the Paramount chief . . . if you have land you are the leader.' Asked about the relative importance of the Ahafo chiefs, Kenyase I hene explained that it was everyone's ambition to be 'a big chief', land and status in the political hierarchy being definitive of this: 'Each chief is in his own town and every man has his master. I am important because I am here on my own land, but the Asantehene is my boss.' His neighbour, Kenyase II hene, laughingly explained: 'You see, I want to be a first-class chief here in Ahafo. But if you go to Mim, the Mimhene will say just what I have been saying now. Same everywhere.' Explaining these ambitions to a European the chiefs find ready parallels in the public bureaucracy, particularly the police force: 'As your town grows, so your title also grows. A policeman would begin as a private policeman then a lance-corporal, then a sergeant – it is a sort of promotion' (Mimhene); 'A policeman who works well is made a corporal . . . We need to have an Omanhene. I should be the first Omanhene as I am the senior chief in the area . . .' (Sankorehene).

a. LAND, ALLEGIANCE AND STOOL INTERRELATIONSHIPS

A well-known Ashanti proverb runs: '*tumi nyina wo asase so*' – 'all power is in the land'. The demographic and material development of a community, and consequently its political growth, depend on the economic resources at its disposal. The distribution of authority within the political hierarchy is certainly dependent on control over these resources, but it is important to note that there is no necessary congruence between proprietary rights in land or claims to political allegiance. One explanation of this may be found in the patterns of community growth; an emigrant from one stool may have sought permission to make a farm on the land of another stool and a new community may have developed, paying tribute to the landowner chief but retaining

224

formal citizenship and allegiance in the original stool. It is on these terms that Mimhene would claim the Goaso lands: 'The land is mine, but they owe allegiance to the Asantehene.' Ownership of the Ahafo lands has been an open political issue for many decades. Map C indicates the conflicting claims to the rights of land deposition among the 28 Ahafo chiefs in 1968–9. Some, but by no means all of these are the subject of outstanding litigation. There are also land disputes involving the claims of chiefs in adjacent areas, and disputes among chiefs outside Ahafo with respect to land in the district. The complexity of these claims and counter-claims has given Ahafo notoriety throughout the Akan area.[2]

The economic and political importance of land is reinforced with a complex of ritual observance, involving the stool ancestors, the fetishes, gods and ultimately Asase Yaa, the Earth Goddess. Land tenure is a corporate affair, but each citizen is entitled to claim exclusive rights to the use of untenanted land sufficient to his needs, and to transmit this farm to his heirs in due course. Acquisition and transmission are ratified by the chief and his stool council on payment of a small fee (*aseda*). The landholding corporation is the family or community segment, represented by an elder, in the first instance, and then the community at large, represented by the chief (*ohene*). Village headmen (*adikrofo*) may control land allocation in the outlying areas of the stool. In the most comprehensive sense the landholding corporation in Ashanti is the state, represented by the Paramount chief (*omanhene*). These levels of proprietary interest are reflected in the distribution of revenue, the authority to settle claims, and residual rights. Perhaps the most significant distinction in landholding is between citizen and stranger, each enjoying distinct kinds of right and obligation. For the former, land is acquired as a birth-right, for the latter it is acquired by contractual agreement. Citizens hold land by virtue of historical tradition, jealously guarding their ancestral rights and evoking the sanction of the fetishes and territorial gods. However, the radial pattern of community growth implies a distinction between the long-established tenancies around the settlement nucleus and the newer farms around the circumference. As these approach the sphere of influence of a neighbouring community, an alien landholding corporation, claims become more equivocal and lay both parties open to political confrontation in the law-courts. Much the same pattern obtains on the intra-community level, segment confronting segment, and individual confronting individual in intricate webs of litigation.

The major contest over proprietary rights in Ahafo lands which has raged for many decades involves the claims of a number of chiefs of the Kumasi state on the one hand, and the Ahafo chiefs on the other. From the former perspective Ahafo is neither a landholding corporation nor a political unit, it is included with parts of Brong to the north among the 'Kumasi Islands',

C1

Territorial claims of Kukuom,
Mim and Noberkaw. Kukuom
claims all of Ahafo.

Mim and Noberkaw each
claims the hatched area
within which it lies.

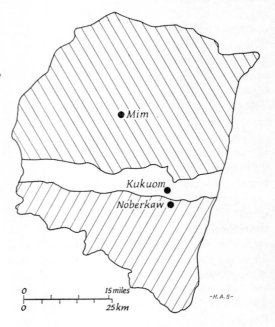

Cautionary note: These maps are interpretations of territorial limits claimed by the Ahafo chiefs and described by them in interviews. They in no way reflect legal title or the deposition of legal claims. Their interest is essentially as an expression of community aggrandisement. Compilation of these maps has also involved some quite free interpretation; a chief may say 'I claim all the land of X' in which case licence has been taken to express this claim cartographically in terms of the area X himself defined as his own stool territory.

Key:

1 Aboum	11 Goaso	21 Nkasaim
2 Acherensua	12 Gyedu	22 Noberkaw
3 Akrodie	13 Hwidiem	23 Ntotroso
4 Anwiam	14 Kenyase I	24 Pomakrom
5 Asufufuo	15 Kenyase II	25 Sankore
6 Ayumso	16 Kukuom	26 Siena
7 Dadiesoaba	17 Kwakunyuma	27 Sienchem
8 Dantano	18 Kwapong	28 Wamahinso
9 Etwineto	19 Mehame	
10 Fawohoyeden	20 Mim	

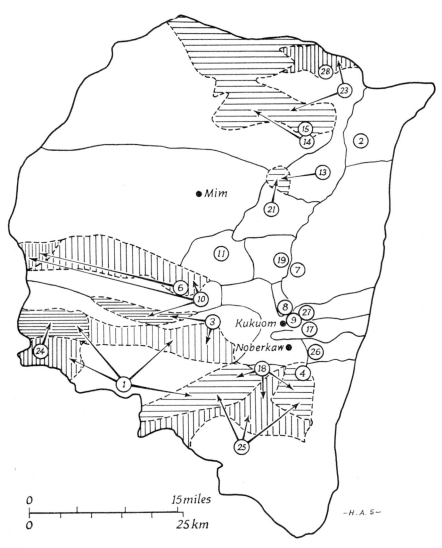

● *Mim*

Kukuom ●

Noberkaw ●

0   *15 miles*

0   *25 km*

–H.A.S–

C2

Territorial claims of the remaining Ahafo stools. Areas *contested* by one or more stools are hatched on this map.

    A stool within a delineated area claims that area. It also claims a *contested* area if an arrow points from it into that area.

    Neither Asufufuo nor Gyedu specify direct territorial claims.

march lands made over to various chiefs in his own immediate state of Kumasi by the Asantehene during the eighteenth and nineteenth centuries. The exceptional nature of this allocation underlies the current proliferation of land disputes in the area.[3] As Ahafo has developed from a region of scattered hunting camps to a prosperous cocoa-farming area, the Kumasi chiefs have had good reason to assert their proprietary interests. The same economic and demographic growth has fostered notions of political integrity within Ahafo, and the view that Ahafo must now be regarded as a distinct landholding corporation. All the Ahafo chiefs are unsympathetic to the claims of the Kumasi chiefs, a few tolerate them, and the seven united around Kukuomhene's leadership reject them outright. It should be noted that the distinction between claims in *land* and claims to *allegiance* means that an Ahafo chief may reject an economic bond with one Kumasi chief while admitting a political bond with another. We shall return to a discussion of this discrimination later. A measure of the stalemate which has been reached was the decision to invest all Ahafo lands provisionally in the President of Ghana in 1961.[4] In the interim most of the revenues accruing have been banked, and the steadily accumulating balance has served only to whet the appetites of the contesting parties.[5]

Political disputes over land allocation and revenue collection have been eased in recent years by diminishing availability in many stools and by the transfer of many aspects of land management to local and central government agencies. Outright sale of land in Ahafo appears to have been very rare, a by-product, perhaps, of the confusion over proprietary rights. The prevalence of customary tenure is no doubt reflected in the public interest in stool politics, and in the wider issues of the Ahafo/Kumasi dispute. The actual process of land allocation and transmission remains at the discretion of the chief and his elders. According to several chiefs the stool okyeame or an elder, accompanied by adjacent landholders, is given the task of confirming the limits of a new claimant's farm. Land is customarily issued in units called *dopen*, which appear to approximate to 8 acres. A citizen acquiring a new farm will be expected to provide a fee, or 'drink', amounting to as much as £9, which sets the seal on the allocation. A stranger would be expected to pay a much larger fee varying, according to the Ahafo chiefs, between £23 and £45 per *dopen* unit. Thereafter the stranger pays annual tribute, or rent, called *nto*. Citizens are not required to pay rent but instead contribute to the special rate currently levied by the town development committees. This is regarded as an updating of the citizen's traditional right to share in the profits and debts accruing to the community, and is charged at a rate of between two and six shillings per headload of cocoa. Strangers are often asked for, and pay, both rent and special rate, although those with little commitment to Ahafo and vested interests in communities elsewhere have complained bitterly about

228

such demands. Until 1962 when a Rent Stabilisation Act fixed the rate of payment at five shillings per acre, rent was agreed between the chief and each tenant individually. In 1966 the National Liberation Council revoked this Act,[6] obliging government Lands Officers to renegotiate all agreements between chiefs and tenants. Rent is normally paid only on bearing cocoa farms, the charge being made per headload of cocoa harvested; according to the Lands Officer in Goaso a rate of Noo.20 (less than 2 shillings) would be a normal charge on a 60lb load worth about NC.6.50. This officer also estimated roughly 55 per cent of all landholders in Ahafo are strangers paying this rent.

The task of rent collection was tranferred from the stools to the new Local Councils under the provision of the Local Government Ordinance of 1951. In 1953 the Local Authorities were also charged with the approval of land issue but shortly after Independence in 1957 their inadequacies in performing these functions prompted the government to transfer responsibility to the Ministry of Justice.[7] In 1961 an office of the Administrator of Stool Lands was opened in Goaso and for the year 1964 the officer in charge reported having collected a total of £16,099, 16s od in rents, royalties and other fees. £13,598 15s od of this consisted of royalties, primarily on timber concessions, the relatively small remainder being rents from stranger-farmers.[8] Until 1962 when ministerial responsibility was taken for making agreements and setting standard fees chiefs enjoyed the right to allocate timber concessions on their land. Many still feel aggrieved over the loss of these privileges although it is clear that they were often exploited and government control assures them more revenue in the long run.

The share-out of revenues has been the subject of persistent debate. In 1939 the Asantehene ruled that of the tribute collected in Ahafo, one third should go to his own stool, four ninths to the Kumasi chiefs owning the land, and two ninths to the 'caretakers' – the Ahafo chiefs.[9] In 1951 the government decided that the new Local Councils, charged with revenue collection, should retain 45%, the 'caretaker chiefs' should be allocated 35% and the 'owner chiefs' (in Kumasi) should have 20%. In 1968 the N.L.C. revised these proportions, earmarking 45% for Development and Scholarship schemes administered by the Local Authorities and 45% for the traditional authorities, a 10% administrative charge being paid to the Consolidated Fund.[10] Until the dispute with Kumasi is resolved all this money, including the Local Authority proportion, is denied to Ahafo. It is particularly for this reason that the secular authorities are as anxious as the chiefs to press for a solution to the problem of an Ahafo constitution.

Ahafo lacks a State Council through which the share of revenues due to 'traditional authorities' might be disbursed, because of the disagreements with the Kumasi chiefs and because it currently has no structure of allegiances of

Dependence and opportunity

its own. In terms of allegiance Ahafo consists, from the Kumasi perspective, of discrete clusters of villages whose headmen are politically subordinate to various chiefs, some senior and others quite junior, in the Kumasi state. Kukuomhene and his six supporters deny this subordination outright, and many Ashanti loyalists disavow the attenuated bonds and humble statuses which these relationships often imply. They acknowledge subordination only to a very senior wing-chief or to the Asantehene directly, and see Ahafo ideally as a state on a par with Kumasi, united within the historic Ashanti Confederacy. Aboumhene dreamed: 'Kokufu, Juaben, Nsuta, Mampong and Bekwai ... they formed the Ashanti nation, hence I was telling you that it is rather that Asantehene adds the name of Ahafo to these five towns to form Ashanti. We, with these five [plus, presumably, Kumasi], making six, all contribute to the maintenance of the Great King.' For Kukuomhene and the advocates of an independent Ahafo the constitutional problems are quite different: the elaboration of an independent state organisation outside the structures and traditions of Ashanti.

Allegiance in Ahafo is indeed 'very complex'[11] and to interpret its involvement in contemporary politics it is necessary to identify the most important principles of which it is comprised. In the most orthodox Ashanti sense, allegiance is the relationship between a divisional and sub-divisional chief, the latter described as the *birempon* of the former.[12] In addition to this, sub-divisional and other chiefs have a special relationship with a particular member of the court of their superior chiefs. It is the duty of this *adamfo*, or patron in court, to entertain the subordinate chief and act as his intermediary, as it would be improper for him to make a direct approach to the paramount chief. In Ahafo, among those chiefs who are campaigning for an independent Ahafo state as well as among those favouring Ashanti incorporation, the distinction between birempon and adamfo is blurred. From the perspective of the Kumasi chiefs, none of the Ahafo chiefs warrants the rank of birempon as none can be regarded as a sub-divisional chief, and indeed until a state council structure is established no Ahafo chief could reasonably lay claim to this title. Most of the pro-Ashanti chiefs speak of their superior relationships in the less specific adamfo idiom:

'We have always passed through the Akroponghene, and it is the same today. My ancestor was related to him. When my ancestors came they lodged with him in Kumasi. Any time you go to town you have to lodge with someone. We see Akroponghene every time we go to Kumasi, before we see the Asantehene. I can go and greet him any time. If the Asantehene summons me I can go to Akroponghene. But I do not need to if I do not want to, it is not like being his servant.'

Fawohoyedenhene's explanation indicates the advantages of the adamfo usage; he speaks of access to the Asantehene through a single intermediary while a birempon in, for example, Mampong state would not be so privileged.

Subordinate chiefs in Ashanti do not necessarily sit in the council of the state to which they belong – hence the function of the adamfo. In discussions of possible Ahafo state council models the tendency has been to simplify allegiance, making all recognised chiefs council members or, in effect, *abiremponfo*. Other trappings of the Ashanti hierarchy are also missing, for example the right of particular citizens to perform special functions for senior chiefs. These offices are separable from the other channels of allegiance, bonding a relatively humble man to the household of a paramount chief, albeit in a nominal way. Several Ahafo chiefs find this an attractive way of expressing fealty directly to the Asantehene, avoiding as it does the need to mention intermediate relationships through the Kumasi chiefs. Thus Asufufuohene claims the task of filling the Asantehene's pipe, while Goasohene is the Asantehene's palmwine-tapper; as an insignia of this office he has an umbrella ornament of a fist clenching a matchet (*twere*). Goasohene explained:

'My stool is the palmwine-tapper, to tap palmwine for the libation of the Golden Stool of Ashanti . . . If you have seen my stool you have looked on the Golden Stool . . . all my family come from Kumasi, my stool too comes from Kumasi. When they see my umbrella they know that the Chief's palmwine-tapper is passing by. The Asantehene's palmwine-tapper (*Asantehene betwani*). Only my stool has this office, I am the only chief who has this *twere*, among the Ashanti chiefs or the Ahafos.'

If political relationships with Ashanti in both land and allegiance are structurally complex, those associated with the independent Ahafo state council may be described as simple. To the Kumasi chiefs Ahafo consists of an ill-defined territory and groups of people related to their state in a number of different ways, but lacking political integrity of its own. The pro-Ashanti chiefs in Ahafo, while averring such integrity, select only those Ashanti relationships commensurate with high political status. The Kukuom protagonists deny all such external bonds and see territorial and political relationships in integral terms. Relationships in land proprietorship and allegiance coincide, all landholding units (stools) having direct political access through the representative functions of their chiefs to the state council. So complete is the idea of political monostructure that congruence between it and modern administrative divisions is either readily assumed or urgently demanded. The dialogue between the two factions about the political incorporation of Ahafo has recently become abbreviated to those who are 'for' Brong–Ahafo Region, and those who are 'for' Ashanti Region. For the latter, the structural complexity of Ashanti relationships has definite disadvantages, fragmenting

TABLE 4. *Allegiance, land and local pre-eminence in Abafo, 1968–9*

Abafo chiefs	Paramount acknowledged by Abafo chiefs [A]	Allegiance to Kumasi chiefs acknowledged by Abafo chiefs [B]	Kumasi chiefs claiming the allegiance of Abafo chiefs [C]	Kumasi chiefs claiming land in Abafo [D]	Claims of local pre-eminence among Abafo chiefs [E]
Aboum	Asantehene	'direct'	Nyinahin	Nkawie Nyinahin	Sankore
Acherensua	Asantehene	'direct'	Ohemaa	Oyokuo	*self*
Akrodie	Asantehene	'direct'	Mentia	Hiawu/Nkawie*	Kukuom
Asufufuo	Asantehene	Nkawie	Nwanmase	Hiawu/Nkawie*	—
Fawohoyeden	Asantehene	'direct'	Akropong	Hia	—
Goaso	Asantehene	'direct'	Akropong	Akwaboa	*self*
Gyedu	Asantehene	Ntotroso and Nkonson	Nkonson	Gyedukumanini	Ntotroso
Kenyase I	Asantehene	Hiawu	Hiawu	Hiawu	—
Kenyase II	Asantehene	'direct'	Hiawu	Hiawu	Mim
Kwakunyuma	Asantehene	'direct'	Domabra	Hia	Mehame
Kwapong	Asantehene	Asuoye Nyuma	Akyina	Hiawu/Asuowin*	—
Mehame	Asantehene	'direct'	Nsuase Nyuma	Akwaboa	*self*
Mim	Asantehene	Akwaboa	Akwaboa	Akwaboa	—
Nkasaim	Asantehene	'direct'	Adum	Akwaboa	*self*
Noberkaw	Asantehene	Akyeamehene	Nsuase Nyuma	Nkawie Nyinahin	*self*
Ntotroso	Asantehene	Gyedukumanini	Gyedukumanini	Gyedukumanini	*self*
Pomakrom	Asantehene	?	Hia	Nkawie Nyinahin	?
Sankore	Asantehene	'direct'	Attipen	(*Sankore*)	*self*
Sienchem	Asantehene	Hia	Hia	Hia	*self*
Wamahinso	Asantehene	Akwamu	Akwamu	Gyedukumanini	Kukuom
Anwiam	Kukuomhene		Buabasa	Nkawie Nyinahin	Kukuom
Ayumso	Kukuomhene		Akwamu	Akwaboa	Kukuom
Dadiesoaba	Kukuomhene		Akropong	Akwaboa	—
Dantano	Kukuomhene		Sewa/Akempem*	Hia	Kukuom
Etwineto	Kukuomhene		Akropong	Hia	Kukuom
Hwidiem	Kukuomhene		Gyedukumanini	Akwaboa	Kukuom
Kukuom	(*self*)		Akropong	Hia	*self*
Siena	Kukuomhene		Akropong	Nkawie Nyinahin	?

the political identity, interests and actions of faction members; in comparison the coherence of the Kukuom protagonists, although fewer, is striking, as has been their solidarity over a long period of time.[13]

Table 4 draws together, for comparative purposes, the various interpretations of allegiance, landownership and claims to local pre-eminence among the Ahafo chiefs as they stood in 1968. Column A indicates the major schism, the paramount chief to whom each chief professed allegiance. Seven acknowledge Kukuomhene as paramount, the others declare allegiance to the Asantehene. Several in this latter group recognise their subordination to a Kumasi chief (column B) but ten do not at the moment acknowledge the reciprocal claims from Kumasi (column C), saying that their relationship to the Asantehene is 'direct'. To the Kumasi chiefs this is laughable, as it implies that a chief like Acherensuahene imagines himself to be an Ashanti paramount. In Ahafo, however, the attitude is considered reasonable on a number of grounds. The Asantehene is reckoned to be sympathetic to the idea of a new Ahafo traditional council in spite of the opposition of his chiefs in Kumasi. As such an organisation is still hypothetical most of the pro-Ashanti chiefs in Ahafo would assert that their chances of leadership are at least as good as each other's – witness the claims to local pre-eminence listed in column E. A further important reason is that since the abolition of the Kukuom–Ahafo State Council in 1966 and the demand that the Ahafo chiefs should 'revert to their former allegiances', it has been considered expedient by both the government and the Asantehene for declarations of loyalty to be made provisionally to the Golden Stool rather than to the various Kumasi chiefs. This has emboldened the Ahafos to speak of 'direct' allegiance to the Asantehene (column A), and has made the demands for their return to the Ashanti fold more palatable. In fact four Ahafo chiefs are known to have

NOTES: to Table 4

* indicates that allegiance or landownership is apparently contested by two parties.
This is as accurate as possible a representation of the situation in 1968–9. Information synthesised in this table is derived as follows:
Columns A and B: Statements from the 28 Ahafo chiefs.
Column C: Derived from a list prepared by Fuller in 1932 (letter to Provincial Commissioner) GNA, D.104, and entries in the Ahafo District Record Book vol II, 1927–51, GNA, ADM 49/5/7, *plus* in some cases where there is apparent doubt, personal confirmation from the Kumasi chiefs.
Column D: Derived from a settlement of Ahafo lands by the Asantehene, agreed by the Kumasi chiefs, dated 25 Oct. 1939, GNA D.1491. No settlement of land with defined boundaries had been made hitherto. Checked against lands revenue collection lists, Goaso Local Council file L.4, p 136, dated 27 June 1957. *Current* lands revenue collection lists are still subject to readjustment but broadly concur with the 1957 lists with the exception that Pomakrom is allocated to Nkawie Nyinahin, not to Hia.
Column E: Derived from the responses of the 28 Ahafo chiefs to the interview question: 'who is the most important chief here in Ahafo'.

reaffirmed their allegiance to their Kumasi overlords: Mim (to Akwaboahene), Sienchem (to Hiahene), Ntotroso (to Gyedukumanini) and Kenyase I
(to Hiawuhene). It is striking that each of these chiefs, unlike any others in
Ahafo, acknowledges claims in both land and allegiance to one Kumasi chief,
and is particularly insistent about the origins of his community from that
stool. It is tempting to conclude, again, that where the constituents of
allegiance coincide in a single relationship which is recognised reciprocally,
that relationship has particular strength. It is certainly a structural principle
favoured in the organisation of the Kukuom–Ahafo State Council.

In the uncertainties of the constitutional crisis the government has chosen to
regard the 28 stools of the disbanded Kukuom–Ahafo State Council as
politically co-equal, a designation more agreeable to the smaller chiefs than to
the likes of Kukuomhene. The latter commented ruefully: 'If I am Kukuomhene and not Omanhene, I am nothing. I used to be their senior, now, because
we are all equal at the moment, some chiefs even try to insult me. Today we
are all equal.' An elder added incredulously that even Mehame was now
regarded as a peer of Kukuomhene. In bowing to government authority
Kukuomhene is well aware that restoration of his paramountcy to him is in
the gift only of the *aban* in Accra, and, apart from fending off the demands
from Kumasi, it is to there that all his diplomatic resources are currently
directed. To any Ahafo chief with a modicum of ambition the present
supposedly egalitarian arrangements are manifestly unsatisfactory and apart
from interest in the frozen Ahafo land revenues the prevalent concern is with
jockeying for relative political status (with implicit economic pay-offs) in
either of the two broad constitutional formulae. The attraction of Kukuomhene's alternative is its relative simplicity both in organisation and the
apparent means whereby it can be achieved, the recent precedent of the
1957–66 Kukuom–Ahafo State Council (however disreputable that may
appear to some), and the full range of state offices in a paramountcy free of the
attenuated and equivocal political relationships which Ashanti incorporation
would imply. If Kukuomhene's claims are obviously a matter for direct
negotiation with the government, the ambitions of Mimhene and the other
pro-Ashanti chiefs could only be satisfied by a lengthy process of compromise
with the Kumasi chiefs and the Asantehene in which the benefits of association with the metropolis would certainly have to be traded off against
relatively humble political status. The most intractable problem would be
within Ahafo itself, few chiefs being willing to admit that any other was as
much as *primus inter pares* (see column E of Table 4). Some progress towards
a solution of that problem has been made in the regional administration's
suggestion that chairmanship of an Ahafo traditional council should rotate
among the 28 stools. Tentatively accepted by some this distinctly un-Ashanti
solution is regarded without enthusiasm by most. It should be re-emphasised

that among the 28 chiefs the unity of Ahafo is not in question – as it is in Kumasi – and that what is at issue is a constitution which justly reflects this unity.

To gain some understanding of the political process among the Ahafo chiefs, in which the state council is the dominant issue, we must refer back to the distinction which is made between the political relationships of the stool and the political actions of its incumbent. In the active sense, politics is squarely the responsibility of the chief as an individual, however much he may enjoy the spiritual and temporal counsel proper to his office. Several interview questions foundered on this distinction, although in the long run meanings became fairly clear. Asked which of the Ahafo stools had the reputation of being the 'most troublesome', Etwinetohene replied: 'I don't know which stool could be the most troublesome, it is men who get trouble, not stools. You may think you are happy, but there are people who are out to do you down.' Asked about his stool's allies, Kenyase I hene queried: 'do you mean the stool or the man sitting on it? . . . The stool itself has no friend, but if I consider that Hwidiemhene and Goasohene have the same mind as I, well, I can take them as my friends. It will depend on myself, and how the other person moves.' The *state* of accord or dissent which may build up between two communities is seen as a long-term product of political interaction: 'I know [the stool's enemies] because I sit on the stool; and if, by his actions, I come to hate him, the stool too will hate him. My stool does not agree with Kukuomhene, and his likewise disagrees with mine' (Kenyase I hene).

The normative view that political communication should be expressed through structures of allegiance rather than in alliance among political equals is stressed in the opinion that it is wrong for a chief to speak of the affairs of another stool. As many chiefs emphasised, to do this is politically provocative, and one of the clearest ways of asserting the subject status of another community is to tell its history (as several Ahafo chiefs in fact did). 'I am a chief here in my own town,' Gyeduhene explained, 'the other chiefs have their own towns too. I cannot speak out about someone else.' Properly it is only through the state council that one may come to hear about, and perhaps participate in the affairs of another stool: 'here in Ahafo, unless a complaint has been lodged with the state council against a certain chief we can not know whether one stool has more troubles than another. I can only discuss what goes on in my town, not someone else's. If something happens to someone in Noberkaw he will not come and tell me about it. If he has a problem he writes about it to the government' (Asufufuohene). In the present state of deadlock it is readily assumed that the state council's functions have been transferred to the government, inevitably to the District Officer in the first instance.

Dependence and opportunity

There are a few bonds outside the context of state council membership between individual Ahafo stools, but these appear to have very little significance in current political action. It might seem that common matriclanship would make for strong political interrelationships, but this is apparently not so. Although a few chiefs described others as 'brothers' by virtue of common clan membership, this had no bearing on alignments in the current state council schism. The three representatives of the Agona clan in Ahafo are Kukuom, Nkasaim and Sankore, stools whose chiefs currently share very few political interests. Some doubt is cast on the relevance of clan identities by instances in which one chief cited as a 'brother' by another claims membership of a different clan. It is also likely that aberrations in 'orthodox' lines of succession have made the association of a few stools with particular clans inconstant. Nevertheless, clanship may be part of the lore of aggrandisement: 'Everyone has his own clan, but I could tell you the [supreme] one for Ashanti. I am Oyoko, and the Asantehene is also Oyoko, so you see, my stool is the most senior in Ahafo. The Asantehene and I are from the same clan so mine is the biggest stool hereabouts' (Mehamehene). Debating the matter with some interest, Ayumsohene came to a more sceptical conclusion: 'There are many clans in Ahafo. The one with the most representatives is the most important, I think ... But everyone here has his own clan, there is no clan which is more important than another.' Most chiefs appeared to endorse this view: 'Everyone is content with his own clan' (Dantanohene); 'Each person has his own clan and it would be wrong to say that one was more important than another' (Gyeduhene).

Marginally more important than clanship are the putative associations arising from settlement history, for example: 'What I know is that we took fire from Asufufuo to establish this village, so he is my brother' (Kwaponghene). However the affirmation of such a bond is as likely to be an indictment of the errant ways of a political rival as an authentication of alliance. Goasohene described how his own and Kukuomhene's stool were cut from the same piece of wood in Akropong, their common town of origin in the Kumasi state, with the blessing of the Akroponghene. Kukuomhene would be unlikely to find this piece of history very apt in the light of his current political endeavours, not least because of the implied parity of status with Goaso. A further example of this kind of historical bond is given in Fawohoyedenhene's account: '[my ally] in the old days was Akrodiehene who ruled alongside my ancestors. He is my best friend. My ancestor who died on the stool and one Asamoah of Akrodie were best friends. As they set about affairs together, whenever you saw one, you would see the other.' This togetherness has not rendered the outstanding land claims between the two stools any less bitter. Often the relationships argued from settlement history are expressed in the idiom of kinship; Dantanohene claimed Dadiesoabahene as a 'brother' because their stools were cut from the same piece of wood; and because he had given Kukuomhene a place to stay, Sienchemhene felt entitled to speak of him as his [errant] 'wife'. Other features with modest and contingent value in expressing inter-stool relationships are the common use of an oath and the possession of fetishes which are reckoned to be in a sense 'relatives'.

If these inter-stool relationships are seen as expressing historical continuities among the Ahafo communities, the competitive political relationships among the chiefs today are seen as distinct, although contributing in the fullness of time to 'traditional' structure. However much they may profess disinterest in each other's affairs, the Ahafo chiefs are hardly strangers on an interpersonal level. According to Mimhene, 'the chiefs of the Ahafo area are all related to each other'. He described his own network thus: 'Akrodie is my personal friend. Nkasaim, too, is my mother's cousin. Hwidiem too is not on my side but paternally is my father's son, my father's brother's son. Kukuom too is a brother paternally – cousin, I may term that. My father's brother's son.' What bearing, we enquired, do these relationships have on the present state council schism? 'Because of our choice, things are difficult, because we the twenty-one [chiefs] are speaking for Ashanti and the others are not. That has made things impossible.' Without much more intensive investigation it would be impossible to relate such interrelationships to the formation of political coalitions. What seems more significant is that the relationships which can be confirmed reciprocally with any precision commonly cross-cut the main factional alignments. Hwidiemhene and Nkasaimhene for example, in opposing camps on the state council issue, agree that they are related affinally, although differing in the way they traced this. It may be worth pointing out that Ahafo is a relatively small area and that intercommunication among all but the most isolated communities is quite intensive. Prior to accession, as 'youngmen', the Ahafo chiefs will have had ample opportunity to establish relationships in other communities. Marriage is clearly of importance here, although details are very difficult to confirm with much exactness. Nineteen of those interviewed reported that they were born in the towns over which they were currently chiefs but, significantly, five of the remainder were born in other Ahafo towns.[14] Until taking chiefly office in the home town of their matrikin, these five chiefs had lived in their paternal households and had usually spent some years earning their living in their town of birth. Goasohene explained:

'[until 1953] I was a farmer in Mim, and when I got money I made a shop. I was in Mim since I was a child – I even have my own home still in Mim . . . When I was with my father in Mim there was no cocoa. I was weaving and selling baskets, I could make and sell many of them and get one and sixpence which was enough for a cloth. In 1947 I had a farm at Mim with my brother. When my

237

cocoa bore I got money and made my shop at Mim. I kept the shop for about six years and divided it into two, one at Adwenase and the other at Domee [sections of Mim]. I was there when they brought me to become a chief at Goaso.'

Land is another personal interest which a chief may have outside his own stool. Hwidiemhene, for example, has property in Ayumso, Goasohene in Mim. Kenyase II hene has timber concessions outside his own realm. The extent of these interconnections and their significance in contemporary politics is hard to ascertain, and one is left with the conclusion that they are more likely to be supportive of a broader Ahafo unity than the coherence of particular factions. In this respect they are quite similar to the historical interconnections of the stools themselves. On the other hand, the contrast with the interrelationships implied by party-political identity is striking. Against the pre-existing pattern of wide-ranging and cross-cutting bonds, which affect ordinary people in much the same way as they affect chiefs, the effect of party membership seems radical indeed. Townspeople, chiefs and whole communities found themselves united or divided (often, it would seem, in wholly unexpected ways) in terms which were not simply local or proper to Ahafo, but which had potent national significance. The effect on the political process, for the chiefs as much as for anyone, was revolutionary.

b. THE POLITICS OF AN AHAFO CONSTITUTION

The economic and political significance of the state council issue is such that ordinary citizens of Ahafo with any interest at all in the affairs of the district are as ready as the District Officer, the Local Council officials and the chiefs themselves to recognise it as the local *cause célèbre*. In the words of Mr S. K. Opoku, Goaso citizen and erstwhile Member of Parliament, this pre-eminent issue is 'all about the position of Ahafo, whether we belong to the Brong–Ahafo Region or to the Ashanti Region . . . We used to have one paramount chief but the present government relinquished his post, so now we have no paramount chief. So this has meant that some chiefs are going to Ashanti while others wish to preserve their position in Brong–Ahafo.' The opinion of Mr Opoku and less politically experienced citizens is that the problem can only be solved by the central authorities. One elderly Goaso resident who favoured the independence of Ahafo was in fact of the opinion that a solution was being obstructed by corrupt officials in Accra who were putting the paramountcy up to the highest bidder. Such citizens would readily agree that without a state council their district is politically deficient. From the government's point of view it is convenient to have a state council as a legitimate body to deal with the allocation of certain economic and political resources; whatever its functions may in fact be it is expedient for it to be there and to have at least a veneer of efficiency. There is thus a measure of agreement with the chiefs themselves that the proper arena for negotiating the distribution of either land revenues or chiefly offices is a formally constituted state council. The chiefs also see good reason why the public at large should be concerned about the resolution of the issue. Never discriminating too closely between the share due to them and the share due to the local authorities for development purposes, they point out that until the questions of allegiance and the proprietary rights in land are resolved the progress of the district as a whole will continue to be impeded. The Local Councils, deprived of income for as long as the sources of revenue are contested, have been actively pressing for a solution in their own interests.

There is substantial agreement between the pro-Kukuom and pro-Ashanti factions about why a council of chiefs in Ahafo is necessary, and what functions it should perform. By far the most common plea is on grounds of financial deprivation, a demand made all the more insistent by rumours of the wealth accumulating in favour of the caretaker or owner-chiefs of Ahafo. The lack of personal allowances was of most immediate concern. Without their rightful share of revenue, the chiefs protested, they had to bear the cost of stool ceremonial and hospitality out of their own pockets. More altruistically, they pointed to the lack of public amenities within their own communities and the district at large. 'A chief like me,' declared Kenyase II hene, 'formerly they paid me £25 a month; now we don't have any sources [of income]. I don't get anything to buy beer or drink for you. Travel allowances, and so on. If a stranger is in town you have to take him and buy him beer. Now we can't get even a penny.' Goasohene complained: 'We chiefs in Ahafo are not paid, but when a visitor comes he lodges with us and we can spend a lot taking care of him. This has brought all the stools in Ahafo into debt. You disgrace yourself if you do not go and borrow money to look after that visitor ... We want the state council so that we can all be paid, all the chiefs in their towns ... We want to be paid so that at the end of every month we can have a shirt on our backs.' 'If I can be paid,' said Sienchemhene, 'I can use some of the money to build a fine palace – two storeys – and buy a palanquin and stool regalia, bracelets and gold for the stool. Then I will be recognised as a good chief.' Apart from these material needs, the reestablishment of the state council was repeatedly urged in the interests of political unity (*kroye*), unity through which autonomy could be expressed, efficient communication conducted and power (*tumi*) derived. Again, this was the attitude of pro-Kukuom and pro-Ashanti chiefs alike. Aboumhene, in the latter faction, remarked: 'We need a traditional council to rule the affairs of the Ahafo area without the interference of any Kumasi chief, or any clan chief from Ashanti. But we all will serve under the great King of Ashanti.' Firmly behind Kukuomhene, Dantanohene observed apprehensively: 'We are worried, we are neither slaves nor servants to anyone ... but someone in Kumasi may be claiming Dantano as his land. This troubles us.' The corporate sense of indignity about the imposed subjection to Kumasi was very widely felt; as one Goaso elder remarked: 'It does not look good for a big district like this to be without its paramountcy.' Many chiefs found the disunity debilitating, both in the sense that the constraints of a formal council structure were lacking and because there was no adequate means of resolving the many minor conflicts of interest among them. The major schism over the state council's constitution was indeed a vicious circle. 'We are not united,' Sankorehene observed, 'but if the government helps us to get a state council we shall elect one man to lead us in a clear way.' We are disunited because we have no Paramount,' said Ayumsohene. Hwidiemhene explained: 'If we have our state council that means we have control over our affairs, our land, everything.' Whatever their opinions about its organisation, all the Ahafo chiefs recognised the Kukuom–Ahafo State Council (1957–66) as the acme of Ahafo independence although few could regard it as a very wholesome expression of unity, dependent as it was on commitment to the Convention People's Party. If a state council is seen as the institutional expression of a measure of independence vis-à-vis the outside world, it is also expressive of certain solidarities within Ahafo. It is the most unequivocal expression of citizenship in a district with so large a proportion of strangers. It also epitomises the distinction between the elders (*mpaninfo*) and the common people (*merante*); thus several chiefs felt that the increasing unruliness of the 'youngmen' constituted a further demand for the stabilising influence of a a state council. 'The chiefs will be able to speak out', declared Goasohene, 'and get back some of their former authority.'

The state council was seen as indispensable to the more general consolidation of chiefly authority: 'Our main problem is to get some authority (*tumi*), for example, by getting a state council so that we can look after our own affairs' (Noberkawhene). 'Only the paramountcy', said Etwinetohene, 'will restore to the chiefs our lost authority'. The council organisation would bring authority to the chiefs corporately, but would also confer authority on each individual chief, partly through the sanction of allegiance to a paramount but more specifically in terms of the formal allocation of offices (*dibre*). The council was thus seen as indispensable to the aggrandisement of individual stools as it was to the district as a whole. Circumlocuting his ambitions, Ayumsohene expressed the hope that the government could make him into a 'senior man' (*opanin kese*) in Ahafo, adding suggestively: 'Where there is a paramountcy it can have a Nifahene, a Benkumhene, an Akyeame panin, an Ankobeahene, a Krontihene ...' Compared with this, the prospect of an attenuated relationship with the Ashanti power structure was decidedly unattractive and provided a sound enough rationale for his commitment to

Kukuomhene's faction: 'If I go to Kumasi they will give me a seat which is not good enough for me. They will have me sit after someone who is really junior to me. For this reason we do not wish to go to Kumasi.' There is thus a sense in which allegiance to the Kukuom or the Ashanti cause is secondary to the interests of stool aggrandisement. Chiefs of very small communities who have thrown in their lot with Kukuomhene are, like Ayumsohene, clearly aware of the inadequacy of their position in any Ashanti constitutional formula. On the other side, ostensible commitment to the Ashanti cause does not mean that a chief like Sienchemhene has not pondered the alternative at length; he feels today that his stool received short shrift in the Kukuom–Ahafo State Council:

'The boy who became a chief during my destoolment [1959–66] was a member of the Kukuom State Council, but the Council did not give promotion (*sic*) to the chiefs, so that man made no progress when he was attending their meetings. He should have been Gyasehene to Ahafo[15] as this village is older than all the others. I have to tell them what to do. Akrodie, Etwineto, Ayumso are still under me. Fawohoyeden, Dantano and I, if there is anything for us we split it three ways and I take two thirds. The rest is shared by all the others, including Kwakunyuma. Now they take no notice of me ... as I went to swear allegiance to the Asantehene, Kukuomhene does not agree with me. During the time of his State Council he never called me when there was something to be discussed. He has forgotten that I gave the place where he has settled to his ancestor.'

For both the chiefs and the government officers a further important function of the state council is its role in consolidating opinion and serving as an organ of communication. Unless they could meet in some formal framework, debate their differences and present their views through effective leadership, the chiefs felt they could not 'speak with one mind' within Ahafo or to external political agents. In this context three of the chiefs used the metaphor of a brood of chickens: if you kill the hen they run about aimlessly unable to find food. According to Fawohoyedenhene the state council 'improves our chieftaincy. It brings the chiefs together so that we can make representations to the government. As we are not united we have no say in government affairs. If the government imposes a law on us which we do not understand, then we can not challenge them. If we had a state council we could all get together.' The unity of the chiefs was seen as bearing directly on the strength of their corporate 'voice'; Ayumsohene recalled: 'Formerly, when there was a state council, the chiefs would meet and write a petition to the D.C., and he would send it on to Sunyani, before it went on to Accra. Now, as we are disunited, each of us writes petitions separately. When we had our state council there were always policemen present, and before we made our decision known to the government they had done so already.' Wamahinsohene also lamented: 'There is no longer anything like getting

Dependence and opportunity

together to petition the government . . . at the moment we do this individually. As I need a water supply [in any town] it is I who have to write on my own behalf. If ever we call the chiefs they can never get together.' For those favouring involvement in the Ashanti hierarchy of allegiance, the communications functions of a council of Ahafo chiefs were no less important: 'I would like us to get our leader so that we can serve the Asantehene. We have no head and if we don't go to Kumasi we don't know what business they are discussing' (Sankorehene). Other forms of representation were not, in themselves, adequate. Kenyase I hene commented: 'We have asked the government to establish a state council so that the chiefs may meet and discuss their problems. This is what we need in Ahafo. As for the Local Council – we have that. We have a D.C. If we have a state council we can meet and discuss things. Without it we are not united.' In fact, the chiefs do not discriminate very exactly between the responsibilities of the local authorities and those of the state council, speaking of the latter as though it was directly concerned with the building of roads and schools and the provision of other public amenities. In terms of the local government reform proposed by the 1968 Constitutional Commission these assumptions would be substantially correct, the intention being to run many local authority and state council functions together. However it is important to recall that for most of today's chiefs these qualities are largely notional; only nine of them have had direct experience of an Ahafo state council and even fewer have participated in the affairs of the local authorities.

The protracted conflict of interests over the Ahafo state council is outlined with economy by Mr S. K. Opoku:

'The people came here for hunting and then later on they started to make their villages and their farms. The paramountcy was created during a certain war so that they could all come together and form a body under a head with the status of paramount chief. As I hear, the proposition was made to Mim chief, but he said he was too much engaged on his fetish (*Mim obuo*) and so he could not take that. So Kukuomhene took up the leadership and later on the colonial government conferred the paramountcy on Kukuom. So all the chiefs later on owed allegiance to Kukuomhene. When the Ashanti Confederacy came into being (1935), to form one big council for the whole of Ashanti, Kukuomhene was not recognised by the Asantehene as a paramount chief. Then at Independence the C.P.P. government restored Kukuomhene as paramount chief. Then, when the counter-revolution came (1966) they said that paramountcies created by the former regime would not be recognised.'

As Mr Opoku indicates the issue in Ahafo has involved, from the beginning, a see-saw of power between Mimhene and Kukuomhene. Mim, the largest and ostensibly the most prosperous Ahafo town has had close and persistent relationships with Ashanti through its allegiance to the Kumasi stool of

Akwaboa. Kukuom, geographically at the heart of Ahafo and the core of a smaller but more coherent faction, has stoutly campaigned for its pre-eminence in an independent Ahafo state. The lesser stools, constituents of a state council notionally independent or part of Ashanti, have allied themselves according to the main schism of interest represented by Kukuom and Mim. To them the alternative can seldom have been more inviting than probable exploitation at the hands of the Kumasis on the one side or exploitation at the hands of the more senior Ahafo chiefs on the other.

The justification of the current political points of view of the two principals, and the factional alignment of the other Ahafo chiefs, are expressed in detailed historical narrative. The pro-Ashanti group account for the political development of Ahafo in terms of a series of events closely linked to Ashanti constitutional history. Variation among these versions may be interpreted in terms of their relative lack of coherence as a political faction. Certainly, there is much greater unanimity among the pro-Kukuom group, whose members speak of an independent acephalous existence as forest hunters terminated relatively recently (the 1890s) by armed resistence to Ashanti colonial intrusions. Mimhene's history dates from the early eighteenth century, the time of the formation of the original Ashanti Union:

'The Asantehene Opoku Ware made a war against the Akims, and while in Akim a message reached him that there had been another man besieging Kumasi town. The Asantehene deputed Akwaboahene and Hiahene to come back and see what had been taking place in Kumasi. They made war against that man. He was by name Abiri Moro and he hailed from the French Ivory Coast. They chased him and he crossed the river Bia, now in our area here. And they chased him right through, nearly to the French Ivory Coast, and then they returned back. On their way back they reached here in Mim and deputed three people to stay here and watch in case another war should come, and the Asantehene was informed. They built their house near this road. There were plenty of palm trees (*mem*) all around, and hence the place was called Mim. From here all around there was no village at all. After that, when there was peace, people used to rush to this area to [live]. Some of these people were hunters, and the head of Mim town showed them where to stay. So, places like Ayumso, Goaso, Mehame, Dadiesoaba, Nkasaim, Hwidiem, Kenyase I and II, were all under this place.'

Kukuomhene's version concerns much later events, around the end of the nineteenth century:

'Each of the communities in Ahafo came from different places and set up hunting camps. The place became populated. Later the Asantehene found that these people were not serving him so he appointed a man called Asibi Entwi to make war against the Ahafos. All the Ahafos met and offered the leadership to Mimhene but he refused it. Then they offered it to my ancestor and he agreed

243

of paramount chief. However, it was in the developing sphere of modern local government that Mimhene achieved pre-eminence. In the 1940s and 1950s he became the spokesman and representative of Ahafo, sitting on the committees and panels which preceded the local government reform of 1951, and thereafter representing 'traditional interests' on both the Ahafo Local Council and the Kumasi West District Council. He was also a special spokes-man for a large area west of Kumasi including Ahafo on the council of the Kumasi State and on the Ashanti Confederacy Council. By virtue of this aggregation of offices, Mimhene clearly exercised extensive authority during this period, contrasting sharply with Kukuomhene who was conspicuously absent from the arenas of public decision making.

The present chief of Mim, Kwaku Appiah, first acceded to the stool on Wednesday, 7 December 1947, an exact recollection typical of this 'semi-educated man' (his own term). He has the distinction of having held this troublesome stool for a total of eighteen years, longer than any other Mim chief this century. The present Kukuomhene, Yaw Frimpong, acceded three years earlier in 1944, and although he has experienced several changes of fortune in the wider political arena of Ahafo, his authority at home in Kukuom has suffered no serious challenge. The contrasting personalities and experience of these two chiefs have undoubtedly had a profound influence on politics in the district. Although lacking Mimhene's educated sophistication, Kukuomhene is seen by his entourage as having all the bearing, attitudes and experience proper to an authentic paramount chief. He has proved able to compensate for his lack of knowledge and tactical skill in confronting the modern political world by mobilising his considerable personal wealth and the wealth of his stool to secure clerical and legal assistance and to consolidate advantageous political alliances. He is, by all accounts, a more astute and determined politician than his predecessor who, it is felt, lacked the political sensitivity to recognise that acquiescence in the re-establishment of the Ashanti Confederacy in 1935 would imply the sacrifice of his paramountcy and the return of Ahafo to the Kumasi yoke. Soon after his accession, Yaw Frimpong set out to retrieve 'what we have lost', mobilising the political resources at his disposal within and beyond the district.

It is clear that Kukuomhene would have met with little success were it not for his association with two political organisations of wider national significance. Until the mid-1950s his plea for the return of his paramountcy was indeed a cry in the wilderness. However, dissatisfaction with the dominance of Kumasi had reached even greater proportions among the Brong chiefdoms along the northern and western periphery of the Con-federacy. Led by the chief of Techiman, they consolidated their opposition to Ashanti by forming a Union of their own, the Brong–Kyempem Federation (the Federation of the Thousand Brong People), in February 1951. In sub-sequent years Kukuomhene developed a close association with these dissident interests, but it was not until 1958, when he had already regained his paramountcy, that he was able to add his own state to a renamed Brong-Ahafo Federation. This common cause with the Brongs was, however, secondary to Kukuomhene's association with the Convention People's Party. The Brong-Kyempem Federation had aligned itself with the C.P.P. long before he had,[21] and it was with the assurance of this partisanship that Techimanhene led the Brong chiefs out of the Confederacy Council in February 1956. It was therefore reasonable that the Asantehene should be persuaded to support the opposition National Liberation Movement, a partisanship which his loyal chiefs, including Mimhene, were only too ready to encourage and to share. Mr S. K. Opoku's account of the infiltration of party political identities into the state council issue in Ahafo is as clear as any: 'The point is that Mim is very much associated with Akwaboahene – Akwaboa stool – and Akwaboahene is close to the Asantehene. And so, well you see they were promised that if they came to the N.L.M. aid they would take the paramountcy from Kukuom and give it to Mim chief.' (When was this?) 'About 1955. Kukuom also became the stronghold of the C.P.P.' (Was Kukuomhene always a C.P.P. man?) 'At the beginning of the N.L.M. he also joined that, and later he withdrew.' (What were his reasons?) 'He foresaw that Mim and Akwaboahene were interested in the paramountcy. By then Kukuomhene was not a literate, but Mimhene was a literate and was representing Ahafo at the Asanteman Council (the Council of the Ashanti Confederacy) and he was taking the opportunity to undermine him. And so he became a protagonist, as Mimhene had gone to the N.L.M. he went to the other side.' While Mimhene had staked his hopes on his Kumasi relation-ships Kukuomhene and his supporters set about bringing pressure to bear on the C.P.P. government of the day. In April 1956 he led a petition, with fifteen signatories, on behalf of the 'chiefs, adikrofo and elders of Ahafo area' to an impressive list of twenty-seven important persons. These included the Governor, the Prime Minister Dr Nkrumah, his Ministerial Secretary, three Ministers and their permanent secretaries, sixteen M.P.s, and the Regional and District administrative officers (see Table 5, column A). The petition explained that the Ahafos had only agreed to join the Confederacy in 1935 on condition that Kukuomhene continued to be recognised as paramount, but that this had not been honoured by the Kumasi chiefs. Ahafo was denied direct representation on the Confederacy Council and, moreover, 'the recent representation of the Mimhene, who was before 1935, the Nifahene of Ahafo a subject to the Omanhene of Ahafo, as a member of the Asanteman council was a political achievement and not customary'. Ahafo had 'derived no benefit from the work of the Ashanti Regional

Development Committee'; prior to 1935 Ahafo had been administered with the Brongs from Sunyani, and if this situation could be restored in the form of a new Region, the Ahafos could wholeheartedly reaffirm their loyalty to the (C.P.P.) government of the day. The petition concluded, rather breathlessly: 'It is felt that (1) the Ahafos have been with the Ashantis for long and yet the Ahafo area is still underdeveloped and therefore Ahafo's can no longer go with Ashantis but want to go with Brongs once more for administrative and development progress and (2) that the Kukuomhene be recognised by the government as the Omanhene of Ahafo.'[22]

This petition was repeated in October 1956, this time addressed specifically to the Minister for Local Government and signed by seven Ahafo chiefs (see Table 5, column B) and 'representatives' of nineteen other communities. In an election year this and similar petitions from the discontented Brong chiefdoms were a political resource the C.P.P. was not disposed to ignore. Assurances of mutual support were exchanged and when they were returned to power as the first government of an Independent Ghana, the C.P.P. leaders, acknowledging how successfully the N.L.M. opposition in the Ashanti sphere of influence had been broken, set about honouring their part of the bargain. In February 1958 the Ministry of Local Government officially recognised Kukuomhene as a paramount chief.[23] These manoeuvres did not escape the attention of the parliamentary opposition; later that year, debating the bill which was to carve the new Brong–Ahafo Region out of Ashanti, the opposition N.L.M. spokesman on local government affairs, Mr Wireko, attacked the Minister's prodigality in handing out paramountcies:

'In this country we have customary laws and tradition governing the creation of paramount chiefs. These *Gazette* paramount chiefs are not paramount chiefs at all according to the real meaning of our custom. The Minister of Local Government

Sources for Table 5
Column A: Petition to His Excellency the Governor and others from the Chiefs, Adikrofo and Elders of the Ahafo Area, dated 17 April 1956, copy in the possession of Kukuomhene
Column B: Petition to the Minister of Local Government and others from the Chiefs and people of Ahafo, dated 28 October 1956, copy in the possession of Kukuomhene
Column C: Kukuom–Ahafo State Council minutes, 25 March 1958
Column D: *Ghana Gazette* no 50, dated 3 June 1958
Column E: Goaso District Office file LA 4, Kukuom State Council Revised Chiefs List, February 1960
Column F: *Loc. cit.*
Column G: Goaso District Office file LA 4, vol 4, undated list (1963)
Column H: Goaso District Office file LA 4, vol 4, Kukuom–Ahafo State Council chiefs list, June 1963
Column I: Various sources – Goaso District Office files and records of the Kukuom–Ahafo State Council
Columns J and K: Kukuom–Ahafo State Council Record Book and National Liberation Council Decrees no 112, 136 and 203
Column L: Interview, and undated list, Goaso District Office

is aware that the definition of a chief in reference to Ashanti is a chief who has sworn the oath of allegiance to the Asantehene or the Golden Stool of Ashanti and must have been recognised by the occupant of the Golden Stool as a paramount chief. The chiefs I have mentioned as listed under schedules 6 and 7 have not sworn any oath of allegiance to the Asantehene so they do not owe allegiance to the Golden Stool, and I wonder why the Minister published their names in the *Gazette* as paramount chiefs. I want the Minister to explain – when he comes to wind up – whether a situation has arisen whereby, he sitting in his Ministry, can elevate or create anybody, including perhaps a person like myself a paramount chief . . .

'It is quite evident in this Bill that the C.P.P. Government having tried to have control over all corporations in this country, over all Municipal Councils, over all Local Councils, and even having had complete control over all sports, are now seeking to have control over the chiefs in order to use them as rubber stamps.'[24]

Kukuomhene, who likes to argue today that his claims to the paramountcy withstood the rigours of parliamentary debate, would argue that the rights of his stool had never been abrogated and that the C.P.P. government had simply confirmed them. Etwinetohene explained:

'The C.P.P. were given power so we all joined it. Nkrumah told us that if we followed him we would get back whatever we had lost. Formerly there was a paramountcy in Kukuom but that was changed during the Confederacy. Because it was not cancelled in the proper way we said that we would help Nkrumah so that we would get back our paramountcy. That is why we joined the C.P.P.'

Identification with the C.P.P. and the N.L.M. (later regrouped as the United Party) served to polarise support and opposition on the state council issue throughout Ahafo. As Nkasaimhene recalled:

'Before the Confederacy we had our paramountcy at Kukuom but the Confederacy did away with this . . . the C.P.P. gave the paramountcy to Kukuom but at that time we were all United Party (U.P.) members, these towns I mentioned were all U.P. members, we did not agree that we should serve Kukuom'.

Although whole communities came to be associated with one party or the other as 'strong C.P.P.', or 'strong U.P.', political opposition in each was such that commitment among townsmen to a single party was never absolute. Partisanship within community segments and even within individual families became political currency with which the state council factions (and other conflicting interests) could play. It is interesting to note that while Kukuomhene and the C.P.P. eventually held sway among the Ahafo chiefs, throughout the 1950s and into the 1960s the U.P. seems to have sustained the majority of popular support in the district.

sition of the pro-Ashanti chiefs. Thus we find the C.P.P. youngmen of Hwidiem berating their chief for having 'failed to negotiate with the Oman-hene to restore your clan position as the Akyeamihene (Chief Linguist) of the State Council . . . against the wishes of your subjects' and being 'a super-lative member of the defunct National Liberation Movement' to boot.[28] It seems that the policy of the State Council was not, at first, to exploit the party conflict rife in the Ahafo communities at the time, but rather to attempt to build a new constitution in terms of a reconciliation of local interests. One of its earliest decisions in 1958 was to appoint a special committee whose terms of reference were 'to settle the differences which have arisen between the chiefs and their subjects within the area, because of politics and to report the result to the Council'.[29] Finding people with the degree of impartiality required for this mission engaged the members in a 'long and heated discussion'. Three laymen and the Ahafo Roman Catholic priest were eventually appointed but it is doubtful whether any of them agreed to act in this capacity. After this initial flight of idealistic fancy the Council capitalised heavily on its loyalty to the C.P.P. With its new authority it could confidently abet and sanction the deposition of United Party chiefs and the installation of C.P.P. successors more amicably disposed to Kukuomhene. Late in 1958 the wave of destoolments was under way and by 1960 eighteen new chiefs had been gazetted and had taken their places on the Council (Table 5, column E).

The offices in the new State Council were a valuable political commodity, but the composition of the Council and the ranking of its members was not without its attendant problems. Kukuomhene consulted the Regional Com-missioner but was assured that such matters were entirely his own affair; beyond the fact that there was a state council there at all, the government was not greatly interested in its constitution so long as its operations were not disruptive. Kukuomhene was obviously drawn, in making appointments, between rewarding his own allies in the recent campaign, offering induce-ment to less sympathetic communities, and observing the pre-1935 consti-tutional precedents on which his own claims to authority so conspicuously rested. Table 5 summarises aspects of the growth of the Kukuom–Ahafo State Council and the political changes involved. Within two years of its establishment the Council had expanded from a small core including only nine Ahafo chiefs, to a body of twenty-three, all but two of whom were chiefs. There are conspicuous omissions from the lists at this time, notably Goaso. In July 1958 the Omanhene sent a letter to the Regional Com-missioner at Sunyani detailing new constitutional relationships within his state. They were expressed in the idiom of Ashanti state organisation, with Kronti, Nifa, Gyase, Benkum and other Divisions. Goaso was designated a subject chief of Mimhene, the Ahafo Nifahene, while so small a community as Dantano was distinguished as the Gyase stool with an impressive list of subject villages: Sienchem, Etwineto, Kwapong, Fawohoyeden, Ayumso (deputy to the Gyase), Dadiesoaba, Mehame, Pomakrom and the rapidly growing village of Tipokrom. It is significant that several of Kukuomhene's key supporters are grouped within this Gyase, or 'household' core, the Division most immediately concerned with the accession and deposition of the paramount himself. The most obvious – and the most contentious – expression of rank was in pay scales (Table 5, column G), ranging from £G 960 a year for the paramount to a paltry £G 120 for the lowest official government grade of chief. There appears to have been little discrimination within the Council chamber, all the 28 chiefs eventually recognised enjoying freedom to participate 'democratically' in discussion and in the transaction of state business. Moreover, there is enough variation in the lists of chiefs which appeared from time to time between 1958 and 1966 to indicate irresolution and inconsistency in the Council's constitution-building. The embarrassment of formal ranking may perhaps be regarded as a reflection of the Council's predicament as a body 'traditional' by definition but largely 'modernist' in intent. Business seems to have been conducted in something approaching a local authority idiom; the Council's first secretary, Mr T. N. Baidoo, who claims to have been extensively responsible for its organisation and the elaboration of its constitution, no doubt applied his experience of the Ahafo Local Council. Lay representatives of various local interests quite often participated at meetings, commonly in the capacity of 'regents', but in April 1958 the Council decided that it would be inappropriate to admit the 'Chief Farmer of Ahafo' as a full member and that 'preference should be given to Chiefs and Stool Elders in an area'.[30]

The status of Mim posed special problems for the State Council's organisers. Mimhene's strong repudiation of Kukuomhene's claims clearly ruled out his participation, but at the same time his stool's right to the status of Ahafo Nifahene was unequivocal. Kwaku Appiah would certainly have to go, and in November 1958 deposition charges were duly preferred by the C.P.P. youngmen of the town in the guise of a 'Mim Youth Association'. They wrote to the State Council declaring authoritatively that Kwaku Appiah and the Mim Queen Mother were both deposed: 'We, being the future rulers, have the right to indulge ourselves in administration and political affairs and also to participate in any matter directly or indirectly affecting the town and its inhabitants.'[31] Although he realised that his elders were being deprived of their conventional role, Mimhene found it expedient to back down quietly, but not before he had complicated matters by handing over the regalia and insignia of his office to his Kumasi overlord the Akwaboahene. Three years later his C.P.P. successors and the Kukuom–Ahafo State Council, frustrated and embarrassed, were still trying to retrieve

disrepair during the years of the reformed Ashanti Confederacy, and required much refabrication. At a lengthy meeting in March 1960 Kukuomhene, Dantanohene and Ayumsohene withdrew to consolidate their interpretation of these traditional matters then returned to announce that Thursday (Yawda), the day of Ahafo's 'war of liberation' against the Kumasis seven decades previously, should be the State oath. Kukuomhene also announced that

'he had chosen the first Thursday following the Akwesida [Sunday] in October each year as State Festival for Ahafo. This day will be celebrated with great pomp and pageantry; peeling (*sic*) of state drums and merry-making will continue up to Sunday. Libation will be poured to the departed souls and the gods of the State; the black stools will be purified in a sacred river. Until after the celebration of this Festival no occupant of a stool in Ahafo has the right to eat new yam.'[38]

Although this home-brewed constitution obviously looked to the organisation of the Kumasi state at least as much as to the obscure traditions of Ahafo it was, and still is, anathema to those who regarded themselves as subjects of the Asanthehene.

Consolidation of the Council's legitimacy and autonomy in other quarters followed more slowly. One may detect a feeling of pique among members that repeated protestations of support for the C.P.P. government were not always reciprocated in terms of clear endorsement of the Council's authority. In 1959 the chiefs were upset to find themselves listed under the Kumasi State Council in a *Ghana Gazette* supplement.[39] Such official equivocation about their autonomy was a continual source of embarrassment, particularly insofar as it re-emphasised that the State Council still had no access to Ahafo lands revenue. This also made for altercations with the Ahafo Local Council which was, until 1960, charged with the collection of revenue. It had no authority to make direct payments to Kukuomhene and his chiefs, and the proportion due to the 'Traditional Authority' responsible for Ahafo was still being paid to Kumasi. As a body the Local Council was certainly not hostile to Kukuomhene who was, as paramount chief in Ahafo, its President. It was, however, put in a quandary when, in 1959, it was instructed by the Regional Commissioner to pay Kukuomhene a £50 monthly maintenance grant. Agreeing that this was fair, the Local Council clerk pointed out that it was not specified from where this money was supposed to come. Shortly after he was obliged to reject quite firmly a State Council request for the purchase of an official car for Kukuomhene.

The much-solicited Brong–Ahafo Region was established in 1959, but the State Council was disturbed to discover that the drawing of the new Regional boundary did not at once resolve the issue of proprietary rights in land. Intensified complaint led to the vesting of Ahafo lands in the President of Ghana in 1961. This was not a very happy compromise, although it did prompt the government to release £10,000 to sustain the Council. Kukuomhene announced that he would match this munificence by agreeing to forego £450 of his annual salary to boost the scholarship budget. By this time Kukuomhene and his advisers had become adept at petitioning and in December 1961 they addressed one of their most assertive pleas to their new landlord, the President. This was inspired by the discovery in July of that year that the new Administrator of Stool Lands in Goaso was continuing to pay a proportion of Ahafo revenues to the Asantehene. In a vigorous debate the Council considered despatching a delegation to Accra but eventually decided on an initial written petition. Kukuomhene's Sunyani solicitor was brought in to compose a long, carefully worded document which insisted that 'We have overwhelming and irrefutable traditional and documentary evidence in support of our contention that no Kumasi Clan Chief has any vestige of title, right or interest in Kukuom (Ahafo) Stool Lands. Neither is the Asantehene the traditional overlord of the Kukuom (Ahafo) Stool Lands.' Kukuomhene's historical claims were stated yet again, scholarly references were made to the works of Captain Rattray and Casely Hayford, the Asantehene himself was quoted in extracts from the minutes of the Ashanti Confederacy Council, and litigation dating back to 1899 was cited in support of the Ahafo claims. The petition concluded:

On grounds of politics, economics and expediency, we submit that our claim to the whole total of Stool land revenue standing to our credit is irrefutable and irresistible. Thanks to your enlightened, progressive, and beneficent regime, we have been restored to our pristine status of paramountcy. This bold act of wise statesmanship, we shall for ever remain grateful to you, Sir.

But, as our proverb runs, 'tumi nyinaa wo asase so' [All power is in the land]. Unless we are fully restored to our old economic independence, our newly-won political independence [from the Ashantis] would not be complete. To strip us of our landed heritage, would be to emasculate us at our re-birth as a paramountcy. We are prepared, able, and willing to put all the revenue accruing from our Stool Lands to good use by launching much-needed self-help projects in our comparatively backward area. Under your wise leadership, we are confident that we can contribute our full quota to the sum total of national effort.[40]

This petition was not in itself successful, and was followed up three months later by another, composed by the State Council's new secretary Mr J. N. Essel and forwarded through the Regional Commissioner, Sunyani. Based on a Council resolution, this explained the chiefs' demand for a full one-third share of Ahafo revenues in terms of the many expenses which they were obliged to meet. Noting that 'the dynamic Convention People's Party' and 'our Selfless LEADER and SAVIOUR OSAGYEFO DR KWAME NKRUMAH' had

These judicial functions are seen as vital to the preservation of unity among the Ahafo communities and as the principal expression of the Council's right to act independently. Noberkawhene explained:

'If two chiefs are disputing something the President meets all the chiefs, they discuss the matter and give their verdict. This avoids strife in the state (*amansosem*). If something crops up in the towns, like a land dispute, they discuss it and decide on the owner. If troubles come between the chiefs and the leaders of a town the elders meet and report the matter to the State Council. If what they have done is not customary they are told so. If the chief acts uncustomarily, they point out his faults to him.'

Peace-keeping is an extension of these functions; in October 1962 the Council authorised Kukuomhene to conciliate between Akrodie and Kwapong who were at odds on an issue of trespass 'to avoid litigation'.

Administratively there might have been more for the Council to do had there been more funds at its disposal. In this sphere, however, it had to restrain its modernist zeal and avoid encroachments on the competence of the local authorities. It was clearly felt to be proper that the State Council should take an interest in the material progress of the district, even if it could not organise and finance development projects by itself. Chiefs today feel that a paramount should tour his realm regularly to assess its needs, very much in the manner of a conscientious District Officer. The Council was expected to reserve a large proportion of what funds it had for the provision of scholarships, administered jointly with the Local Councils and subject to ministerial approval. The chiefs tended to feel that the money was in their gift and could therefore be used with their own interests in mind, although this did not necessarily make the allocation of scholarships free of contention:

'Nana Kwesi Appaw – Gyasehene moved that he was against the Standing Committee's recommendation of the 19th April 1962 that an amount of £3,000 should be given to Mr Isaac Amoako Ababio, a Royal to the paramount stool of Kukuom who is at present studying in the United Kingdom as scholarship ... he suggested that if there was any money available at all it should be used in putting up council hall and offices as the Council has nowhere to hold its meetings.'

This was defeated on a counter-motion that as a Kukuom royal 'It is the duty of this Council to look after him while in the United Kingdom pursuing further studies as he will be useful to the Ahafo area after his studies.' This was passed with 7 votes for, 3 against and with 3 abstentions.[45] As a supplementary estimate was necessary the decision was passed on to the Regional Commissioner where it encountered Local Council objections that scholarships were supposed to be administered jointly and that £3,000 was too large a slice of the budget to be allocated to a single client. The District Commissioner wrote to the State Council suggesting that Kukuom should use its private funds to support Ababio.[46] From the Council's point of view, a precedent had been set in its heavy investment in the education of Mr. B. K. Senkyire, a Kenyase royal and former Member of Parliament who trained in law in Britain and in due course became a C.P.P. Member of Parliament for Ahafo. In July 1963 Mr Senkyire wrote to the State Council expressing his 'deep appreciation and gratitude to the Council for the unavoidable help and fatherly love shown to him while in the United Kingdom', and asking whether the Council could assist him with a further £2,000 loan for a car, the better to ply his trade. The Council agreed, but again the Regional Commissioner declined to sanction this expenditure.[47] A more serious rebuff was still to come; the Council decided to recoup its investment in Mr Senkyire by appointing him 'Counsel and Legal Adviser to advise the Council in all matters of importance and to defend it in cases where legal implications were involved . . . with a yearly remuneration of FIVE HUNDRED POUNDS (£500)',[48] but once again the government refused. Whatever confidence the Council may still have had in the political value of its educational investments must have been reduced further by the Local Council's insistence that large disbursements to a select few should now yield in favour of smaller grants and scholarships to approximately thirty students.

A good deal of the Council's time was spent discussing the apportionment of the other moneys at its disposal. Travel allowances and ceremonial expenses appeared frequently on the agenda, sometimes involving large sums. In September 1961 the Council resolved to increase the subsidy for the annual first-fruit ceremonies from £400 to £700.[49] Some of this budgeting was regarded as unorthodox and in April 1964 the Regional Commissioner instructed the D.C. at Goaso (and his colleagues elsewhere in Brong–Ahafo) to attend the session at which the State Council debated its annual estimates, and to offer advice to the chiefs.[50]

Although the limits of its competence were not clearly understood by the chiefs, the State Council proved itself quick to challenge anything which seemed like an encroachment on its 'traditional' functions. On one occasion, hearing that the Game Department was culling elephants in Ahafo, the Council resolved that it should claim from the government tribute of a tusk, an ear, a hind leg and the tail of each animal killed.[51] Again, having ruled that fishing should be prohibited in the Tano river, the Council felt entitled to complain very sharply to the Asunafo Local Council for issuing permits to three local fishermen.[52] In general the Council seems to have sought to avoid any direct confrontation with the local authorities and was discouraged by the District Commissioner from taking too close an interest in their affairs. Instead it adopted an attitude of friendly patronage, the concrete expression of which was Kukuomhene's annual appearance as President at the opening session of the Local Councils. The State Council sent a formal expression of

town to town to induce and to persuade certain people to rebel against our socialist governement'.[59] The chiefs exchanged details of their own personal encounters with this kind of dissent; Dadiesoabahene reported that U.P. members were 'meeting day and night' in his town 'to discuss matters which are detrimental to the progress and security of the Ahafo State and the Ghana Nation as a whole'. These people should be 'brought to book' at once, to prevent their malignant influence spreading to other towns. A list of twenty names and addresses was drawn up and forwarded to the regional office with a plea that the culprits should be 'removed from the Ahafo area and detained so that peace and tranquility might reign'. The Regional Office remained unresponsive and in December the Council held an emergency meeting at which the charges of conspiracy were presented in new and compelling terms. If its fears could not be justified to the administration in terms of the subversion of the authority of loyal C.P.P. chiefs, they would undoubtedly receive more attention if the villains were recast as a direct menace to the party, the government and the President. Sixteen Ahafos, eight of whom had appeared on previous lists, were accused of plotting one night in the clinic at Kukuom to assassinate Dr Nkrumah, blow up his statue in Accra and overthrow the government by force. It was alleged that they had contributed four pounds each 'to cover transport and other incidental expenses' involved in this ambitious excursion. The Council's recommendations, on this occasion addressed directly to the Minister of the Interior, called for 'drastic and stringent measures . . . against the plotters', and concluded: 'the Council seriously demands the arrest and detention of the people whose names [are] mentioned herein at no distant date so that peace and tranquility might reign in Ahafo in particular and Ghana in general'. The troublemakers were 'United Party members and followers of the irresponsible minority opposition members who had wanted to turn this country into a state of anarchy and chaos'.[60] In spite of the high drama of this plea, the Council was again to be disappointed by the government's inaction.

United Party scapegoats could hardly be found for all the political problems confronting the Council, and by 1964 the plausibility of charges of U.P. subversion in stool disputes was wearing thin. Dismissing a case against Aboumhene the State Council declared that they were becoming bored with repeated accusations of this kind and that if the plaintiffs felt that the chief was indeed plotting for the return of Dr Busia they should take the matter to the police and have criminal charges preferred. Slapping on a stiff pacification fee of £23 8s od and four bottles of Schnapps the Council warned both parties that it was 'taking initiative to be a watch-dog henceforth at Aboum'.[61] These sentiments may have reflected waning enthusiasm for some of the operations of the C.P.P.; the Council members can hardly have welcomed a compulsory annual deduction of between £60 and £84 from their salaries as a contribution towards the Regional Secretariat building fund.[62] However, a much greater threat to the Council's coherence was the recrudescence of inter-stool rivalry, apparent in the minutes barely three years after its inception. It is unlikely that the chiefs were often as menacing as Ayumsohene who 'told the Council that unless the boundary dispute between the Ahafo chiefs are solved, any body entering into his land would be fired at with gun'.[63] This threat, plainly addressed to the stools adjacent to Ayumso and to its old rival Goaso in particular, indicates that the conflicting interests of economic and political aggrandisement which had lain dormant for some time were returning to the fore. The tacit agreement that the elusive land revenues should be held in common among all the Ahafo chiefs[64] did not deter them from making individual territorial claims, primarily expressed in the right to allot land to new tenants. On this occasion Noberkawhene, sufficiently distant from the contending parties to be regarded as a fair arbitrator, persuaded Ayumsohene to withdraw his threat. Mr T. N. Baidoo, visiting the Council in his capacity as D.C. and Chairman of the (District) Working Committee of the C.P.P. also urged the chiefs to 'co-operate and try to embrase the State Council and make it a success'.

A little over a year later in April 1962 the D.C. (Mr Baidoo's successor at Goaso) was again urging the chiefs to 'sink their indifferences' and avoid the crippling cost of land litigation. By this time inter-stool rivalry was clearly apparent, particularly among the smaller towns which had acquired young and outspoken C.P.P. chiefs. The cold war of stool aggrandisement became more open and in one significant move, initiated by Ayumsohene and the chief of Kenyase II, the Council was asked to recommend to the government that some more of them should be raised to the status of paramount – while still declaring allegiance to Kukuomhene. Ayumsohene 'moved that Ahafo is a vast area comprising about 32 towns and villages, therefore an approach or representation [should] be made to the Government for additional Paramount chiefs to be created i.e. some of the chiefs at present under the Omanhene of Ahafo to be raised or up-graded to the status of Paramount chiefs . . . under the present Paramount Chief of Ahafo'.[65] A major attraction was undoubtedly the £960 salary of a paramount, yet it is clear that the prestige of supremacy within enhanced Ahafo Divisions, with the implication of the allegiance of neighbouring stools and the recognition of superior rights in land, were at stake. Kwaponghene, one of those unlikely to gain anything from such plans, objected strenuously to this idea, pointing out that Kukuomhene was by tradition the only paramount. However, others were plainly intrigued by the possibilities implicit in Ayumsohene's proposal and, carefully sidestepping the issue of who should be upgraded, the Council debated the number of chiefs to be elevated. Ntotrosohene, plainly angling for the north eastern paramountcy, proposed

deposition. As a staunch C.P.P. member he had sustained authority in this predominantly U.P. town with moderate success, but on his departure the political fever mounted. Mr J. K. Bofah, identified as both a commoner and a stranger, was recognised as regent by the State Council, 'being a neutral person'.[70] Eventually the Mim elders proposed one Kofi Kwarteng as the new chief. Kwarteng had already occupied the Mim stool for a short period in 1935, was now aged 70, was illiterate and – to the concern of the State Council – was a United Party supporter. The local C.P.P. branch executive proposed another candidate, Mr J. K. Owusu, and pressed his case in a petition addressed directly to the Minister of Justice. 'As a result of this absence of a chief in Mim', they declared, 'We have been existing like "Sheep without a shepherd".' They continued to explain:

That recent signs of the adverse effect of this vacancy are manifested by unrest and confusion among the populace.

That we have discovered that there is little unity in the town: the elders have often reported acts of disrespect by citizens towards the elders.

That on enquiry we have discovered that the cause of this direspect is the inability of the elders to instal a chief at Mim for this long period.

That we members of the Executive of the Mim branch of the Party have been approached by all classes of the society and asked what efforts are being made to solve this disturbing problem.

That many disputes which are in the province of the chief have been left unresolved because there is no chief in Mim.

That the customary rites have been left unperformed due to this vacancy as a result of which a lot of unrest has been caused.

That after consultation amongst ourselves we have picked 1 (one) person from among us who we think will be the proper person to occupy the long vacant stool of Mim, namely Mr James Kwaku Owusu of Mim.

That the said Mr James Kwaku Owusu is a native of Mim and a member of the clan eligible to occupy the Mim stool.

That not only is the said Mr James Kwaku Owusu a loyal, staunch and ardent member of the Convention People's Party, but is a hard working, intelligent and highly respected young man, whose progressive ideas will help us to develop the town of Mim.[71]

To the chagrin of the Party branch the Judicial Commissioner appointed to investigate the problem decided in favour of Kwarteng, the State Council was obliged to accept his installation, and he was duly gazetted by the government.

However, the C.P.P. chairman and his executive in Mim were not prepared to let the matter rest there. In May 1963 they addressed a letter to Dr Nkrumah himself, asking him to reverse the decision in favour of Owusu. They felt that it 'would be unfortunate and retrogressive to enstool the said

Nana Kofi Kwarteng, a staunch member of the defunct United Party, as Mimhene'.[72] They were sure Kwarteng was so unpopular that he did not command the support of as many as a tenth of the inhabitants of Mim. They recommended a referendum, warning that 'it is our strong belief, born of hard experience and loyal devotion to the cause of the Party, that upon the peaceful solution of the Mim stool case will now depend the fate of the Party in and around Mim. Kofi Kwarteng as Mimhene would spell down on the Party . . . the loyal devoted, and Party actionist, Mr J. K. Owusu would assuredly boost the future of the Party.' A further petition, purporting to come from three members of the Mim royal family, was sent to the Regional Commissioner at Sunyani, and was followed up by a letter of endorsement from the branch executive, again 'vehemently protesting against the enstoolment of Nana Kwarteng' and claiming to speak on behalf of '90% sincere and loyal party members in the town'. They warned that Kwarteng was 'strongly determined to crush down the Convention People's Party in Mim', and that on his accession 'the town will once more be dominated by the United Party die-hards'.[73] The Regional Commissioner took up their case with the State Council which, 'after lengthy discussions on the matter . . . agreed to issue Form 2 for the destoolment of NANA KWARTENG AMANIAMPONG I, Mimhene and Nifahene of Ahafo'.[74]

This did nothing to cool the debate in Mim. At length Mr F. K. Osei, Mr T. N. Baidoo's successor as D.C. at Goaso, called a meeting of all the parties concerned at Goaso to pursue a settlement. The outcome could hardly have been in doubt. Kwarteng was not called to attend and his main advocates among the Mim elders chose to absent themselves, explaining in a letter to the D.C. that they would prefer to put their case to him separately three days later. Those present 'viewed the contents of the letter and the line of action taken by the petitioners as an attempt to delay the efforts being made by the Six Stool elders for the enstoolment of Comrade J. K. Owusu as the chief of Mim and detrimental to peace and unity in Mim'. The one-sidedness of the morning's business was rationalised by Mr Osei who 'explained . . . that it was incumbent on the part of members present to guard against those who act as middlemen whenever there was a stool dispute in town'. The main objective of the meeting, he declared, had been to meet the elders and the Town Committee members to reconcile the supporters of Kwarteng and Owusu. As the Town Committee at this time was the C.P.P. executive by another name the occasion was plainly a Party affair – suggesting why Kwarteng's supporters had preferred to absent themselves. A 'Town Committee Representative' declared at the start of the meeting that all parties to the dispute, bar those absent, 'had agreed at a meeting the previous night to bury all differences and help in the administration of the town by supporting Mr J. K. Owusu to be sworn in as Mimhene'.[75] Customary drinks were

chief and the queen mother, Mehamehene stood accused of behaviour improper to a chief. In March 1967 Mimhene was obliged to write to the Regional Administrative Officer in Sunyani complaining of persistent challenges to his authority from the ex-chief Kwarteng and his followers: 'Your honour, if nothing is done to check these people there will be no peace at all at Mim. These people still go about writing petitions upon petitions . . . they are vindictives and unless they are checked there will be a source of danger to the town of Mim. They are all members of the C.P.P. hence they do not understand themselves.'[80] Later the dissidents in turn petitioned the administration, protesting against Kwaku Appiah's determination to renew his allegiance to Akwaboahene and the Asantehene. They pointed out that 'at present Mim is not under any Traditional Council through which to present its case and as such we deem it expedient to send this Complaint to you to call the Mimhene Nana Kwaku Appiah, and the Complainants and investigate this serious complaint for us before it was too late, i.e. to avoid our land being taken away from us . . .'[81] Saddled with many of the functions of the abrogated Kukuom–Ahafo State Council, the District Administrative Officer was obliged to devote increasing attention to deposition charges and renewed arguments about proprietary rights in land. As petitions piled up and the need to hold special meetings to unravel the complexities of stool disputes became more frequent, the more he was disposed to abet the re-establishment of a council of chiefs for Ahafo.

In December 1966 the D.A.O. circularised all the Ahafo chiefs as follows:

At the request of the majority of Chiefs in the Goaso (Ahafo) district I have deemed it fit to convene a meeting of all the Chiefs in the district to take place at Goaso on Thursday, 29th December 1966.

2. With the dissolution of the Ahafo (Kukuom) Traditional Council it is considered that there should be a forum for Chiefs in the district to meet and discuss matters of common interest pertaining to Chieftaincy, the general development of the district, and the proposed Constitution for the Chiefs and people of Ghana.[82]

With Kukuomhene's fortunes reversed, it was not long before the true political character of this forum became apparent. Mimhene declared in interview: 'I am the chairman and was responsible for starting it. As we have no traditional council this is a way of getting the chiefs together to discuss the affairs of Ahafo.' Certainly, Kukuomhene and his followers regarded the new body with suspicion from the outset, although they did agree to attend the third of these meetings. This was no doubt in response to the D.A.O.'s exhortations for unity among the Ahafo chiefs and for the patient pursuit of a solution to the state council issue which might satisfy them all. For a month or two there was some semblance of concerted action and then the pro-

Kukuom/pro-Ashanti schism made itself sharply obvious. Cash was collected to commission a lawyer to act on the chiefs' behalf, but it soon became apparent that he had been persuaded to take a decidedly pro-Kukuom point of view. The pro-Ashanti chiefs, who had been attempting to consolidate their own position in Kumasi, were understandably chagrined when the lawyer, Mr A. A. Munufie, successfully defended Kukuomhene against the demands of the Asantehene and went on to become the Progress Party Minister of Rural Development. Those chiefs who saw Dr Busia's Progress Party as the natural heir of the old United Party's interests were undoubtedly taken aback by Kukuomhene's new alliance; any hopes that the P.P. would do for Mimhene and his followers what the C.P.P. had done for Kukuomhene were certainly thwarted, and there must have been feelings of despair in the pro-Ashanti faction about the intractability of parties in power. With the Progress Party government ousted in 1972, however, they were prepared to try their luck again with a petition to the National Redemption Council of Colonel Acheampong.

In 1967 Kukuomhene had good reason to lose faith in the Ahafo chiefs' forum when Mimhene and his followers submitted a petition in the name of 'Chiefs within Ahafo District, Brong–Ahafo' calling for the creation of 'three paramount chiefs in the Ahafo area to serve under the Otumfuo, The Asantehene'. The petition requested 'that lands and mineral resources within Ahafo area be entrusted to the Traditional Councils concerned', and concluded: 'the Ahafo area as a whole, has a population of 86,000 with Secondary Schools, Teachers' Training Colleges, Timber Companies and other enterprises; and since we are now in a new Ahafo other than erstwhile Ahafo, we humbly crave for your Otumfuo's consideration for the creation and etc. in respect of our humble request.'[83] By this time the chiefs meeting at the Goaso District headquarters were exclusively of the pro-Ashanti persuasion and had revived their earlier title 'the Association of Ahafo Chiefs'. In August 1967 they elected Mimhene chairman and Goasohene vice-chairman.[84] They had some success in persuading the Asantehene to take up the cudgels on their behalf against Kukuomhene, and were delighted when the latter was summoned to Kumasi to declare his allegiance to the Ashanti state in person. Kukuomhene's stout refusal to comply, even in the face of a police summons, and his lack of contrition were reflected in a new petition of his own addressed to the chairman of the new Chieftaincy Secretariat in Accra, boasting no less than forty signatories including many elders from such towns as Mim, Goaso and Noberkaw. This document was boldly entitled: 'Unanimous Support of Kukuomhene's Nomination as Representative of Ahafo in Brong/Ahafo House of Chiefs' and commenced: 'From time immemorial the Kukuomhene has been the Paramount Chief of the Ahafo District with the Mimhene as his Nifahene and the Noberkawhene also as his Benkumhene.' Having outlined the historical background to his claims, Kukuomhene asserted that 'The Chiefs who are at present against the Kukuomhene are the few chiefs who were recently brought back to their stools by the N.L.C. Decree No 112 of 1966, but being individuals in their respective towns and villages they have no power to override the majority and impose anything upon them against their will, because we are now in a Democratic State of Ghana'. The petition concluded: 'We categorically state that all the Chiefs, elders, youngmen and women in Ahafo Area are strongly united behind the Kukuomhene to be their representative in the Brong–Ahafo House of Chiefs, and also want the return of Ahafo Lands to them as well as the reopening of the Ahafo Traditional Council at Kukuom, with Kukuomhene as its Chairman.'[85]

The battle of petitions had now been joined and a week later Mimhene led the Ahafo Chiefs Association in a counter-petition addressed 'through Otumfuo the Asantehene . . . to the Chairman, National Liberation Council, Accra'. This again decried Kukuomhene's claim to the Ahafo paramountcy and drew attention to his intransigence in observing the N.L.C. Decree 112, which stipulated that chiefs should return to their 'former allegiance'. This petition re-emphasised, however, that the underdevelopment of Ahafo was 'due to lack of a Traditional Council', and suggested that a single traditional council of chiefs for Ahafo should be established without delay.[86] By this time the request for three paramountcies had been dropped in favour of a Council with a chairman appointed from among the chiefs either in rotation or by election. It was also apparent that the Association was now united more in terms of its outright opposition to Kukuomhene than in terms of any other common sentiments. In June 1968 they could bring to the Asantehene's attention their 'humble but painful grievances . . . in connection of the maltreatment, injustice, suppression and oppression being accorded to us by the chiefs who do not like to come to Ashanti to serve Otumfuo the Asantehene or owe any allegiance to the GOLDEN STOOL as their predecessors or ancestors did in the olden days'. These enemies were 'finding ways and means to destool us one by one' and the petition recommended that 'strong measures be taken against them to bring them to justice'.[87] At this time, however, the Association of Ahafo Chiefs was again falling victim to the schism of interests characteristic of the Ashanti cause in Ahafo. It was rumoured that some of the chiefs had struck bargains with their respective Kumasi overlords to get a share of land revenues, rather than committing themselves to concerted action with the others. Several chiefs objected to the prominence of Goasohene in the Association; Sankorehene expostulated: 'At the moment we have no master but any chief can write you a letter telling you to come. Goasohene is the Chief's [Asantehene's] palmwine tapper. Because he is in the town where the D.C. is he has written me a

letter telling me to come. But here in Ahafo there is no-one greater than I.'
Inevitably this waning enthusiasm in the Association was blamed on subversion by the Kukuom faction. Goasohene, whose authority was under
serious challenge in his community, asserted 'Kukuomhene and Hwidiemhene are the most troublesome people in Ahafo, they question our going to
Kumasi, we disagree with them. They trouble us; the common people are
also troubling us but it is through the influence of these chiefs that they are
acting like that.'

d. AN AHAFO SUMMIT CONFERENCE

Perhaps the most vivid way of illustrating the political processes described
in this chapter is to examine in some detail a recent meeting of the Ahafo
Chiefs Association. This may suggest how political relationships among the
Ahafo chiefs are actually conducted, how political means and ends are
identified, and how political issues are interpreted. The meeting to be
described is of particular interest in that it focusses on a problem of communication, an investigation of the process of petitioning on which the chiefs
have pinned their hopes for the realisation of their ambitions. The importance
of the event and the sense of the occasion to the participants was obvious.
Even after just ten months' fieldwork it was clear to us that virtually every
utterance in the one hour and forty-six minutes of discourse was charged with
political meaning and that transactions were taking place which were quite
beyond the ostensible frame of reference of the meeting.

The meeting of the Ahafo Chiefs Association was held one morning in
March in the committee room of the District headquarters in Goaso. It was
called at the instance of the vice-chairman Goasohene; Mimhene, the chairman, was absent, supposedly unwell although this was viewed with some
suspicion. It was attended by the chiefs of Goaso, Fawohoyeden, Kenyase I,
Aboum, Mehame, Sienchem, Gyedu and Ntotroso, and the senior elders of
Nkasaim and Akrodie. Neither of these last two participated directly in
discussion, although by calling the meeting to order respectfully when it
became unruly they showed that they were not without influence. A few
spectators, who sat at the rear of the room, were brought by four of the
participants, and made no contribution to discussion. An important witness
to the proceedings in this era of police–military rule was a corporal of the
Special Branch. Ourselves, our assistants and our recording equipment were
also ranged around the main table where the chiefs sat.

Goasohene, the convener of the meeting, was the first to arrive and was
soon joined by Fawohoyedenhene. The pair launched into a lengthy conversation in which Goasohene expressed mistrust for Mimhene's current

attitude and disdain for Kukuomhene's refusal to declare allegiance to the Asantehene. The chiefs had been foolish to allow Kukuomhene to swindle them out of their lands revenue. Now he was back at his old tricks – Goasohene could cite several cases of deals he had tried to make with the pro-Ashanti chiefs in an effort to break up the Association. Fawohoyedenhene said he felt assured that the new paramountcy, when it was established, would eventually go to Goaso, a prediction which Goasohene received with smiling approval. Fawohoyedenhene also pointed out that the Association plainly enjoyed the support of the District Administrative Officer, an assumption on which Goasohene felt less sanguine. The Secretary of the Goaso Town Committee, a local school teacher, arrived complaining that Goasohene had no right to summon him from his work to take the minutes of the meeting. He declared that it was not his wish to 'meddle in chieftaincy affairs' and reminded the chiefs that they should make sure the District Administrative Officer attended to allay suspicions that they were plotting against the government.

Scheduled for 9.00 a.m., the meeting eventually got underway after mid-day. The round-table pattern of seating emphasised that the participants were peers. Aboumhene, literate in English, set himself up as secretary, spreading pens, papers and his briefcase authoritatively around him. Kenyase I hene called the participants' attention, pointed out that the presence of a European warranted clear and restrained discussion, and reminded Goasohene that he was to act as chairman. Goasohene in turn asked Mehamehene to open the meeting with a short Christian prayer, and then explained why he had called the chiefs together:

'Chiefs (*mpaninfo*), I called the meeting because we have met already and sent a petition that Otumfuo must let the government know that Ahafo is not little. There was a State Council at Kukuom and all the chiefs got paid through this. Now the government has done away with this but now we want the government to give us a Traditional (*sic*) Council. We have already told the government that we do not want any Omanhene in Ahafo because Kukuomhene had oppressive power over us. We want to be President turn-about. We wrote about this to the Government. He [the Asantehene] signed and the letter was sent to the government. We have been waiting patiently until today without getting any reply as to whether or not it will be set up for us. I thought the chiefs should meet again either to send another petition or to go there ourselves to see what is being done about the matter. That is why I called you here. How are we to go about getting our traditional council? Also, we can discuss any other business.'

After a pause the chiefs, led by Kenyase I hene, gave their opinions one after the other around the table and the following points emerged as debatable issues:

(1) Should another petition be sent?

278

(2) Should a delegation be sent – and if so, how many members should it have?

(3) How much money should be collected as expenses for the delegates?

(4) Should the Asantehene be consulted first and the petition, or the delegation, be channelled through him?

(5) Should publicity be sought in the form of an open letter to the *Graphic*?

The central purpose of the meeting, stated and restated several times, was to lay hands on the impounded land revenues. The project with which the meeting was immediately concerned was the establishment of a traditional council, recognised by the chiefs as the only means by which funds could be released. From time to time speakers redirected the attention of participants to this project: 'It is the state council we are after; if we can get that the lands will follow' (Kenyase I hene). The public rationalisation of these needs was elaborated at various points in discussion when it appeared that attention had been diverted to more contentious matters. The chiefs and the stools were 'starving' and the development of the district as a whole was sadly neglected. A large part of the meeting was concerned with what had become of the previous petition and with the content and style of communication with the government. Was writing petitions not a weak and ineffective strategy? Would direct personal representation not make for greater impact? To whom might such a representation be made?

In the initial exchanges several concise statements were made which seem to have been the elements of subsequent decisions, for example:

'As we have sent a petition we must now send a reminder (*sic*)' (Aboumhene).

'Appoint some people and give them something for travelling expenses' (Fawohoyedenhene).

'Before we go to Accra we must first see the Asantehene' (Sienchemhene).

'We shall make this an open letter to the *Graphic* before we send delegates to Accra' (Aboumhene).

A need for insistence in the prosecution of their case was also asserted – 'I want us to be persistent' (Sienchemhene) – and reiterated throughout the meeting. Aboumhene, who had strong opinions on the communications issues, stressed the need for unanimity: 'We must discuss this together and reach a joint decision.' He favoured written approaches to the government, in contrast to Fawohoyedenhene who asserted 'If we say we are going to write a letter it will just cause delay ... We should go ourselves to the government and find out from them if they have got our letter and have decided to set the council up for us.' Sienchemhene recalled that previous approaches to the Asantehene had met with little success, nevertheless it would be improper to visit Accra without first declaring their intentions in Kumasi, Fawohoyedenhene agreed: 'If we go there [Accra] without first seeing the Asantehene he will be angry with us. It would indicate that we are not serious when we say we want to serve him.' Gyeduhene felt that a delegation of three or four should be picked at once, recalling that 'when you tie sticks into a bundle it is very hard to break them'. A single representative who was well briefed might speak out well on the chiefs' behalf but there was also a chance that in refreshing himself after his journey he might get drunk and forget his mission. Two or three delegates could act as a restraint on each other.

Still advocating a documentary approach, Aboumhene explained the value of publicity in the press:

'We must write something like an open letter to the *Graphic* so that the N.L.C. can get to know about it. They can read then in the *Graphic* about our problems and the predicament in which they have put Ahafo. A stool cannot be looked after. Even a government employee who is suspended for getting into trouble is paid until they hear his case. But the stools, they have been here all this time...'[88]

Goasohene expressed his misgivings about this: 'It is not necessary to do this *Graphic* thing,' and Aboumhene sought to convince him:

'Let us do something to show the government we are disturbed about the matter, that we have met and when we met we took this decision. We are wasting time here – if we put something into the *Graphic* there are people who will read it and the government may even be afraid and give us a reply within a short time. We may get to hear about it through the District Administrative Officer. We shall make this an open letter (*sic*) to the *Graphic* before we send the delegates to go to Accra.'

Kenyase I hene appears to have resolved the matter by declaring 'It should go into the *Graphic*. But we must first inform the man that we shall be coming to see him on such-and-such a day.' This appears to have reminded the chiefs that they were not aware who 'the man' might be, or even whether he had received the first petition. Discussion of this revealed another important link in the chain of communication: 'We met last time and sent our petition through the Asantehene. As Darkwah is the Asantehene's secretary we must go to him to discover where our petition was sent' (Mehamehene). The suspicion gained ground that their plea might have got no further than Darkwah's desk.

Aboumhene was not convinced of the value and the necessity of campaigning for the state council through the chiefly hierarchy.

'We have done what is customary and sent our names to Otumfuo, and he has sent them on to the government. But at the moment we are discussing how to get the council and our pay. If we get Darkwah to understand, he has no authority over us, he can't go and speak on our behalf to the government...Let us not forget that Brong–Ahafo Region still exists; before we get our state council it will have to come to us through Brong–Ahafo. When something customary crops up, Akwasida or something, and a chief is making a celebration, we have to go and serve at Kumasi. That is how the custom goes. But still we shall be under Sunyani.'

Adopting a conciliatory tone he continued:

'The best thing is to go and tell Darkwah that we are going to find out about our letter. It all depends on the government. It will tell us how to handle our affairs in Ahafo. We will eventually get to know whether it was the Lands Department or the Asantehene who has withheld our pay.'

Fawohoyedenhene, still advocating a direct approach, declared:

'We must get hold of Darkwah and say ... we are fed up sending petitions, so he must tell us what is to be done, in our presence. He must show us where he has been sending our letters in Accra so that we can go and find out what has happened to them. He may say that he is unable to accompany us, but "go to this and that office and you will find your letters".'

Kenyasehene again cautioned against alienating the Asantehene:

'If someone is ruling over you and you try to take his power (*tumi*), he will not be ready to share it with you. It is up to us just to inform him, for after all they are not really trying to give us our share of power. We must not put all our trust in Darkwah.'

'They' in this context was a plain reference to the Kumasi wing-chiefs.

Angrily, Fawohoyedenhene demanded to know why there was continued talk of petitions when the purpose of the meeting was supposedly to send a delegation to Accra. Mehamehene sternly told this young and impetuous chief 'you must not speak like that', and in the heated exchanges which followed Aboumhene took a placatory role. Returning to his opinions about communications he declared: 'We must first see the [District] Administrator. Because it was a chieftaincy matter we sent it straight to the Asantehene. This time, even though it is a chieftaincy matter, as the traditional council is involved we must send it through the D.C. In fact the letter should have been sent through the Administrator in the first place.' Somewhat self-righteously redirecting the meeting to what he took to be the main issue, Fawohoyeden-hene announced: 'We should go to Kumasi and if Darkwah says he is not going then we can go ourselves. Let us cut this long chit-chat and pick the people who are to go.' This was followed by series of short statements of a reiterative nature which appear to embody decisions: 'are we agreed that we should go to Accra . . .' (noises of assent) '. . . to see whether our petition got there or not?' (Goasohene). 'And to take up the matter of our pay and our council?' (Fawohoyedenhene). 'Don't worry about your pay, when you get the council your pay will come' (Kenyase I hene). Mehamehene put in: 'I must say, you have been prolonging this matter. Let's agree to go to Kumasi and Darkwah will tell us what to do.'

After a brief pause, Kenyase I hene reintroduced the question of the size of the delegation. Goasohene announced 'many people are no use, four are enough'. Fawohoyedenhene enquired: 'who are to be appointed?' to which Goasohene replied 'Kenyase I, myself . . .' Aboumhene asked Mehamehene if he had time to go, and Mehamehene said he could. Later Fawohoyedenhene was added to the list because he had a relative in Accra with whom the chiefs could conveniently (and economically) lodge. In the event, Aboumhene also joined the delegation. 'But for lack of money,' Fawohoyedenhene remarked, 'we might all be going.' Inevitably this refocussed attention on the prime motive of the meeting: 'We must have the state council before we are paid. We have not got the state council, that is why we are not paid.' Reunited in terms of this common need the chiefs expatiated to one another on the difficulty of performing ritual and social duties and the danger of neglecting stool ceremonial. Warming to the theme, Fawohoyedenhene suggested that further details of these problems should be despatched to 'the man' in Accra. He was encouraged by Goasohene and Kenyase I hene: 'let him say whatever is on his mind', 'we all want our affairs to improve, let him speak'. Fawohoyedenhene concluded '. . . when we get no money to pour libations this can be dangerous, and can harm the area'. 'Do you not think,' Kenyase I hene cryptically enquired, 'that there is money for you somewhere?'

Taken aback, the chiefs rounded on Kenyase I hene. In the clamour he explained: 'The money which was there has been taken to the Kumasi State Council.' The exchange continued:

Goaso: 'For whom is the money there?'
Kenyase I: 'They have shared it out already.'
Fawohoyeden: 'That means they have not sent ours to us?'
Kenyase I: 'I have had mine already, so don't think there is money there for you.'
Fawohoyeden: 'Have you gone for yours?'
Goaso: 'You have offended us!'
[uproar]
Kenyase I: 'I heard that your money has been sent to you already. What little shares we get, everyone has gone for his.'
Fawohoyeden: 'How much did you get?'
Kenyase I: 'What little I get, I got.'
Goaso: 'Tell us how you managed to get yours!'

In another placatory speech, Aboumhene acknowledged that he knew this had been going on, and rebuked Kenyase I hene: 'You should have told us how and when you got yours so that we might also fight for ours. What do you get out of hiding this from us?' Kenyase I hene excused himself: 'What money I got was less than what I was due,' but was challenged by Fawohoyedenhene: 'Didn't you get about £2,000?' 'I got mine, so don't pester me' was the reply.

In a lengthy speech, Kenyase I hene sought to direct attention away from his own dealings with his Kumasi overlord to the question of the state council.

'What I am driving at is that you must have your state council before you can get your pay. Without the state you will never get your pay. But if the state is not there the Asantehene may have a part of his land revenue which he might give you. But I can't talk about your affairs, I don't know how you are set up on your lands. Maybe it is given to someone before it is divided up and given to you – I don't know.'

Goasohene was not to be consoled: 'This suggests that you dislike us, this is why we are unsuccessful in everything we do.' Again attempting to calm the uproar, Aboumhene observed that as usual the Kumasi chiefs were behaving in an underhand way, undermining the unanimity of the Ahafo chiefs and depriving them of their rightful revenues. Kenyase I hene had done no more than look after his own interests as a chief properly should. The trouble was, the Asantehene was obliged to pander to the pressure of his Kumasi chiefs;

'Some time ago' [he confided], 'I wrote a letter condemning all the Kumasi wing-chiefs and saying that all the troubles in Ahafo have arisen through them, and litigation is rife in the area. They were sorry, and called me in the night and begged me to withdraw my petition. The Asantehene said that it was through my letter that he had got to know that Ahafo had been let down because of his wing-chiefs. He said 'I have never spoken against any Ahafo chief who has come to me. Even many of them do not know me. This has informed me that because there are some chiefs in Ahafo who do not want to come to me, the wing-chiefs are to blame. I will keep an eye on what crops up now.' What Nana Kenyase I hene has just said is a typical example.'

Kenyase I hene followed this up:

'When we were at a meeting in Kumasi I told Darkwah that if Hiawuhene tried to cheat me in money matters I would not sit idle if he allowed it. Since I have become a chief it has been Darkwah who signs my cheques; when I went there he knew I would make trouble if I was not paid so he got in touch with the appropriate man and I was paid.'

As the meeting was settling down again, Kenyase I hene remarked to Fawohoyedenhene: 'Don't pin your hopes on that money.' Through the ensuing disorder, Fawohoyedenhene retaliated: 'Last time we collected money and entrusted it to you. It is now time you accounted for this, so we know how much is still left.' Kenyase I hene turned on Goasohene: 'There has to be a fall-guy in all ventures. Last time we had a collection of £5 each I remember Goasohene never paid up.' He recalled the unfortunate excursion to Sunyani to find a lawyer only to discover that 'Kukuomhene was fighting to become a paramount chief', and that 'this lawyer was just helping Kukuomhene to get the land'. 'If we keep on like this,' interjected Mehamehene acidly, 'we shall be at it for three days. Goasohene rambles on, Kenyasehene rambles on . . .' 'But he has got the money,' complained Goasohene. The Nkasaim Krontihene, respectfully loosening his cloth from his shoulder, stood up and begged the angry chiefs: 'Please, we are here on the matter of the council and not previous money matters we don't need to hear about. You should be talking about the travel expenses for the delegates.'

A discussion of the money to be collected ensued, but Kenyase I hene was still nettled about the discussion of his Kumasi relationships and Goasohene's challenges, 'I want you to know,' he grumbled, 'that you can't speak more than I. When I speak in public I don't fear anybody's face.' Other chiefs, he complained, were being less than frank and were putting the burden of collecting money and petitioning on the conscientious few. Aboumhene agreed: 'Before we can progress we have to have fall-guys. We who have met here bear the expenses.' Sienchemhene disagreed: 'Mimhene who is the chairman is sick and they say he couldn't come, but he should have sent a deputy. He should have led us in our campaign.' On the basis of Aboumhene's computations, it was decided that a £5 contribution from each chief would suffice.

Kenyase I hene then questioned the necessity of a new petition to 'the man' in Accra: 'Are you going to write a letter and at the same time sit down and explain things to him?' Aboumhene explained, patiently and authoritatively:

'The Europeans speak of a "reminder" (*sic*). Before you go to enquire about a petition you must send a "reminder". You quote the reference number of the petition and explain everything in the "reminder" to him. When you meet him to discuss the matter you will convince him your needs are serious. Because of that you have come to him. But what the Europeans call "verbal speech" – well, if you just go along and talk to the man as if he were your son, he will never listen to you. We should write our petition once more.'

He appealed for confirmation to the Special Branch Officer, who declined to give an opinion. 'I don't think the present government is willing to give us our state council,' declared Gyeduhene gloomily.

After some reiteration of decisions apparently reached the meeting concluded with two unrelated items, Goasohene's suggestion that the Chairman of the National Liberation Council should be invited to Goaso and Aboumhene's proposal that the chiefs should go as a body to pay their respects to the sick and elderly chief of Nkasaim. Both were received without enthusiasm on financial grounds: 'here we are trying to scrape up money to go to Accra and you bring this up!' complained Kenyase I hene.

With only eight chiefs in attendance the signs of disunity within the Ahafo Chiefs Association were apparent from the start of this meeting. Discussion of the most effective means of communication was framed by a series of oppositions. The chiefs were against Kukuomhene and his supporters who had duped them in an earlier bid to secure the state council. They were hostile to the Kumasi wing-chiefs and suspicious of their influence on the Asantehene. They mistrusted Darkwah, their intermediary with both the Asantehene and the government. The chiefs were as suspicious of the pro-Ashanti chiefs who had absented themselves as they were of Kukuomhene and his followers. What was the nature of Mimhene's indisposition – a deal with the Akwaboahene in Kumasi, perhaps? At times such doubts divided the participants themselves, making them mutually wary of motives and methods. A mood of consensus was fragile and could be sustained only with effort. The release of land revenues was a goal to which all of the chiefs could commit themselves, a theme which could be evoked when discussion became divisive. In this context the state council was construed as the means to the financial end, glossed over not because of its unimportance but because of its deeply contentious implications. Unlike the money, the state council could bear little exposure to open debate if any semblance of unity was to be sustained; any reference to details of its organisation could lead too quickly to discussion of the differential allocation of authority.

The style and content of discourse, and the roles established by the participants suggest the meeting was not simply negotiation towards an immediate end, it was one episode in a much more lengthy political process. Throughout the meeting there is much evidence of the dialecticism of the values of unity and of aggrandisement. This is highlighted in the ill-disguised duplicity of Kenyase I hene; Fawohoyedenhene's self-righteous outrage at the threat to concerted action is made the more acute by his obvious chagrin at being outmanoeuvred by another Ahafo chief. Above all, the meeting was an exploration into political *terra incognita*, a definition of the opportunities which were available and the means by which they might respectably be exploited. The principal opportunity was presented by an *aban* of policemen and soldiers ostensibly sympathetic to the interests of non-C.P.P. chiefs. Strategies of despatching a delegation, of backing this up with a 'reminder' and an open letter to the *Graphic*, were assessed in the light of a range of political responsibilities: to the Asantehene, the Regional and District Administrators, the various stool communities. If, objectively, we may readily imagine the delegates, that awkward bundle of Ahafo twigs, losing themselves and their petition in the ministerial corridors of Accra in their quest for the elusive 'man', it must be because our identification of the means and the ends is, curiously, less sanguine and precise than theirs.[89]

CHAPTER 7

THE GROWTH OF LOCAL GOVERNMENT IN AHAFO

a. LOCAL COUNCILS

One October morning in 1953, a year after the new system of local authorities had been established in the Gold Coast, the clerk of the Ahafo Local Council 'read and explained' to the assembled councillors a booklet issued by the Ministry of Local Government and Housing entitled *Your Council and Your Progress*.[1] 'Local Government', the booklet asserted, 'is not a new idea just thought of in the Gold Coast. There has however been a big re-organisation carried out by the introduction of the new system, in order to fit the changed circumstances of the Gold Coast.' In its eleven pages the booklet gave a simplistic rendering of what the central authorities would have the councillors and the public at large understand about local government. It was also a reassessment after the first year of the new system, an attempt to relate the abstract specifications of the 1951 Local Government Ordinance to the hard realities of establishing councils in the rural districts. As the title suggests, it was an exercise in public relations, playing on the sentiments, real or supposed, of those involved in the new system.

Alluding to the 'Local Problems' arising from political party opposition, extracting rates from the public, and the confusion in functions and representative roles, problems which were 'preventing each area of the country becoming a healthier and better place', the booklet insisted somewhat naively that 'the tasks of local government are practical'. It described these tasks as the provision and management of 'services' ('by "services" are meant such things as clean, good latrines and markets, minor roads, etc.'). Distinguishing central and local government functions, the booklet pointed out that 'local people are in a better position than anyone else to decide the places where such "services" are most urgently needed in their areas, and to say just how they should be built, considering how much money can be afforded on each item'. Dwelling on the confusion of roles which had arisen the booklet insisted that

Councillors are not to be thought of as a new sort of Chief; and they should not, either in Council or as individuals, attempt to interfere with the customary position and work of Chiefs. Nor should Councillors, as individual members, even interfere with the work of the officers and employees of the Council . . . Chairmen of Council have not in any way 'inherited' rights or powers from Chiefs . . . Similarly Chiefs and Chairmen of Councils have different parts to play, and it is wrong for Chairmen to try to take upon themselves powers to which they are not entitled.

The clerk of the Ahafo Local Council may have had difficulty reconciling this with another passage in the booklet which read 'Councillors, whether traditional representatives or special members, have exactly equal and similar tasks and responsibilities.'

As this, and other apparent contradictions in the text of the booklet suggest, the organisation of local government is not much clearer from the perspective of central authorities than it is from the point of view of Ahafo, even though there may be similar ideas on both sides about what a proper local council should actually do. The development of a democratic representative system of local government has been the most important project of the colonial and postcolonial governments in Ahafo during the past twenty-five years. The credentials of Ghana as a modern nation state have, to a large extent, depended on the success of this project. Although few might deny that the Local Councils have essential tasks to perform, the 'services' spelled out in the booklet, it must generally be agreed that in both organisation and operation they have failed. The modern local government project dates from political unrest in the late 1940s which obliged the colonial authorities to undertake a critical appraisal of the constitutional development of the country. A new, more educated generation expressed its dissatisfaction with colonial overrule and the continued dependence in local government on the chiefs and elders. The reforms of the 1950s proved a formidable task, implying as it did the unification of the many discrete political units within a coherent national structure. However strong the current of national, democratic idealism may have been, it was clearly acknowledged that changes were not to be effected without compromise with pre-existing political authorities.[2] The political resources of the country were such that local government without the participation of the chiefs and the continued control of local political officers was unthinkable. The single, secular authority structure has not yet appeared and government in the districts of Ghana remains vested in an historical amalgam of traditional, colonial and modern elected institutions.

Nevertheless, the Local Government Ordinance of 1951 established a system which was quite new. The continuity with the past, noted in the booklet, may be taken to refer mainly to the Native Authorities which had been set up in Ashanti in 1935. These were primarily judicial bodies, and lacked both the financial resources and trained personnel to enable them to undertake the provision of local amenities. In the late 1940s an Area

Committee (including a large part of Western Ashanti) was set up to assist
the regional administration in the planning of local projects. This consisted of
the political officers, some chiefs and a few hand-picked laymen, but could
hardly be described as representative and clearly meant very little to the
ordinary citizen. The 37 District and 229 Local Councils which were established throughout the country in 1951 and 1952 were quite different from
these earlier, highly selective experiments in popular participation. Ahafo
became a Local Council Area consisting of twelve wards, each of which
elected a representative. The Local Council itself elected members to serve
on the new Kumasi West District Council. On both bodies the chairman
and two thirds of the councillors were popularly elected, the remaining
members being chiefs all of whom were appointed by the State Council in
Kumasi. In fact, the requirement that participants at the District level should
be literate obliged the Kumasi State Council to co-opt three laymen to serve
as 'traditional representatives' of Ahafo, so short was the supply of educated
chiefs. One of these representatives was Mr A. W. Osei who later became a
Member of Parliament for the Kumasi West area.

The first full meeting of the Ahafo Local Council was held at Goaso on
1 August 1952. The President was supposed to be the local paramount chief,
which Ahafo lacked until Kukuomhene was reinstated in 1958. Requiring
little more than attendance at the annual inaugural meeting of the Council
the role was not prominent and was fulfilled initially by the Government
Agent and then by several chiefs on a rota basis. In due course Kukuomhene
became President of all three Local Councils in Ahafo. The first of the Local
Councils lasted from 1952 until 1958 with only minor changes of personnel.
Full elections were held in 1958, a year after Independence, on a political
party basis. The United Party won 8 seats, the Convention People's Party 4,
a total of six new members joining the Council. By this time there were no
chiefs on the Council, partly because of the crisis which was affecting chiefship (see chapter 6) and partly because of impending local government
reform. Table 6 and Fig. 1 are arranged to indicate the various local government bodies which have operated in Ahafo over the seventeen years up to
1969, reflecting the repeated organisational change. The politicisation of
Council affairs made for turbulent meetings and appears to have hastened
the takeover of its business by a small Management Committee in May 1959.
This consisted of the Government Agent, the Kenyase I hene (a young and
educated chief who had become a prominent member of the newly
established Kukuom–Ahafo State Council) and Mr T. N. Baidoo who had
been chairman of the Ahafo Local Council for five years. In the six months
of their interregnum they met thirteen times and dealt with nearly four times
as many items of business as the full Council had tackled during the last six
months of its life. This was the first of three periods during which select

appointed committees under the direction of the District Officer have acted for the Local Councils. The most lengthy of these periods of deputisation has been from 1966 to the present day, and it is significant that for well over a third of the time since the inauguration of the new local government system in 1951 its operations have been entrusted to non-elected managers. It is clear that they have proved efficient and economical in despatching business, but in spite of such virtues they are hardly in accordance with the democratic terms of the local government project in Ghana.

Elections were held in 1959 for the Brong–Ahafo South Local Council, the old Ahafo Local Council in its new regional guise. The District Councils were abolished and the new Council came under the aegis of the regional administration at Sunyani. The C.P.P. carried every ward, reflecting a rise in the party's fortunes nationally and locally and a general refusal of the United Party to commit itself to elections. Recently installed as paramount chief, Kukuomhene presided over the first meeting in December 1959 and Mr J. Opoku, who had joined the Council after the 1958 elections, was elected chairman. After barely three years the Council was again dissolved pending the implementation of the 1961 Local Government Act. In an effort to achieve economies of scale the Act reduced the number of Local Councils in Ghana drastically to 69, but population increase in Ahafo was sufficient to justify the division of the existing Council Area into the two new Asutifi and Asunafo units. On paper at least, Council organisation was quite well-defined, with new staff regulations, financial controls, a local government inspectorate and other measures designed to enhance efficiency. In practice there was a steady decline in Council efficiency, marked by poor attendance and infrequent meetings. The Councils were subsumed by the C.P.P. to the extent that they tended 'to *become* the constituency party organisation',[3] a change which appears to have done nothing to enhance their executive and decision-making efficiency. As before, the system depended on the surveillance of the District Commissioner, but when this became a party office control of Council affairs suffered further from the inadequacies of those appointed.

From June to September 1962 local authority business was again transacted by a management committee, consisting of the District Commissioner, a senior party official and a literate elder from Mim who was also a C.P.P. activist. Meanwhile elections were held for the two new Councils; candidates were in fact chosen by the district branches of the party and returned unopposed. It is notable that none of them had served previously on the Ahafo Council. The division of assets and liabilities arising from the creation of the Asutifi and Asunafo Councils has proved very difficult, aggravated by the creation of the third Local Council in 1965. On the recommendation of the Boison Commission enquiring into electoral areas, Asunafo was divided into

TABLE 6. *Items of business discussed in the various Ahafo local councils according to the official minutes, 1952–68*

Category of business considered	Ahafo Local Council	Ahafo L.C. Management Committee	Brong-Ahafo S. Local Council	B.-A. S. L.C. Management Committee
	%	%	%	%
A. Public amenities				
1. Schools	5	7	4	17
2. Health	5	6	5	—
3. Roads	2	6	3	—
4. Other amenities	17	15	12	11
5. Other expenditure	1	3	—	5
B. Committee/officers' reports				
6. Sub-committee reports	10	—	16	—
7. Council officer's reports	4	2	4	—
C. Local government relations				
8. Relations between L.A.s.	—	—	—	—
9. General communications	4	7	6	—
D. Revenue				
10. Council income	7	11	5	6
11. Control of finances	11	6	9	6
E. Council organisation				
12. Staff matters	7	16	12	49
13. Council members	15	6	7	—
14. Staff/members expenses	2	3	—	—
15. Procedural matters	3	—	3	—
16. Visits and addresses	4	1	8	—
F. Other business				
17. National affairs	—	1	1	—
18. By-laws	1	—	1	—
19. Traditional matters	—	—	—	—
20. Other business	2	8	3	6
Total	100	100	100	100

Asunafo Local Council	Asunafo L.C. Management Committee	Goaso L.C. Management Committee	Asutifi Local Council	Asutifi L.C. Management Committee	Kukuom L.C. Management Committee	Total
%	%	%	%	%	%	% [29.6%]
8	19	15	1	15	7	9.0
5	9	6	2	6	4	4.7
—	4	5	3	7	5	4.1
3	5	13	5	7	10	11.0
1	3	—	—	—	—	0.8
						[10.5%]
11	—	—	10	4	2	5.8
10	—	2	9	4	9	4.7
						[5.4%]
2	—	—	2	1	5	1.1
11	2	1	—	3	8	4.3
						[18.9%]
8	10	15	6	10	12	9.5
9	6	11	12	10	6	9.4
						[31.9%]
13	24	17	22	20	18	16.0
6	1	2	5	1	4	5.7
—	10	8	6	2	2	3.4
—	—	—	1	2	—	1.2
9	3	1	15	7	3	5.6
						[3.7%]
1	—	1	1	—	—	0.6
2	—	1	—	1	4	1.1
—	—	1	—	—	—	0.3
1	4	1	—	—	1	1.7
100	100	100	100	100	100	100.0

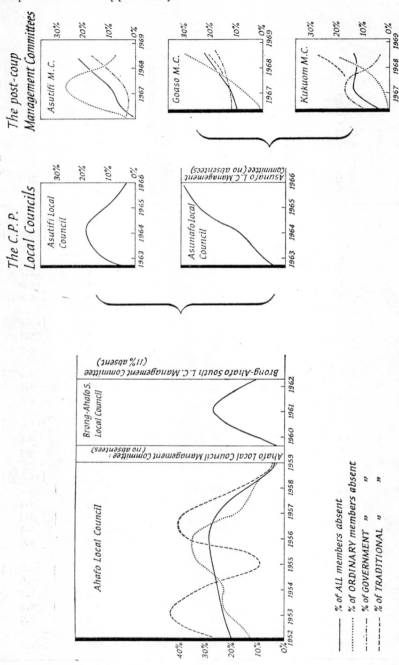

FIGURE 1. *Percentage of members absent from meetings of Ahafo local councils 1952–68*

the Goaso and Kukuom Council areas, reflecting the government's policy of making local authorities congruent with parliamentary constituencies. This supposedly enhanced party control over Council affairs, and when the C.P.P. regime was ousted by the police-military coup d'état of 1966, changes made on the recommendation of the Boison Commission were revoked, including the Kukuom Local Council which had only held a single meeting. On the strength of appeals from Kukuomhene, the District Administrative Officer and others it was re-established later in 1966 on the authority of the National Liberation Council.

After the coup d'etat, small management committees were appointed to transact the business of the disbanded Councils, but these were reconstituted and enlarged in 1968 when it became clear that the re-establishment of a democratic local government system would be long delayed. The new management committees consisted of ten men and a 'woman representative', and operated under the close supervision of the District Administrative Officer. Each Council retained its executive staff, led by the clerk and treasurer and other employees such as rate collectors continued to carry out their normal functions. It was intended that the new management committees should give the appearance of popular representation, but there was no question of elections and little opportunity to cast membership in terms of clearly demarcated segments of the public.

These restless changes suggest one good reason why a Local Council means little more to the ordinary citizen of Ahafo than a body which extorts rates with tiresome frequency or, very occasionally, builds a school classroom or patches up a local road. Council organisation has been changed six times in seventeen years, quite apart from such incidental developments as the rise and fall of the C.P.P.; local authority areas, personnel, bases of representation, staffing arrangements and administrative relationships have altered frequently enough to confuse the most informed citizen. Ahafo has so far experienced local government by a mixed traditional-elected Council, by a Council elected on a competitive political party basis, by Councils appointed by the local organisation of a single ruling party, and for over a third of the time by the appointed committees of management. In 1968 it appeared that the wheel might turn full circle, for the Commission under the chairmanship of Mr Justice Akufo-Addo called upon to design a new constitution for the second republic of Ghana recommended a three tier system of local government with Local Councils, District Councils and Regional Development Committees, very similar to the system established by the 1951 Government Ordinance. It was subsequently agreed that two thirds of the members of the Local and District Councils should be popularly elected, one third being nominated 'Traditional Representatives'. The Commission also advocated a complete integration of traditional and secular affairs at the Local Council level, an arrangement which 'would have the effect of infusing modern ideas into the institution (chieftaincy) by making it possible for a number of popular representatives to be associated with the election, installation or deposition of chiefs, thus lending the institution a more democratic outlook'.[4] Although the proposed system was never put into effect it is significant that the central authorities should have returned to the earlier view of local government reform as essentially the transformation of a pre-existing, traditional authority. To many in Ahafo this would seem very reasonable; chiefs tend to regard the Local Councils as supplementing their own functions and, organisationally, as capricious youth assuming some of the authority of the elders. The sense of precedence is made clear: 'It was the chiefs who started local councils long before local government (*sic*) took over. I feel that if the chiefs are not there the local council is of no importance' (Wamahinsohene).

The vagueness of popular understanding of Council organisation may be contrasted with the clarity with which its proper functions are perceived. The Council should provide the amenities which have become the modern requisites of communal aggrandisement, latrines, clinics, schools and roads. Implicit in this is the opinion that if the Council should direct an amenity to a community other than one's own it has behaved unscrupulously. From the Council's perspective its operations are a complicated exercise in political economising, the allocation of extremely scarce resources among too many specific and insistent communal wants. From both points of view failure and success turn on the collection of money. The individual may see his own contribution and those of his neighbours as financing his community's needs handsomely. He grudges the Council its running costs and readily assumes (at times with good reason) that its operations are corrupt. For their part Council officials see themselves as over-charged with the provision of local amenities, and complain of the intransigence of the ratepayers: 'They want their improvements before they pay for them,' complained the Kukuom Council clerk. 'There are always the righteous ones who say "I paid my rates of £3". Can you build a road for £3? You must get all the ratepayers to pay their rates. If the 31,000 people in this Local Council Area all paid as they ought, that would mean no problems at all.' During the seventeen years of their existence there is evidence of a steady decline in the financial position of the Councils. In June 1955 the chairman, Mr T. N. Baidoo, could boast 'My Council stands without compare as far its financial position is concerned. The Council has in this financial year estimated an expenditure of £82,000 as against an annual revenue of £75,364. Its surplus funds have risen to £2,886 and reserve funds £7,000.'[5] In spite of vigorous 'Pay-Your-Rates' campaigns, disillusionment among the ratepayers gained ground, and government grants provided a decreasingly adequate and reliable source of income. In June 1961 the District Commissioner remarked: 'The Council's sources of revenue were very limited' and added that 'this unhappy situation and the execution of annual recurrent expenditure leaves the Council in a perpetual unhealthy financial position'.[6] By 1966 the Councils were bankrupt.

In terms of statutory and popular expectations, the actual operations of the Local Councils bear some examination. Table 6 is an analysis of all the items of business minuted by the various bodies in Ahafo between 1952 and 1969. It is striking that nearly a third of the items discussed have been concerned with processes internal to the Council itself. Observation of the present management committees certainly suggests that matters concerning the members and the staff make for the most animated discussion. Perhaps the public would interpret the fact that only 30 per cent of items discussed concern the provision of local amenities as expressive of dereliction of duty. Compared with the amount of time devoted to the conduct of the staff and the discussion of travelling expenses, such a view might be justified, but would overlook the fact that many aspects of public amenities are dealt with by sub-committees and presented to the full Council in the form of reports and minutes. Considerable attention is devoted to the collection of revenue and its management when it reaches the Council's coffers – matters which are the most contentious aspect of its activities from the public point of view. The promulgation of by-laws absorbs relatively little time nor do national affairs loom large, although a substantial 5.6 per cent of the agendas refer to official speeches and addresses by visiting dignitaries, particularly in the Councils dominated by the C.P.P. The avoidance of 'traditional affairs' clearly reflects repeated injunctions from the government that this does not fall within their competence.

It is notable that the various management committees have, on the whole, dealt more extensively with public amenities than the Local Councils. However they have also quite consistently paid more attention to staff matters, largely because they have been obliged to clear up the administrative disorder generated by the Councils. In 1962 the Brong–Ahafo South Local Council Management Committee devoted nearly a half of its business to a purge of the staff. An entire meeting of the Ahafo Local Council Management Committee in 1959 was spent on what amounted to a trial of the clerk for corruption. Efficient staffing has for long been regarded as one of the main shortcomings of local government development. It is worth recalling that between each three or four hour session of the full Council as many as eight weeks may elapse in which business is entirely in the hands of the salaried officers. Inadequate training and organisational weaknesses may account for some apparent dishonesty but can hardly justify such abuses as led to the turnout of the entire Asutifi Local Council Staff in August 1964. In the customary oblique prose the minutes recorded that 'an anomaly . . . has crept into the Council with regards to some funds which have unaccountably gone out of the Council's Coffers unconstitutionally'.[7] However damaging these misdemeanours may be to the public reputation of the Council, some sympathy may be spared for the role-dilemmas of the staff. They tend to see themselves as scapegoats for both the government and the ratepayers:

'The trouble is, the ratepayer does not know what the central government is. They don't know who the Minister for Finance is. They probably don't even know who General Ankrah is. But everyone knows who the clerk of Council is and they all come here to abuse him. When the roads maintained by the regional administration are damaged in the rains – the clerk is blamed. It is much easier to go to Kukuom and abuse the clerk of Council than to go to Accra and abuse the central government. What the central government must realise is that the main population is in the villages, not in Accra, Kumasi or even Sunyani. They do not know the people, and the people certainly don't know them. The Local Council staff are looked on with suspicion. Even if I appear in my car the people say I am cheating them. The clerk of Council is held responsible for all the faults of the government' (clerk of Council, Kukuom).

Nevertheless, the authority of the clerk may become quite firmly established, more as a consequence of personal attributes than the properties of the role. This is particularly true in the Council chamber where his experience and training may give him many tactical advantages over the Councillors. The clerk also transacts on a face-to-face basis a large proportion of the Council's dealings with its public and this may also determine his wider reputation. The present Goaso clerk, a personable and well-qualified officer, was rated by a wide range of people as one of the most important 'government men' in Ahafo. A curious expression of this prestige was the decision of the Ahafo Local Council in March 1958 to appoint the clerk President in the absence of an appropriate chiefly candidate for the office. The clerk declared: 'I feel within me that I have been elevated to a never-expected position which does not befit me as a mere servant of the Council; but since it is your will I am to do it. I call this day a momentous occasion.'[8] In his presidential address he appealed to the Councillors' 'good senses of honesty, duty and justice to decide development projects and their location irrespective of the political creed of the place', and concluded 'I thank you, my Masters'. The occasion was enhanced by the attendance of the Government Agent and two Members of Parliament, Mr Joe Appiah and Mr A. W. Osei, who both exhorted the new, predominantly C.P.P. Council not to take advantage of the U.P. minority. The acting President was plainly nervous about his own position for in a final statement which was later deleted from the minutes he urged the Councillors 'not to concern themselves with the talks of the outsiders that employees would be dismissed because they are suspected as supporters of one party'. Two meetings later the minutes, in their usual inscrutable style, announced that the clerk had fled from Goaso and that his appointment should therefore be terminated.[9]

The elected Councillors were not immune from corruption and were from time to time removed for taking bribes or using their status to extort money. Many of the District Officer's addresses to the Council contained pointed references to dishonesty, for example: '[the Government Agent] finally asked the Council to work harder and to clear up the many rumours circulating against some of the Councillors, many of the allegations, he hoped, were unfounded.'[10] Later C.P.P. District Commissioners gave similar warnings: 'It is not for money-making that the Councillors were elected to serve the community.'[11] In his annual presidential address Kukuomhene invariably gave councillors down to earth advice against regarding the Council as their milch cow. After the 1966 coup d'etat the District Police Superintendent delivered a harsh epitaph on the latter-day C.P.P. Councils: 'Most of the people so picked to serve on the Council sought their own interests and enriched themselves at the expense of the man in the street, the poor taxpayer. These representatives' motto was to make hay while the sun was shining ... They in fact preached "socialism" but practised "capitalism" in its highest sense.'[12]

In an effort to confine some of these shortcomings the central authorities have sought to exert progressively greater statutory control over the local authorities. At the same time they seem to have recognised that the most pronounced weakness of the Councils has been the very low sense of responsibility of members to their electorates. From the outset Council operations have been encapsulated in a way which is contrary to their formal democratic specifications, the public having little access to and exerting very little control over the activities of the Councillors and staff. Nevertheless, public interest in what the Council *should* be doing is very keen. The chiefs, who feel they are more directly charged with the interests of communal aggrandisement than a Local Councillor ever has been, and know that they are much more directly responsible to their people, have strong views on this.

'Those whom we elect to represent us on the Local Councils do not speak the truth, but the chiefs seek the progress of their towns. If the chief cannot rule well, he is destooled. You have to do well to keep sitting on the stool for long' (Sienchemhene).

Mimhene, one of the most experienced Local Councillors in Ahafo, explained:

'To the ordinary people, chiefs are the most useful. Because people dislike the order of the Local Council sometimes they go about saying ill words against the Local Council – "what I am after is [this], but the Local Council won't do [it]" – so they go about speaking ill words against the Local Council. But the chief who is supposed to be the father of all people, he can easily be touched and asked why this is not done. Even this morning many have come to me to ask – "look, the Local Council, when you go there to ask you won't meet the chairman and the members are also scattered away to their own places and you can't get in touch with them" – so they prefer the chief to any other people.'

Kenyase I hene summed up the situation incisively:

'At the moment the help [the Council] have given us has just come from our own cocoa-surtax, to build the latrine. The nightsoil shifters were employed by them and sometimes they clear away the bush around the town. Otherwise I have not seen anything which they have done for us. About four years ago the Council built two blocks for our school. Now when we ask them about school buildings they tell us they have no money. We developed this town with our own cocoa-surtax. Because they are part of the government if you go and consult them they tell you there is no money, so you have to come home and sit put. You have no power over them when they say there is no money... we have used our own strength to build things because we seek the prosperity of our town.'

Such feelings of frustration prompt many to argue that if the Council does nothing it might as well be abolished:

'The Council is bad... there are three Councils here, and if you went now to any one of them you would find everyone lying about asleep. They misappropriate our money freely... I want the government to scrap the Local Councils and put their business in the hands of the Social Welfare department... we want the Social Welfare department to do the Council's work' (Kwaponghene).

Barely three years after the establishment of the new local authority system, Hannigan wrote of 'the fear of the new system of representation as opposed to the old one of delegation. The African is used to sending a delegate who has to consult with those who sent him before coming to a major decision. This is quite different from the British system of representation.'[13] Hannigan cited the case of a Legislative Assembly member from Ashanti who was upbraided by his people for voting without first consulting them. The reference to 'fear' is perhaps inappropriate here; in Ahafo it would be more apposite to speak of the irrelevance of Local Council representation. One obscuring feature has been the categories into which members have been grouped. The participation of chiefs, obliged to speak out for abstruse 'traditional interests', has been particularly problematic. They have been exhorted repeatedly to 'behave like Councillors' but have been reprimanded when they have spoken out [as chiefs properly should] for their own communities. It is clear that criteria for their co-option to Local Councils and management committees have not involved any inherent 'traditionalness' so much as literacy and an ability to adapt, like Mimhene, to the ambiguous and inexplicit expectations of them. One reflection of the role dilemma is that absenteeism has been higher among the 'traditional representatives' than any

298

other category of member (see Fig. 1). If the central authorities have been concerned to direct the chiefs away from the articulation of parochial interests towards some unspecified modernist participation, they have also been much exercised in persuading the elected Councillors that they are not 'a new sort of Chief' – as we have seen from the 1953 brochure quoted above. From the point of view of the Ahafo people the analogy of chiefship is perfectly reasonable, more so than some of the imagery used by visiting officials to define the Councillor's role. In December 1965 the Regional Commissioner 'defined the word "Best Councillors"' to the members of the Asutifi Council; 'councillors should note that they are not chiefs,' he observed, 'but are like "Zoo-Keepers" who are to satisfy all the animals in the zoo'.[14]

The problem of membership categories has been emphasised by the establishment of 'representative' management committees in 1968. These have consisted of six ordinary (literate) citizens, one of whom was appointed chairman, two 'traditional' members, the local Health, Education and Social Welfare officers and a single 'woman representative'. Many of the procedural traumas which these committees have experienced may be related directly to confusion about who is representing which interests, and whether these interests are admissible. The ordinary members were painstakingly selected by the administration to cover the Local Council area as fully as possible, yet at the inaugural meeting they were warned by the District Administrative Officer, as the chiefs had been warned before them, that 'not being elected representatives of any wards, [they] must seek the common interests of the larger community of the Council area as a whole and endeavour to eschew allowing selfish and parochial consideration to cloud their judgment'.[15]

Given that the central function of a local authority is the collection of money and the allocation of amenities, one might expect ward representatives to compete with one another when annual estimates are prepared for the resources available in various categories. However, the ward system has proved a very inadequate framework for this economising in Ahafo. Clearly, Local Council viability has depended on the creation of relatively large units, and democratic interests have insisted that these should be roughly equal demographically. Consequently a number of separate communities have been aggregated to constitute a ward. In terms of the pattern of community identities described in chapter 1, it would be more reasonable to expect rivalry than unity of interests within such groupings. The Ahafo Local Council ward of Goaso, Fawohoyeden and Ayumso cannot have had much political coherence. Kukuom, Dantano and Etwineto, long-term political allies, seems a more promising combination as ward 5 of the Asunafo Local Council, but it is difficult to imagine much 'we-group sentiment' being generated in a ward defined as 'Mim East, from the Methodist schoolhouse including the sawmill quarters'. At elections a candidate from a neighbouring community cannot have been supported with much confidence or enthusiasm. Nor was the situation eased when candidates were elected on a comparative political party basis, a community identified as 'strong C.P.P.' being understandably aggrieved if a U.P. candidate was elected for the ward as a whole. Latterly the C.P.P. appointment of Local Councillors took much of the heat out of representation, and with it most of the public interest in modern local government.

Community concern about the demarcation of local government units is reflected in petitions to secede from wards or from Council Areas. In the latest of a series of petitions against inclusion in the Asutifi Area, Mehamehene argued 'on behalf of the people of this town/village' that his community was much closer to Goaso than to Kenyase, the Asutifi headquarters:

'We shall be at a great disadvantage to be included in the Asutifi Local Council Area. For several years the people of Mehame and the inhabitants of Goaso have formed a community of interest. The people of Mehame sent their foodstuffs and other agricultural products to Goaso where they sell them and buy goods from the stores. All these have come about because of proximity of the two towns which have therefore become an inseparable community.'[16]

There are similar petitions from Nkasaim, Pomakrom and Akrodie, all including references to the strong rational argument of problems of travel. Pleas for the secession of a whole (traditional) state from a Local Council Area have been quite common in Ghana;[17] although this question has never arisen directly in Ahafo there are chiefs like Sankorehene who in conversation express a desire for 'a Local Council of my own'. More generally, a directly contrary sentiment prevailed in Ahafo. Nkasaimhene and Noberkawhene both argued in favour of a return to a single Ahafo Local Council:

'We used to have just the one Local Council at Goaso but now it has been divided into three. During the next two years I should like to see us uniting under Goaso Local Council again. If we all get together it would reduce the staff so that we could get labourers sent here to clear the bush . . . we have about 40 clerks working and all the money is going to them' (Nkasaimhene).

'Our former Ahafo Local Council used to be about the richest, after Kumasi. One clerk of Council should be employed, one treasurer, but more tax collectors. We have one clerk and treasurer at Kukuom, the same at Goaso and at Asutifi. The money is spent on all of them instead of just one' (Noberkawhene).

A Goaso citizen complained in a similar vein:

'I think that the staff is too much. I don't think the purpose of this set-up is to find employment for people. Too much money goes to the staff instead of projects for the public.'

300

Perhaps the best example of the enduring pre-eminence of community identities over ward or party identities is a controversy which brought business in the newly established Asutifi Local Council to a standstill in 1962 and 1963. The minutes of the inaugural meeting in October 1962 record the familiar exhortations to unanimity from the D.C. and Kukuomhene, but end on this ominous note: 'immediately after the election of the chairman and vice-chairman respectively, the undermentioned Councillors walked out unceremoniously at 2.30 p.m. in protest of the seat of the Council at Kenyase No I ... The meeting was adjourned indefinitely at about 2.25 p.m.'[18] The dispute which proceeded to rage on the subject of the location of the Council headquarters had the rather negative advantage of sustaining public interest and preventing Asutifi from succumbing to the same kind of torpor which was afflicting Asunafo at this time. The dispute reflected a profound schism of interests within the Asutifi area, particularly the long-standing rivalry between Hwidiem and Kenyase. Hwidiem felt that its situation on the main road to Kumasi, its larger population and greater number of modern facilities warranted the location of the Council head-quarters there, and that Kenyase had taken unfair advantage of its C.P.P. contacts, notably Mr B. K. Senkyire who was an M.P. and a Kenyase royal. A letter purporting to come from President Nkrumah himself was produced, sanctioning the choice of Kenyase, and peace was grudgingly made. At a meeting of the Council in December the chairman exhorted members

'to bury the differences between themselves, if any, and to start the new year with vigour coupled with the entire co-operation of the staff who do the most important work of the Council. He further advised them not to forget that, it was the Party that had made them Councillors and as such their support to its leader Osagyefo the President must ever be unflinching.'[19]

The first items of business of the Council were thereupon transacted.

The next meeting of the Council in February 1963 again folded up 'unceremoniously', and there followed a long period of recrimination in which the authenticity of Dr Nkrumah's instructions were called to question by the dissident members. The ubiquitous Mr T. N. Baidoo, now District Commissioner for Asutifi, succeeded in smoothing things over, but the location of the headquarters has remained a sore point even after the 1966 coup d'etat and a complete change in Council personnel.

The problems of representation are clearly reflected in the performance of Councillors. In an early local authority circular, the Chief Regional Officer Ashanti observed: 'Many allegations have been made that Councillors are not keeping in touch with their wards. I think most of these allegations are made by persons who have got an axe to grind and that they are not necessarily true but I hope Councillors will keep in close touch with their electors.'[20] The circular also recommended the posting of agendas on Council notice boards to encourage the public to attend discussions if they wished – a privilege which, by all accounts, they have rarely exercised. Similar, if less specific advice has been dispensed regularly ever since, for example: '[the D.C.] further advised all Councillors to be faithful and loyal to their respective towns and villages'.[21] There is much verbal but little documentary evidence of complaints from the public about the behaviour of their Council representatives, but one detailed and specific challenge merits description here. In May 1953 the Town Committee of Goaso, led by the chief, requested the Goaso Local Council to dismiss Mr T. N. Baidoo, the representative of ward 4 which included their town. The petitioners claimed that Mr Baidoo, then chairman of the Council, did not tour his ward to tell his people about the development projects which would affect them, did not discuss rates and levies with them, did not respect his chief and was discourteous to the community elders. They claimed, furthermore, that when his constituents came to consult him he always looked very gloomy, an attitude which 'lends a stain to his character' and 'is also against democracy'. 'He claims', they asserted, 'to be the over-lord of Ward 4'.[22] Plainly sobered by the fact that this petition was addressed to a wide range of public persons from the Prime Minister down, Mr Baidoo wrote a careful reply to the Town Committee with copies to the Government Agent and the Local Council. He retorted that the petition was a personal vendetta launched against him by the Goasohene and that most of the signatories were not even registered members of the electorate. He begged to point out that he did tour his ward – including the other villages within it – and gave much attention to the requests and complaints of those he represented. He observed, however, that 'It is not necessary that a Councillor should at all times accede to the request of the mass of the men and women who, at the electoral period gave the ultimate direction to the event. I am a Councillor, and at the same time the Chairman of the Council; and I should not be partial in my decisions.' Mr Baidoo observed that he laughed when he saw fit and could not see what glumness had to do with democracy. On the 'personal grudge' of the Goasohene, he pointed out that the chief and the Ayumsohene were at daggers drawn and that his efforts to represent his ward impartially might have appeared to suggest disloyalty to the traditional authority of his native town. Keeping in touch with his townsmen meant that 'I am always in groups of youngmen and women, who elected me' but that this should not be construed as 'an attempt to making a division among the chief, Elders and youngmen'. Mr Baidoo remarked that the Goasohene was involved in a dispute with his elders and that perhaps the chief suspected his complicity. Whatever the extent of Mr Baidoo's involvement in stool affairs may in fact have been, he remained ward representative and Council chairman for five more years, while the Goasohene was deposed a few months after.[23]

It is clear that Mr Baidoo had considerable influence on the Ahafo Local Council in its early days. He attributed his success to a sound working relationship with the Government Agent and a thorough knowledge of the statutes: '[the Government Agent] explained the Local Government Ordinance to me. I hadn't seen a copy, so when he had a copy he called me and explained all the ordinances. This was the reason why I was able to be the chairman for such a long time, I quite understood what the ordinances were.' Although Mr Baidoo was undoubtedly conscientious in his interpretation and application of formal rules, much of the Council's proceedings seems to have been conducted in an *ad hoc* manner. As late as 1956 it was pointed out that the Council still had no standing orders.[24] One cannot, of course, learn a great deal about the actual process of decision making from the written records of the Council; our attendance at Management Committee meetings in 1968–9 made it clear that the impassive style of the minutes could bear no relationship to the traumas experienced in the Council hall. The framework for decision making has been the familiar western committee style of procedure, with agendas, the inspection and approval of minutes, the tabling of questions and motions and the conventional rules of order. Although statutorily expected to make decisions by the majority vote[25] there is much evidence of preference for consensual styles of decision making. If we are to follow the arguments of F. G. Bailey[26] we would regard this as indicative of an 'elite' council at work, although the formal specifications correspond to the contrasting 'arena' type. Certainly there are many indications that the 'elite' model is an appropriate description of the less formal features of Local Council organisation: members have been selected on elite criteria of literacy and chiefship, and the segmental, egalitarian ward system of representation has been ineffectual. To a large extent the interests of members have been 'inward looking' to processes and relationships within the Council itself. This is reflected in the detailed minuting of the election of chairmen and vice-chairmen and the appointment of representatives to the District Council. Members have watched over these office-bearers jealously, checking them when they appeared to overstep their authority. On one occasion the chairman and his vice were dismissed for failing to inform members of their participation at a meeting in Sunyani.[27] It is very clear that members dealt with one another less as the equal representatives of segments of the public and more as subtly differentiated individuals.

The District Officer has loomed large in all processes of communication affecting the Local Councils, and has dominated the activities of the various management committees. He has been responsible for filtering all communications to and from prior authority, and official instructions to the

Councils have repeatedly insisted that these formalised channels be rigorously adhered to. This has generated a tendency among members to regard decisions as being made 'for the District Officer' rather than 'for the public' in the first instance. It is a measure of the inadequacy of Local Council representation that the public too regard a direct approach to the District Officer as by far the most effective local political initiative.

It might reasonably be argued that elections on a competitive party-political basis could have enhanced Local Council representation. However, both at the time and retrospectively there has been wide agreement that this was not and could not be so. One post-coup management committee member and former C.P.P. activist described party politics in local councils as 'completely deleterious', while for Ronald Wraith it was 'so manifestly bad'.[28] During the 1950s Councillors were repeatedly exhorted to 'keep Council business above politics', and during the relatively short period when members were elected on party tickets they were explicitly charged not to carry their partisanship from the hustings into the Council chamber. As they were almost by definition party activists this advice must have seemed unrealistic as well as confusing. In the following years when local government was subsumed by the Convention People's Party organisation and opposition was obliterated the tune was radically changed and party loyalty became an imperative. In 1962 the Asunafo chairman could confidently pledge his Council's 'loyalty and unflinching support to Osagyefo Dr Kwame Nkrumah and his Convention People's Party Government'.[29] Two years later the Goaso D.C. 'in a golden tribute to the Councillors urged them to uphold their loyalty to the Party, the Government and the Nation. He said, in the course of his speech that it is not sufficient for a Councillor to forget the Party after having been voted into power.'[30] Shortly before the 1966 coup d'etat the Asutifi Councillors were exhorted by no less a person than the Minister of Local Government to 'attend regular meetings and rallies of the Party' and educate the 'masses' in Party ideology.[31]

When they were first elected in 1962 the Asutifi Councillors were all registered as 'staunch Party activists',[32] an identification which, as we have seen from the headquarters dispute, was not a guarantee of their unanimity. 'C.P.P.–fication' does not seem to have diminished the encapsulation of interests within the Council, which now came to be expressed vis-à-vis the other organs of the Party. Perhaps the most interesting example of this is a controversy which raged over the appointment of a chairman to the Brong–Ahafo South Local Council.[33] In December 1961 the district branch committee of the C.P.P. claimed the right to appoint office-bearers in the Local Council, and the members hotly defended their right to make their own elections. The Council minutes record that the new (C.P.P.) District Commissioner, Mr G. O. Boateng, addressed the Councillors in the following terms:

Although the Local Government Act (1961) provides that it was for a Council to elect her own officers; the Government Party of which he is a representative, had the overall power to direct the conduct of such annual [Council] meetings, as all the Councillors were Government Party members. He went on to say that, in view of his explanations above the District Working Committee of the C.P.P. had submitted a proposal of the composition of the Council's new officers to the Regional Steering Committee for approval which should be adopted by the Council.

The minute continues:

The Councillors vehemently objected to this new procedure which they said was at variance with the requirements of the Local Government Act and argued that they should have been consulted in the submission of the Working Committee as they were the only people who could better recommend new officers in view of the fact that they have come to know themselves as Councillors. After some minutes of heated argument, the President of the Council, Nana Yaw Frimpong II, Omanhene of Ahafo, ruled that the procedure as explained by the District Commissioner be adopted as all the Councillors were Government Party members.[34]

The meeting was adjourned, a further meeting was postponed, but eventually on 29 December it was reported that the Party Working Committee was insisting on the appointment of the new chairman, Mr C. K. Opoku: 'When this was announced, a heated argument and confusion ensued, and the meeting ended in deadlock.'[35]

The trouble seems to have turned on the rivalry between two Councillors, Mr J. Opoku and Mr C. K. Opoku. The former had been a Council member since 1958, and from December 1959 until the present crisis had been chairman. Mr C. K. Opoku had been a member of the original Ahafo Local Council during its first year and was re-elected as a C.P.P. candidate in 1959. At the next meeting the Councillors resolutely rejected the Working Committee's interference and once again the session 'ended in confusion'. At this point the Working Committee seems to have capitulated; the Councillors held elections at the following meeting and Mr J. Opoku was appointed chairman with 7 votes to Mr C. K. Opoku's 6.

From 1961 onwards there are many signs of diminishing interest in Local Council activities. Meetings became infrequent and poor attendance made it difficult to attain a quorum. The Brong–Ahafo South Local Council held 15 meetings during 1960, and 11 in 1961. In 1962 a management committee took over in preparation for the creation of the new Councils; thereafter the Asunafo Local Council held 6 meetings in 1963, 6 in 1964, and only 3 during 1965. This decline was matched by a sharp increase in absenteeism in the Asunafo Local Council (see Fig. 1). Each new local government body established in Ahafo has experienced declining attendance after an enthusiastic start; no doubt stimulated by interest in impending elections or reorganisation, attendance improves again towards the end of each body's career. Periods of crisis may have much the same effect, as in the Brong–Ahafo South Local Council during 1961 or the Asutifi Council in 1964.

By 1966 there can not have been many people in Ahafo who regarded the local government project with much enthusiasm. The management committees which took over after the coup d'état were uncomfortably aware of the Councils' insolvency, reputation for corruption, and inadequacy in providing for public needs. Continually reminded of this heritage by a zealous District Administrative Officer, members could draw little comfort from him or from the prevailing public mood of cynicism, although they might reassure themselves with the thought that they were the hand-picked servants of their country in its hour of need. Mr A. W. Osei, the Goaso Management Committee chairman concluded one long and at times fraught meeting with an indulgent sigh: 'Let us thank ourselves for wasting our time about the nation's business.' It would probably be unfair to judge so intricate a venture as the establishment of Local Councils a failure; perhaps success may only be assessed fairly in the long term and on such incidental criteria as the extent to which Council experience has contributed to the maturation of local politicians or whether it has enhanced the political relationship between the locality and the state. There is, however, one largely incidental success of the local government project which may be recognised quite clearly today – the vigorous growth of Town Development Committees in Ahafo. This is attributable to no great insight on the part of central government planners but rather to a marked lack of formal control. Given considerable freedom to establish their own organisation and operations the Committees have been at least as much the product of an Ahafo initiative as the product of government institution-building. As such they have acquired considerably greater significance to the Ahafo citizens than the Local Councils. There is a much more direct and obvious connection between the gathering of funds, the application of labour and the achievement of concrete results under the aegis of the Town Committee than is the case with the inscrutable operations of the Local Council. We may recall Kenyase I hene's complaint about the Council: 'You have no power over them when they say there is no money ... we have used our own strength to build things because we seek the prosperity of our town.' This is certainly not to say that all Town Committees are efficient and enjoy public support, but it is clear that accessibility and amenability to interests within the community have done much to enhance their political role. Nevertheless the Committee is recognised as an extension of modern governmental processes into the community, potentially a valuable political organ; as such it is not only a means of satisfying communal needs, it has also become in itself one of the criteria of communal aggrandisement.

b. THE TOWN COMMITTEES

The Town Committees have been remarkable for their growth in national political stature as well as for their proliferation in districts such as Ahafo. Provision for the establishment of the Committees under local authority supervision was first made in the 1951 Local Government Ordinance:

A council may appoint such town, village or area committees within the area of its authority as it may deem necessary or expedient, and may delegate ... with or without restrictions or conditions, as it thinks fit, any function exercisable by the council with respect to the area of authority of the town, village or area committee, except the power of making bye-laws, approving annual estimates, levying a rate or issuing a precept, or of borrowing money.[36]

The Ordinance also specified that the Council could control the number of Committee members, their terms of office and method of selection, and could lay down standing orders governing the place, frequency and conduct of Committee meetings. Predictably, the first Committee in Ahafo was established in Goaso, in October 1952, under the watchful eye of the Government Agent and on the initiative of Mr T. N. Baidoo (a Goaso citizen and chairman of the new Local Council), and the energetic, semi-literate chief. The latter summoned 'a meeting of the inhabitants of Goaso town', took the chair and supervised the drawing up of a Committee :

Messrs A and B were asked by the odikro and his elders to find out suitable candidates who could run the town. These two headmen presented eight men to the meeting this evening. The composition was found to be bad as most of the candidates could not read or write. This technical objection was raised by Mr T. N. Baidoo, seconded by Mr C... The meeting retired into consultation and the following candidates were elected by popular votes: [6 men plus three nominated by the chief and elders]. It was found that the composition of the Committee was quite in order. It was also agreed in principle that the Chairman of the Ahafo Local Council should be invited whenever possible to give advice to the Committee on the duties and limitations of such a Committee.[37]

The meeting was important in that it set a precedent which other Ahafo communities were quick to follow. Certain features which were to characterise Committee growth were already apparent: the patronage of the chief, the guidance of the Local Council, the need for popular representatives and the *ad hoc* selection procedure. The model of the Local Council was followed, with appropriate quotas of commoner and traditional members, although there were no official stipulations to this effect. The consequent spread of Committees within Ahafo was quite predictable in terms of inter-community political relationships; it would be an affront to Mim if Goaso had a

Dependence and opportunity

Committee and it did not; Kukuom could not let its arch-rival Mim take any advantage; and so by March 1953 the Local Council clerk reported to the Government Agent, with some apprehension, that applications for formal recognition had been received from nine Committees. 'You will be pleased to hear that all over the area both towns and villages are anxious for authority to form village committees,' he observed, adding: 'The snag in it, I am sure, is that it will give room for unnecessary pressure to be brought to bear on the Council.'[38] The Assistant Government Agent reassured him that it was the Ministry of Local Government's policy to accord formal recognition sparingly.[39]

The ambivalent official attitude to Committee growth is well expressed in a letter from the Government Agent to the new Mim Town Committee: 'As I have pointed out several times before although the Mim Town Committee is not officially recognised, it is a voluntary organisation playing at least the role of a consultative machinery, I am willing to give it rather unofficially all the support I can.'[40] The problem had been to control Committee growth in a respectable bureaucratic manner. There had been a rash of 'Committees' with strange organisation and strange names – the Mim Improvement Association, the Kenyase Kroye Kuo (Unity Association). Within three years the Local Council had registered 22 of the more orthodox Committees and was obliged to form a Development Committee of its own to attend to their affairs. This mainly involved the collection and disbursement of the 'special rates' which each Committee, with public approval, had agreed to levy. The considerable sums involved (in excess of £1,000 a year for Goaso) brought the Council/Committee relationship under severe strain with accusations of abuse from both sides. By the late 1950s it was clear that the Committees had become more than the Council could handle, and subsequently the District Officer was given more direct control over their registration and activities. The Council's ambivalent attitude was that a well-organised Committee could greatly assist such vital operations as rate collection and the transmission of information to the public, but could be difficult to control and could provide a means of harassing the Council. However, the Council can not be said to have discouraged Committee growth, indeed it established an annual conference of Committee members, the first of which was held in April 1961. Ninety-two delegated from 30 Committees attended, and it seems that the occasion was of value more for the enthusiasm which was generated than for any exchange of substantive information. The Council chairman defined a Committee as 'a body of persons appointed for the progress of the town' and offered the by now very familiar advice that 'to be a member of a committee is no chieftaincy, but rather to serve as a servant'.[41] The Council/Committee relationship remains tense: 'I am often puzzled,' the Goaso Committee secretary confessed.

308

'Often the Local Council lays all their burden upon us...but the Town Committee is only supposed to supplement where [the Council] is weak. The Council is a government arm, we can't force it...they are our bosses, I would say they are our government from which we take our inspirations. The townspeople expect us to oppose inimical regulations from the Local Council . . . they expect us to petition the Local Council, but if we don't also take care we fall into trouble with the government. We are to help the Local Council with the administration of the place but we are not to interfere. We are between and betwixt, you see'.

Section 34 of the 1961 Local Government Act transferred responsibility for the regulation, appointment and registration of Town Committees to the Ministry. The following year a cabinet decision that every community irrespective of size should have its own Committee led to the promulgation of the first specific regulations.[42] The levying of special rates was made subject to cabinet approval and Committee budgeting, a source of much ill-feeling, was taken over by the Ministry from the Local Councils. Further ministerial instructions specified that Committees should consist of up to eleven members, and that the chairman should be the chief or headman of the community.

In the late 1950s the Town Committees were as affected by the prevalent party-political strife as the Local Council. As community interest groups were subsumed by the party dichotomy Committees were set up and toppled all too frequently. In contrast, the 'C.P.P.-fication' of local government which followed in the early 1960s had an atrophying effect on the Committees – and on the system at large. In 1964, when Ghana became a one-party state, the District Commissioner at Goaso announced that 'Osagyefo Dr Kwame Nkrumah had instructed that a town or village development committee should be made of the chairman and the secretary of the town or village Party branch and five other appointed members.'[44] The chief was grudgingly allocated a nominal, presidential role. Although meetings became infrequent and public interest flagged, the Committees were certainly not killed by 'C.P.P.-fication'; their enduring importance was recognised after the 1966 coup d'etat, and in May of that year the National Liberation Council ruled that provisional Committees consisting of the chief and up to four of his elders should be established, with the Council clerk and Community Development officer attending all meetings. Later regulations re-established full Committees with a majority of ordinary members appointed from the community.[45]

The relative freedom with which Town Committees have been allowed to grow has made for some diversity in their form and functions throughout Ahafo. In general it would be agreed that the competence of a Committee today extends to discussion of the public amenities required by the community, and the organisation of the money and labour needed to obtain these. Occasionally Committees have dealt with such matters as the allocation of land and the settlement of local disputes, but they have never been authorised by the government to do so. In an address to the Local Council in 1961, the District Commissioner 'remarked that in his short stay in the District, he had observed that some town and village committees exercised some functions without the knowledge of the Council. In support of this allegation, he mentioned a contract agreement which had been entered into between the Apenimadi Village Committee and a Contractor in respect of a feeder road.'[46] However, the District Officer and the Local Council were not normally disposed to enquire too closely into Committee activities so long as they did not (as was the case with the Apenimadi feeder road) clearly fall within the competence of another local government body. In December 1967 the District Administrative Officer received without comment a report of one Committee undertaking which from any point of view, 'modern' or otherwise, must have appeared eccentric. The Mehame Committee had sponsored a fund-raising football match between the 'Mehame Women XI' and their Dadiesoaba counterparts, a novel inter-community encounter which had been frustrated by the failure of the Dadiesoaba XI to present themselves. Undaunted, the Committee had 'divided Mehame Women into two parts and played the match', collecting three Cedis for the National Trust Fund.[47]

From a public point of view the principal value of the Committee is as an instrument of communal aggrandisement. Because any community is entitled to form one, the Committee may become a significant means of expressing political interrelationships. An example of this was a meeting convened by the Goaso Committee in 1969 to try to persuade the Committees of its subject villages to contribute to the extension of the town Middle School. The villages were more inclined to favour the long-term development of their own than the immediate facilities in Goaso. Debate was wide-ranging and at times heated, and after an injudicious reminder from a Goaso elder that the villages were, after all, finally subject to the authority of the Goasohene, negotiations broke down. However accurate this claim may have been, the subject villagers, through the authority of their respective Committees, had the right to contemplate developments which were in their own best interests. Communities throughout Ahafo have shown some independence in the size, methods of selection, composition and style of officeholding of their Committees. Although the Local Council has served as an approximate organisational model, efforts to cast the Committees in a truly 'modern' idiom have occasionally produced strange hybrids. In 1962 the Committee of the small town of Dantano appointed Ministers of Education, Finance, Health, and Transport-and-Communications, prompting the District Commissioner to enquire 'May I know if you are forming another government over there?'[48] Other Committees have registered a wide range of officeholders, from sub-treasurers and internal auditors to chaplains and porters.

We have discussed Committee growth and its significance in the Ahafo communities elsewhere.[49] Here it may be sufficient to emphasise the contemporary importance of the Committee in public decision-making processes. It has provided a means for articulating community interests in a contingent rather than a categoric manner; the effectiveness of the Committee has come to depend on the opportunities which it affords for a wide range of intra-community interests, strangers, elders, religious bodies and occupational groups, to express themselves when occasion demands. A preference for implicit rather than explicit representation has gained ground, interested parties being anxious to 'have a voice' when a particular issue arises, but there being little concern that individual members should be specifically charged to speak for this or that group. Political parties or factions for and against a chief may upset this delicate balance and indications of bias may weaken the Committee's authority to make decisions. Such considerations are in evidence when Committee members are selected. During 1968–9 this was carried out in the context of a public meeting in the community convened by the District Administrative Officer and attended by the Local Council clerk. Nominations were called for from the crowd, and in each case assent was taken when a convincing-looking number of people raised their hands in support. Thus seven to eleven individuals were accumulated, each declared 'unanimously elected' in the sense that there was no explicit dissent. Some candidates showed little enthusiasm but usually responded to cajolery from the Administrative Officer or the townspeople around them. Only if no nominations were forthcoming would the District Administrative Officer call for proposals in terms of specific categories: a literate member to act as secretary, an elder, a representative of the zongo, a woman. Occasionally he was obliged to intervene to prevent a single interest group being obviously over-represented.

The Stool Council in each community has certainly been affected by Committee growth. The chief, as chairman of both bodies, is a direct link between the two but as his authority derives in the first instance from his Stool Council his primary responsibility is to his elders. The dual role disposes many chiefs to feel uneasy about participation on the Committees, which are often designated as being essentially 'for the youngmen' rather than 'for the elders'. Participation in two distinct community organisations is sometimes seen as jeopardising the chief's cardinal function as moderator of competing interests. As Nkasaimhene bluntly declared: 'A chief can not have two posts.' Attendance at Committee deliberations was also regarded as incompatible with the chief's role as the final sanctioning authority in the town: 'The chief should be the one to whom the Committee reports its proceedings' (Akrodiehene). 'What I would like is for a common man to be elected as their chairman, so that after their meeting he can report to me. But if I don't understand I shall call the townspeople and put the matter before them. But if I go and meet with them to discuss the matter – how can can it be advanced?' (Ayumsohene). However, in public decision making the competence of the Stool Council and the Town Committee is never too closely distinguished, local explanations tending to depict both as engaged in a single process. When an issue arises within an Ahafo community it is almost invariably put before an elder or the chief in the first instance, and thus tends to come before the Stool Council first. It may then be referred to the Town Committee where it is discussed and refined. If it has not yet been resolved the issue may finally be presented, cut and dried, to a meeting of the community at large, attended by the chief, his elders and the Committee members. In a year there may be as many as five of these public meetings in a community, and they are generally considered as important authorising instruments in matters of public policy. Kenyase I hene described his own role as 'manager' of this process in these terms:

'Before I discuss developments in the town with the Committee I discuss things with the elders ... The Committee represents the common people in the town but I discuss matters with the elders before I submit them to the Town Committee and the gong is beaten to arrange a meeting of the people ... If I discuss something with the Committee without informing the elders it is difficult for me to tell the people of the town about it.'

Ultimately the decision is made when the chief pronounces it, but he takes virtually no part in the actual discussions; the tenet that a chief is never wrong implies that he should never be given the opportunity to be wrong. In an orthodox Ashanti Stool Council the chief communicates, as a safety measure, through his official spokesman (the okyeame) on all formal occasions. In the Committee and at public meetings the secretary serves very much the same function. Ideally the presence of the chief exerts a strong restraining influence at all meetings: 'If you offend a chief a sheep will be slaughtered and you will get a big [law] case ... The people are careful with their words. If you offend a chief you offend the whole town' (Goaso Town Committee secretary).

Asked to specify the functions of the Committee an ordinary citizen will almost invariably reply that its business is to 'attend to the progress of the town'. This is hardly in itself a novel preoccupation. Although he may not follow its activities very closely the same citizen would be surprised if it were suggested that the Committee was superfluous. The unobtrusive but useful role the Committee has come to play is at least as much a consequence of 'Ahafo-isation' as of 'modernisation'. If the success of the Committee from a central government point of view must be attributed to the ways in which its organisation and operations have fused with other political processes in the community, its significance from the local point of view rests reciprocally on the fact that it is in some measure an extension of modern government into the community.

CHAPTER 8

PARTY POLITICS IN AHAFO

Much of the political activity in Ahafo over the last two decades has continued to follow the channels established in the preceding half century of
colonial rule. The maintenance of central political control was as much a
preoccupation for the postcolonial government bureaucracy in the face of
Ahafo as it had been for its colonial predecessor. The furthering of local
political purposes today, as earlier, remains largely the prerogative of the
Akan institutions of local political action which still serve formally to define
the communities of Ahafo. Chieftaincy and central government have both
shown themselves flexible and inventive political interests, neither of them
immune to autocratic tendencies but both sensitive over time to the necessity
to offer intelligible services to those whom they controlled, if their own
power was not to be depleted. There have been substantial periods of time even
since 1951 – one of them being at the time of writing – when these two
institutional traditions have in effect monopolised the formal politics of Ahafo.
But there have also been periods in the same two decades – thus far, rather
longer periods – in which a third set of institutions has purported to syn-
thesise central government and local community by providing a representative basis for the allocation of control over central government. As far as
local communities are concerned the representation of their interests to the
central government is not so much a convenience as it is a necessity. But, as
might be expected of a necessity, it is not a service which communities have
allowed to become dependent solely on a system of government which has
proved to be liable to regular suspensions by those who are the more direct
heirs of the colonial state power. If the system of representative democracy
bequeathed to Nkrumah and resuscitated by the first military government of
1966–9 was the legal legatee of the colonial order, the more substantial
elements of the colonial estate passed concretely into the hands of the civil
service and, even more directly, into those of the forces of coercion. In 1969
– and very possibly still today – the legitimacy of the Ghanaian state in the
eyes of its ordinary rural citizens[1] appeared to depend on its long-term
conformity to the model of representative democracy. But it was also clear that
the prudential and moral requirement of obedience to whatever was currently
the government was a much more definite and salient political precept for all

but the most politically engaged than any vague conception of how the polity ought legitimately to be organised. Elections, political parties and a representative legislature have all, accordingly, entered prominently into the articulation of political interests in Ahafo since 1951. They have served to illuminate many aspects of the social basis of power in the area and they have undoubtedly contributed substantially to the ability of groups of local residents to organise themselves collectively to defend their interests. Individual parties have established themselves with some firmness in the hearts of a few as foci of loyalty and have spread widening but weakening ripples of affection and antipathy out to much larger proportions of the population. We have, the N.A.L. chairman for the Asunafo constituency explained in the course of the 1969 election campaign, 'two different sorts of people: United Party people and C.P.P.' But distinct though these party allegiances now often are, they have not as yet altered the basic orientation of the population towards the agencies of the central government. The mood of moderate optimism about the future of representative government which reached out to Ahafo in the summer of 1969 appeared to be shared in an unexacting way by almost all those with any interest in modern political processes who did not happen to be dedicated members of the former C.P.P. political apparat. In public indeed the latter were at pains to exhibit an equal level of optimism, as the campaign began. But the extensive political proscription lists issued by the military government and the low level of political commitment to the C.P.P. interest of most parts of Ahafo gave their professed confidence more than a tinge of bravado. In retrospect the summer of 1969 is likely to appear an even more atypical moment of political consciousness in Ahafo than it seemed to be at the time. Such atypicality certainly does not in any way diminish the illumination of a period, however brief, in which the Ahafos were politically free to choose for themselves, just as Rousseau had noted the English to be in the eighteenth century.[2] No doubt the illusion of persisting liberty faded briskly enough after the election of August 1969 and neither it nor the prospects for effective elective representation are likely to have been exactly revived by more political developments.

The election of 1969 has been studied at length elsewhere[3] as an expression – imperfect and evanescent as all such expressions necessarily are – of the political will of Ahafo as a political entity. In the context of a study which attempts to grasp the political development of Ahafo over three quarters of a century, the imperfection and evanescence of the form in which the will was expressed matters more than the content of the will itself. The discussion of modern politics in Ahafo must have a definite historical position in such an account. For drama of event and for the novelty and glamour of the roles which emerged from it modern politics has held a prominent position in the recent history of Ahafo. But in the treatment of structural change, even

315

over the last twenty years, modern politics has no such privileged place. Ahafo today cannot do without passable roads or supplies of petrol. It would find the gravest discomfort in any cessation of the import into the area of tinned milk or aspirin or even – over a period of any length – of the salaries of school teachers and local administrators. By contrast interference with the formal opportunities for modern political activity or impediments to the pursuit of the careers of politicians can be accepted with complete equanimity by the great majority. For all except the most politically engaged any plausible theory of political legitimacy in Ahafo today would incorporate a considerable element of providentialism. It is hardly likely that there can be extensive zest for military government today in an area which had been so close to the heart (and so well placed to tug at the purse strings) of the previous civilian government; but except among those who had been directly allied to this particular governing party, it is not to be supposed that there is much active resentment of the new government either. Politicians come and politicians go, but government goes on for ever and it is scarcely now conceivable to the Ahafos that it might fail to do so. There are few displaced Ahafo politicians whose theology would be likely to convince them to make destiny their choice;[4] but the great majority of the population has less wilful expectations of the part which its choices are due to play in the constitution of governments and accepts the government as it accepts the universe: because it had better.

The initial advent of modern politics in Ahafo was undramatic. The area formed part of the Kumasi West Rural constituency in the first legislative election of 1951. It lacked traditions of modernist political activity, such as characterised the coastal towns or Kumasi itself; and it was devoid of the sort of local notables for whom the C.P.P. political style and success was in itself an affront to their status and who formed the basis for the main political opposition to the C.P.P. in the south.[5] But it was wealthy enough and involved enough with the expansion of the local market to see the new politics as prospectively an opportunity and not, as much of the impoverished and secluded Northern Territories appear to have regarded it at first, as a threat.[6] The beginnings of local initiative in the promotion of development had helped to develop skills of organisation and to foster the rhetoric of communal betterment, as well as raising the aspirations of a number of energetic local personalities for the securing of public – and perhaps of private – goods.[7] Ahafo initiative in the formation of Area Development Committees and other agencies of local betterment won the respect of the first Ghanaian D.C. in the area, A. L. Adu, in the late 1940s[8] to such an extent that he advanced them as a model for emulation elsewhere in the Gold Coast.[9] The Secretary of the first Ahafo development association, the Ahafo United Association, was a member of the Goaso chiefly family, T. N. Baidoo, who became C.P.P. Chairman of the Ahafo Local Council from 1952 to 1957. His earlier career had been exceedingly varied. Educated for two years at Mim and then for six years at a Methodist school in Kumasi between 1925 and 1931, he returned to Goaso and in 1940 was acting as a bailiff in the Magistrate's court in Goaso.[10] In 1943 he was arrested and prosecuted for smuggling perfumes and other goods across the Ivory Coast border to sell them in Ahafo. He was sentenced to a fine of £6 (or two months in gaol) after an elaborate defence designed to show that he had purchased the smuggled goods in Kumasi (an opportunity which appeared from the evidence to have been no harder to come by in 1943 than it would be today).[11] He had also worked for a time as a cocoa broker and appeared by 1951, in the list of representatives elected by the individual sub-districts to the electoral college in the Parliamentary election, as a farmer and public letter-writer. Another prominent campaigner for Ahafo development who later became a leading C.P.P. dignitary assisted Baidoo in 1951/2 in the formation of the Ahafo Youth Association as a comprehensive local pressure group, Baidoo himself becoming Chairman and the newly returned B. K. Senkyire from Kenyase became Secretary.[12] Senkyire was a younger man, born in 1928, a Kenyase royal who had followed up his seven years' primary education in Kenyase by moving on to a secondary school, Ghana National College, at Cape Coast, where he began to take an active interest in politics as a student in form III in 1948. This experience as a student in Cape Coast gave him political contacts with the party leadership which were later to prove invaluable and it helped to mould a political approach which contrasted to some degree with that of Baidoo. When he returned to Ahafo after completing his schooling to take up the post of Clerk of the Ahafo Local Council, he proceeded to organise the entire Council staff in August 1952 into a trade union, the Ahafo Local Authority Employees Union which fixed its own regulations, hours of work, attendance and times of payment.[13] In the development of Ahafo, the roles of local representative and salaried employee of the locality hardly seemed to require precise differentiation. Senkyire saw himself as having returned to serve his community, denying that at the time he had entertained any ambition of entering national politics. In the idiom of Ahafo values at this point, his return was a proper response to the calls of duty, an acceptance of the precept *noblesse oblige*, though without prim overtones of nobility having to be its own exclusive reward. A prosperous scion of the royal house with the good fortune to receive a modern education had the obligation to bring the benefits of modernity to his people, though the latter in return might expect to pay for the privilege. To be Clerk of Council was to be an expert in modernity, a prerogative of literacy. Trade unions, too, were at the time a form of modernity warmly favoured by the enthusiastic student followers of the C.P.P. The Ahafo Local Authority

Employees Union in self-proclamation might appear to be a striking example of workers' control; but under the gentle admonitions of the government official stationed in Ahafo, it was accepted as a valuable instrument of workers' self-discipline with firm guidelines as to the disciplinary requirements of the government.

If these two men and their organisational projects may be taken as symptomatic of viable local political energies and of widespread local political aspirations it is not difficult to see how natural the initial appeal of the C.P.P. in Ahafo was certain to be. The C.P.P. aspirations for the end of colonial control and for that local access to the economic privileges of colonial rulers which was expected to accompany this end hardly generated the same inebriated expectations among the cocoa farmers of the forest as it did among the youthful unemployed and ex-servicemen of the coastal cities. In Ahafo it seems to have been taken as offering the pursuit of the same goals of local development as were already accepted locally – but by instrumentally superior means. No doubt there was an element of the pursuit of private goods to supplement the motivational purity of this concern with wholly public goods; but it is clear from the extreme placidity of most of the electoral process in Kumasi West Rural constituency that the role of Member of the new Legislative Assembly had not yet been identified by many as the entry to a potentially lucrative career. In these conditions the national apparatus of the C.P.P. had little difficulty in linking up with the aspirants to modernist political leadership in Ahafo itself. The C.P.P. candidate for the constituency, B. F. Kusi, hailed from Bisease, a village on the eastern edge of the constituency near Kumasi but had close family connections in Acherensua, Kenyase I and II, Mim, Ntotroso, Gambia, Bediakokrom, Akrodie and Ayumso.[14] Kusi was an energetic young trader in Kumasi, importing arms and ammunition, hardware and haberdashery. Born in 1922, he had been educated in Kumasi, finishing his middle school education in 1942 with the economic assistance of one of the most perceptive younger British administrators, Peter Canham.[15] Kusi's interest in politics went back to the period of the founding of the United Gold Coast Convention (U.G.C.C.) and he had been one of the group of young activists who encouraged Nkrumah in his breakaway to found the C.P.P. A member of the C.P.P. National Executive, he had been actively engaged in organising support for the C.P.P. in Ashanti from 1949 onwards and had built up a formidable personal political base in the Kumasi West Rural constituency. His nominators came from Acherensua, Teppa and Nkasaim, while those of his opponent George Kingsley Owusu, also described as a Kumasi merchant, all came from two adjacent houses in Goaso and appear to have been closely associated with the stool of Goaso, one being the Linguist (*okyeame*), Kwabena Antwi.[16]

Registration of voters had been held in the last two months of 1950. Despite the prevalence of a number of rumours (such as that the government was trying to complete a list of cocoa farmers' names in order to facilitate the destruction of their trees) it was successful – at least from a simple numerical viewpoint. But the Goaso D.C. expressed considerable doubts as to whether the figures indicated any real understanding of the issues involved and noted, perhaps more materially, that 'in many places it appears that the odikro beat gong-gong ordering all to register and it seems probable that many registered because of fear of the consequences'.[17] Information teams with a loud-speaker van visited Teppa, Kenyase, Goaso, Mim, Kukuom, Hwidiem and Acherensua from 23 to 25 January to explain the process of voting and all civil servants were warned elaborately and with great emphasis of the need to appear wholly impartial and not under any circumstances to discuss the qualifications of candidates.[18] When it came to the election itself in February 1951, it was held in two stages. The constituency was divided up into sub-districts in which representatives were elected to an electoral college which met two or three days later at Teppa. Fifty-seven of these elections were uncontested (representing a total of 13,620 registered voters), while in only seven of the sub-districts (a total of 1,330 registered voters) was there in fact a contest.[19] In these seven, 764 votes were cast in all. One Assistant Returning Officer who had supervised the elections in Nkasaim, Hwidiem, Wamahinso, Ntotroso, and the two Kenyases, found that in each case a single candidate was nominated and returned unopposed.[20] The formalities were not always observed with much accuracy; but they were clearly conceived very much as formalities. 'In the above villages it was clear that the matter of selecting a candidate had been unanimously agreed upon before polling day. As a result only a few people were present at each election; the rest of the voters had gone about their normal business.' The only serious complaint about the conduct of the election came from Nyinahin, a village outside the Ahafo area, in which it was alleged that thousands had been effectively dis-franchised by a drastic shrinkage in the list of electors between registration day and polling day.[21] The very small number of active contests indicates the absence of effective political organisation on the national level to combat the C.P.P. Such contests as did occur resulted for the most part not from the enticement of a national political organisation reaching down into the villages but from the absence at the time of the election of any stable and accepted local hierarchy of influence in the village in question. Many sub-districts, it is clear, simply adopted their normal communal spokesman in public negotiations as their delegate to the electoral college.[22] A list of the delegates selected by the Ahafo sub-districts gives some indication of the range of economic experience on which political influence at the village level might be based (see Table 7). The heavy dependence on the growing and

TABLE 7. *Delegates chosen by the Ahafo communities to Teppa electoral college,
1951 Parliamentary election*

No.	Sub-district	Person elected	Occupation
31	Acherensua	Yaw, Nkansah Appawu	Farmer and Trader
32	Hwidiem (West)	S. K. Adai	Co-operative Secretary
33	Hwidiem (East)	Mensah, Isaac Francis	Farmer
34	Kenyase I	Dankwa Boakye	Farmer
35	Kenyase II	J. K. Asamoah	Merchant
36	Ntotroso	Kontor, Matthew	Teacher
37	Jedu/Wamahinso	Mensah, Isaac	Produce-buyer
38	Nkasaim	Asumadu, D. K.	Farmer
39	Goaso	Thomas Nelson Baidoo	Farmer and Letter-writer
40	Dantano	Anomako, Paul	Farmer and Cocoa-buyer
41	Kukuom (West)	Kofi Poku	Farmer
42	Kukuom (East)	Charles Oduro	Farmer and Produce-buyer
43	Noberkaw	Mansoh, Peter K.	Farmer
44	Mehame/Dadiesoaba	Robert Kwabena	Farmer
45	Akrodie	Awuah Kojo	Trader
46	Mim (West)	Ahensua, Kofi Alfred	Chief Farmer
47	Mim (South)	F. K. Donkor	Farmer and Produce-buyer
48	Mim (North)	Nsiah, Alexander Michael	Farmer
49	Mim (East)	Samuel K. Ankrah	Pupil Teacher
50	Ayumso/Fawohoyeden	Albert Kwabena Owusu	Poultry Farmer
51	Kwapong	Safo, B. K.	Letter-writer and Produce-buyer
52	Sankore	Donkor, E. K.	Farmer
53	Abuom	Buruma Yaw	Carpenter

marketing of cocoa and on the literate skills which are at such a premium in
organising the latter stand out with some clarity. If ever political mobilisation
should come to focus round the needs of cocoa-producers, as had already been
shown by the success of Ahafo United Association propaganda over the
distant threat of cutting out for swollen shoot, Ahafo plainly offered rich
possibilities for recruitment. But in February 1951 national political goods
were very little differentiated in the minds of Ahafo electors. When the
electoral college met at Teppa on 8 February 1951, B. F. Kusi was duly
elected by the votes of 59 delegates to one.[23]

As a constituency Member, Kusi was extremely active, taking part for
example in efforts to settle a dispute over the special rate at Mim and in the
setting-up of a Farmers Association.[24] Many of the themes which he espoused

in the Assembly set the pattern for the representation of Ahafo's claims on the supply of public amenities: the tarring of roads, above all the main Teppa–Mim road, the provision of clean water supplies, hospitals, schools, police stations, telephones, post offices, the depredations of the expatriate timber firms, above all the Mim Timber Company, the degree of government economic expropriation from the cocoa sector, the general backwardness of the rural areas and the lack of knowledge about or concern over their needs felt by those who controlled the central government.[25] These were all themes which were resumed with more or less tact by subsequent Ahafo M.P.s and Kusi himself returned to them in detail in relation to Ahafo even after he had become the parliamentary representative of another area. At no point in the period of C.P.P. rule was there any lack of persistent parliamentary critics, whether inside or outside the governing party, of the distributive pattern of government expenditure between rural and urban areas or of the rate of government investment in the areas which they personally represented. The representation of local interests was the central theme in the local obligations of a parliamentarian, just as solid obedience to the orders of the party leadership was the central theme in the government's view of his duties. The gap between norm and performance was probably little wider in the case of these peripheral obligations than it was in the case of the central ones on which a parliamentarian's future career depended. Kusi himself adopted with some speed the only theoretical solution to the potential conflict between these duties by resigning from the governing party in the wake of a number of other prominent young members on the National Executive, notably Saki Scheck.[26] The dispute which led to his resignation was ostensibly over personality clashes and the style of Nkrumah's leadership, but it naturally acquired a more ideological dimension in retrospect. Kusi found his constituency visited by government ministers, including the Minister of Education and the Prime Minister himself and alleged that his constituents had been promised extensive development expenditure, including the tarring of their main traffic artery, if they disposed of him in future and threatened with corresponding deprivations if they were unwise enough not to do so.[27] He attacked dictatorial tendencies in the C.P.P., criticised the allocation of Cocoa Puchasing Company loans to farmers on the basis of support for the C.P.P. and spoke out so vehemently for the interests of Ashanti ('I represent the Ashanti nation') that he earned the charge of tribalism from none other than Krobo Edusei.[28] During 1953 Kusi acted as Chief Whip for the opposition.

When it came to the 1954 election the Kumasi West Rural constituency was divided between Ahafo (including Asunafo, Ahafo Ano and Teppa) and Kusi's own home area. Kusi naturally stood for office in the latter. Even there his candidacy was unsuccessful in the face of C.P.P. sponsorship of his opponent (John Baidoo, C.P.P. 3,203; B. F. Kusi, Ghana Congress Party

1,708).[29] In Ahafo itself there were three candidates – B. D. Addai, a leading Kumasi entrepreneur in the marketing of cocoa for several decades and a former member of the Legislative Council (described as a merchant and nominated by a Kumasi farmer, a magazine keeper from Goaso and the Ahafo Native Court Registrar from Goaso) who stood for the Ghana Congress Party; the young Ahafo Local Council Clerk, Senkyire (nominated by the Council Chairman T. N. Baidoo, the Secretary of the Co-operative Society in Goaso and a Kukuom farmer) who stood for the C.P.P.; and A. W. Osei, a trader from Goaso and a relative, like Baidoo, of the Goaso royal house, nominated by three Goaso cocoa farmers, who stood as an independent candidate.[30] Osei was 42 years old at this time and had spent twenty-four years of his life, from the age of sixteen on, working for the government Health Department all over the country as a nurse.[31] When he retired from the nursing service in 1952 he had undertaken a number of different lines of work, including the establishment of a small nursing home at Goaso which was visited once a week by a doctor from Kumasi, Dr Hastings Banda. It had become clear by 1954, unlike 1951, that the position of a parliamentarian in the ruling party was potentially the gateway to many prosperous lines of enterprise. Competition between the C.P.P. for the ruling party nomination had become competition for a resource which was recognised as the more scarce precisely because it was now widely perceived to be so much more substantial. Nor was this necessarily at all a matter of technical corrruption. Perfectly legal opportunities for gain, as well as – for those who cared to use them – a good number of somewhat less legally impeccable openings came with some readiness to the C.P.P. Member in the Legislature. Accordingly, while in many parts of the country, it still took an intellectual or a lawyer to have intrinsic ideological reasons for opposing the C.P.P. – and the candidature of a man such as Addai could be substantially interpreted as a result of pique at the blow to his status implied by the continuing C.P.P. government – there were many with solidly egoistic grounds for contesting the party nomination with real vigour. Osei and Senkyire both made strenuous attempts to secure the C.P.P. nomination. Both were well enough connected in terms of traditional affiliations and modern commercial linkages, to say nothing of their considerable personal talents, to be perfectly plausible candidates. But Osei had been away from the constituency for most of his adult life, only returning two years before the election, and he was in consequence less well known to younger men in the constituency than the ubiquitous Senkyire. With the best will and the purest bureaucratic dedication, neither of which was likely in practice to be available in such a competition, it is no easy matter in a huge rambling rural constituency with a largely illiterate electorate and very poor communications to see that the nominating process for party candidates is conducted with firm regard for constitutional proprieties. The Ahafo dispute was only one of a very large number of disputed nominations which had to be transferred to the Party Executive at the coast for resolution. But once it had been transformed in this way Senkyire's superior access to the party leadership, his more modernist political style and his record of close co-operation with the party chairman on the Local Council, T. N. Baidoo (Osei's cousin and bitter personal enemy), were likely to give the younger man a decisive advantage. It is unnecessary to invoke in explanation of his victory in securing the nomination (though it would be naive to exclude the possible truth of) the allegation, still maintained a decade and a half later by his subsequent U.P. opponents that the key factor in deciding the nomination was the payment of a sum of money on his behalf to a leading party influential.

Disappointed at this result, Osei campaigned fiercely for the seat as an Independent. Because of the recency of his own C.P.P. allegiance, he was in no position to mount a serried ideological assault upon the party. The two main issues were consequently reduced, as Senkyire himself subsequently put it, to 'the candidate himself and what he could do for the area'. Individual representative efficacy was an entirely plausible criterion for the selection of a representative in the absence of ideological dissent. The 1954 election was the last Ghanaian election in which, because of the proportion of independent candidates who were simply unsuccessful candidates for the C.P.P. nomination, individual representative adequacy could be regarded as the main basis for electoral choice. Once there existed serious opposition parties, it was abundantly clear that affiliation with the party which proved to be victorious was a necessary condition for any representative effectiveness at all. Even in 1954 the official support of the C.P.P. machine was a formidable asset for a candidate. As Senkyire put it, 'The C.P.P. in those days had an image and that alone was a help for me.' Osei maintained in later years that he had in fact authentically won the election but had been cheated of his victory by the theft or destruction of his ballot papers by his opponents. It is not inconceivable that there were some electoral irregularities, but it is difficult to believe that as early as 1954 they can have made a crucial difference to the result of an election in which Senkyire was officially regarded as victorious by 5,400 votes to 1,744 for Osei and 579 for Addai, out of a registered electorate of 16,665.[32] During the next year the political placidity of Ahafo, along with numerous other parts of Ashanti, was severely disrupted by the rise of the National Liberation Movement (N.L.M.), the Kumasi-based political movement to raise the producer price of cocoa and protect the political power of Ashanti. As an immigrant area in which the permanent landholders were largely recruited by origin from Ashanti and as a locus for heavy investment by such leading N.L.M. personalities as Bafuor Osei Akoto himself, Ahafo was speedily drawn into the vortex of this violent

323

political storm. At the point at which the C.P.P. had been the only effective national political équipe with the organisational capacity to muster the support of a large rural constituency the internal divisions of Ahafo had failed to provide a focus for very bitter electoral conflict. But as soon as the formation of the N.L.M. had produced a wealthy, energetic and enthusiastic rival and one with superlative political contacts, in chiefly, commercial and farming ranks in Ashanti, with the apparent blessing of Manhyia Palace itself, Ahafo was eminently open to counter-organisation in opposition to the C.P.P. Senkyire was an able and enthusiastic young politician who enjoyed strong traditional and popular support in the section of Kenyase from which he came. But he was no Krobo Edusei.

Because of the defection of B. F. Kusi from the C.P.P. ranks, the relationship between the C.P.P. government and Ahafo did not have, even in 1954, the quality of solid mutual service which had been established in the Sekyere constituency centred on Edusei's home town of Kumawu, a long-standing traditional rival of Kumasi. The C.P.P. did, of course, possess a number of assets in the competition which ensued in Ahafo, notably its control over the liquid funds of the official Cocoa Purchasing Company (C.P.C.), later explored in the Jibowu report.[33] C.P.C. loans on farms, allocated from November/December 1953 onwards, were intended to be protected by an elaborate process of guaranteeing, surveying and indentures and they were supposed to be used for the improvement of farms. But they were envisaged in many cases simply as a means of acquiring capital for trading and some farmers clearly expected never to have to repay them. Often the produce of the farm pledged could not in principle suffice to repay the loan within the period specified, even if it were to be exclusively devoted to that purpose.[34] It is difficult to estimate how much effect this facility did have in political terms in the Ahafo area. But some indications of the flow of resources involved can be gathered from the fact that in the summer of 1969, a decade and a half later, there were still ten C.P.C. loans outstanding in the Goaso area (including at least one of over £500, one more of over £400 and two more of well over £300), while in the Kukuom district there were a further twelve and in Mim district a further seventeen. However this particular form of leverage was soon to some degree neutralised by the countervailing efforts of the Ashanti Farmers' Union, a political affiliate of the N.L.M., which likewise made its reports direct to the Asanteman Council. The two largest subscribers to the deposit for the hire-purchase Land Rover which the A.F.U. used for campaigning purposes were both from Teppa, Opanin Kobina Nimo and Opanin Yaw Boadu, the Teppa Chief Farmer.[35] The first constituency tour reported by the A.F.U. was led in fact to Goaso and Mim by the Ashanti Chief Farmer, Opanin Kofi Buor, 28 February 1955.[36] Large rallies were held in both towns and enthusiastic support was reported from chiefs and people. Militant Chief Farmers were elected and installed in all major centres of population. Between mid-May and mid-July 1955 the A.F.U. van and General Secretary were heavily engaged in the first major trial of strength between C.P.P. and N.L.M., the Atwima/Nwabiagya by-election, in which they saw to it that 'the farmers were educated to vote solidly for their cocoa trees'.[37] The N.L.M. drafted in for the election large numbers of Atwina farmers from their new farms in the Ahafo area.[38] The C.P.P. campaign was led by a group which included Bediako Poku, currently Loans Manager of the C.P.C. and there were vehement accusations of the use of C.P.C. lorries by the C.P.P. on voting day to match the equally vehement allegations of N.L.M. mustering of unregistered voters. The power of the new Ashanti machine was shown by the fact that B. F. Kusi contrived only a year after the election of 1954 to reverse its verdict, defeating the new C.P.P. candidate B. K. Kufour, a wealthy cocoa broker and farmer by 3,998 votes to 1,758.[39] Later in the same month of July the Ashanti Farmers' Union, reporting on their progress to the Asanteman Council, recorded that they had managed to offset the flood of C.P.C. loans in Ashanti by raising a loan of no less than £70,000 from Cadbury and Fry 'upon strong negotiations coupled with some very outstanding immovable and worthy securities'.[40] These sums had been advanced to sympathetic farmers in a number of areas in Ashanti including Ahafo in proportion to their cocoa output and were to be liquidated by prompt deliveries of cocoa from the beneficiaries to the nearest Cadbury and Fry centre at the time of harvest. 'By this the Union have been able to liberate the farmers from the depressing and deceptive clutches of the C.P.C.'

As far as the finances of individual cocoa farmers were concerned, one set of clutches was presumably no more depressing and deceptive a source of advances than any other, the indispensable achievement being to be clutched at all. But to those who were attempting to engineer a sense of moral solidarity among farmers as a group it was certainly essential to be able to prevent the defection of individuals who set immediate and concrete personal advantages above long-term potential collective gains. It was hardly possible in the long run for the accumulated cocoa wealth of Ashanti to outbid the resources for positive and negative reinforcement available to the central government of the Gold Coast. Indeed the N.L.M. did remarkably well to offset the impact of external finance in Ashanti to the extent to which they succeeded in doing so in the period leading up to the 1956 election. Their comparative success meant that in Ahafo at least C.P.P. control of the votes could no longer be anticipated on a platform of pure nationalism, augmented by the judicious distribution of individual incentives. To supplement their wilting support the ruling party was obliged to seek for new followers in the quarters in which the N.L.M.s greatest strength appeared to lie, among the traditional leaders of local communities. Most Ahafo chiefs had responded eargerly enough to the new political initiatives radiating from Kumasi, the more so because in this instance their Kumasi traditional overlords did for once appear to be seeking their economic and political assistance for purposes which were potentially as much in the interest of the citizens and communities of Ahafo as they were in those of metropolitan Ashanti. However the experience of reintegration into the restored Confederacy had not always proved at all eloquent of the moral solidarity of Kumasi power with Ahafo impotence. Even (or perhaps especially) among traditional officeholders there were those who could reasonably hope to advance their interests by an alliance with what was currently the central government against the forces of Kumasi. Above all the stool of Kukuom stood to gain from the reworking of Ahafo allegiance along a pattern closer to that which had prevailed in the first third of the century when the Kukuomhene had been Omanhene of the whole of Ahafo. Senkyire accordingly negotiated an alliance between the Kukuom stool (as a traditional representative of Ahafo localism) and the Brong chiefs from the areas in which C.P.P. control was more firmly established.[41] He also attempted to consolidate local support for the party on the platform of secession from Ashanti to form a part of a separate Brong–Ahafo region. In Parliament in August 1955 he attacked the credentials of Kukuom's arch-rival, the Mimhene, as Ahafo representative on the Asanteman Council, pointing out that he had been nominated, not popularly elected, and claiming that he lacked the support either of his chiefly colleagues or of their people.[42] In May 1956 he proclaimed Ahafo support for the reconstitution of the old colonial administrative division of the Western Province, Ashanti as a separate region with its capital at the former colonial administrative centre of Sunyani, asserting that Ahafo had been neglected by the administration, left unvisited by the Chief Commissioner for Ashanti for the seventeen years up to 1952, and exploited by Kumasi, and alleging that the Kukuomhene and his subjects had been blackmailed to pay £1,500 to the N.L.M. because of their failure to support the Ashanti demand for a federal government.[43]

By the time that the C.P.P. government was forced into the election of 1956 Ahafo had become the scene of bitter political conflict and of intermittent coercion and violence. Brawls between rival groups of party activists became common and the lives of leading political figures were threatened, though in Ahafo at least none of them seems in fact to have been terminated and the worst attacks against both Osei and Senkyire, involving bomb-throwing and the dynamiting of a house, both took place oustide the constituency, in Kumasi. But at a less elevated level few communities escaped without substantial threats of violence against those who stood out against the *pars major et valentior* of the community in which they lived.[44] There is no reason to assume any greater reluctance on the part of the supporters of one party than those of the other to have recourse to physical coercion or the threat of it. Oral tradition is not at its most dependable when it comes to the assessment of levels of communal violence and more precise information was naturally often not collected at the time. But it seems likely that in this early period of the struggle the greater weight of violence was deployed by those best placed to deploy it, the party which had won control of the majority of Ahafo communities and their electors. Senkyire himself admitted in retrospect that he had not expected to win because of the dominating character of the cocoa price issue. Indeed he had managed to insure his future even before the election by applying for a British Council scholarship to study co-operatives at Loughborough, a possibility suggested to him at an Easter school which he had attended by a visiting UNESCO dignitary. The total registration for the election was slightly larger than it had been in 1954 – 17,554 electors as against 16,665[45] – and Senkyire's own vote was cut by some 50 per cent to 2,854, while his former opponent, Osei, now standing as an official N.L.M. candidate more than quadrupled his showing to 7,248.

Thus in Ahafo the N.L.M. won a major victory. But it failed to establish electoral control even of the whole of Ashanti and in the country at large was heavily defeated by the C.P.P. The struggle to impose a federal constitution to safeguard the political autonomy of Ashanti had failed. With the coming of national independence in 1957, the C.P.P. was left in full possession of the governmental machine and it was able to set itself to reimpose its political control at its leisure over Ahafo and other dissident areas. Communities in Ahafo which had supported the C.P.P. throughout, like Acherensua, a convenient road-block on the Kumasi road, and Kukuom duly received their rewards in the form of major items of government development expenditure, like the secondary school provided by the Ghana Educational Trust, or in the control of traditional status and the land revenues which go with it. It is possible to measure the rate at which party control was in fact reimposed in a variety of dimensions, the destoolment of chiefs who had favoured the N.L.M., the extinction of effective opposition at times of public electoral 'choice', the cessation of formal opposition in Parliament or Local Council. In none of these dimensions did the N.L.M. forces in Ahafo go under without a struggle. In Parliament Osei was one of the last handful of M.P.s to remain formally in opposition and he continued to make speeches criticising many aspects of the regime, particularly its cavalier attitude to detaining people without trial, despite threats and blandishments from the government and an occasion in 1960 when he was beaten up by a mob of his local opponents in the police station in Goaso.[46] Only the proclamation of a one-party state and the holding of elections in which only C.P.P. supporters

Dependence and opportunity

were permitted to stand as candidates removed Osei from Parliament early in 1965. In temperament he was a man of great courage and determination; but it seems clear also that it would only have been possible for him to persist in formal opposition for so long in a constituency in which popular attitudes to the C.P.P. regime remained for the most part deeply unenthusiastic. The position of parliamentary representative, however, was defensible in the N.L.M. (or, as it subsequently became, the U.P.) interest for much longer than other prominent positions of local authority which were more essential to the maintenance of political control or for which the occupants were selected at a point when the C.P.P. could exercise heavier pressure than they had proved able to do in 1956.

The last election in which the opposition interest succeeded in resisting the C.P.P. pressure was the Local Council elections at the beginning of 1958 in which eight United Party members were elected as against four for the C.P.P. and in which the U.P. chief of Mim was chosen as the traditional member of the Council.[47] In the same first quarter of 1958 the Kukuomhene was raised to the paramountcy which his predecessor had lost in 1935.[48] Most of the other Ahafo chiefs sent protest letters to the Regional Commissioner. No State Council had yet been established and the Government Agent doubted that they would be willing to serve under the Kukuomhene. In June of this year the membership of the new State Council was published and in July Goaso was re-established as the seat of a separate district headquarters within Western Ashanti, a move which was greeted with enthusiasm by the Kukuom interest as a token of official administrative recognition of Ahafo autonomy from Kumasi.[49] In August the Regional Commissioner Yeboa-Afari met the Kukuomhene and a number of other Ahafo chiefs in the Government Agent's office in Goaso to discuss the formation of the Ahafo State Council.[50] As he reported to the Prime Minister at the end of the following month,

I am anxious that Mim, Kenyase I and II, Acherensua, Noberkaw, Sankore, Ntotroso, Akrodie, Dantano and Hwidiem Chiefs should all serve the Kukuomhene and eventually form the Ahafo State Council. The majority of the Chiefs present at the meeting at Goaso asked for time to consider the proposed membership of the State Council. Present indications are that there is considerable opposition to the Kukuomhene being accepted as their overlord, but four of the Chiefs present have already agreed to serve the newly created Omanhene.[51]

The report by the Goaso Government Agent for July/September was less discreet.

A number of Ahafo Chiefs expressed a strong opposition to the creation of the Kukuom state and refused to be included in the Council. Prominent among these were the Chiefs of the following places: Goaso, Mim, Hwidiem, Sankore, Kenyase

328

I and II. Various villages reacted against Chiefs who refused to declare their support for the government by destooling them.[52]

Three destoolments of U.P. supporters and enstoolments of C.P.P. adherents reported for this quarter were those of Nkasaim, Noberkaw and, most notable of all, Mim.[53] In the last quarter of 1958, the same process was repeated in Ntotroso, Kenyase I, Mehame, Kwapong and Hwidiem and new chiefs were also installed in Akrodie and the U.P. stronghold of Sankore.[54] In the Regional Assembly elections of October the U.P. boycotted the elections, partly in protest at the constitutional erosion of the powers of the proposed Assemblies and partly in fear of the increased commitment of governmental resources within the electoral process.[55] Only C.P.P. candidates stood for the two Ahafo seats and in only one of these was there a contest of even a purely technical kind, J. K. Asamoah being elected unopposed for Ahafo East and Bediako Frimpong securing 3,908 votes as against 80 for Twumasi Ankrah who had been frustrated by a technicality from withdrawing in his favour. The election aroused correspondingly little interest and produced no 'incidents'.[56]

The process by which the C.P.P. consolidated its control in Ahafo from this time onwards was complex and not always gentle. Local farmers' co-operatives were compulsorily expropriated by the C.P.P. affiliate, U.G.F.C. Local C.P.P. officials revived and adopted for themselves the colonial title of District Commissioner, T. N. Baidoo, the former Council Chairman appearing naturally as the first party D.C. in Goaso itself. In the early 1960s the party youth branch, the Young Pioneers, was duly established in the constituency.[57] In 1965 the first elections under the one-party state returned three C.P.P. members from the Ahafo area including S. K. Opoku, a primary school teacher and party branch chairman from 1962, and Senkyire himself, returned to the country after extended legal studies in Great Britain. Senkyire even became Minister for Co-operatives. Organized and overt opposition to the C.P.P. thus came to an end. But the formally monolithic façade of party rule masked the weakness of a political organisation whose effective powers of action were as deficient as its powers of repression were locally ample. Party control was less severe in Ahafo, despite the fierce conflicts of 1955/7, than it was in many other parts of the country, Baidoo in particular being praised in retrospect even by his opponents for his reluctance to invoke the more feared of the party's repressive instruments, notably the Preventive Detention Act. But not all of Baidoo's local colleagues were as chary to invoke force in order to get their way. In retrospect the C.P.P. regime was presented locally even by those without sympathy with its political opponents as being bullying in its approach, as well as corrupt in its methods, compared with the ensuing military government. The major

329

Dependence and opportunity

grounds of resentment towards it were described as its bullying, its fanning of generational conflict within families (setting children to spy on parents) and its flouting of traditional norms (destooling 'legitimate' chiefs and substituting youthful party men who were often alleged to be traditionally ineligible for succession to the stool). All of these grievances, however, offered opportunities to some residents of Ahafo. In the last case, the installation of younger and usually better-educated Chiefs, it seems entirely possible that the populace at large benefited from the change. Certainly the removal of the C.P.P. cohort and their replacement by their now rather aged predecessors, imposed by N.L.C. Decree 112 after the 1966 coup, was seen as regressive by local civil servants as well as by supporters of the displaced C.P.P. regime. The boast made by Baidoo for example in 1969 that the C.P.P. because of their greatly superior knowledge of the local population were much better placed to organise it than the civil service and the restored chiefs did carry some conviction.

There were even aspects of the administrative and constitutional changes involved in the prising of Ahafo away from Ashanti and the establishment of C.P.P. hegemony – the creation of the Brong–Ahafo Region and the restoration of Kukuom to the paramountcy – about which even the opponents of the C.P.P. were at most equivocal. When Goaso was re-established as a district headquarters in 1958, instead of serving merely as a sub-district of Kumasi, the Kukuom interest hailed the shift as a political triumph for themselves; but, as the Government Agent reported, 'Even the opponents of the Western Ashanti Region felt proud to have a Government Agent in their District once more and were pleased that it would no longer be necessary for them to travel all the way to Kumasi to discuss their affairs.'[58] Even over the establishment of the independent Brong–Ahafo Region itself, a key item in C.P.P. strategy, there was some suggestion that N.L.M. feeling in Ahafo was not altogether blind to the potential advantages which their locality might expect to derive from it. When Senkyire was advocating the formation of the new region in the Assembly by revealing the heinous details of the N.L.M. blackmailing of Kukuom, Krobo Edusei, the leading C.P.P. politico from Ashanti, also vouched for Ahafo solidarity with the Brongs by producing in the Assembly (to the accompaniment of a certain amount of mirth) a petition dated 17 April 1956 from the Ahenfie, Kukuom, and signed by 'all the Ahafo Chiefs', affirming their desire to secede from Ashanti and regain their own Omanhene.[59]

By 20 March 1959 when the bill establishing the Brong–Ahafo Region was once again before the House, the elected representative from Ahafo was no longer a member of the C.P.P. Yet not only Krobo Edusei hmself but also the C.P.P. member for Wenchi East, C. S. Takyi, claimed that the Ahafo representative A. W. Osei had given them assurance either orally or

330

in writing of his entire support for the new administrative arrangements. Takyi indeed also claimed that Dr Busia, the leader of the United Party, who was himself an M.P. from Wenchi, had proclaimed his support for it; and Krobo Edusei went so far as to claim Osei's complete agreement with his entire speech.[60] But three months later on 11 June Osei asked unavailingly in the House why 'the Ahafo constituency was included in the Brong/Ahafo Region, although the people of that constituency objected to their inclusion in that region in a petition to the Minister?'[61] It is more plausible to see these contradictory opinions as representing a compliant bending before the force of two very different pressures than as invention in the one case and simple veracity in the other. Both Dr Busia himself and the local leaders of his party, the P.P., in Ahafo at the election of 1969 were at considerable pains to lay the *canard* that Busia as the lackey of the Ashantis would be committed on coming to power to the dissolution of the Brong–Ahafo Region. It was recognised that such an expectation was politically enormously damaging, whatever the popularity of varying solutions to the problems of the local traditional constitutions might be, because the status of a separate region was in itself a guarantee of governmental commitment of a larger quantity of administrative resources than the same area would otherwise enjoy and because it was felt, with considerable plausibility, that to the guaranteed increment of administrative resources there would over any long period of time be added a corresponding increment in the allocation of governmental development expenditure. Not only are government administrative personnel in the localities in themselves a public good of a kind, they also attract over time a flow of other goods of a more unambiguously utilitarian character.

The attraction of governmental development resources was the common ideological goal for both C.P.P. and their opponents. Other grounds of dispute – whether over the location of modern power or of traditional status – appear to have been more factional than ideological in nature, adopted on the basis of their tactical advantages for the competing political organisation with which the chooser was affiliated – in the expectation that he would in due course benefit from his affiliation. The only issue dividing the C.P.P. from the N.L.M. which was genuinely an issue of policy was the producer price of cocoa (and the consequent proportion of value produced in the cocoa sector expropriated as a cess by the central government). It would be plausible if all cocoa producers eligible to vote had been perfectly informed and had acted rationally to explain the victory of N.L.M. over C.P.P. in Ahafo (in what was the only open election which the two fought in the constituency) as a result of the correct calculation that the rewards for those paid individually by the C.P.P. for their support could not in principle match the resources which would accrue to the constituency from an overall rise in the producer price. Such a calculation would clearly be most convincing to those who produced the largest quantity of cocoa from their farms and would be least convincing to those who were paid a money wage which would not necessarily rise because of any increment in the cocoa price. But several factors militated against any strong patterning of electoral allegiance in terms of class stratification. First (and perhaps least important) it would be naive to assume that while the rich supporters of the N.L.M. could expect to benefit most from an N.L.M. victory, it was not in fact – and indeed in expectation – the rich supporters of the C.P.P. who could in turn expect to benefit most from a C.P.P. victory. Payments for securing electoral support were plainly apt to be proportioned to the quantity of electoral support provided. With the exception of small groups of semi-professionals with recognised skills at public persuasion and organisation, an instrumental necessity for either party and one which might at times be particularly striking, the mobilisation of electoral support on a large scale in a predominantly illiterate rural constituency was carried out by the manipulation of more or less informal clientages. In the more retired areas of the constituency, the control of such clientages was almost invariably related to the control of large quantities of land. Chiefs and larger landholders could expect to be able to influence much more substantial blocks of votes than those of less elevated status or economic position. Hence they could also demand substantially larger prospective rewards in return for their political support. To those from whom much was asked, much would have to be given (or at least promised).

Even in the larger centres of population, Mim, Goaso, Hwidiem, in which there were many voters who were not direct economic dependants of other Ahafos, the skills and experiences which would most facilitate the accumulation of a viable electoral following, literacy and wide social contacts, were also strongly related to prospects for economic success. Larger store-owners, often with extended credit-clientages, or Co-operative Society Secretaries, were both eminently plausible political organisers but neither came from the ranks of those whom their normal economic prospects would compel to offer their services to the first comer on the cheap. Furthermore it was just as much a natural perspective for such persons as it was for landlords to see a rise in the cocoa price as a prospective advantage for themselves, since their own takings, formal and informal, could be aptly seen as a percentage of local cocoa profits. A rise in the producer price of cocoa spread its benefits gradually but very visibly throughout the whole Ahafo economy and a fall spread equivalent ripples of gloom. There is no direct evidence of how large a proportion of the Ahafo population understood this relation in the mid-1950s. But it was clear by 1969 that even those Ahafo adults with the haziest image of economic processes were well aware of their direct interest in the producer price and there is every reason to suppose that such understanding must have been widespread a decade and a half earlier. A further impediment to the success of any C.P.P. strategy for large-scale accumulation of votes on a fee-for-service basis was that a large proportion of those in Ahafo who are landless labourers employed by cocoa or food farmers, the group to which most of the poorest inhabitants belonged, were in fact citizens of foreign countries, the Ivory Coast, Upper Volta and Nigeria in particular. These were ineligible to vote in Ghanaian elections, though this did not always debar them from doing so in practice – particularly when it came to the acclamatory elections of the later C.P.P. period. Others, who came from Northern Ghana, were often short-term migrants and as such were not likely to be in the constituency at both the time of election and that of registration. Among those who were not disfranchised in one or other of these ways the status of 'stranger' and impermanent resident did militate against much interest in the results of Ahafo elections, while those most likely to have an interest in voting were precisely those whose employers, with whom they were in a condition of direct and at times semi-domestic dependence, were most eager to get them to vote and correspondingly readiest to exert their energies to cement the political affections or coerce the political compliance of their clients. Those voters to whom C.P.P. inducements were most likely to be effective at the level of simple economic gain, the cheapest potential votes, were either for legal reasons not potential votes at all or else were rendered by the social structure peculiarly inaccessible to direct political mobilisation except by their 'patrons'. When it is said in the text that the political will of Ahafo took a particular form, it is not suggested that most of the area necessarily felt the slightest intrinsic interest in the issues concerned, still less that they autonomously reflected upon and decided about the issues. What *is* implied is merely that among the small proportion of the local population – perhaps 10 per cent at the outside – who concerned themselves with or exerted themselves over national political disputes, the *major et valentior pars* had adopted the view in question.[62] Once the factional struggle had begun, others would be drawn into its vortex as voters or strong-arm men. They were not necessarily in any sense inauthentic members of the factions to which they belonged. But their allegiance was mediated through ties of patronage to individuals and did not rest directly upon independently identified political principles.

With the single exception of the cocoa price issue the constitution of political factions in Ahafo had in many ways an extremely adventitious air. But once the dynamic of factional conflict had been powerfully established, it necessarily left some enduring legacies. Physical intimidation was by no means an intrusive novelty in the political processes of Ahafo communities. But the scope of individual commitment demanded by the institution of universal suffrage, however shallow in depth most individual commitments might actually be, ensured that the effort to establish control would prove more exacting – and hence more pervasive in its effects – than a corresponding project in the competition for traditional office. In 1954 it was a matter of little significance to a large majority of those in Ahafo what national political organisation controlled the government of the Gold Coast. By 1958 it had become a matter of urgent practical importance to most Ahafos in their daily lives whether their village was predominantly of C.P.P. or of U.P. allegiance and hence which of these two équipes was eventually to achieve lasting and decisive control of the national government. Enduring patterns of factional conflict within lineages, communities and groups of communities associated in traditional political conflict had been elaborately superimposed and solidified. Lines of division were seldom entirely stable at any point or at any level of political organisation; but the great bulk of affiliations displayed by 1958 a very substantial fixity over time. A disinterested neutrality became an increasingly exhausting posture to maintain. In earlier stages of N.L.M. expansion while the *major et valentior pars* was disciplining its forces for the combat, the dynamics of coercive consolidation served to impose upon the communities involved the ethos of embattled virtue. Party political competition was presented as displaying the community at war. Those who, for their own factional reasons, dissented from the interpretation of communal interests advanced by the incumbent political leadership were portrayed as a potential fifth column and interpreted, if their time eventually came at some later point, as actual quislings. Available methods for the accumulation of electoral support, once serious competition had emerged for such accumulation on the national level, guaranteed that the struggle between political parties should became transported at the local level largely into a struggle between communities affiliated to the different parties. Once this transposition had taken place the norms of communal solidarity in the struggle between communities made the norms of democratic electoral free competition seem not so much an exotic curiosity as a cultural atrocity. When there is a war on, electoral voluntarism exercised in favour of the enemy is indistinguishable from treason. It is important to realise that it is not the sustained amorality of the techniques of communal integration which produces these effects so much as the persisting moral substance of the integrative value. Coercion from within the community is only likely to be effective over any long period of time, in absence of a specialised police apparatus to enforce it, where a considerable proportion of the community approve of it more than they disapprove of it. This is even more plainly the case when the organisation from within the community is conducted in the face of the powers of the national government. When a political organiser is looking for votes wholesale it is scarcely remarkable that he should approach the chief in a community where the latter happens to be influential and popular. Nor is it in any way in tension with the traditional norms of interest-representation which sanction his office that a chief approached in this way should attempt to sway his people's support to whichever side he thinks most likely to prove victorious and hence able to return to his subjects a due reward for their allegiance. But once the structure of traditional authority within a community has been tied in this way assault upon the party to which it is tied that happens to come from within the community is also automatically assault upon the structure of traditional authority within it. When the chief in question is not either popular or influential his support may easily prove an electoral liability and the use of violence by his supporters may be more likely to hasten his destoolment than to augment the votes of the party which he supports. Even where he is himself popular, once the party competition is temporarily over and one side has established conclusive control of the government machine, a chief who has committed himself irreversibly to the losing party might be thought to have imperilled his traditional title to rule. Chiefly authority in Ahafo today is hardly conceived of as deriving from divine right; but it is certainly subject to providential erosion. Losing the mandate of Accra may not be explained in terms of spiritual forces today, any more than it was in the colonial period; but crude functional considerations make it apparent that it is hardly possible to lose the mandate of Accra for any time and retain that of Heaven. Hence, once a war has been unequivocally lost, the norms of contemporary chiefship do not merely permit, they might even be said to *require* unconditional surrender. The chiefs who refused to accept the Kukuomhene's return to paramountcy in 1958 were asking for destoolment, even if they retained the sympathies of their people. But if prudence required submission to what was now the direct application of the will of the central government (however mediated by its local supporters' observance of the traditional procedures for destoolment), honour certainly did not demand any change in the emotional attitudes of the local population to the war and its outcome. All Ahafo communities eventually knuckled under to the central government. But the great majority felt no particular inclination to turn their coats. In the summer of 1969 they were happy to demonstrate at the ballot boxes which party it was to which they still felt allegiance.

Evidence of widespread intimidation in the consolidation of party support in Ahafo between 1955 and 1958 is easy to come by today and some of it has long ago been printed elsewhere.[63] The experience of intense communal conflict was vividly (perhaps over-vividly) recollected more than a decade later. It had made itself felt at the time with varying violence in virtually every village and every agency of local administration or justice. Late in 1955 the lines of division were still extremely confused. Allegations of partiality by the Ahafo Native Court Registrar in a case in Sankore which involved conflict between the N.L.M. chief and a C.P.P. plaintiff elicited anxious demands for an investigation to vindicate the neutrality and propriety of his conduct from the Registrar in September of that year.[64] In November it was even possible for a group of Cocoa Purchasing Company farmers petitioning the Prime Minister himself against the rate of local exploitation by the authority which owned their land, the Kukuom stool, to imply that the money was being extracted to further the political interests of the N.L.M.[65] By the early months of 1956, however, conflicts had become both more open and more violent. A directive from the Ashanti Regional Office gave instructions that 'whilst the present political tension continues in Ashanti', all criminal cases 'arising from or in the course of the tension' should be withdrawn from Native Courts and transferred to Magistrates' Courts because of the likelihood of improper pressure being exercised or thought to be exercised in the Native Courts and because of the risks of violence at their sessions. In addition any cases of a political character should be removed from the hands of Native Authority police and transferred to those of the government police.[66] At the same time the institutions of local government began to be severely affected. The effects were not always immediately harmful – the meetings of the Kumasi West District Council 'lost much of their usual vitality due to the absence of a reasonably large number of C.P.P. councillors', but both Committees and full Council continued to meet regularly and its administration was described as 'very satisfactory'.[67] But the lower level institutions suffered more, the Ahafo Local Council failing to meet at all for the three months up to 19 January, because of the political tension. Levels of conflict outside formal political institutions also rose. 'An attempt by the C.P.P. to reexert itself in the Ahafo area led to a number of clashes at Akyerensua and Goaso in which several persons were injured. In one of these a saloon car belonging to the Mim Timber Company had its windscreen smashed as it passed through Akyerensua and as a result it ran off the road and sustained considerable damage.'[68] In February the chief of Akrodie was convicted on an extortion charge 'in connection with political matters'. In the second quarter of the year matters grew worse rather than better. Neither the full Ahafo Local Council nor any of its committees contrived to meet in April or May because of the atmosphere of violence. Early in May the Council Chairman T. N. Baidoo fled from Goaso to Kenyase I 'for fear of physical attack by his political opponents'[69] and threats of violence kept the known C.P.P. members of the Council's staff from going to work for several days. One of these, the Assistant Registrar of the Native Court, J. N. Essel, also fled to Kenyase I,[70] where he remained beyond the middle of August despite frequent and peremptory instructions to return to his duties.[71] He had been for some time at daggers drawn with the Registrar, an N.L.M. supporter.[72] During May in any case the Ahafo

336

Native Court 'could not sit at such places like Kukuom, Hwidiem and Kenyase I believed to be C.P.P. strongholds' as attempts were made to beat up panel members who were known to be members of the N.L.M. Similarly litigants from the C.P.P. towns and villages could not come to Goaso which was dominated by the N.L.M.[73] The dilemmas presented by this degree of conflict were brought out forcibly by a petitioner who was due to appear before the court on a civil writ over the ownership of a cocoa farm. 'This political crisis had given way to certain people at Goaso to beat litigants who are natives of Akyerensua, Kenyase nos I and II etc who attended court at Goaso to hear their cases.'[74] In view of this he and his witnesses were afraid to attend court at Goaso and wished to be heard at Hwidiem or Kenyase I since both parties to the case lived at Acherensua. 'If Goasohene is afraid to come to Hwidiem or Kenyase no I' (both of which were centres of C.P.P. support as well as being geographically closer to Acherensua), then the case ought to be postponed until political tensions had abated. It was not until the last quarter of 1956, following Essel's resignation, that the Ahafo Court began to function effectively once again and that instances of violence against panel members by C.P.P. sympathisers ceased.[75]

In May and June violence was most acute at road bottlenecks through which the inhabitants of an enemy village might have to travel. Virtually all traffic from Ahafo to Kumasi had to pass through the strongly C.P.P. village of Acherensua, while all traffic from another leading C.P.P. bastion, Kukuom, had to pass through the strongly N.L.M. town of Goaso. In compensation all traffic to the strongly N.L.M. village of Noberkaw had to pass through Kukuom. Early in May the Kukuomhene wrote to the government representative in Goaso that he had heard that 'all Goaso people have determined to damage any lorry which comes from Kukuom and then beat anybody from this place'[76] and asked the representative to 'give a fair advice to the Chief of Goaso and his people about this harmful act as he belonged to his own party and I am not. As all Drivers here are afraid to come here with their lorries.' Shortly after this the Kukuomhene complained again of groups of men in a jeep hired by the Goaso chief who travelled to Kukuom to beat up its citizens, pointing out that it was the responsibility of the government to maintain peace.[77] Goasohene was ordered to beat gong-gong and to announce that all were free to pass through Goaso and that no one was to be molested under any pretext.[78] Slightly later the Kukuom Krontihene wrote again to point out that a number of Kukuom political activists were due to appear in court at Teppa in the near future and that the 'Chief of Goaso and his people has seized every lorry from Kukuom travelling to Kumasi or either any where else and anybody in the lorry from Kukuom will be flogged and damage the lorry.'[79] He also alleged that plans had been made at a meeting in Goaso to watch the road for three days before the Teppa hearing and either prevent anyone from Kukuom passing through the town or beat them to death. In the circumstances no Kukuom lorry drivers were prepared to convey the defendants to Teppa and the Krontihene requested the authorities to provide a lorry with a police escort to enable them to make the journey in safety. At the same time the chief of Noberkaw whose people had to travel through Kukuom if they wished to reach Goaso and Kumasi and who admitted in the letter to his personal support for the N.L.M. requested the government representative to instruct Kukuomhene to prevent the latter's subjects dragging stranger farmers from Noberkaw out of the lorries in which they were travelling through Kukuom and beating them up.[80] A little earlier the government representative had succeeded in persuading the N.L.M. not to hold a proposed rally at Noberkaw because it would imply party supporters from villages like Nkasaim passing through Kukuom and would be likely to provoke a riot.[81] Later on, in July, police patrols had to be sent to Noberkaw because of political troubles there.[82] Similar tussles took place even further into the forest, the government representative writing for example to the Chairman of the C.P.P. branch in Aboum on behalf of an old lady who alleged that she was being molested because of the N.L.M. allegiance of her children.[83] Her age and general physical weakness, he pointed out, made it unlikely that she could participate actively in political conflicts and it was hardly fair that she should be made to suffer as a result of them. The chief of Asufufuo also approached the government to transfer a case between his sister and some C.P.P. members of his community from Kukuom Native Court (where strenuous efforts to assault her had only been frustrated by sending a police escort to accompany her back to Asufufuo) to Goaso Native Court.[84] He claimed that women from the village of Anwiam who supported the N.L.M. had already been gratuitously beaten up at the Kukuom court without the Native Authority police being able to intervene on their behalf. Closer to Kumasi, at Hwidiem, the conflict appears to have been even more acute. Late in April some twenty-five C.P.P. members from Mim, Kenyase I and II, and Acherensua had come to Hwidiem with 'sticks, bottles and stones' and had been arrested at the chief's behest for causing damage and provoking a riot. While the case was pending before the magistrate's court the chief had thought it prudent to retire to Kumasi. At the same time 'the C.P.C. loans supervisor by name Mr Asamoah who because of his troubles being giving to the people of Ahafo/Goaso has been driven away from the town...has now gone and stayed at my Town Ahafo Hwidiem to cause the same troubles to my subjects in the town. I therefore request police's action with this matter by advising him to quit.'[85] More urgently, he had learnt that the C.P.P. from the neighbouring villages were proposing to come to the town in the immediate future to hoist their party's flag, an action which would be certain to provoke the

N.L.M. supporters into attempting to reciprocate by raising their own party flag and thus to result in a major riot. Accordingly he begged the police chief for the whole Ashanti region to send a large detachment of police to Hwidiem and to establish a permanent police post there in order to preserve civil order and to prevent the disruption of that vital Hwidiem public facility for the whole of Ahafo, the new mission hospital.

The situation of Hwidiem within relatively easy reach of the C.P.P. strongholds of the two Kenyases and Acherensua clearly made the position of its N.L.M. chief especially exposed. It was natural for him in his quest for coercive assistance to attempt to tie his own position closely to that of an important public service. But there is clear evidence that other public agencies were also disrupted by prevailing violence. The Agricultural Officer complained to Goasohene that his field staff were being molested by N.L.M. Action Troopers from Goaso, apparently on the grounds that as civil servants they were intrinsically associated with the party which happened to control the government.[86] The Local Council was under particularly heavy pressure. The Odikro of Kenyase I attempted to secure a postponement of the Council elections because the prevailing political disturbances had prevented him and his elders from selecting a candidate and he refused to take any responsibility for the physical safety of any candidate who did stand in the area until order had been restored.[87] There were a number of petitions by defeated candidates in the local elections on such grounds as that their successful opponents had retained (and abused) the position of Basic Rate Collector, while standing for Council Office.[88] Two defeated C.P.P. candidates in Mim alleged that

the Mimhene, a staunch member of the U.P. at Mim Ahafo caused a 'gonggong' to be beaten by one Kofi Korkor on Monday two days before the voting day that the Mimhene swears the 'Yawoada'[89] that anybody who does not vote for the U.P. whose symbol is green cocoa tree with yellow pods and a white background would be dealt with by him...This caused many illiterate and ignorant people to refrain from voting and over 500 registered voters which might have voted for the C.P.P. did not vote for fear that Mimhene would deal with them according to the gongong beaten.[90]

In August the Government Agent assessed the distribution of party strongholds in the villages as for C.P.P. Acherensua, Kenyase I and II, Ntotroso, Kukuom, Wamahinso, Aboum and for N.L.M. Mankranso. Teppa, Mabang, Goaso, Mim, Gambia, Nkasaim, Dadiesoaba, Mehame, Noberkaw, Kwapong and Sankore. 'The "sensitive" spots at present are Kenyasi I and II, Ntotroso, Hwidiem (this town is dominated by both parties), Acherensua, Teppa, Kukuom and Mim. Since the announcement of the results of the General Election clashes have occurred at Kenyasi no I (whose Odikro has been detained by the police for shouting at a mob of C.P.P. adherents alleged to have attacked the Odikro in his house), Hwidiem, Noberkaw, and Aboum.'[91] At this time the preponderance of N.L.M. support was still very evident.

By the first quarter of 1957 the conflict had moderated appreciably in intensity; the number of complaints against decisions of the Ahafo Native Court, for example, decreasing, although most of them continued to come from C.P.P. supporters convinced of the N.L.M. partialities of the court members.[92] By the middle of the year the political conflicts could still serve as an especially convincing reason for objection to the level of local cocoa taxation, an objection which many residents of communities clearly felt without such directly presentable validation. Complaints came from Kukuom that the cocoa surtax collected from stranger and native farmers on Kukuom lands ostensibly for the construction of a medical dressing station in Kukuom appeared to have been spent in its entirety on some other project. At a public meeting held in June to discuss the current year's cocoa surtax Kukuomhene

told us bluntly that he had spent much money in his claim for paramountcy in the Ahafo Division and also in organising his party – the C.P.P. – and so we must endeavour to pay it so as to give him a relief! We said that we knew that whatever cocoa taxes were collected, they were meant for projects such as latrines, schools, roads etc which are in the interest of all the inhabitants from whom they were collected, but not politics. We therefore resolved that in view of that statement we were no longer going to pay the taxes until when agreement had been reached on the project for which the taxes were intended. Opanin Yaw Boateng, a linguist to Kukuomhene, rose up and, in turn, told us that if we would not pay the taxes for the purposes suggested by Kukuomhene, we must quit from the town.[93].

Accordingly the petitioners had refused to pay any more taxes until the Kukuomhene had abandoned his announced intentions to expend the taxes on his political expenses and until he had accounted for the taxes which had been collected in the previous year. But, in general, the conflict had become more desultory by this time: as the government representative put it 'rather incoherent and somewhat dissipated'. Kukuomhene had submitted a petition for the paramountcy and was actively backing the Brong–Kyempem Chiefs, while the majority of chiefs in Ahafo and its immediate vicinity remained firmly opposed to this venture, notably the chief of Mabang. There was 'a good number of lesser Chiefs still owing varying degrees of loyalty to the Golden Stool'.[94] The Local Council had also returned to normal. 'Victimisation of employees with political bias different from the councillors is uncommon in this area. The Ahafo Local Council has a C.P.P. Chairman (= T. N. Baidoo) with predominantly N.L.M. members. The efficiency of the Council, however, in no way suffers from this motley accretion.'[95]

But the relative calm of 1957 proved to be only a lull before the storms of 1958. National strategy for the C.P.P. resulted in the creation of a separate Region for the Brongs and Ahafos in this year and also in the restoration of the Kukuomhene's paramountcy. The local N.L.M. hegemony established in the struggles of 1956 was thus overturned from the outside as a result of decisions taken by the central government and a new local order had to be created to replace it. In the creation of this new order the civil service of the new government was not at first a comprehensively available instrument. When the opposition to local taxation in various Ahafo communities was discussed at a meeting at Goaso in April 1958, the government representative who presided over the meeting, the Secretary to the Regional Commissioner for Ashanti, was a British civil servant and it was still possible for the representative of Kukuom objectors to the taxes, Charles Oduro (who had been one of the two Kukuom delegates to the electoral college at Teppa in the 1951 election), to argue publicly that Kukuom taxes were being illicitly deflected to paying the Kukuomhene's personal political debts. If the government representative did not show himself convinced by the argument, there is no reason to suppose that he had any grounds for his scepticism besides the fact that the evidence produced by Oduro for his claim was not particularly convincing.[96] By the time that the Party's control was symbolically affirmed by T. N. Baidoo's appointment as District Commissioner for Goaso in May of the following year,[97] the administration had largely ceased to enjoy the independence which enabled it to 'arbitrate' local political disputes. In May 1958 the government representative reported 'a wave of dismissals in all Local Council areas almost all of them stemming from political motives' and noted that to be valid such dismissals had to be reported to the Regional Commissioner (a party official).[98] During the next year the administrative officer was obliged to send monthly security reports to the Regional Commissioner,[99] the guns of the local population remained impounded[100] and Goaso, Mim, Kenyase I and II, Teppa, Aboum and Ntotroso continued to be regarded as potential flashpoints. By the middle of 1959 when C.P.P. chiefs had replaced their political opposite numbers in most Ahafo communities, though often without succeeding in securing the stool paraphernalia from their predecessors,[101] the Peace Preservation Ordinance had been applied within three years to Goaso, Fawohoyeden, Ayumso, Kokofu, Dechem, Kukuom, Dantano, Sienchem, Etwineto, Hwidiem, Acherensua, and Kenyase I and II.[102] Not only major communities were riven by what the government representative aptly called 'bitter and bloody political strife',[103] but even tiny villages like Dechem and Etwineto which were little more than clusters of huts in the forest.

Nothing which has happened since in the politics of Ahafo has even approached in importance the impact of the three years 1956–9. It is essential to grasp two paradoxically contrasted aspects of them. No previous political experience in the history of Ahafo had elicited a level of political commitment from individuals as protracted, as intense and as broad in its scope. In one aspect this was a direct product of the fact that for the first time in their history the communities of Ahafo were presented with an opportunity to organise effectively to secure a measure of control over the central government of the modern state, the policies of which did directly and pervasively affect the interests of Ahafo. From the point of view of representative democracy, nothing could have been more rational than that the inhabitants of a cocoa-growing area should have chosen to give their entire support to a political party which proclaimed its dedication to recapturing for the cocoa sector a larger proportion of the surplus produced within it. But on the other hand the extent of Ahafo political commitment to the N.L.M. (or as it was later named, United Party) interest was also in its consequences a major political disaster for the area. Whether it was necessarily bound to prove an economic disaster in the long run is a controversial question. If the C.P.P. strategy for economic development by fostering import-substitutive manufacturing in an enlarged international African market had proved to be successful in the long run, it is conceivable that within two or three decades' time the Ahafo population might have been reconciled completely by the expansion of economic opportunities for their children which resulted from the public investment funded by their own earlier cocoa surplus. But even if the C.P.P. government had been a more trustworthy and effective agency of economic development and even if the global gains for the Ghanaian economy from the diversion of the cocoa surplus had proved to be decisively more positive than they did in practice, it is by no means certain that they would have been regarded as genuinely public goods by the Ahafos. Indeed, given the geographical and ethnic bias of recruitment to novel roles in modern industry[104] and the exceptional comparative advantages of Ahafo as a zone of cocoa production, it is not at all clear that it would have been correct for Ahafos whose sense of economic value was individually or locally egoistic to regard the expansion of modern industry as a genuinely public good. It is exceedingly naive to suppose that an intricate extended family system in a capitalist economy fosters pervasive economic altruism. Where competition between individuals, kin groups, communities and larger units of traditional political action for economic goods is conceived firmly (and in the short run quite accurately) so much in terms of a zero-sum game, it is a real achievement of the political imagination to grasp the rationality of uniting at a constituency, divisional or regional level for the struggle. But where the economic role of the government is seen primarily as that of a distributor of largesse, a greater level of popular participation in political action may automatically represent a diminution in the government's capacity to choose a strategy for economic development which is rational in view of the interests of all areas of the country.

But whatever the actual or potential economic benefit of the C.P.P. victory, either for Ahafo in the fullness of time or for the country as a whole more immediately, the political costs for Ahafo can scarcely be denied. Once the majority of Ahafo communities had been successfully organised from the inside for factional struggle against a political interest which was convincingly represented as battening on their wealth, and once these communities had been victorious in the battle within Ahafo itself but their opponents had prevailed in the war as a whole, the political damage was well and truly done. The mechanics of clientage-mobilisation and the tactics of communal blackmail by which the struggle was conducted no doubt looked to many of those involved as amoral from the inside as they are likely to appear from the outside. But the very fact of uniting the local factions into an Ahafo-wide coalition around a convincing moral theme gave a heavily affective tone to the victorious coalition and meant that the victory of their opponents on the national level wore a grimly contingent air to Ahafo. It is possible that a more resolutely ethical governmental power than the C.P.P. might have erased in time – even without the benefits of dramatic economic advance – this grim image of the triumph of Vice over Virtue. But, if Ahafo political practitioners themselves were never likely to prove hypnotically compelling as embodiments of virtue, the C.P.P. both nationally and locally contrived to sustain its Ahafo image of delinquency with some bravura. Only a taxing authority which was truly above suspicion would have been likely to convince the Ahafos that the expropriation of their wealth by the government was a moral act. The public face of the C.P.P. was raffish enough to confirm in many Ahafo eyes that any gap between world market prices and producer prices of cocoa was simply a gain for those thieves whom history had seen fit to make best placed to steal it. As an interpretation, it was plainly in some measure unjust. Yet there is little difficulty in grasping how it came to be espoused.

It is clear that having won the election, the C.P.P. had to recapture political control of Ahafo. It is also clear that the only readily available machinery for doing so was the use of governmental power to overturn those currently victorious in the local factional struggles in Ahafo and replace them by others who were committed to the C.P.P. interest. Since in many communities the leaders of N.L.M. factions or their most powerful supporters happened to be the Chiefs of the communities and these were now in effect in open opposition to the government, it was natural that the C.P.P. authorities should set themselves to destool these and to replace them with new chiefs who had a better sense of their responsibilities to the government. This was in effect no more than the British colonial government had done when confronted with obdurately insubordinate chiefs. A British Commissioner had shown no more hesitation in disposing of Beditor of Mim than the C.P.P. did in removing the N.L.M. Mimhene, Kwaku Appiah. Nor was there any shortage of precedents in British practice for the alleged C.P.P. insouciance over whether their replacements for the destooled were in fact proper 'royals' of the stools in question, there being few stools whose traditions were not contested enough to lend sanction of some sort to any necessary innovation. What was new and what was in fact a direct result of the introduction of democratic political organisation for electoral choice into Ahafo was the scale of reversal to which the government now had to commit itself in order to restore its authority. The consequences of this were dire in their implications. Paradoxically the C.P.P. national triumph in the 1956 election fastened upon Ahafo a regime which in local eyes was more plainly and pervasively a quisling regime than any which had resulted from the direct application of British colonial power. It was a quisling regime in the sense that those who now held local power, the C.P.P. District Commissioners, branch chairmen and newly enstooled chiefs had replaced in the majority of Ahafo communities those who had succeeded in a relatively open if often undecorous competition in mustering the support of the greater part of the populations of these communities. It was not of course a quisling regime from the viewpoint of *all* Ahafo communities. The mechanics of Ahafo schism guaranteed that no powerful external political pressure exerted on the area could fail to enlist local allies with the hope of advancing their own relative position within the area by serving as outriders for the invaders. Nor should it be assumed, as has already been emphasised, that political affiliation to the blatantly vanquished would prove particularly durable in Ahafo communities. The luxury of persistent and obdurate resistance to the national government was not one which the cocoa farmers of Ahafo expected to be able to afford nor one for which most of them showed any inclination to pay the costs. In the course of history a great many communities have learned to live with quisling regimes and the Ahafos had never shown themselves particularly fanatical in their loyalties or antipathy to the great magnetic centres of power towards which they were compelled to orientate themselves. However, the C.P.P. political style did have distinct appeal for some groups in Ahafo, especially among the young. If the world market price of cocoa had continued to bring ever larger quantities of governmental cargo to land, instead of inducing a growing fiscal crisis, it is perfectly possible that the Ahafos might collectively have come to feel as much affection for their C.P.P. masters as they had for the motley array of political groupings which had preceded the C.P.P. in their control. In the event, however, the economic misfortunes which beset the C.P.P. as a government, aggravated by their own visible economic misdemeanours, did little to dissipate the initial political perception of the re-establishment of C.P.P. domination. The scale and persistence of political mobilisation within Ahafo communities during the struggles of 1956–8 was without parallel in previous traditional conflicts or in the establishment of British colonial control. The reasons for this level of commitment were the combination of democratic electoral opportunity and the identification of a clear interest for the locality which was to be represented by the elected member. It was precisely the relevance and reality of representative politics which made the U.P. triumph locally so likely and which made the C.P.P. triumph nationally so strongly resented in Ahafo.

When the C.P.P. rule came to an end with the military coup of February 1966, there appear to have been few in Ahafo outside the ranks of the holders of party office and their friends and relations who much regretted its passing. The latter do not seem to have been greatly bullied for their past deeds – though party officials and M.P.s were detained for a time and T. N. Baidoo had an unpleasant experience with one irritable civil servant. The military regime of the N.L.C. had many of the characteristics of a return of the colonial state. If it was not exactly loved by anyone in Ahafo, it did not appear to be especially resented by anyone either. Even the staunchest members of the C.P.P. locally were inclined to admit that the rule of the party had degenerated at times into tyranny, particularly in its use of detention without trial. It was assumed by all who bothered to think about it (and apparently by many who did not) that civilian and elective government would return in the fullness of time. But no one in Ahafo seems to have been consumed with impatience to hasten its arrival. Only one major political issue affecting the area continued to hold attention during these three years, the traditional constitution of Ahafo and the land revenues the disposal of which it controlled. By Decree 112 of the National Liberation Council all chiefs destooled by the C.P.P. government were restored to their office and all relations of traditional allegiance which had been abrogated by the C.P.P. government were resurrected. The first of these provisions was simple enough to apply in Ahafo, the former U.P. chiefs simply displacing their C.P.P. rivals. But the second was more awkward. The N.L.C. government had no wish to annul the creation of the Brong–Ahafo Region, although some of its most influential advisers from the former United Party were vigorous partisans of Ashanti interests. The Kukuomhene was deprived of his paramountcy and he was also summoned to pay his homage to the Golden Stool. This he refused to do, claiming to be an independent chief and denying that he was in any way subordinate to the Asantehene. At the same time the restored U.P. chiefs, although for the most part hostile to Kukuom-hene's pretensions, were also deeply unenthusiastic at the prospect of Ahafo land revenues again passing out of the area (which meant out of their hands). The majority of the Ahafo chiefs accordingly petitioned for the establishment of an Ahafo State Council, though not of course one permanently chaired by the Kukuomhene as Omanhene of the area. They were supported by the resuscitated Ahafo Youth Association, a literate pressure group for the interests of the area in which old U.P. politicians like Osei and young unaffiliated 'scholars' from the area like Badu Nkansah and Osei Duah joined forces. The recapture of control over local development resources was an uncontroversial political goal for all groups, though the strategy favoured for pursuing it was plainly influenced by considerations of comparative factional advantage. The government's efforts to arbitrate in the conflict remained indecisive under the strong factional pressures from both sides. The Kukuomhene's case was speedily withdrawn from the hands of the Chieftaincy Secretariat, the respectable body of experts in tradition which the government had set up to keep traditional disputes out of the politics in which it was supposed that Nkrumah had corruptly immired them. It was treated as a matter of national political significance by the N.L.C.: the state prosecution of the Kukuomhene for failing to pay his homage, presented by the Department of the Attorney General Victor Owusu, the leading Ashanti politician closely associated with government, was neither abandoned nor pressed with precipitate speed. A government Commission of Inquiry, the Bannerman Commission on Brong–Ahafo lands, met on a number of occasions and took evidence about traditional allegiance and landownership from several Ahafo chiefs, before being discreetly put into indefinite cold storage. No clear settlement of the dispute had been reached by the time of the official resumption of party politics in the summer of 1969. It was indeed in the course of the election campaign itself that the state prosecution of the Kukuomhene in the High Court in Sunyani was completed and the court verdict announced.

The fact that the High Court judge contrived to resolve the contradictions of Ahafo's history into the clear verdict that the Kukuomhene had no traditional allegiance to the Golden Stool did not turn out in the fullness of time to be legally at all conclusive. The Attorney General's Department in the new Busia government carried its appeal against the court verdict up to the Court of Appeal and showed no inclination, once the Department had returned into the hands of Victor Owusu, to reconcile itself to Kukuom autonomy. But the acquittal during the election campaign itself, whatever its causes or its legal status, may have been an important element in the case with which the political leaders of Ahafo contrived to elicit a sense of local solidarity at the ballot box not long after. This solidarity could not have been solely an Ahafo creation, although it was apparent that the most widespread and deeply felt political value among the local population was the urgent desire for communal peace, an attitude which certainly reflected the experience of bitter communal conflict in the mid-1950s. In addition to this ready appeal of local solidarity, it was a major preoccupation of what emerged nationally as the most effective political équipe to contest the election, Dr Busia's Progress Party, to restrict the impact of continuing local schisms on the articulation of a national campaign. It was by no means a foregone conclusion that Dr Busia should have emerged at the head of the national political party which was best able to present itself as successor to the U.P. – two leading U.P. luminaries, Joe Appiah and Modesto Apaloo, in fact refused to join the party precisely because Busia had emerged at its head and many others must have come close to doing so. But in the event Busia did succeed in collecting together a considerable preponderance of the best political brains and the most influential political personalities in most parts of the country, among them A. A. Munufie, the Kukuomhene's lawyer and in due course Regional Chairman of the Progress Party and Minister for Rural Development in the Busia government. Among the erstwhile supporters of the C.P.P. the consolidation of clientages for the coming fray had to be executed under much less favourable conditions than was the case for former U.P. elements. Not only were some of the wealthiest of the C.P.P. ministers still prudently out of the country or incarcerated on corruption charges, but many others were individually proscribed from taking part in politics. Furthermore the more enterprising efforts which they did contrive to make to organise for the elections were liable to further disruption from the military and police government which might be internally split over the objects of its enthusiasm but was at least united in a reluctance to hand over power to those whom it had removed from office by force of arms. Senkyire, the leading C.P.P. figure from Ahafo and a courageous and vigorous exponent of the party's populist heritage, was himself automatically on the list of those proscribed: but he played a major part in the attempt to organise a legitimist C.P.P. party for the election, until these efforts were decisively suppressed by the government. The only significant party which was in the event permitted to organise itself for the election in a (carefully refracted) variant of the C.P.P. tradition was K. A. Gbedemah's National Alliance of Liberals. It is a nice issue in Ghanaian politics how far this party could be seen as a legitimate offspring of the C.P.P. Certainly to Nkrumah himself, on the air from Conakry, and to his close friends and associates, it did not appear that the mantle of Elijah had fallen upon Elisha (something much closer to Judas Iscariot). In the politics of the C.P.P. court Gbedemah was the arch traitor, a renegade so low that he had not even scrupled to co-operate with the perfidious Busia in his exile struggle against the Osagyefo. But in the provinces these tense issues of personal fealty were not so evident. When it became clear in Ahafo that N.A.L. was going to be the nearest to the C.P.P. which was to be permitted to contest the election, efforts were made by the former local organisers for the C.P.P., notably T. N. Baidoo, to put the best possible face upon this outcome.

Dependence and opportunity

Gbedemah's party was probably on a national scale not the most electorally viable of potential reincarnations for the C.P.P., though it is possible that its added appeal among the Ewe seats in the Volta Region may have more than compensated for this in the total of seats which it secured. Since no party avowedly committed to the return of Nkrumah was permitted to contest the election the residue of the C.P.P. mantle amounted merely to the personnel of a somewhat debilitated organisation. Ideologically it was hard to detect any trace of difference between the proclaimed positions of the contesting parties which were permitted to take part, though substantively Gbedemah's party may have envisaged a less fervently rationalist path for the development of the Ghanaian capitalist economy. In these circumstances the electoral task for the leaders of the resuscitated U.P. in Ahafo, the Progress Party as it was now called, was one of singular simplicity. Given the degree of effective consolidation of former U.P. personnel at the national level achieved by Busia there was no strong divisive pressure extending down from the national level to disrupt U.P. solidarity within Ahafo, while the confusion nationally as to how far (and in what form) C.P.P. supporters were to be permitted to contest the election at all gave the C.P.P., or as it was now termed the N.A.L., campaign in the constituency a belated start and a rather surreptitious and lacklustre air throughout. Only the personal visit to Ahafo of the magnificent presence of Gbedemah himself a fortnight before the polls brought a fleeting glamour and confidence. The Progress Party candidates for the two Ahafo constituencies and one at least of the N.A.L. candidates were all young and active members of the Ahafo Youth Association, a new political generation marked in particular by a higher level of education than their predecessors of a decade and a half before. The last open challenge of the older generation in Asunafo was the unsuccessful candidature of A. W. Osei against Badu Nkansah, a young Ahafo secondary school teacher and graduate of the University of Ghana, for the post of Ahafo representative in the Constituent Assembly at the end of 1968. The actual work of political oragnisation for the two parties remained to some degree in the hands of older men, Osei and his friend Boame for the P.P. and T. N. Baidoo and Kojo Bonsu, Senkyire's brother, deposed chief of Kenyase and N.A.L. candidate for Asutifi, for N.A.L. Much of the voting for both parties also seems to have been inherited directly from the memory of past campaigns. Only the assessment of the criteria for representative efficacy in the new legislature had shifted: to give greater recognition to the presumed skills imparted by higher education. One further aspect of the campaign, of minor significance in Ahafo but arguably more important in the Akan areas outside Ashanti and Brong–Ahafo and potentially perhaps of even greater significance after the eviction of the Busia government, was the appearance of a politically novel ethnic fissure. It is not clear (nor is it perhaps particularly important) which party was the first to introduce the issue explicitly into its campaigning. What is beyond dispute is that the basis of support which N.A.L. contrived to attract outside the ranks of formerly active adherents of the C.P.P. was predominantly confined to two ethnic groups, the Ewes and the Krobos, and that among the Ewes this support was overwhelming. The United Party had enjoyed valuable support in the past from Ewe separatist feeling and the P.P. certainly did not expect before the campaign began to be so heavily trounced in the Ewe areas. In the closing stages of the campaign in other areas the Progress Party certainly did begin to react to the disquieting evidence of Ewe solidarity with the invocation of a solidarity of the Akans, a tactic which suggested itself the more readily because there are so many more Akans than there are Ewes. But whichever party was responsible for the *explicit* introduction of this ethnic rift into public campaigning, its place in the Ahafo campaign was far too marginal to affect the result in any significant way. A number of Ewes and Krobos in Ahafo certainly voted for the N.A.L. candidates and did so on the basis of intimations from beyond the borders of Ahafo; but they seem in most cases to have been sympathetic to the C.P.P. and hostile to the U.P. well before any campaign began. We did not find one case of someone initially sympathetic to the Progress Party who switched their support to N.A.L. in the course of the campaign for ethnic reasons nor anyone who did the same in reverse from N.A.L. to the P.P. Indeed there are good grounds for supposing that in the election campaign in Ahafo (as in most other election campaigns in most other places) a majority of those who favoured one side or the other had done so well before the campaign began. The novelty as far as Ahafos were concerned in the 1969 election was the question of just what form the U.P. and the C.P.P. were to take in it. By this time that this form became clear locally it was evident that Ahafo U.P. solidarism, reinforced by the experience of C.P.P. rule, had given the inhabitants of the area altogether more central and important matters to cast their vote about than which way the Ewes were throwing their suffrage. The P.P. victory in the two Ahafo constituencies was crushing, though little more crushing than in most of the Ashanti and Brong seats. When broken down by polling station[105] it revealed how completely the party had contrived to prevent a resumption of the fission between communities which had marked the struggles of the 1950s. No single significant population centre in the whole of Ahafo aligned itself with the N.A.L. interest. The lessons of 1956 had been learnt all too well. Ahafo had 'done something' for the Progress Party and waited happily for the Progress government to 'do something' for it.

Its inhabitants were not disappointed. Whatever its failures on the national scale, the P.P. government with its Brong Prime Minister and its Brong Minister of Finance cannot be accused of having stinted the Brong–Ahafo

Dependence and opportunity

Region. Projects for rural water supplies and the tarring of roads (the latter a theme of urgent Ahafo pleas for many years), the promise of a new secondary technical school in the district to be sited at the home town of the Asunafo M.P., Akrodie, even the opening of new daily service by two huge State Transport Corporation buses from Kumasi to Mim, the government's largesse

1969 Voting figures in Ahafo constituencies

Asunafo	A. Badu Nkansah (P.P.)	13,039	81 polling stations
	J. K. Osei (N.A.L.)	2,715	P.P. wins 79
Asutifi	I. K. Osei Duah (P.P.)	6,026	42 polling stations
	Nana Kojo Bonsu (N.A.L.)	1,707	all won by P.P.
	Kwame Anane Obinim (U.P.P.)	124	

to the people of Ahafo was on an ample scale. The young Asunafo M.P. Badu Nkansah became a Ministerial Secretary and appeared set for a prosperous career though he was somewhat troubled by anxieties that his colleague for Asutifi, Osei Duah, who had become embroiled with the Mim Timber Company and who had alienated part of the Asutifi party executive was planning to supplant him in the Asunafo seat in the next election. Only one major Ahafo interest (apart from the cocoa price to producers which was effectively restricted by the unsatisfactory prices on the world market) remained troublesome, the question of the traditional constitution. In part it clearly remained so because, while it was somewhat unsatisfactory for all that it should still be unresolved, there was in fact no solution possible for it which would not be decisively *more* unsatisfactory for some important group. Delicate considerations of regional autonomy, accentuated by the political power of the region which was threatened, competed with imperious traditional claims voiced by the political unit with the proudest political pretensions in all Ghana and the resolute legalism of an Attorney General's Department restored to the control of Ashanti's most powerful politician, Victor Owusu. That final control of Ahafo's 'traditional' land revenues should pass into the hands of the traditional authorities of another region could hardly be acceptable either to the traditional authorities of the Brong–Ahafo Region, the Brong–Ahafo House of Chiefs, or to its 'modern' political bosses, the Party's Regional Chief, A. A. Owusu in Sunyani, the Ahafo M.P.s and above all the powerful Brong Minister for Rural Development. On the other hand it was not easy to reconcile Ashanti to the loss of control over this now extremely prosperous sector of its periphery. Under these circumstances the Attorney General's Department continued to press its case against the Kukuomhene despite the reversals which it had suffered in the lower courts and the government officials in Ahafo, under political direction from the

350

regional capital, acted discreetly to hold in abeyance further Kumasi initiatives against other local chiefs who supported the Kukuomhene. In a characteristic combination of mediation and procrastination, Dr Busia established in the summer of 1971 a further committee entrusted with the task of finding a solution to the dispute. It consisted of six chiefs, three from Brong–Ahafo and three from Ashanti under the diplomatic chairmanship of William Ofori-Atta, Foreign Minister and scion of the Akim stool. But there had been no indication by August 1971 of any weakening in the wills of either side and no sign that a compromise distinguishing landownership from formal allegiance, favoured by the Brong–Ahafo interests, would satisfy Kumasi demands. When the Busia government was removed from office by the army some months later no public settlement had yet been reached. The group which had the keenest reasons to be dissatisfied with this situation were the U.P. loyalist chiefs who had never wavered in their loyalty to the Golden Stool (though they were willing enough to keep the bulk of Ahafo traditional land revenue at their own disposal) and who had supported in a discreet manner the Progress Party victory in the 1969 election. For them the understanding between the Progress Party and the Kukuomhene was deeply unwelcome: yet further testimony to the glaring incapacity of national political organisations for loyalty in local traditional struggles. It was perhaps with some relief that the Mimhene and his band of anti-Kukuom chiefs greeted the new and as yet less locally partisan military regime with a petition for Ahafo to be allowed to return properly to the only wholly reliable allegiance in traditional politics, its overlords in Kumasi.[106] If in 1968 the U.P. chiefs might have seemed quite the least likely beneficiaries in Ahafo of a forcible military removal of a duly elected U.P. government, their resurgent optimism in the early months of 1972 speaks eloquently of the continuing gap between the morality of localism and the morality of the nation. To a local interest in Ghana the only morally dependable national political ally remains one utterly devoid of the power to act. Impotence is hardly bliss for Ghanaian national politicians; but it is plausibly still a necessary condition even with the most moral will in the world for the reliable appearance of virtue at the local level.

It is not plausible any longer in Ahafo that the rift between local and national communities resembles that which Professor Bailey has identified in his researches on the peasantry of Orissa.[107] The manipulative and accumulative aspirations of Ahafo's peasants are not culturally very far from those prevalent in most parts of the government bureaucracy or the party structures which confront them. The 'brokers' between local communities and national organisations are too many, too various and in many cases too locally prominent for their roles to be seen as socially interstitial between rural locality and urban authority any longer. Status within the local community, either 'modern' or 'traditional', is not separate from the activity of brokerage. Today it is closer over time to being a precondition for and a reward of success in that activity. When Ahafo is led politically it is led by Ahafos and if Ahafos sufficiently attuned to the national community to be effective as leaders are recognised as being potentially unreliable from a moral point of view, it is simple romanticism to suppose that they do not fully share this characteristic in popular imagination with all other Ahafos with whom anyone's interests are potentially in conflict, not least the members of an individual's nuclear family. A genially Hobbesian view of human nature does not preclude uniting for shared political purposes, even where it is recognised that some of those who share the political purposes stand to benefit more handsomely from political success than do others. The Ahafos do not expect the society in which they live to be economically egalitarian nor do they give any indication under close questioning of feeling that it *ought* to be so. It is not the prevalence of a certain realistic cynicism about politics which has posed a major threat to the viability of electoral democracy in Ahafo. What made the second Ghanaian experience of democracy such a brief one was the failure of the policies of the elected government to handle the crisis of the country's economy, a failure unrelated to its disposition towards Ahafo and one which any government in the near future will do well to avoid emulating. The politicians who represented Ahafo did not betray the interests of Ahafo. Indeed the regional disparities in the distribution of development resources in the 1971 budget favoured the Brong–Ahafo Region so heavily as to evoke mild dismay in some of the party's leading members nationally. Only in the field of conflicts over traditional status did the party's rule betray some of its supporters in Ahafo – and here the only way in which a government could fail to betray some of its supporters would be for it to draw its supporters solely from one side in any traditional dispute. The very solidarity which the Progress Party contrived to amass in Ahafo as a representative of the modern interests of the district as a whole, taking in the support of both Kukuom and anti-Kukuom factions, was a guarantee that in power it could only temporise indefinitely or betray some of those who had given their loyalty to it.

CHAPTER 9

CONCLUSION

The Ahafos were opportunistic indeed when, in 1896, they sought out the British at Cape Coast and made their marks on a contract of friendship and protection. As their flexible loyalties in succeeding years suggest, it is unlikely that a declaration of dependence to officers of the British crown rather than to agents of the Kumasi chiefs was construed locally as anything other than a matter of immediate expediency, however momentous the agreement with the former might appear in retrospect. The justice of this rejection of 'traditions' of Ashanti dependence was, of course, entirely relative, but it is interesting how concerned both parties to the 1896 treaty were that the new arrangements should appear respectable ('traditional', one might say). What we know of Ahafo, then and now, points to lenient interpretation of the opportunities which it is respectable to seize. The exploitation of opportunities is compulsive, the main protagonists impelled not simply by personal interest but by communal responsibilities, the keenness of competition bringing politics frequently to the limits of what any party may consider respectable. Opportunities are inevitably unpredictable and frequently novel – 'modern' in a very real sense. The astute politician in Ahafo is watchful for such opportunities, however unfamiliar they may be. Nevertheless he is also aware that political success may still require the justification of opportunities seized or contested, even if ideas about what is respectable have little coherence beyond immediate contingencies.

Medicine, said the great German philosopher Leibniz in one of his less conventional formulations, is concerned with the pleasant, politics with the useful, and ethics with what is just.[1] Medicine and politics as these are now understood might appear to be novelties brought to Ahafo by the colonial order. Certainly, Ahafo conceptions of what is pleasant and what is useful have been deftly deflected to meet the requirements of dependency on a world market. Easy though it may be to sneer at this cultural shift, it remains true that soft drinks[2] and photographs[3] and wheeled transport have brought much pleasure to those who live in Ahafo. In return for this deflection ('modernisation' it might be called) much that meets these criteria of use and pleasure has been returned to Ahafo by the all too visible hand of the world market. But what has perhaps not been brought to Ahafo by either colonial or postcolonial rulers has been the more elusive commodity of ethics. So long as their eminently realistic recognition of dependency on forces unintelligible to them in detail precludes the Ahafos from any very inventive identification of how they would now choose to live for themselves – let alone any drastic effort to begin to do so – there will be no reason to see their situation in the world as a whole as just. It is all the more paradoxical that if the view is confined within Ahafo itself and a choice were to be made between the forest in 1890 and the forest today, it might be perfectly possible to vindicate the choice of the second by the stern criterion that no one affected should fail to benefit on balance by the change.[4]

NOTE ON DOCUMENTARY SOURCES

The published literature directly concerned with Ahafo it too scanty and for the most part too slight to justify the presentation of a bibliography. Full bibliographical details are given for all works cited in the first citation from each in the notes to each chapter. One agreeable full length work on Ahafo, R. A. Lystad's *The Ashanti, A Proud People* (New Brunswick, N.J., 1958), which we have not had occasion to cite at any point should perhaps be drawn to the reader's notice. The main documentary source employed has been the government records in the Accra, Kumasi and Sunyani branches of the Ghana National Archives. The contingencies of physical survival and re-organisation can make these difficult for a beginner to employ. Many crucial documents appear simply to have been lost. However, the variety of types of document can serve to some degree to repair the damage suffered by any individual type. The scope of annotation offered here is designed, in addition to its more direct function, to emphasise the rich possibilities for reconstructing in detail the history of areas of Ghana from the records of the colonial regime. We found the diaries kept by different grades of the colonial hierarchy particularly valuable for identifying the differences in perspective on local happenings at varying distances from the locality. Court records and records of administrative ventures in road-building, public health and agricultural extension work have provided particularly valuable perspectives on local interpretations of colonial initiatives. We have tried throughout to depend closely upon documentary files or upon our own opportunities for direct observation. Several important features of the political process which we have tried to study necessarily leave few systematic traces in government archives, notably (as was pointed out to us by an acute critic) the formation of debt clientages and the change in local consciousness produced by increasingly insistent exposure to the machinery of a centralised state. We have not been able to find any clear way of subjecting either of these two processes to systematic historical investigation on the geographical scale with which we have been concerned. It would plainly be possible to discover much about both from extensive interview work on a very much smaller area.

NOTES TO THE TEXT

Abbreviations used in the Notes

ACCA   Acting Chief Commissioner, Ashanti
ACWPA Acting Commissioner, Western Province, Ashanti
ADC   Acting District Commissioner
ADM   Administrative Records
CCA   Chief Commissioner, Ashanti
CNWDA Commissioner, North Western District, Ashanti
CWPA   Commissioner, Western Province, Ashanti
DCG   District Commissioner, Goaso
GNA   Ghana National Archives
PRO   Public Record Office, London
WPA   Western Province, Ashanti

1. Introduction, pp 1–9

1 PRO, CO 96/275, 30 June 1896, Davidson Houston, report, p 27.
2 Cf. Aristide R. Zolberg, *Creating Political Order. The Party States of West Africa* (Chicago 1966); David W. Brokensha, *Social Change at Larteh, Ghana* (Oxford 1966).
3 Quoted by Donald Macrae, 'Populism as an Ideology', in Ghita Ionescu & Ernest Gellner, *Populism: Its Meanings and National Characteristics* (London 1969), p 161.
4 Cf. A. F. Robertson, 'The Development of Town Committees in Ahafo, Western Ghana', in A. I. Richards and A. Kuper (eds.), *Councils in Action* (Cambridge 1971).

2. 'Changing communal identities', pp 10–40

1 Cf. R. S. Rattray, *Ashanti* (Oxford 1923), pp 172–202.
2 J. C. Caldwell, 'Population: General Characteristics', in Birmingham, I. Neustadt and E. N. Omaboe (eds.) *A Study of Contemporary Ghana*, ii (London 1967), 128.
3 B. Gill and K. T. de Graft-Johnson, *The 1960 Population Census of Ghana*, vol v *General Report* (Accra 1964).
4 A. F. Robertson, 'Histories and Political Opposition in Ahafo, Ghana', *Africa*, XLIII, 1 (1973).
5 J. K. Fynn, 'The Rise of Ashanti', *Ghana Notes and Queries*, ix (1966), 24–30.
6 Personal communication, the Asantehene Sir Osei Agyeman Prempeh II.
7 GNA Accra, ADM 54/1/1, 59/05.
8 The earliest timber concession of which the Ahafo conservator of forests has records is one allocated to the Glicksten Company in 1947.
9 A good illustration of the expansion of farmland along a line of communication may be found in the maps accompanying W. H. Beckett's study, *Akokoaso* (London 1944). Akokoaso is a cocoa-producing village some 100 miles east south east of Ahafo.
10 M. Fortes, *Kinship and the Social Order* (London 1970), p 155.

11 S. A. Darko, 'Changing Settlement Patterns in Ashanti, 1873–1966', Ph.D. thesis, University of London, 1971.
12 GNA Accra, D.894, 12 Aug. 1906.
13 Cf. Polly Hill, *Migrant Cocoa-Farmers of Southern Ghana* (Cambridge 1963), pp 44–46.
14 It seems that land in Ahafo is issued in units of measurement called *dopen*, usually translated as 'pole'; one or two *dopen* units apparently constitute an average-sized farm and, where square-measure is implied, approximates to nine acres.
15 F. R. Bray, *Cocoa Development in Ahafo, West Ashanti* (Achimota 1959), p 20.
16 M. J. Field, *Akim–Kotoku: an Oman of the Gold Coast* (London 1948), p 1.
17 Mr J. K. Boame (interview in English).
18 According to its present chief, Asufufuo was also established by a woman.
19 A. W. Cardinall, *In Ashanti and Beyond* (London 1927), pp 83–4.
20 K. A. Busia, *The Position of the Chief in the Modern Political System of Ashanti* (London 1951).
21 Population figures relate to the town itself and not to its dependent villages within the stool unit.
22 In 1932, for example, the D.C. observed that he had no clear idea of the extent of his District to the west. GNA Accra, D.104, Fuller to Chief Commissioner Kumasi, 11 Sept. 1932.
23 Kukuom–Ahafo State Council minutes, 14 Feb. 1961.
24 Goaso District Office file LA10, vol 2, p 68, letter from Sankorehene to General Secretary UGFC.
25 Goaso District Office file LA10, vol 2, passim, letters between D.C. Goaso, D.C. Nkawie, Kukuom–Ahafo State Council and Nkawiehene.
26 A. A. Y. Kyerematen, *Inter-State Boundary Litigation in Ashanti* (Leiden 1971), 48–51.
27 D. E. Apter, *Ghana in Transition* (New York 1963).
28 *-suro*, which may be translated either as 'fear' or as 'respect'.

3. 'Economic development of Ahafo'

a. 'Cocoa', pp 41–66

1 G. B. Kay (ed.), *The Political Economy of Colonialism in Ghana* (Cambridge 1972), p 334.
2 *Ibid.* p 336.
3 Figure supplied by Goaso Administrative Office, July 1971.
4 GNA Kumasi, Acc 2293, letters of 21 July 1916 and 2 Aug. 1916.
5 GNA Kumasi, Acc 1850, diary CWPA, 1 and 3 Feb. 1919.
6 GNA Accra, ADM 49/5/2, diary, 23 July 1930; ADM 54/1/1, letter 111/03, 136/03, 3/04 etc.; ADM 49/4/9, case of 28 April 1943 against T. N. Baidoo, etc.
7 See Polly Hill, *Studies in Rural Capitalism in West Africa* (Cambridge 1970), cap 2, and especially her classic *The Migrant Cocoa-Farmers of Southern Ghana* (Cambridge 1963).
8 David Kimble, *A Political History of Ghana 1850–1928* (Oxford 1963), pp 24, 30; Kay (ed.), *Political Economy of Colonialism*, pp 20–1.
9 See esp. Ivor Wilks, 'Asante Policy towards the Hausa Trade in the Nineteenth Century', in Claude Meillassoux (ed.), *The Development of Indigenous Trade and Markets in West Africa* (London 1971), pp 124–39.
10 GNA Accra, ADM 54/1/1, letter 26/0/6.
11 *Annual Colonial Report. Ashanti, 1902*, p 2.
12 *Annual Colonial Report. Ashanti, 1904*, p 16.
13 GNA Kumasi, Acc 2123, CWPA to CCA, 31 Jan. 1913 – commenting on Conservator of Forests' report for the third quarter of 1912 on his tour of the Western

Province; GNA Accra, ADM 54/1/5, 454/11; GNA Kumasi, Acc 1730, 27 Jan. 1913 (Conservator of Forests to Colonial Secretary), and see Note 24 below.

14 GNA Accra, ADM 54/1/1, 284/04, CWPA to CCA: 'There is some hesitation on the part of chiefs to grow cocoa and cotton; with apparently a certain amount of justification for it. They ask the question "How much should we get for a load of 60 lbs cocoa?" and when the reply 16/- is given them they contend that a man can gather 60 lbs of rubber in 25 days and get £4-15-0 for it at Kumasi, and what is the good of growing cocoa at 16/- a load which takes from 6 to 10 days to transport to Kumasi, before it can be sold, the tree taking 3 years to bear, the virgin forest to be cut, ground tilled and weeded. I have pointed out that it is the quantity, and facility for growing, which will ultimately pay them. They still seem somewhat sceptical, but intended to try the experiment.'

15 *Loc. cit.* 'I have instructed all the Chiefs in my district both verbally and by letter to get ground prepared by the beginning of the next rains for the purpose of planting the cocoa.'

16 GNA Accra, ADM 54/1/1, 59/05.

17 *Loc. cit.*

18 *Loc. cit.*

19 *Loc. cit.* 205/05.

20 *Loc. cit.* 206/06.

21 *Annual Colonial Report. Ashanti, 1906,* p 20, and *1907,* p 22.

22 *Annual Colonial Report. Ashanti, 1907,* p 22.

23 *Annual Colonial Report. Ashanti, 1908,* p 10.

24 GNA Kumasi, Acc 654, para 4. 'In Wam and Ahafo there should be great development in the future. Cocoa has been extensively planted. Rubber is there and I hope will be planted and if the Government decide to open the Tano waterway for timber, judging from Thompson's report, I should gather there should be a great future for the timber from the Ahafo forest. These trades alone would in my opinion justify the Government's approval of a subsidiary district.'

25 GNA Accra, ADM, 54/1/5, 433/11, para 8.

26 *Annual Colonial Report. Ashanti, 1907,* p 22.

27 GNA Accra, ADM 54/1/5, 434/11.

28 *Loc. cit.* 474/11.

29 GNA Kumasi, Acc 574, diary Oct. 1912, Remarks.

30 GNA Kumasi, ADM 11/1309, report 19 Aug. 1913 to CWPA, para vi.

31 GNA Kumasi, Acc 612, diary 17 March 1914.

32 GNA Kumasi, Acc 612, 17 April 1914.

33 GNA Kumasi, Acc 2231, Curator of Agriculture to CCA, 16 Jan. 1915.

34 GNA Kumasi, Acc 612, 13–15 March 1914 and 1 March 1914.

35 GNA Kumasi, Acc 377, diary CWPA, 20–21 Sept. 1918.

36 GNA Kumasi, Acc 1850, diary, 1 Feb. 1919.

37 GNA Kumasi, Acc 1850, 3 Feb. 1919.

38 Kay (ed.), *Political Economy of Colonialism,* pp 338–9.

39 GNA Accra, ADM 11/1317, CCA to Col. Sec. report on tour in N & W of Ashanti.

40 GNA Kumasi, Acc 2472, ADC Goaso to CWPA, 19 April 1923.

41 GNA Accra, ADM 45/5/1, Prov. Record Book, WPA, 671, Agriculture 1923/4.

42 Cf. Joan Robinson, *Economic Philosophy* (London 1962), p 45.

43 GNA Kumasi, Acc 215, 5 Dec. 1923, DCG to CWPA. Acherensua was the furthest market to the south in Ahafo at this time (GNA Accra, ADM 45/5/1, 671, Agriculture 1924/5).

44 Kay (ed.), *Political Economy of Colonialism,* pp 338–9. Figures for 1931–6.

45 GNA Kumasi, Acc 1928, 6 Feb. 1931. Cf. 19 Nov. 1930.

46 GNA Kumasi, Acc 215. This continued at least up to 1932 and 1933 (GNA Kumasi, Acc 533).

47 GNA Kumasi, Acc 1926, 5 Feb. 1931.

48 GNA Kumasi, Acc 13, Annual Report 1935/6.

49 Such an insight was, of course, seldom an exclusive determinant of the behaviour of the administration which always perforce had other matters on its mind than the cultivation of its self-image.
50 GNA Kumasi, Acc 612, diary, 10 Oct. 1914.
51 *Annual Colonial Report, Ashanti, 1961*, p 8.
52 GNA Kumasi, Acc 1121, CWPA to CCA, 9 May 1917.
53 *Annual Colonial Report. Ashanti, 1918*, p 7.
54 GNA Kumasi, Acc 2511, 24 Dec. 1929, Report of Superintendent of Agriculture to Superintendent, Plant and Produce Inspectorate, Accra.
55 GNA Kumasi, Acc 2168, General Report on Instructional Work, April–June 1921, Western Province.
56 See Peter C. Garlick, *African Traders and Economic Development in Ghana* (Oxford 1971), esp. caps VII and VIII.
57 GNA Kumasi, Acc 802, ACWPA to CCA, 5 Sept. 1912.
58 GNA Kumasi, Acc 796, Fell to Chiefs, 8 Jan. 1913.
59 GNA Kumasi, Acc 814 and Acc 391, 25 Aug. 1917, Director of Agriculture, Aburi, to CCA.
60 GNA Kumasi, Acc 391, CCA to Director of Agriculture, 7 Sept. 1917.
61 GNA Kumasi, Acc 497, 17 Oct. 1925, CCA's circular.
62 *Loc. cit.* 25 Jan. 1928, CCA to Col. Sec.
63 *Loc. cit.* letter of 26 July 1926.
64 GNA Kumasi, Acc 1699, 10 Nov. 1928, p 2.
65 K. A. Busia, *The Position of the Chief in the Modern Political System of Ashanti*, 2nd edn. (London 1968), pp. 189–90. And see list of five land cases in late 1937 (Ahafo District Record Book, II (1927–51), GNA Kumasi, Relation of Kumasi Clan Chiefs to Ahafo, Oct., Nov., Dec. 1937) – one of which had already cost the Chief of Acherensua 'anything up to £1000 to date'. 'In every case mentioned a Kumasi chief is involved and every case has been or is due to be heard in Kumasi and each case will probably cost the Ahafo village concerned a sum of money that will mean years of debt and pledged cocoa farms.'
66 GNA Kumasi, Ahafo District Record Book, II *loc. cit.*
67 GNA Kumasi, Ahafo District Record Book, II, Financial Relationship between Clan Chiefs and Ahafo Villages.
68 See note 66 above, *loc. cit.* Esp.: 'In the days before the Yaa Asantewa war these Ahafo villages owed service in war to the Asantehene through their clan chiefs who were their commanders. Now that the clan chiefs are no longer in any sense leaders of the Ahafo people and have to a great extent lost touch with them except for the purpose of extortion, it seems that the modern parallel to the old national service is now obviously a contribution to the central revenue of the Golden Stool.'
69 *Loc. cit.* 'General', Esp.: the attribution of blame for the Ahafo debt to the 'land disputes, humbug and extortion of the Clan Chiefs'.
70 GNA Sunyani, Goaso District Files, Acc 64/1969, letters of 4 and 19 April 1940.
71 See note 67 above, Oct.–Dec. 1939. See also Asanteman Archives, Manhyia, Kumasi, Acc 626, Cocoa Tribute, letters of 20 Oct. 1938, 9 March 1940, 6 March 1940, 11 Dec. 1939, 23 Jan. 1940, 13 Jan. 1940, 16 Nov. 1939 etc., and GNA Sunyani, Goaso District Files, C.50.
72 Asanteman Archives, Acc 626, letter of 13 Jan. 1940.
73 GNA Sunyani, Goaso District Files, Acc 56/1969.
74 GNA Sunyani, Goaso District Files, Acc 44/1969.
75 GNA Sunyani, Goaso District Files, Acc 48/1969; Cocoa Surtax 1957/8.
76 Institute of African Studies, Legon, Ashanti Court Records, vol 1, no 13, 16 Dec. 1957, p 3.
77 GNA Accra, ADM 49/4/1, 521–5, 13 June 1923.
78 GNA Accra, 49/4/2. There were 24 debt recovery cases in the corresponding quarter of 1928, most of which arose out of cocoa-broking (ADM 49/4/1).

79 GNA Accra, ADM 49/4/1, 521–5.
80 GNA Kumasi, Acc 1215, Frame's African Agency to P.C. Sunyani, 19 Dec. 1926.
81 GNA Accra, ADM 49/4/1, 521–5; and ADM 49/4/2, 13–18 (21 March 1922), 108–9, etc. The cases recorded in the Civil Record Book give extensive insight into the development of the purchasing system.
82 GNA Kumasi, Acc 2115, June and July 1927, Oct. and Nov. 1927 (J. Lyons & Co.); GNA Kumasi, Acc 2380, 14 Dec. 1931; GNA Accra, ADM 49/5/3, 26 Nov. 1930 (Cadburys).
83 GNA Kumasi, Acc 1928, CWPA diary, 5 Feb. 1929.
84 GNA Kumasi, Acc 4, Report of Acting Provincial Superintendent of Agriculture, 24 Dec. 1929.
85 *Loc. cit.*
86 *Loc. cit.* 'I consider the area most suitable for cooperative marketing; in fact I feel certain that it is the only safe remedy; the people should be lifted out of their present state of helplessness before it is too late and I am making recommendations regarding this to the division concerned.'
87 GNA Accra, Acc 1960/289.
88 Kay (ed.), *Political Economy of Colonialism*, p 411.
89 *Ibid*. p 268.
90 *Ibid*. p 271.
91 At a purely factual level the government's anxiety might have been entirely well-judged. Cf. Polly Hill, *The Gold Coast Cocoa Farmer* (London 1956), pp 130–1: farmers 14, 15, 16 and 17 in Hwidiem who spent between £50 and £200 in the year 1954 alone.
92 Kay (ed.), *Political Economy of Colonialism*, p 111.
93 GNA Kumasi, Acc 415, Col. Sec. to CCA, 8 Oct 1915. And see Kay (ed.), *ibid*. pp 111–14.
94 GNA Kumasi, Acc 415, CCA to Col. Sec., 18 Oct. 1915.
95 GNA Kumasi, Acc 1115, Col. Sec. to CCA, 20 Sept. 1916, and Acting Governor's minute, 16 Dec. 1916.
96 Kay (ed.), *Political Economy*, pp 108, 113–14.
97 GNA Kumasi, Acc 1115.
98 Kay (ed.), *Political Economy*, pp 115–17.
99 *Ibid*. p 121.
100 See the comments of the Basel missionary Ramseyer in 1905 and the agitated response of the colonial administration to them, recognising that Chief Commissioner Fuller's rules over domestic slavery and pawning condoned breaches of the criminal law of the Gold Coast Colony and were incompatible with the Brussels Act of 1890 (GNA Kumasi, Acc 234). Cases of pledging children for debts occur in court records as recently as 17 March 1942 (GNA Accra, ADM 49/4/9).
101 For a brief account of the share-cropping system (*abusa*), see Hill, *The Gold Coast Cocoa Farmer*, cap 1.
102 For a useful survey see Polly Hill, *The Occupations of Migrants in Ghana*, Museum of Anthropology, University of Michigan, *Anthropological Papers*, no. 2, 1970 and literature cited there.
103 GNA Kumasi, Acc 612, CWPA diary, 18 and 21 Oct. 1916.
104 GNA Kumasi, Acc 1719, Unofficial statistics of Muslims, returned on forms for enumerating Christians. Kukuom area had 89, Mim area 9, Noberkaw area 18. In 1911 only 2 Muslims were recorded for Ahafo as a whole. The population recorded for Kukuom in the census was judged obviously excessive in the following year (about double), *loc. cit.* DCG to CWPA, 3 Nov. 1922.
105 GNA Kumasi, Acc 2071, 9 Sept. 1926.
106 GNA Accra, ADM 49/5/1, Dec. 1929, para. 51; 25 Nov. 1929; ADM 49/5/2, 6 August 1930.
107 GNA Accra, ADM 49/5/1, Nov. 1929, para. 41.
108 GNA Accra ADM 49/5/2, 18 July 1930.

109 *Loc. cit.* 19 July 1930.
110 GNA Kumasi, Acc 1699, 3 Feb. 1930.
111 GNA Kumasi, Acc 2509.
112 *Loc. cit.* Figures for Goaso:

	pre-puberty boys	virile men	non-virile men	girls	women[1]	women[2]
Ashantis	70	149	11	76	100	39
Nkramos	24	132	3	16	23	2

(girls = girls pre-puberty.   Women[1] = women producing.
Women[2] = Women past producing.)

113 GNA Kumasi, Acc 2509, p 13.
114 GNA Kumasi, Acc 76, Report on Social and Economic Progress of the People of West Ashanti 1932, paras 10 and 11.
115 GNA Kumasi, Acc 215, 17 April 1929, Dept. of Agriculture to Col. Sec., Accra.
116 J. C. Muir, 'Crop Surveys, Gold Coast', *Department of Agriculture Bulletin*, 20 (1930), 180.
117 GNA Accra, Ahafo District Record Book, vol 1, DM 49/5/6, Agricultural Survey, Ahafo Goaso (WP 28/29), Table 1, summary.
118 J. C. Muir, 'Survey of Cacao Areas, Western Province, Ashanti', *Department of Agriculture Bulletin*, 22 (1930), 63.
119 *Ibid.* p 61.
120 However, the accounts of the 1928/9 survey given in the two articles cited suggests that the later information, though comparatively restricted in reference, is much more reliable so far as it goes.
121 Polly Hill's investigation of a section of the cocoa farmers of Hwidiem in the 1954/5 season (Hill, *The Gold Coast Cocoa Farmer*) and the more protracted and systematic study organised by F. R. Bray over two and a half to three years up to 1958 (F. R. Bray, *Cocoa Development in Ahafo, West Ashanti* (Achimota 1959).
122 Hill, *The Gold Coast Cocoa Farmers*, p 126. Evidence of the scale of Kumasi colonisation of Ahafo at this time may be taken from the fact that half of the farmers surveyed for the village of Kokoben near Kumasi had new farms in the Ahafo area (*ibid.* pp 46, 125).
123 *Ibid.* p 20.
124 *Ibid.* Table, p 23.
125 *Ibid.* p 24.
126 *Ibid.* p 35, Table 7.
127 *Ibid.* p 46, Table 10.
128 *Ibid.* p 89.
129 *Ibid.* p 91.
130 *Ibid.* p 91.
131 *Ibid.* p 90.
132 *Ibid.* pp 130–1, farmers 13, 16, 20.
133 *Ibid.* p 91.
134 *Ibid.* p 125.
135 *Ibid.* p 94.
136 *Ibid.* p 95, Table 20.
137 Bray, *Development of Cocoa Farming*, p 25.
138 *Ibid.* p 25.
139 *Ibid.* p 26.
140 *Ibid.* p 27.

141 *Ibid.* p 27, Table III.

Size group	Average area			
	0–7 yrs	8–15 yrs	16–30 yrs	30 yrs +
small (under 5 acres)	2.0	1.9	2.0	1.9
medium (5–50 acres)	11.5	14.9	16.5	18.7
large (over 50 acres)	67.2	85.4	96.5	121.1

	Percentage distribution of farms			
small	58	49	48	36
medium	41	48	44	54
large	1	3	8	10

	Percentage distribution of acreage			
small	19	9	5	3
medium	76	65	45	42
large	5	26	50	55

142 *Ibid.* p 27.
143 *Ibid.* p 28.
144 *Ibid.* p 28.
145 Goaso District cocoa purchases, Total (in tons)

Year	Main crop (from 1947/8)	Mid crop (from 1948)	Year	Main crop (from 1947/8)	Mid crop (from 1948)
1948	8,843	15	1960	30,650	1,022
1949	12,510	116	1961	30,795	20
1950	14,055	4	1962	42,214	347
1951	17,159	7	1963	48,857	5,337
1952	13,074	5	1964	*	7,014.3
1953	15,123	7	1965	39,062.1	1,268.1
1954	15,148	9	1966	33,364.1	512.2
1955	17,044	361	1967	24,067.5	905.7
1956	19,283	166	1968	38,796.4	1,809.1
1957	20,896	32	1969	**	**
1958	14,901	1,099	1970	36,044.1	906.8
1959	29,825	3,328	1971	35,412.9	

Note: Figures up to * are drawn from annual reports of the Cocoa Marketing Board. Figures between * and ** were drawn up specially for me by the Produce Inspection Division in Teppa. The final figures are those of the District Administrative Office in Goaso.

b. 'Other products', pp 67–76

1 The details of Salamu Mossi's life are taken from his interview with A. F. Robertson in August 1968.
2 A similar career is suggested by one of Polly Hill's informants in the early 1950s (Polly Hill, *The Gold Coast Cocoa Farmer* (London 1956), p 130, Farmer 15). For *dawa-dawa* as a food asset see Kwamina B. Dickson, *A Historical Geography of Ghana* (Cambridge 1969), p 72.
3 See for example the file Cocoa Farm Labour (Asanteman Archives, Manhyia, Acc 89). The figures cited there for 1948 do not compare unfavourably, when due allowance has been made for changes in the value of money, with those paid today.
4 See esp. Ivor Wilks, 'Asante Policy towards the Hausa Trade in the Nineteenth Century', in Claude Meillassoux (ed.), *The Development of Indigenous Trade and Markets in West Africa* (London 1971), pp 124–39; and R. S. Rattray, *Ashanti Law and Constitution* (Oxford 1929), pp 109–11.

5 GNA Accra, ADM 12/3/6, 20 July 1896, Gov. to Col. Sec.
6 For the origins of this see the very informative file on the drawing of the Sefwhi/ Ahafo boundary (GNA Kumasi, Acc 706). It was still involving Sankore in expensive legal wrangles and the D.C.s in protracted administrative labour twenty-five years later.
7 GNA Sunyani, Goaso District Files, G. 41/29, Diamonds; GNA Accra, ADM 49/5/1, 22 Feb. 1930.
8 Kwame Yeboa Daaku, *Trade and Politics on the Gold Coast 1600–1720* (Oxford 1970), p 27; J. K. Fynn, *Asante and its Neighbours 1700–1807* (London 1971), pp 62–3.
9 Davidson Houston, report 30 June 1896, Attachment A (PRO, CO 96/275).
10 F. R. Bray, *Cocoa Development in Ahafo, West Ashanti* (Achimota 1959), pp 82–3.
11 Davidson Houston, report (cited note 9 above), p 15.
12 *Ibid.* p 11.
13 For bushmeat see Bray, *Cocoa Development in Ahafo*, pp 10–12. For fish see GNA Accra, ADM 49/4/1, 593–605, 22 April 1924, Dadiesoaba/Sienchem fishing dispute. For snails see A. W. Cardinall, *In Ashanti and Beyond* (London 1927), pp 78–80, etc.
14 Davidson Houston, report (cited note 9 above), p 8.
15 See the description of Kumasi decay in 1888 quoted in William Tordoff, *Ashanti under the Prempehs 1888–1935* (London 1965), p 31. But for an emphasis on the partial recovery of the city under Prempeh see Francis Agbodeka, *African Politics and British Policy in the Gold Coast 1868–1900* (London 1971), cap 7.
16 Dickson, *Historical Geography of Ghana*, pp 162–4.
17 GNA Kumasi, Acc. 936, Stewart's judgement of 27 Feb. 1899 in D.C. Kumasi's letter of June 1926.
18 This award was still being cited in full in 1971 in petitions of the Ahafo Youth Association, urging the re-establishment of the Kukuom paramountcy over an autonomous Ahafo.
19 GNA Accra, ADM 54/1/1, 284/04.
20 GNA Accra, ADM 54/1/2, 225/07 and ADM 54/1/4, 220/09.
21 Compare the tables of export volumes and prices in G. B. Kay (ed.), *The Political Economy of Colonialism in Ghana* (Cambridge 1972), pp 336–9.
22 *Annual Colonial Report. Ashanti*, 1902, p 2.
23 *Annual Colonial Report. Ashanti*, 1906, p 20.
24 See the prominence of the issue in the D.C.'s diaries for 1929–31 (GNA Accra, ADM 49/5/1–3).
25 See note 13 above.
26 Davidson Houston, report (cited note 9 above), Attachment A.
27 GNA Accra, ADM 54/1/1, 284/04.
28 See letter quoted in the first section of this chapter, 'Cocoa' (3a), note 14.
29 *Annual Colonial Report. Ashanti.* 1906, p 20.
30 In September 1905 the number of animals and loads passing through the Kukuom toll collection point per year was estimated at: horses 10; cattle 500; calves 100; sheep 500; lambs 100; donkeys 50; trade loads 10,000; and kola loads 1,500 (GNA Accra, ADM 54/1/1, 219/05). Tax rates on these were set in December 1905 at: Gin 5s a load; cattle 4s each; calves 2s each; sheep and goats 1s each; lambs and kids 6d each; and rubber 3s a load (*loc. cit.* 329/05). The estimates of trade flows for January and February 1906 (GNA Accra, ADM 54/1/2, 173/06) suggest that the 1905 estimates for Kukuom in relation to Wenchi had been well below the mark.
31 *Annual Colonial Report. Ashanti.* 1906, p 20.
32 *Annual Colonial Report, Ashanti.* 1907, p 22.
33 *Annual Colonial Report, 1908*, pp 6–7.
34 *Ibid.* p 10.
35 GNA Accra, ADM 54/1/4, 251/09.
36 GNA Kumasi, Acc 1429, CWPA to CCA, 7 Sept. 1910.

37 Most of the kola was still head-loaded to the north and the administration had no means of assessing the total quantity of this traffic with any accuracy.
38 *Annual Colonial Report. Ashanti, 1911*, p 6.
39 GNA Accra, ADM 54/1/5, 433/11.
40 GNA Kumasi, Acc 612, 5 Oct. 1914.
41 *Loc. cit.* 13 and 14 March 1914.
42 Kay (ed.), *Political Economy of Colonialism in Ghana*, p 338.
43 *Annual Colonial Report. Ashanti, 1918*, p 8.
44 GNA Kumasi, Ahafo District Record Book, ii, ADM 49/5/7. See Ahafo Court, Jan.–March 1938. 'During the cocoa holdup' is used as a chronological reference point in a court case in January 1941 in Goaso (GNA Accra, ADM 49/4/2, p 359).
45 GNA Kumasi. Acc 612, 14–17 March 1914.
46 GNA Kumasi, Acc 179, half-yearly report, 30 Sept. 1926, Trade, C.
47 GNA Accra, ADM 45/5/1, p 155. Grey and white monkey skins reached up to 7s each in 1923, though their normal average price was around 3s in the early 1920s. Chewsticks were sold to Kumasi traders for 3d a 2½ ft stick.
48 GNA Kumasi, Acc 1928, 23 March 1931. Oranges are now exported from the area on a small scale.
49 GNA Accra, ADM 45/5/1, pp 674–5.
50 GNA Sunyani, Goaso District Files, Acc 103/1969, pp 82, 95, 104–5 (items 21–23).
51 GNA Kumasi, Acc 321. Cf. the comparative optimism of mid-1920s (GNA Accra, ADM 45/5/1, pp 674–5).
52 GNA Accra, ADM 45/5/1, pp 674–5.
53 GNA Accra, ADM 45/5/1, p 155, 1925–6.
54 GNA Kumasi, Acc 1928, 25 Nov. 1930.
55 GNA Accra, ADM 45/5/1, 671-, Ahafo District, 1923–4.
56 *Loc. cit.* 1924–5.
57 J. C. Muir, 'The Cola Industry in the Western Province of Ashanti', *G.C. Department of Agriculture Bulletin*, 22 (1930), 218–24.
58 The information was collected in the course of the cocoa survey by visiting all villages in the kola-growing area and enquiring at each house as to the average sale of kola.
59 GNA Kumasi, Acc 1699, Handing Over Report, 30 Aug. 1929.
60 GNA Kumasi, Acc 1926, 11 Sept. 1931.
61 GNA Accra, ADM 45/5/2, 18-, Kola.
62 Stress on the necessity of civil order as a precondition for profitable trade in the economic urge for imperial expansion (see e.g. Trevor Lloyd, 'Africa and Hobson's Imperialism', *Past and Present*, 55 (May 1972), 130–53), has important implications for the availability of a local entrepreneurial welcome for an effective imperial power.

c. 'Timber', pp 77–84

1 Interview (Robertson) with Senior Assistant Conservator of Forests, Apaloo, Sept. 1968.
2 Davidson Houston, report, 30 June 1896 (PRO, CO 96/275), Attachment A. Goaso had 80 huts; Noberkaw 450; Kukuom 250; Anwiam 20; Bediako 15; Mim 550, etc.
3 GNA Accra, ADM 54/1/5, 545/11, p 6.
4 *Loc. cit.* p 1.
5 GNA Kumasi, Acc 569, 31 Jan. 1913.
6 GNA Kumasi, Acc 1730, 27 Jan. 1913, Conservator of Forests to Col. Sec.
7 GNA Kumasi, Acc 1312, Conservator of Forests to Gov.
8 GNA Accra, ADM 11/1317.
9 GNA Kumasi, Acc 1312, Col. Sec. to CCA, 6 Sept. 1912.
10 GNA Kumasi, Acc 13, Annual Report 1934/5, Forestry.
11 GNA Kumasi, Acc 233, Annual Report 1937/8, Forestry, Sunyani District. For the

area of Ahafo forest reserves in 1953/4 see land revenue figures of £315 on a total
of 315.4 sq. miles in the nine forest reserves listed in GNA Sunyani, Goaso District
files, Acc 91/1969, p 42.

12 GNA Kumasi, Acc 233, Annual Report 1937/8, Forestry.
13 Institute of African Studies, Legon, Ashanti Court Records, vol 1, 9, 15 Oct. 1937,
p 2, Akwaboahene's grievances, 3.
14 Details of the progress of the Mim Timber Company operations are taken (except
where otherwise indicated) from information supplied in interviews cited in
notes 1 above or 22 below. See also J. Adomako-Sarfo, 'The Development of Cocoa
Farming in Brong Ahafo South with Special Reference to the Migration of
Farmers', M.A. thesis, Institute of African studies, p 31. The Mim Timber
Co. was reported in Parliament in 1960 (*Debates*, vol 18, 63–4) as the fourth largest
timber firm in Ghana, with 644.78 sq. miles of timber in forest reserves and
502.42 sq. miles outside them.
15 Figures given by District Agricultural Extension Officer (Ansah) in interview with
Robertson, Sept. 1968.
16 Interview cited in note 1 above.
17 Adomako-Sarfo, M.A. thesis, pp 16–19, 30–2.
18 This impression is reinforced with particular strength by consultation of current
government files on the main Teppa–Mim road in the regional headquarters of the
Public Works Department in Sunyani and the District Administrative Office in Goaso.
19 *Debates*, 1952, 7 March 1952, 1435; 1953, 5 March 1953, 965–6; 1954, 8 Feb. 1954,
174–5; 1954:2, 6 Aug. 1954, 208: vol 42, 20 Dec. 1965, 250–1.
20 See e.g. GNA Sunyani, Goaso Files, Acc 150/1969, esp. pp 1–5.
21 See (Accra) *Daily Graphic*, 25, 29 March 1972, 11, 20 April 1972. For further evidence
of political pressure on Mim Timber Company concessions see *Daily Graphic*, 22 Feb.
1972. See also *West Africa*, 8 Jan. 1973, p 47.
22 Information on the career of W. K. Ennin is based (except where otherwise indicated) on an interview with him at his house in Asokwa, Kumasi in the summer of
1971.
23 GNA Sunyani, Goaso District Files, Acc 91/1969, p 91, 24 Jan. 1957, Ahafo Local
Council to Conservator of Forests, Kumasi.
24 GNA Sunyani, Goaso District Files, Acc 136/1969, p 161, 32, Farm and Timber
Inspectors.
25 GNA Sunyani, Goaso District Files, Acc 41/1969.
26 GNA Sunyani, Goaso District Files, Acc 54/1969.
27 Asanteman Archives, Manhyia, Personal File 128.
28 *Loc. cit.* letter of registration 7 Aug. 1952.
29 Asanteman Archives, Manhyia, Personal File 128.

4. 'Colonial transformation of Ahafo'

a. '*Military control and public order*', pp 85–95

1 William Tordoff, *Ashanti under the Prempehs, 1888–1935* (London 1965), pp 64,
83–4; and GNA Accra, ADM 12/3/6, Gov.'s despatch to Col. Sec., July 1896.
2 GNA Accra, ADM 12/5/159, Intelligence Report 1922, 1900 War: 15 April Ahafos
part of the revolting tribes; 10 October Mim surrenders.
3 GNA Accra, ADM 11/1137, Armitage's report to Resident, 2 Aug. 1901 on reasons
for increasing Ahafo indemnity: 'although the people had joined the rebels during
the fighting no punitive expedition had been sent against them and having lost
but few of their fighting men they returned to their villages to find them just as
they had been left.'
4 Tordoff, *Ashanti under the Prempehs*, pp 138–9.
5 GNA Kumasi, Acc 936, Stewart's judgement, 27 Feb. 1899, cited in D. C. Kumasi's
letters of June 1926.

6 Tordoff, *Ashanti under the Prempehs*, p 89.
7 *Loc cit.* note 5 above.
8 GNA Accra, ADM 11/1137, Resident, Kumasi to Col. Sec., 4 Aug. 1901.
9 *Loc. cit.* Armitage's report to *Resident*, 2 Aug. 1901, paras 20 and 21.
10 *Loc. cit.* Residents, Kumasi to Col. Sec., 4 Aug. 1901.
11 GNA Accra, ADM 12/5/159, Intelligence Report, Jan.-June 1930.
12 GNA Accra, ADM 11/1137, Armitage's report, 2 Aug. 1901, para 14.
13 *Loc. cit.*
14 *Loc. cit.* Armitage's report, 2 Aug. 1901, para 9.
15 GNA Accra, ADM 54/1/1, 111/03.
16 *Loc. cit.* 136/03.
17 *Loc. cit.* 3/04.
18 *Loc. cit.* 229/04.
19 *Loc. cit* 284/04, Annual Report for 1904.
20 *Loc cit.* 42/05.
21 *Loc. cit.* 81/05.
22 GNA Kumasi, Acc 2205.
23 GNA Accra, ADM 54/1/2, 242/06.
24 *Loc. cit.* 297/06.
25 GNA Accra, ADM 54/1/4, 139/09.
26 *Loc. cit.* 439/09.
27 GNA Accra, ADM 54/1/3, 20/10 (NB. This volume of the Duplicate Letter Books, Sunyani is not in series with vols 1–2 and vol 4). The distribution of these by village is interesting: Asufufuo 10, Hwidiem 24, Acherensua 24, Kenyase 43, Akrodie 56, Ayumso 27, Dadiesoaba 70, Kukuom 51, Aboum 13, Nkasaim 42, Goaso 45, Fawohoyeden 39, Sankore 88, Sienchem 24, Kwapong 85, Noberkaw 25, Kwakunyuma 5, Mim, 185, Anwiam 14.
28 GNA Kumasi, Acc 1429, CWPA's report to CCA, 7 Sept. 1910.
29 GNA Accra, ADM 54/1/3, p 73.
30 *Annual Colonial Report. Ashanti, 1906*, p 4.
31 *Annual Colonial Report. Ashanti, 1912*, p 3.
32 GNA Kumasi, Acc 158, CWPA to ACCA, 25 May 1914 and Acc 612, 22 Aug. 1916. Indications of the colonial government's confidence in the military reliability of Ashanti can be found in the fact that no effort was made in the event of wartime to call in the weapons registered five years earlier – in contrast with the level of military preoccupation revealed in the fact that the French authorities in the Ivory Coast had at one time destroyed, as the intelligence Officer of the Gold Coast Regiment in Kumasi noted, all dane and cap guns they could find – a total which had reached 104,828 (GNA Accra, ADM 11/1164). Registered dane and flint-lock guns in Ahafo numbered 1,140 in 1929 (Kukuom 365, Mim 640, Noberkaw 144) in contrast with figures like 728 for Wam (=Dormaa), 1,816 for Berekum (=Sunyani District 2,544) and 256 for Wenchi, 130 for Tekyiman, 250 for Gyaman (=Wenchi District 636) (GNA Accra, ADM 45/5/1, WPA Provisional Record Book). The government was, however, somewhat more nervous about the possible effects of introducing compulsory recruiting into Ashanti during the 1914–18 War, despite urgent requests for troops for despatch to East Africa (GNA Kumasi, Acc 1117, coded telegrams, 4 and 8 Dec. 1916). There was some signs of unrest in metropolitan Ashanti at the prospect (GNA Kumasi, Acc 1268, entries in Jan., March and Nov. 1917). The Commissioner of the Western Province picked up one or two volunteer recruits in 1914 (GNA Kumasi, Acc 612, 21 and 22 Sept. 1914), and he did hold meetings to explain the recruiting system when touring Ahafo in May 1917 (GNA Kumasi, Acc 1121, letters of 9 May 1917). But there seems to be no record of any recruits being raised within Ahafo itself: an index of the very limited character of its practical links with the colonial regime, as far as the lives of most of its inhabitants were concerned, rather than a token of any peculiarly vivid hostility towards it.

33 GNA Kumasi, Acc 654.
34 Private letters of Johnstone (D.C. Goaso) sent by CWPA to CCA (GNA Kumasi, Acc 158) and see GNA Accra, ADM 54/1/3, pp 60–2, letters of 16 March 1914; 1914; GNA Kumasi, Acc 1722, letters of 16 Sept. 1913, 9 and 10 April 1913 on need to open prison with armed warders in Ahafo when D.C. begins to reside there.
35 GNA Kumasi, Ahafo District Record Book, vol II, July 1949.
36 *Loc. cit*, and see *ibid.* pp 109–, education, July 1949.
37 GNA Accra, ADM 11/1137, Armitage's report, 2 Aug. 1901, para 17. The behaviour of Hausa detachments had been one of the major causes of acute Ashanti resentment in 1897 (Tordoff, *Ashanti under the Prempehs*, p 87).
38 GNA Accra, ADM 54/1/1, 99/04.
39 GNA Accra, ADM 54/1/2, 238/06 and 241/06.
40 GNA Kumasi, Acc 612, 25 May 1914 and 16 June 1914.
41 GNA Accra, ADM 54/1/3, 16 March 1914.
42 See e.g. GNA Kumasi, Acc 1124, letters 5 Oct. 1929 – 2 Goaso Policemen imprisoned for extortion and 2 others transferred: 'I am of the opinion that if it is necessary for this station to be left without a Commissioner it should, as far as the Police are concerned, be closed down and the men temporarily transferred to Sunyani.' See also GNA Kumasi, Acc. 2499, Handing over reports for 13 March 1926 and 31 March 1929 on Goaso police behaviour without adequate supervision from a resident D.C.
43 GNA Kumasi, Acc 1699, Handing over reports, 12 March 1929, Religion: 'There are various small Churches in the District representing Wesleyan, Presbyterian and Roman Catholic beliefs. None of these to my mind are very satisfactory institutions, as they are rarely supervised by a European Minister.'
44 Cf. the discussion of Kofi Pong's part in advancing the prosecution of the Bungulu fetish in 1908 (GNA Kumasi, Acc 2111) with the judgement in 1911: 'Kofi Pong has been sent to prison for 6 months. As you know this man was once given a present of £5 for information he gave to the government with regard to the Bungulu fetish in a case tried by the C.C. in Kukuom. Since then he appears to have become a liar and extortioner and I am surprised that no one in Ahafo complained about his actions before (GNA Accra, ADM 54/1/5, 440/11).
45 GNA Accra, ADM 54/1/1, 278/04.
46 GNA Kumasi, Acc 1124, letter of 5 Oct. 1929.
47 GNA Accra, ADM 49/4/1, case on Kenyasi Christian/pagan brawl of 1915 (pp 133–141).
48 GNA Kumasi, Acc 612, 18 and 21 Oct. 1916 and the violent brawl in Mim between Ashantis and N.T. men initiated by a northerner persisting against threats in dancing an Ashanti dance. The Ashantis threatened to shoot the northerners and one man attempted to push a stick up the rectum of an individual whom he had beaten up (GNA Accra, ADM 49/4/8, case of 27 Dec. 1941).
49 Kenyase divisions go back at least to 1930 (GNA Accra, ADM 49/5/2, July and Aug. 1930).
50 See chapter 8 below.
51 See chapter 6 below.
52 These deficiencies were clear to the administration as early as 1937. See Political Officers' Meeting, 26 and 27 Feb. 1937 (GNA Sunyani, Sunyani District Records, Acc 477, Political Conferences).
53 GNA Accra, ADM 54/1/1, 205/05.
54 GNA Accra, ADM 11/1309, Ross's report of 19 Aug. 1913, para 1.
55 *Loc. cit.* passim.
56 GNA Kumasi, Acc 17, Appendix A.
57 GNA Kumasi, Acc 35, passim.
58 Except briefly and for very direct reasons between September 1969 and January 1972.

b. *'Hygiene and respectability', pp 96–120*

1 A. W. Cardinall, *In Ashanti and Beyond* (London 1927), pp 75–6.
2 GNA Accra, ADM 12/5/159, Internal Intelligence Report 1922 on population.
3 Cardinall, *Ashanti and Beyond*, p 71.
4 For extensive details see Philip D. Curtin, *The Image of Africa: British Ideas and Action, 1780–1850* (Madison, Wisconsin 1964), esp. cap 7.
5 Cardinall, *Ashanti and Beyond*, p 70.
6 GNA Kumasi, Acc. 1928, 21 and 30 Nov. 1930 and 1 Dec. 1930.
7 See esp. Medical Officer's report on visit to Goaso of 2 June 1926. The latrine for European officials' servants, the night-soil deposit, the area within which rubbish was burnt, the bush, the native clerk's quarters, the police lines and indeed the village as a whole are all separately judged to be too close to the D.C.'s bungalow in this report (GNA Kumasi, Acc 2426.)
8 Cardinall, *Ashanti and Beyond*, p 64.
9 GNA Kumasi, Acc 158, CWPA to CCA, 25 May 1914.
10 GNA Accra, ADM 11/1309, report, 19 Aug. 1913 to CWPA: 'Kukuom itself has undoubtedly diminished. There are fewer houses and some are deserted, the only building of any pretension to repair or permanancy being Braimansu's house, which is a large, new, two-storied building built by skilled labour and roofed with iron and standing a monument to his affluence amidst surrounding squalor.'
11 GNA Accra, ADM 54/1/1, CNWA to CCA, 16 Jan. 1906, Native Affairs.
12 Cardinall, *Ashanti and Beyond*, pp 82–3.
13 GNA Kumasi, Acc 1429, 7 Sept. 1910, CWPA to CCA, para 5.
14 *Loc. cit.* para 6.
15 GNA Kumasi, Acc 1429, CCA's minute.
16 GNA Accra, ADM 54/1/5, 448/11, para 3.
17 GNA Accra, ADM 54/3/5, 155/12, cf. Cardinall, *Ashanti and Beyond*, p 65.
18 GNA Accra, ADM 54/1/5, 169/12.
19 *Annual Colonial Report. Ashanti*, 1912, p 17.
20 GNA Kumasi, Acc 2161.
21 GNA Kumasi, Acc 377, 3 and 6 Dec. 1918.
22 *Loc. cit.* 27 Dec. 1918.
23 GNA Accra, ADM 45/5/1, pp 135–7, Medical 1924.
24 See e.g. Perry Miller, *The New England Mind: From Colony to Province* (Boston pb. edn. 1961), cap xxi; John Blake, 'The Inoculation Controversy in Boston, 1721–22', *New England Quarterly*, xxv (1952), 489–506; Genevieve Miller, *The Adoption of Inoculation for Smallpox in England and France* (Philadelphia 1957).
25 Niyazi Berkes, *The Development of Secularism in Turkey* (Montreal 1964), pp 120–121.
26 GNA Kumasi, Acc 10, CWPA's report, p 27.
27 GNA Accra, ADM 45/5/1, pp 135–7, Medical 1928–9.
28 GNA Sunyani, Goaso District Files G. 22/1928, Infectious Diseases, Dec. 1928.
29 *Loc. cit.*
30 *Loc. cit.*
31 GNA Kumasi, Acc 2050, 4 Aug. 1928, CWPA to ACCA.
32 GNA Accra, DMA 45/5/1, pp 135–7, Medical 1926.
33 *Loc. cit.* 1926/7.
34 GNA Sunyani, Goaso District Files, G. 22/1928, Infectious Diseases 1929. GNA Accra, ADM 49/5/1, 15, 19 and 23 Oct. 1929.
35 *Loc. cit.* 23 Oct. 1929.
36 *Loc. cit.* 25 Oct. 1929.
37 GNA Kumasi, Acc 219, Annual Report 1929/30, Public Health, para 90.
38 GNA Kumasi, Acc 1699, Handing Over Report, 1 Oct. 1929.
39 GNA Accra, ADM 49/5/1, 24 March 1930.

40 GNA Accra, ADM 49/5/2, 23 June 1930, para 31.
41 *Loc. cit.*
42 GNA Accra, ADM 49/5/2, 24 June 1930.
43 *Loc. cit.* 23 June 1930.
44 This claim is based on observation and on the responses of a large proportion of illiterate men and women in interviews.
45 GNA Sunyani, Goaso District Files, G. 22/1928, Infectious Diseases, 1939.
46 Interview with A. W. Osei.
47 GNA Accra, ADM 49/4/2, pp 274ff.
48 GNA Accra, ADM 49/4/6, Sept.–Dec. 1937.
49 GNA Accra, ADM 54/1/4, 345/09.
50 GNA Sunyani, Goaso District Files, Acc 56/69.
51 *Loc. cit.* Area Committee Meeting, 21 Dec. 1949.
52 GNA Accra, ADM 51/5/6, pp 330–2, Ahafo Area Committee.
53 *Loc. cit.* p 354, Ahafo Area Committee, July–Sept. 1950.
54 *Legislative Assembly Debates*, 1953 (1), 11 Feb. 1953, 118–19; 1953 (3), 5 Nov. 1953, 86; 1954 (1), 3 Feb. 1954, 60–1.
55 *Legislative Assembly Debates*, 1953(1), 5 March 1953, 965–6; 1953(2), 14 July 1953, 376–7, 17 July 1953, 643; 1954(1), 8 Feb. 1954, 174–5. GNA Sunyani, Sunyani District Files 515, Ahafo Information Service Panel Meeting, 13 Dec. 1952. Interview with B. F. Kusi, Summer 1969.
56 *Debates*, 1954(3), 5 Nov. 1953, 87–8.
57 *Debates*, 1954(3), 28 Oct. 1954, 117.
58 GNA Sunyani, Goaso District Files, Acc 50/69, Jan.–March 1956.
59 *Loc. cit.*
60 GNA Sunyani, Goaso District Files, Acc 114/69, 5 and 6.
61 GNA Sunyani, Goaso District Files, Acc 136/69, p 33, item 10.
62 *Parliamentary Debates*, vol 6, 7 June 1957, 622, 13 June 1957, 814–16, 26 June 1957, 1359; see also vol 11, 23 July 1958, 931.
63 GNA Sunyani, Sunyani District Archives, File 518, Inspecting Pharmacist, Ashanti to Principal Medical Officer, Ministry of Health, Kumasi, 23 Sept. 1957.
64 *Parliamentary Debates*, vol 3, 21 Jan. 1957, 138–9.
65 *Debates*, vol 23, 8 May 1961, 429.
66 *Debates*, vol 11, 28 July 1958, 931–2.
67 The details of the progress of the administrative decisions on the Goaso Health Centre were given to me in interviews with senior civil servants in the Ministry of Health in 1969. But I was (very properly) not permitted to inspect the files in question myself.
68 *Debates*, vol 12, 10 Dec. 1958, 313.
69 GNA Sunyani, Sunyani District Files 518, 29 June 1959, Kukuomhene to Medical Officer, Central Hospital, Sunyani.
70 *Debates*, vol 21, 23 Nov. 1960, 36.
71 Though a little more information was provided, ungraciously enough, in 1962 (*Debates*, vol 26, 9 Feb. 1962, 269–70). The defensive tone of C. E. Donkoh, C.P.P. member for Wenchi, who had worked in Goaso as research assistant with the American anthropologist Lystad some years earlier perhaps indicates an awareness of the lack of moral plausibility of the government's planning at the receiving (or, as in this case, the non-receiving) end.
72 *Debates*, vol 35, 17 March 1964, 202.
73 *Debates*, vol 33, 20 Sept. 1963, 82.
74 *Debates*, vol 23, 27 April 1961, 263 and vol 26, 15 Feb. 1962, 395.
75 District Administrative Office, Goaso, File GS.4, Water Supply General, is the source of all subsequent details on the water supply problems of Ahafo.
76 See e.g. Polly Hill, *The Gold Coast Cocoa Farmer* (London 1956), pp 130–1.
77 GNA Accra, ADM 11/1309, report, 19 Aug. 1913 to CWPA.
78 GNA Kumasi, Acc 1722, CWPA, to Supt. Prisons, Accra, 9 April 1913, paras 3

and 5 and CWPA to CCA, 16 Sept. 1913; GNA Kumasi, Acc 158, CWPA to CCA, 16 March 1914.
79 GNA Kumasi, Acc 1722, CWPA to Supt. Prisons, Accra, 9 April 1913, para 3.
80 GNA Kumasi, Acc 158, 12 and 22 Aug. 1913.
81 *Loc. cit.* 15 Dec. 1913.
82 *Loc. cit.* 16 March 1914, para 2.
83 GNA Kumasi, Acc 612, 14 and 15 March 1914.
84 *Loc. cit.* 14 March 1914.
85 GNA Kumasi, Acc 158, 16 March 1914, para 1; GNA Kumasi, Acc 612, 15 March 1914.
86 Cardinall, *Ashanti and Beyond*, p 70.
87 GNA Kumasi, Acc 612, 12, 13 and 19 Oct. 1914.
88 Cardinall, *Ashanti and Beyond*, pp 70, 75.
89 GNA Kumasi, Acc 612, 26 and 27 Feb. 1915 and 1 March 1915.
90 *Loc. cit.* 25 and 27 Feb. 1915.
91 *Annual Colonial Report. Ashanti, 1916*, p 20.
92 GNA Kumasi, Acc 1900, 3, 5 and 7 Feb. 1917.
93 GNA Kumasi, Acc 491, 14 May 1926.
94 GNA Kumasi, Acc 1633, Census on Compounds.
95 GNA Kumasi, Acc 1719, Census Report, sections 47–51.
96 GNA Kumasi, Acc. 2499, Handing Over Notes, May 1923, Section 5: Rebuilding of Towns.
97 GNA Kumasi, Acc 2426, 2 Jan. 1924.
98 *Loc. cit.* 7 Dec. 1923.
99 For the use of residential resettlement as a means of control see e.g. Georges Balandier, *Sociologie actuelle de l'Afrique noire* (2nd edn., Paris 1963), pp 172–4, 362–3; and for a more extreme example see Pierre Bourdieu and Abdelmalek Sayad, *Le Déracinement* (Paris 1964). The control aimed at in Ahafo was an altogether less nervous and more delicate matter.
100 GNA Accra, ADM 45/5/1, pp 151–2. But note the dramatic retrenchment in 1930/1.
101 *Loc. cit.* pp 135–6.
102 *Loc. cit.*
103 GNA Kumasi, Acc 2276, 6 March 1923, CWPA to CCA.
104 GNA Kumasi, Acc 1699, Handing Over Notes, 21 Dec. 1927, 16: Sanitation.
105 GNA Kumasi, Acc 1688, 12, 19 and 23 Aug. 1927, 12 Land 17 Sept. 1927; GNA Kumasi, Acc 2517, item 100, 26 Oct. 1929.
106 GNA Kumasi, Acc 2426, Sanitary Report, Ashanti, 1926/7, p 28.
107 GNA Accra, ADM 49/5/2, 14 July 1930.
108 GNA Accra, ADM 45/5/2, pp 40–1; GNA Kumasi, Acc 2509, Report on Sunyani & Goaso districts, p 4.
109 GNA Kumasi, Acc 2270, items 4–10, esp. letters 18 Feb. 1930, 1 and 11 March 1930; GNA Accra, ADM 49/5/1, 10 and 12 March 1930.
110 GNA Kumasi, Acc 2426; GNA Kumasi, Acc 10, Sanitary Report, p 25.
111 GNA Accra, ADM 45/5/1, pp 135–7, April–Sept. 1926.
112 *Loc. cit.* 1926/7.
113 GNA Accra, ADM 49/5/1, 2 Nov. 1929.
114 GNA Accra, ADM 49/5/2, 6 Aug. 1930: 'As a reminder that orders are to be obeyed I am going to knock down his own dilapidated compound together with seventeen others.'
115 *Loc. cit.*: 'I find these people when they say a thing unlike some of the Ashantis usually intend carrying it out.'
116 GNA Accra, ADM 49/5/2, 23 July 1930.
117 GNA Accra, ADM 12/5/37, 10 June 1931.
118 GNA Kumasi, Acc 1928, 27 May 1931.
119 GNA Kumasi, Acc 2499, Handing-over notes, 3 Dec. 1927, p 18.
120 GNA Kumasi, Acc 2426; 31 Dec. 1926, CWPA to M.O. Sunyani.

121 GNA Kumasi, Acc 1928, 26 May 1931.
122 GNA Accra, ADM 49/5/3.

c, i. '*Godliness*', *pp 121–36*

1 No D.C. was stationed permanently in Ahafo until 1914; but frequent visits were made from 1896, and more especially from 1901 onwards. Daily diaries of local commissioners for periods after the early 1930s have not been found in the archives.
2 Cf. Robert Ricard, *The Spiritual Conquest of Mexico* (Berkeley, Calif. 1966), esp. part III; Richard E. Greenleaf, *Zumárraga and the Mexican Inquisition 1536–1543* (Academy of American Franciscan History, Washington D.C. 1961), esp. caps III, IV, VII and VIII; Pierre Duviols, *La lutte contre les religions autochtones dans le Pérou coloniale* (Lima 1971).
3 GNA Kumasi, Acc 612, diary CWPA, 26 Feb. 1915.
4 *Annual Colonial Report. Ashanti, 1906*, p 4.
5 David Kimble, *A Political History of Ghana, 1850–1928* (Oxford 1963), pp 79–80. For Northern Nigeria, see James S. Coleman, *Nigeria: Background to Nationalism* (Berkeley 1963), pp 133–40. For contrasting interpretations of the commitments of the British administration in the area see Robert Heussler, *The British in Northern Nigeria* (London 1968) and I. F. Nicolson, *The Administration of Nigeria, 1900–1960* Oxford 1969).
6 GNA Accra, ADM 1137, Typed notes on the country of Ahafo, 10 July 1899.
7 T. C. McKaskie, 'Innovational Eclecticism: The Asante Empire and Europe in the Nineteenth Century', *Comparative Studies in Society and History*, 14:1 (Jan. 1972), 30–45.
8 Ivor Wilks, *The Northern Factor in Ashanti History* (Legon 1961), pp. 14–29 and *idem*, 'The Position of Muslims in Metropolitan Ashanti in the early nineteenth century', in I. M. Lewis (ed.), *The Influence of Islam in Tropical Africa* (London 1966), pp 318–39.
9 'insolent disposition of the lower orders of Ashantees ... is as vexatious to him as to you' (letter of King of Ashanti to Governor Smith of Cape Coast, 31 Aug. 1817), in Edmund Collins, 'The Panic Element in 19th century British Relations with Ashanti', *Transactions of the Historical Society of Ghana*, v, 2 (1962), 135.
10 GNA Kumasi, Acc 23.
11 A. H. M. Jones and Elizabeth Monroe, *A History of Ethiopia* (Oxford 1966 reprint), pp 97, 73.
12 Heussler, *British in Northern Nigeria*, cap 2.
13 See Norman Daniel, *Islam and the West: The Making of an Image* (Edinburgh 1960) and more briefly R. W. Southern, *Western Views of Islam in the Middle Ages* (Cambridge, Mass. 1962). For the development of this heritage in the period of Imperialism see Norman Daniel, *Islam, Europe and Empire* (Edinburgh 1966).
14 GNA Accra, Sunyani Duplicate letter book, ADM 54/1/2, 145/06.
15 *Loc. cit.* 279/06.
16 GNA Kumasi, Acc 2111, passim.
17 GNA Kumasi, Acc 654, passim.
18 GNA Accra, ADM, 54/1/2, 226/07.
19 GNA Kumasi, Acc 1699, May 1928, Extra handing-over notes by Capt. A. W. Norris, para 6.
20 The irregularity of Beditor's dominant position in Mim as fetish chief was obvious in terms of official Ashanti political norms, a point emphasised in the period after the restoration of the Confederacy (a time when Ahafo was more fully integrated into the forms of proper Ashanti practice than anyone had ever bothered to make it previously), when the Asantehene in his court publicly reaffirmed the complete political subordination of the Komfo stool in Mim to the Mimhene (Institute of African Studies, Legon, *Ashanti Court Records Transcripts*, vol 1, case 9, p 4).
21 GNA Kumasi, Acc 158, esp. letters of 25 May 1914 and 2 June 1914.

22 GNA Kumasi, Acc 612, diary CWPA, 27 May 1914.
23 GNA Accra ADM 45/5/1, WPA Record Book, 109–12.
24 *Loc. cit.*
25 GNA Accra, ADM 11/1309, letter of 1 Aug. 1913, ADC to CWPA.
26 GNA Kumasi, Acc 17, Appendix C, item 6, letters 10 May 1916.
27 GNA Kumasi, Acc 2499, Goaso District handing-over notes, August 1928: Native Affairs.
28 Asanteman Archives, Manhyia, Kumasi, File 7: Ntotroso Native Affairs, 27 June 1940.
29 GNA Accra, ADM 49/5/2, diary 5 June 1930.
30 GNA Accra, ADM 49/5/1, diary Dec. 1929, para 13; and ADM 49/5/2, diary 5 Sept. 1930.
31 GNA Accra, ADM 49/5/1, diary 21 March 1930.
32 GNA Accra, ADM 49/5/3, diary 4 and 6 Nov. 1930.
33 GNA Kumasi, Acc 425.
34 GNA Accra, ADM 11/1309, letter of 19 Aug. 1913.
35 GNA Kumasi, Ashanti District Record Book, 11, Relation of Clan Chiefs to Ahafo, Oct.–Dec. 1937.
36 GNA Kumasi, Acc 2331, pp 153–5.
37 GNA Accra, ADM 49/4/9, Criminal Record Book, Charges against Kwame Wiredu & 8 others, Dec. 1942.
38 GNA Sunyani, Goaso District Files, case 17/37: Fetishes.
39 *Loc. cit.* letter of 28 Aug. 1949.
40 GNA Kumasi, Acc 1719, Administrative Report on Ashanti for 1911, p 15.
41 GNA Kumasi, Ahafo District Record Book, 11, Schools, 109-, Nov. 1943 and July 1949.
42 GNA Kumasi, Acc 377, 28 Sept. and 11 Dec. 1918.
43 GNA Accra, Ahafo Civil Record Book, ADM 49/4/1, 28 March 1922, pp 347–71. The first proper mission community established in Ahafo, the Wesleyan mission at Kukuom under the ex-railway clerk Williams in 1914, began the association between Christianity and the invasion of the Tano (CWPA diary, 21 March 1914–GNA Kumasi, Acc 612). 'Missioner asked to catch fish in Tano R. I told him he could do so at his peril. He asked me to order people to school. Refused but enlarged upon advantages of education.'
44 GNA Accra, Ahafo Civil Record Book, ADM 49/4/1, 28 March 1922: 'The arrangement was to be that the Omanhene of Kukuom has got the Tano river as a sacred thing since the time of our ancestors and if anyone went and fished in it he would be charged £16 and £4 sheep.'
45 The priest himself did not appear in the case as a witness and was presumably. not subpoenaed by either side.

c, ii. '*Good learning*', *pp 137–52*

1 T. C. McKaskie, 'Innovational Eclesticism: the Asante Empire and Europe in the Nineteenth Century', *Comparative Studies in Society and History*, 14:1 (January 1972), 30–45, p 33.
2 Interview, B. F. Kusi, Kumasi, Summer 1969.
3 B. K. Senkyire, Interview, Accra, August 1971.
4 A. W. Osei, speech, Progress Party election rally, Akrodie, 13 July 1969.
5 GNA Accra, ADM/1137, Typed notes on the country of Ahafo, 10 July 1899.
6 GNA Accra, ADM/1137, Armitage's report, 2 Aug. 1901, para 18.
7 *Loc. cit.* para 14.
8 Cf. Richard Cobb, *Les Armées Révolutionnaires* (2 vols Paris 1961–3), vol 2, 645.
9 Given the very heavy archival bias towards the colonial administration's view of the history of its presence in Ahafo.

10 GNA Accra, ADM 12/5/116.
11 See Robert A. Lystad, 'Marriage and Kinship among the Ashanti and the Agni: A Study of Differential Acculturation', in William R. Bascom & Melville J. Herskovits (eds.), *Continuity and Change in African Cultures* (Chicago 1959), p. 190, on the comparative educational development in 1950 of Ahafo and the Agni district centred on Abengourou.
12 GNA Kumasi, Acc 2025, Alleged Christians at Teppa.
13 GNA Kumasi, Acc 35, CWPA to CCA, 25 March 1907; 'after all we are dealing with savages'.
14 GNA Kumasi, Acc 2025; GNA Accra, ADM 54/1/3, letter 12/10. The instructions under discussion in this letter of 11 February 1910 were stigmatised by the Provincial Commissioner Fell as bound to result immediately in 'the subversion of the Chief's authority'.
15 *Annual Colonial Report. Ashanti, 1911*, p 15.
16 GNA Kumasi, Acc 2078, letter of 24 Sept. 1914, D.C. Goaso to CWPA.
17 *Loc. cit.*
18 GNA Kumasi, Acc 2078, letters of CWPA to CCA, 28 Sept. 1914 and CCA to Col. Sec. 5 Oct. 1914. The Governor in fact decided that the school could not be opened for the next year but held out some hopes for 1916 (GNA Kumasi, Acc 1300, letter of 16 Nov. 1914, Col. Sec. to CCA).
19 GNA Kumasi, CCA to Col. Sec. 5 Oct. 1914.
20 GNA Kumasi, Acc 2978, Director of Education's Minute, 14 April 1917.
21 *Loc. cit.* CCA to Col. Sec. 25 April 1917.
22 GNA Kumasi, Acc 377, CWPA diary, 7 Sept. 1918. See diary for 4 to 10 Sept. 1918 for further details of the dispute.
23 *Loc. cit.* CWPA diary, 13 Aug. 1918.
24 The mission superintendent Waterworth threatened to take the matter to the Secretary of State if the decision went against him at Sunyani, Kumasi and Accra *loc. cit.* 5 Sept. 1918.
25 GNA Kumasi, Acc 1719, Census Report 1921, sect. 47–51.
26 *Loc. cit.*
27 GNA Accra ADM 49/4/1, Ahafo Civil Record Book, pp 347–71, 28 March 1922.
28 *Loc. cit.* pp 457–62, 14 March 1923.
29 GNA Accra, ADM 45/5/1, Provincial Record Book WPA, pp 601–2.
30 GNA Sunyani, Sunyani District Record Acc 477, Political Conferences, 4 Sept. 1924. GNA Kumasi, Acc 491, CWPA diaries, 9 Sept. 1924.
31 GNA Kumasi, Acc 179, Half-yearly reports WPA, 1 April 1926–30 Sept. 1926, p 22; GNA Accra, Provincial Record Book WPA, ADM, 45/5/1, Schools 1925–6, pp 601–2.
32 GNA Accra, *loc. cit.* 1926/7.
33 GNA Kumasi, Acc 1699, Handing over reports, Ahafo, 30 May 1927: Education, and 27 June 1927: Education; GNA Kumasi, Ahafo District Record Book, II (1927–1951), p 109.
34 GNA Kumasi, Acc 1699, Handing over report, 17 Oct. 1927.
35 GNA Kumasi, Acc 167, Ahafo Native Affairs, Jan.–Feb. 1928.
36 GNA Kumasi, Ahafo District Record Book, II, 109, 5 June 1928 and Acc 1699, 22 Sept. 1928: Education.
37 GNA Gumasi, Acc 2153, District Agricultural Committee WPA, D.C. Sunyani to CWPA, 29 Feb. 1928.
38 GNA Accra, ADM 45/5/1, Provincial Record Book WPA, 1923–30, p 701; Native Jurisdiction Ordinance, April 1928.
39 GNA Kumasi, Acc 1699, 12 March 1929: Education and Religion.
40 GNA Kumasi, Ahafo District Record Book, II, 109, 1930. By August 1930, however the Omanhene was once again being pressed by an African Presbyterian priest to build (GNA Accra, ADM 49/5/2, D.C.'s diary, 21 Aug. 1930, para 45).
41 GNA Kumasi, Ahafo District Record Book, II, 109-, 1930.

42 GNA Accra, ADM 49/5/2, D.C.'s diary 30 July 1930; GNA Kumasi, Acc 2509, Census of 1931, p 9: Goaso schools.
43 GNA Kumasi, Acc 2509, p 8.
44 GNA Accra ADM 45/5/1, Provincial Record Book WPA, pp 601–2: 1928 General.
45 GNA Accra, ADM 49/5/2, 19 June 1930.
46 GNA Accra, ADM 49/4/2, pp 194–6.
47 GNA Kumasi, Acc 1040, list appended to summons for 6 July 1937, item 11. Kojo Frimpong was destooled in 1935.
48 GNA Kumasi, Acc 76, Annual Reports 1931–2, Report on the Social and Economic progress of the People of West Ashanti, para 9: 'So long as these conditions remain progress on the right lines is assured.'
49 GNA Kumasi, Acc 215, Cocoa, 15 May 1924.
50 GNA Kumasi, Acc 92, Annual Reports 1935–6, Report on the Social and Economic Progress of the People, p 4: 'Education it is hoped will develop public spirit, dissipate animosities, and emphasize obedience to the native authority in the same way as loyalty is today shown to the Crown.'
51 GNA Kumasi, Ahafo District Record Book, II, 387–8: Relation of Kumasi Clan Chiefs to Ahafos, Sept. 1944 (for high hopes initially set upon it as an effective representative against Kumasi); GNA Accra, ADM 51/5/6, Kumasi District Record Book, 330–2, April–June 1950.
52 Though it would be naive to suppose that the normative level has as yet had a great deal to do with the *causation* of its ebbs and flows.
53 Informal questionnaires, Summer 1969.
54 Totals taken from school attendence registers of all Goaso schools, June 1971.
55 GNA Kumasi Ahafo District Record Book, II, 109-, May 1937–March 1938.
56 *Loc. cit.* April 1939.
57 *Loc. cit.* II, Goaso Native Affairs, Sept.–Dec. 1939.
58 *Loc. cit.* II, 387–8: Relation of Kumasi Clan Chiefs to Ahafos, Sept. 1944.
59 GNA Sunyani, Sunyani Schedule C, Acc 219, Ahafo Sub-district Education Committee.
60 GNA Sunyani, Acc 1969, 56/69, Ahafo Area Committee, etc.
61 Lystad in Bascom and Herskovits (eds.), *Continuity and Change*, p 189.
62 GNA Sunyani, Goaso District Schedule C, File C.77, 117 and 119.
63 GNA Sunyani, Goaso District Files, Acc 1969/48, Notes on meeting at Ahafo Court House, 9 April 1958 – claims of stranger-farmers from Dechem etc. and of those from Fawohoyeden.
64 Lystad in Bascom and Herskovits (eds.), *Continuity and Change*, p 201.
65 GNA Kumasi, Ahafo District Record Book, II, 137, 7 Dec. 1953.
66 *Legislative Assembly Debates* (Kusi), 26 March 1953–1962. Senchirey 1954(2), Supplement, 9. Osei, *Parliamentary Debates* 1964, vol 37, 25 Sept. 1964, 85.
67 Interview with Mr Michael Asiedu, Ministry of Education, Accra, 1969.
68 Interviews with B. A. Yeboa-Afari and S. W. Yeboah, former Regional Commissioners for Brong–Ahafo, August 1971. Yeboa–Afari as Regional Commissioner went personally to demarcate the area for the school.

d. 'Political control and political administration', pp 153–73

1 The title of the official representative of the central government charged with administering a district has varied over the last twenty years between District Commissioner, Government Agent and District Administrative Officer. The term 'Administrator' is used here, unless it is important to draw specific attention to the title used at the time in question.
2 These attitudes appeared in a variety of contexts in extended interviews about local political attitudes conducted in Goaso in Spring and Summer 1969.
3 These differences are discussed in chapter 8: 'Party Politics in Ahafo'.
4 See e.g. GNA Accra, ADM 54/5/1, 1,274/04, 13 Dec. 1904: 'It is not possible always to comply with Government Regulations' over the receipt of presents from chiefs.

See also the scale of maximum permissible gifts set for Ashanti as a whole by Commissioner Fuller in 1910 (GNA Kumasi, Acc 1305, 7 June 1910). For more direct corruption see e.g. the reference to the 'fees' taken by Mr Fell's interpreter in Sienchem/Dadiesoaba fishing case (GNA Accra, ADM 49/4/1, 22 April, 593–605).

5 See chapter 6.

6 It is illuminating to contrast the scope of the District Administrator's role with that of the party 'cadre' in the more ideologically ambitious control programme of the Chinese Communist Party, as presented by Franz Schurmann, *Ideology and Organization in Communist China* (2d edn. pb., Berkeley, Calif. 1968).

7 GNA Kumasi, Acc 612, 25 Feb. 1915: 'sounds like too much searching for undercurrents of native intrigue not properly understood and spying on the people with native spies'. And see Governor Clifford's scorn: GNA Accra, ADM, 11/1161. But cf. the Colonial Secretary's minute to the Governor, 1 Oct. 1913, item 3 (GNA Accra, ADM 11/1309).

8 And which no doubt affected even these when they were seen from the dizzy heights of London.

9 See esp. R. Furse, *Acuparius: Recollections of a Recruiting Officer* (London 1962); R. Heussler, *Yesterday's Rulers: The Making of the British Colonial Service* (New York 1963); J. M. Lee, *Colonial Development and Good Government* (Oxford 1967).

10 GNA Accra, ADM 54/1/1, 26/06; GNA Kumasi, Acc 1900, Feb. 1917; GNA Kumasi, Acc 2499, Handing-over notes, 25 Sept. 1925; GNA Kumasi, Acc 202, Quarterly Report on Native Affairs, Sunyani & Goaso District, 17 Oct. 1931, General. Goaso District office was still closed in March 1934, when the district was added to Sunyani district. In April 1937 it was transferred to the Kumasi district (GNA Accra, ADM 54/5/2, p 504).

11 GNA Kumasi, Acc 1624, 12 Sept. 1919.

12 GNA Kumasi, Acc. 1116, 17 Oct. 1916.

13 Quoted by V. G. Kiernan, *The Lords of Human Kind* (pb. edn., Harmondsworth 1972), p xxxiii.

14 GNA Kumasi, Acc 35, 25 March 1907.

15 GNA Kumasi, Acc 1926, 22 Nov. 1931: 'the first thing that struck me was that the Queen Mother looked the best "man" of the lot'.

16 GNA Accra, ADM 49/5/3, 26 and 27 Sept. 1930.

17 GNA Accra, ADM 54/1/1, 42/05, 3 Feb. 1905.

18 *Loc. cit.* 88/05, 17 March 1905.

19 GNA Accra, ADM 54/1/2, 177/07, 2 May 1907. In Ahafo Kukuomhene already had a message stick and two pairs of handcuffs at this time and it was decided to present Beditor with a message stick (one of the new plainer type, not one of the old ones with a raised crown, like Kukuomhene's) and *one* pair of handcuffs (GNA Kumasi, Acc 1926, 19 Dec. 1931).

20 GNA Kumasi, Acc 1926, *loc. cit.* and GNA Accra, ADM 54/1/4, 436/09, CWPA to Kukuomhene: 'I do not understand your complaint as to Chief Beditor and his "Royal Staff" as you call it. Chief Beditor was given a Govt message stick, as were all the other subchiefs in the Province and there was no need to give you any information as to his receiving it.'

21 GNA Kumasi, Acc 6, 4 Jan. 1906, p 40.

22 GNA Kumasi, Acc 1928, 3 Dec. 1931.

23 GNA Kumasi, Acc 377, 3 Sept. 1918.

24 GNA Accra, ADM 1/1309, 24 Dec. 1929, CCA to Col. Sec.

25 Cf Walter Ullmann, *Principles of Government and Politics in the Middle Ages* (London 1961), esp. Introduction.

26 In interviews conducted in Goaso in 1969 the performance of the Administrator was assessed with much more favour than that of chiefs by most ordinary citizens. But only a small proportion of those who were not themselves literate government officials gave any indication of viewing him as someone whose aid might be accessible to them at an individual level.

27 GNA Accra, ADM 49/5/1, 18 March 1930.
28 GNA Kumasi, Acc 1928, 21 Aug. 1930, CCA to CWPA; and see discussion of his diary with D.C. Goaso by CWPA, *loc. cit.* 7–9 June 1930.
29 GNA Accra, ADM 49/5/2, 11 Aug. 1930.
30 The classic commentary on colonial fantasies of control – in no way invalidated by historical study of the vicissitudes of colonial rule in Ahafo – is Joyce Cary's *Mister Johnson* (pb. edn., Harmondsworth 1962).
31 GNA Accra, ADM 11/1309, Col. Sec.'s minute to Governor, 1 Oct. 1913.
32 *Loc. cit.* Governor's minute, 17 Nov. 1916. And note the complaint of the Secretary for Native Affairs, seven years later, in his minute of 16 Aug. 1923 that the government in Accra had never been informed either of the deposition of one Omanhene or of the election of another.
33 GNA Accra, ADM 49/5/1, 19 Sept. 1929.
34 GNA Accra, ADM 54/1/4, 153/09, 13 April 1909.
35 GNA Accra, ADM 49/5/1, 26 Nov. 1920 (looking for a suitable tree for a flagpole in Goaso – 'the present pole is too short') and GNA Accra, ADM 54/1/5, 467/11, 10 Dec. 1929.
36 GNA Accra, ADM 54/1/1, 95/05, 8 April 1905.
37 GNA Kumasi, Acc 491, 30 June 1925 (Princess Marie Louise); GNA Accra, ADM 49/2/1, 15 May 1925 (Governor), etc.
38 See notes 19 and 20 above.
39 GNA Accra, ADM, 49/2/1, 25 May 1927; GNA Sunyani, Goaso District Files, G. 14/28, Empire Day celebrations.
40 *Parliamentary Debates*, vol 9, 19 Feb. 1958, 11.
41 GNA Kumasi, Acc 2378, 12 May 1925, ACWPA to CCA.
42 GNA Sunyani, Sunyani District Files, 515, Public Relations Advisory, Meeting of Ahafo Information Service Panel, 13 Dec. 1952, chaired by T. K. Impraim, the Government Agent, later Secretary to the President until the February 1966 coup. 'A member stated that he had been informed by the Odikro of Teppa that during the Prime Minister's last visit there the latter enquired whether those who attended the meeting were the entire subjects of the Odikro as apparently the Prime Minister had been disappointed at the size of the crowd; the Odikro had shown some concern at the Prime Minister's query and so wanted to know whether an Odikro and all his subjects must necessarily turn up to meet the Prime Minister, whenever he was touring the country in his capacity as leader of his party. The Chairman replied that he did not know whether the Odikro was being queried as a member of the Convention People's Party or as a Chief; if as a member of the party, then the matter was a purely private one and did not concern the Panel. But if the Prime Minister implied that the whole subjects of a state should turn out to meet him as leader of the Convention People's Party irrespective of the fact that such subjects were not all members of that party, then the point needed establishing. The meeting therefore decided that the Assistant Information Officer should take up the matter with the authorities concerned to see whether a ruling could be obtained.'
43 *Loc. cit.*
44 GNA Kumasi, Acc 2134.
45 GNA Accra, ADM 54/1/5, 440/11, 26 Sept. 1911.
46 GNA Kumasi, Acc 612, 21 Oct. 1914.
47 GNA Kumasi, Acc 377, 25 May 1918.
48 GNA Kumasi, Acc 2131; GNA Accra, ADM, 49/5/1, 9 Oct. 1929; GNA Kumasi, Acc 1699, Handing-over report, 19 Nov. 1928, p 3 (896 new poppies received for sale in Ahafo this year); GNA Kumasi, Acc 491, 22 Oct. 1925, CWPA diary: 'Distributed Poppies to be sold on Poppy Day. Informed that Omanhene of Goaso (*sic*) will guarantee £20, so send this amount to him with letter of thanks. If other Amanhin follow his example this Province will do well.'
49 GNA Accra, ADM 49/5/3, 10 Dec. 1930.
50 GNA Kumasi, Acc 377, 4 Sept. 1918. And see GNA Accra, ADM 49/5/2, 12 Sept.

1930: 'The Odikro of Ntotrosu arrived. I explained the arbitration and gave him the paper I wish him to sign that he might go away and read it. His remark was "we black men are not good yet and with an African Arbitrator Atroni will probably be rude and I may be annoyed and be rude too." I am afraid there is something in what he says.'

51 GNA Kumasi, Acc 1926.
52 GNA Accra, ADM, 12/4/12, 1 April 1947, unlawful assault case at pp 200–22, involving Chiefs of Ayumso and Goaso, Native Authority Police and the Tribunal Registrar, James Nyarko Essel (currently stool clerk in Kukuom). All the defendants were in fact acquitted on the evidence of the Kukuomhene. Essel was accused of having said that the victim of the assault could be beaten until he died. For earlier examples of irregularities see e.g. GNA Accra, ADM 49/5/3, 4 Oct. 1930, Kukuom clerk and two N.A. policemen accused of locking up two men in the Chief's prison and extorting money from them on the pretext of their having unlicensed guns. Reports of violence in the vicinity of *Ahenfie* are common in relation to the major political clashes of 1956/7.
53 GNA Kumasi, Acc 377, 25 May 1918.
54 See e.g. GNA Accra, ADM 49/5/2, 20 May 1930.
55 GNA Kumasi, Acc 1928, 30 Dec. 1931.
56 This process has been admirably chronicled in relation to Ashanti in William Tordoff, *Ashanti under the Prempehs 1888–1935* (London 1965).
57 GNA Kumasi, Ahafo District Record Book, II, 1927–51, Financial Relationship between the Clan Chiefs and the Ahafo Villages, and Goaso Native Affairs, April 1938–Dec. 1939. Cf. also the charge that the Ntotrosohene had been 'uncustomary' in not sending fines for sanitary offences to the Asantehene (charges against Ntotrosohene, D.C. Kumasi to Asantehene, 17 May 1940, Asanteman Archives, Manhyia, File 7, Ntotrosu Native Affairs).
58 Tordoff, *Ashanti under the Prempehs*.
59 GNA Kumasi, Acc 1699, Extra handing-over notes by Capt. A. W. Norris, 28 May 1928.
60 The precision of the administration's historical tradition also sometimes left something to be desired.
61 In the first three decades of colonial rule in Ahafo the main themes of boundary disputes were rights of hunting and gathering over land: ivory, game, fish, rubber and above all the snail harvests. Thousands of hours of Administrator's efforts must have been consigned in these years to the arbitration of rights of snail-gathering alone. In more recent decades boundaries have been slightly less easy to shift by political or commercial pressures (though a change of national government still arouses the optimism of many). Furthermore the increase in the potential rewards in terms of the control of cocoa land and timber has been so considerable that the skein of traditional ownership is still being tugged fiercely in different directions.
62 GNA Kumasi, Acc 377, 26 and 27 Sept. 1918.
63 GNA Accra, ADM 49/5/1, 22 Dec. 1929: 'I suppose that, as usual, the man who can bribe the Elders most heavily will get the stool.'
64 GNA Kumasi, Acc 1699, Handing-over notes, 27 June 1927, 17: Mim Subdivision Native Affairs.
65 GNA Kumasi, Acc. 167, 68 (diary for July 1928, *e*).
66 PRO Davidson Houston's report, CO 96/275, 30 June 1896, Treaty IV.
67 PRO Vroom's report, CO 96/295, 19 June 1897 (incl. in Maxwell to Chamberlain, 14 July 1897, p 37).
68 *Loc. cit.* p 6.
69 GNA Accra, ADM 54/1/2, 144/06.
70 GNA Kumasi, Acc 1068, Kukuomhene's letter, 11 Dec. 1909.
71 GNA Accra, ADM 54/1/5, 11, 13 Nov. 1911.
72 GNA Accra, ADM 11/1309, Col. Sec.'s minute to Governor, 1 Oct. 1913.
73 GNA Kumasi, Acc 1850, 26 April 1919: Akwaboa chief illicitly visiting Mim for

six months – on pretext of attending funeral which took place some time before he set out – and interfering in stool affairs, sitting with the elders to try the chief, etc.

74 See the whole file GNA Kumasi, Acc 27.
75 GNA Kumasi, Acc 612, 12 Dec. 1916.
76 See chapter 6, below.

5. 'Chiefship and the community', pp 174–222

1 Essay by John Felix Aidoo, Acherensua secondary school.
2 National Liberation Council Decree, no 112, December 1966.
3 This commission, under the chairmanship of Mr Justice Bannerman, was set up in 1967 to enquire into boundaries and proprietary rights over Ahafo lands. Its activities were suspended in 1968.
4 Essay by Attah Effah Frimpong, Acherensua, Acherensua secondary school.
5 M. J. Field, *Akim-Kotoku: an Oman of the Gold Coast* (London 1948), p 29.
6 R. S. Rattray, *Ashanti Law and Constitution* (Oxford 1929), p. 1.
7 *Ibid.* p. 88.
8 Essay cited in note 4 above.
9 Nkasaimhene explained: 'Before, only the Asantehene, Kokofuhene, Juabenhene, Mamponghene and Kumawuhene [the states of the Ashanti Confederacy] had Sanaahene. The Sanaahene used to be treasurer but we as villagers had no money so there was no need for this. The Sanaahene was formerly in the big towns but not, as now, in the villages . . . I don't get paid so there is no need for Sanaahene.'
10 Anwiamhene explained: 'When there is trouble [the elders] have to sit together and settle it. When something comes in from outside they have to tackle it. They are always close to the stool and when trouble crops up they have to settle it.'
11 Cf. K. A. Busia, *The Position of the Chief in the Modern Political System of Ashanti* (London 1951), pp 9ff.
12 *Memorandum on the Proposals for a Constitution for Ghana* (Accra 1968), sects 643 and 644.
13 *Loc. cit.* sect 637.
14 Ministry of Local Government and Housing circular no LAC 12/52, 4 Dec. 1952.
15 The State Councils (Ashanti) Ordinance, no 4 of 1952, sect 2 (1).
16 The Chieftaincy Act, no 81, 1961, sect 2.
17 *Loc. cit.* sect 1.
18 Circular from the Permanent Secretary to the Ministry of the Interior and Local Government, no 689/SF.8, 21 Nov. 1961.
19 Legislative Instrument no 309 of 1963.
20 GNA Kumasi, 30/59, letter from the Secretary to the Regional Commissioner Sunyani to the D.C.s of Sunyani, Wenchi, Goaso and Atebubu, 30 July 1960.
21 Kukuom–Ahafo State Council minutes, 16 Aug. 1962.
22 *Memorandum on the Proposals for a Constitution for Ghana*, sect 635, 643, 644 and 646.
23 *Constitution of the Republic of Ghana* (Accra 1969), sect 153.
24 Essay by John Arhin, Acherensua secondary school.
25 A. F. Robertson, 'Histories and Political Opposition in Ahafo, Ghana, *Africa* XLIII, 1 (1973).
26 These 'sons' of the Tano river are discussed in detail by R. S. Rattray in *Ashanti* (Oxford 1923) and *Religion and Art in Ashanti* (Oxford 1927).
27 These were: 7 Roman Catholics, 6 Methodists, 1 Anglican, 1 Seventh Day Adventist, 2 members of spiritual churches, 1 unspecified 'Christian', 1 lapsed Moslem. Previous affiliations had included the principal Christian churches as well as more ephemeral sects such as 'Nkansah the Miracle Man'.
28 Essay by S. K. Amoako, Acherensua secondary school.
29 The Ashanti Confederacy Council, pressed by the Colonial authorities, enquired into these affairs in detail in 1952, eventually drawing up a new schedule of regula-

tions. There is not much evidence, at least at the lower levels of chiefship, of these regulations being adhered to. Cf. the Report of the Committee Appointed by the Asanteman Council at its June 1952 Session to Study and make Recommendations as to Native Law and Custom with Special Reference to the Enstoolment and destoolment of Chiefs. Typescript in the Asanteman archives, Kumasi.

30 On one occasion when we had arranged a meeting with a chief in this predicament he received us lying on a mattress outside his room, speaking feebly and refreshing himself with orange juice. The drama of his contrived malady was dissipated by the helpless mirth of the townspeople who had followed us into his courtyard.

31 Kukuom–Ahafo State Council record book, Sienchem Destoolment Dispute, 10 May 1966.

32 Goaso Local Council file N3, copy of letter dated 30 Sept. 1958.

6. 'Politics of the Ahafo State', pp 223–85

1 In 1960 the Aniwiamhene declined an invitation to a durbar of chiefs at Sunyani on the grounds that he was engaged in land litigation with the Ashanti chief of Nkawie and was therefore reluctant to appear in public. Kukuom–Ahafo State Council minutes, 6 Dec. 1960.

2 A. A. Y. Kyerematen, *Inter-State Boundary Litigation in Ashanti* (Leiden 1971), p 50.

3 Cf. *ibid*. pp 48–51.

4 Executive Instrument no 46 (Stool Lands Instrument, 1961), supp. to the *Ghana Gazette* no 12, 3 March 1961

5 In May 1968 the 45 per cent share of revenue constituting the Development and Scholarship fund due to the three Local Councils in Ahafo amounted to NC25,034.39. A similar proportion was withheld in respect of the 'traditional authorities' of Ahafo.

6 National Liberation Council Decree no 49 of 1966.

7 The Administration of Lands Act, no 123 of 1958.

8 Goaso District Office file LA4, vol 2, 149.

9 GNA Kumasi, D1491, District Commissioner Butler to Chief Commissioner Ashanti, 14 Dec. 1939.

10 National Liberation Council Lands Secretariat circular letter no 18198/4/63, dated 6 May 1968.

11 W. Tordoff, *Ashanti under the Prempehs 1888–1935* (London 1965) p 162n.

12 Cf. R. S. Rattray, *Ashanti Law and Constitution* (Oxford 1929), 94ff.

13 This aspect of the current schism in Ahafo is discussed in detail in A. F. Robertson, 'Histories and Political Opposition in Ahafo, Ghana', *Africa*, XLIII, 1 (1973).

14 Aboumhene was born in Mim, Dantanohene in Mim, Goasohene in Mim, Kwakunyumahene in Dadiesoaba, Wamahinsohene in Kenyase I. Asufufuohene was born in Nkawie, and Ayumsohene in Antoa, both in Ashanti.

15 He was in fact made a subject chief of Dantanohene, who was ranked as Gyasehene to the state.

16 GNA Accra, D. 166, 9 June 1932.

17 Copy of document in the possession of Kukuomhene.

18 GNA Accra, Ahafo District Record Book, II, 1927–51, ADM 49/5/7.

19 Cf. K. A. Busia, *The Position of the Chief in the Modern Political System of Ashanti* (London 1951), pp 192–3.

20 As late as November 1957, when conflict with the Kukuomhene over the state council issue was at its height, Mimhene was moved to address a complaint to the Asantehene about the conduct of the Kumasi wing chiefs. Goaso Local Council file L4, letter dated 9 Nov. 1957.

21 Meyerowitz reports the establishment of an entente between Techimanhene and Dr Nkrumah as early as December 1952. E. L. Meyerowitz, *At the Court of an African King* (London 1962), p 230.

22 Copy of document in the possession of Kukuomhene.
23 *Ghana Gazette*, LN 47, no 14, 8 Feb. 1958.
24 *Hansard*, 11 cols 326–9.
25 Document in possession of Kukuomhene, dated 7 March 1958.
26 *Ghana Gazette* no 50. 3 June 1958.
27 Goaso District Office file L.52, letter dated 1 Sept. 1958.
28 Goaso Local Council file N3, letter dated 30 Sept. 1958.
29 Kukuom–Ahafo State Council minutes, 10 April 1958.
30 *Loc. cit.*
31 Goaso Local Council file N3, letter dated 3 Nov. 1958.
32 Goaso District Office file L.52, letter dated 21 March 1959.
33 Kukuom–Ahafo State Council minutes, 15 July 1958.
54 *Loc. cit.* 16 Nov. 1962.
55 *Loc. cit.* 27 Sept. 1959, 14 June 1962 and 4 Aug. 1964.
36 Kukuom–Ahafo State Council minutes, 28 Dec. 1959.
37 Goaso District Office file L.47, vol 2, dated 30 Sept. 1960.
38 Kukuom–Ahafo State Council minutes, 8 March 1960.
39 *Ghana Gazette* no 496, 7 March 1959.
40 Goaso District Office file LA10, letter dated 5 Dec. 1961.
41 *Loc. cit.* letter dated 3 March 1962.
42 *Loc. cit.* vol. 2, letter dated 24 March 1965.
43 Kukuom–Ahafo State Council minutes, 14 June 1962.
44 One of which we were permitted to attend in 1968.
45 Kukuom–Ahafo State Council minutes, 30 April 1962.
46 Goaso District Office file LA19, letters dated 4 May 1962 and 7 Aug. 1963.
47 Kukuom–Ahafo State Council minutes, 7 July 1963.
48 Kukuom–Ahafo State Council Standing Committee minutes, 20 Sept. 1963.
49 Kukuom–Ahafo State Council minutes, 28 Sept. 1961.
50 Goaso District Office file LA19, letter dated 15 April 1964.
51 Kukuom–Ahafo State Council minutes, 16 Aug. 1966.
52 *Loc. cit.* 1 Oct. 1964.
53 *Loc. cit.* 16 Aug. 1962.
54 *Loc. cit.* 16 Nov. 1962.
55 *Loc. cit.* 27 Sept. 1959, 14 June 1962 and 4 Aug. 1964.
56 *Loc. cit.* 28 Dec. 1962.
57 *Loc. cit.* 16 Nov. 1962.
58 *Loc. cit.* 28 Dec. 1962.
59 *Loc. cit.* 28 March 1961.
60 *Loc. cit.* 18 Nov. 1961
61 Kukuom–Ahafo State Council Record Book, 5 July 1965.
62 Kukuom–Ahafo State Council minutes, 4 Aug. 1964.
63 *Loc. cit.* 6 Dec. 1960.
64 *Loc. cit.* 29 Aug. 1966.
65 *Loc. cit.* 22 March 1962.
66 Press release issued by the Ministry of Information and Broadcasting on behalf of the Ministry of Justice, no 731/60, Goaso District Office file LA47, vol 2.
67 Kukuom–Ahafo State Council minutes, 2 April 1962.
68 Goaso District Office File LA4, vol 6, letters from the queen mother and elders of Nkasaim to the Chairman of the Brong–Ahafo Regional Administrative Committee, dated 4 June 1966.
69 Goaso District Office file LA4, vol 4, letter dated 6 May 1963.
70 Kukuom–Ahafo State Council minutes, 10 Feb. 1962.
71 Goaso District Office file LA4, vol 4, letters dated 26 March 1963.
72 *Loc. cit.* letter dated 6 May 1963.
73 Goaso District Office file LA4, vol 7, letter dated 31 Oct. 1963.
74 Kukuom–Ahafo State Council minutes, 28 Nov. 1963.

75 Goaso District Office file LA4, vol 4, 'Minutes of a meeting held at Goaso on Saturday 15th February, 1964, by Mim Stool Elders'.
76 Kukuom–Ahafo State Council Record Book, 5 April 1966.
77 Kukuom–Ahafo State Council minutes, 10 March 1966.
78 *Loc. cit.* 16 Aug. 1966.
79 Mainly by National Liberation Council Decrees nos 112, 136 and 203, but also in five cases on the initiative of their own townspeople.
80 Goaso District Office file LA4, vol 7, letter dated 2 March 1967.
81 *Loc. cit.* letter dated 3 Feb. 1968.
82 *Loc. cit.* letter dated 21 Dec. 1966.
83 *Loc. cit.* petition addressed to the Asantehene dated 12 March 1967.
84 *Loc. cit.* 'Summons to Meeting – Ahafo District Chiefs', 3 Aug. 1967.
85 Copy of a petition dated 26 April 1968, in the possession of Kukuomhene.
86 Goaso District Office file LA4, vol 7, petition from the Association of Ahafo Chiefs, dated 3 May 1968.
87 *Loc. cit.* letter dated 11 June 1968.
88 On to May 1968 an 'Open Letter to Otumfuo Asantehene' from Aboumhene was published in the '*Pioneer*', a Kumasi daily newspaper. Aboumhene's suggestion that a second open letter should be sent to the *Graphic*, a daily national newspaper published in Accra, was apparently cognate with the meeting's intention to pursue the matter of the state council through to the highest levels of government.
89 The sequel to this meeting was an excursion to Kumasi where Darkwah apparently telephoned 'The Ministry' and discovered that 'the man' was none other than the N.L.C. member Inspector General of Police Mr Harlley, and that the chiefs were to 'wait for some time so that he could go through the paper'. The delegation returned to report back to the Chiefs' Association, but had already agreed provisionally to go to Accra to satisfy themselves that Darkwah was not deceiving them.

7. 'Growth of local government in Ahafo', pp 286–313

1 *Your Council and Your Progress*, published for the Ministry of Local Government and Housing by the Information Services Department (Government Printer, Accra 1953).
2 Cf. Report to H. E. the Governor, Committee on Constitutional Reform, Chairman J. H. Coussey (Colonial Office, London 1949).
3 R. Wraith, *Local Government in West Africa* (London 1964), p 59.
4 *Memorandum on the Proposals for a Constitution for Ghana* (Accra 1968), sect 663.
5 Ahafo Local Council minutes, 30 June 1955.
6 Brong–Ahafo South Local Council minutes, 29 June 1961.
7 Asutifi Local Council minutes, 17 Aug. 1964.
8 Ahafo Local Council minutes, 7 March 1958.
9 *Loc. cit.* 27 May 1958.
10 *Loc. cit.* 18 March 1959.
11 Asunafo Local Council minutes, 1 Oct. 1962.
12 Asutifi Local Council Management Committee minutes, 30 July 1966.
13 A. St J. J. Hannigan, 'Local Government in the Gold Coast', *Journal of African Administration*, vii, 3 (July 1955), 120.
14 Asutifi Local Council minutes, 14 Dec. 1965.
15 Goaso Local Council Management Committee minutes, 16 May 1968.
16 Goaso District Office file A9, vol 4, petition to the Permanent Secretary, Ministry of Local Government, 31 July 1966.
17 Goaso District Office file D1, Ministry of Local Government circular LG166/10, '*Requests for permission to secede from existing enlarged local councils*', 16 Aug. 1961.
18 Asutifi Local Council minutes, 1 Oct. 1962.
19 *Loc. cit.* 21 Dec. 1962.

20 Goaso Local Council file A. 0039, circular dated 20 Dec. 1952.
21 Brong–Ahafo South Local Council minutes, 29 June 1961.
22 Goaso Local Council file A.0060 vol 1, petition dated 30 May 1953.
23 *Loc. cit.* letter dated 11 June 1953.
24 Ahafo Local Council minutes, 22 June 1956.
25 Cf. the Local Government Act no 54, 1961, Cap 24, subsection 1.
26 F. G. Bailey, 'Decisions by consensus in councils and committees', in M. P. Banton (ed.) *Political Systems and the Distribution of Power* (London 1965) p 9ff.
27 Ahafo Local Council minutes, 24 June 1958.
28 Wraith, *Local Government in West Africa*, p 61
29 Asunafo Local Council minutes, 1 Oct. 1962.
30 *Loc. cit.* 2 Oct. 1964.
31 Asutifi Local Council minutes, 30 July 1965.
32 Goaso District Office file LA22, Asutifi Local Council election returns, 5 July 1962.
33 The successor to the Ahafo Local Council.
34 Brong–Ahafo South Local Council minutes, 12 Dec. 1961.
35 *Loc. cit.* 29 Dec. 1961.
36 Local Government Ordinance no 29 of 1951, Cap 44, subsection 1.
37 Goaso Local Council file A. 0054, 12 Oct. 1952.
38 *Loc. cit.* letter dated 6 March 1953.
39 *Loc. cit.* letter dated 28 April 1953.
40 Goaso Local Council file F16, letter dated 25 March 1955.
41 Goaso Local Council file F25, vol 2, Programme and minutes of the first delegates' conference of town/village committees held at Goaso, 29 April 1961.
42 Legislative Instrument no 19 of 1962.
43 Legislative Instrument no 262 of 1963.
44 Goaso Local Council file F25, vol 3, Minutes of the second annual delegates' conference of town/village development committees in Brong–Ahafo South Local Council area, held on Friday 13 April 1962 at Goaso.
45 Legislative Instrument no 540 of 1967.
46 Brong–Ahafo South Local Council minutes, 29 June 1961.
47 Goaso District Office file A9, vol 4, letter dated 4 Dec. 1967.
48 Goaso District Office file A9/SF vol 1, letter dated 24 Sept. 1962.
49 A. F. Robertson, 'The Development of Town Committees in Ahafo, Western Ghana', in A. I. Richards and A. Kuper (eds.) *Councils in Action* (Cambridge 1971), pp 130–70.

8. 'Party politics in Ahafo', pp 314–52

1 The judgements on popular attitudes in 1969 were based on over sixty lengthy interviews with Goaso residents and on informal observation, particularly during the months leading to the election.
2 Jean Jacques Rousseau, *Du Contrat Social*, Bk III, cap xv (*Political Writings*, ed. C. E. Vaughan (Oxford 1962), II, 96).
3 See John Dunn, 'Politics in Asunafo: From Democracy to Representation, an interpretation of a Ghanaian election', in Dennis Austin and Robin Luckham (eds.), *Ghana's Second Republic* (O.U.P. for R.I.I.A. forthcoming).
4 The providential foundation of political legitimacy was an intellectual assumption for many in the seventeenth-century England (see, for a particularly lucid sketch, John Wallace, *Destiny His Choice. The Loyalism of Andrew Marvell* (Cambridge 1968), cap I). The resemblance which is here suggested is one of social expectation and, to some degree, social sentiment, *not* one of overt ideology.
5 The best available account of the basis of opposition to the C.P.P. up to the 1951 election remains Dennis Austin, *Politics in Ghana 1946–1960* (London 1964), caps 2 and 3.

6 See e.g. J. A. Braimah and J. R. Goody, *Salaga: The Struggle for Power* (London 1967), cap 22.
7 For the notion of a public good as used here see Mancur Olson, *The Logic of Collective Action* (Cambridge, Mass. 1965), cap 1. It is not clear how far an expectation of individual economic advantage from membership in the Legislative Assembly influenced candidates in the 1951 election in offering their services. But it is obvious that Senkyire's support from the Kukuom State Council and Osei's timber-felling enterprises reflect the economic advantages accruing to a politician, whether in government or opposition, from the contacts open to an M.P.
8 Mr Adu kindly described his experiences as D.C. in Ahafo to the author in the summer of 1971.
9 This information was given by T. N. Baidoo in an interview in the summer of 1969. All information relating to Baidoo's career which is not otherwise identified is derived from this interview.
10 GNA Accra, ADM 49/4/8, p 4, 14 Sept. 1940.
11 GNA Accra, ADM 49/4/9, 28 April 1943 (and ADM 49/4/10, pp 9–14).
12 Mr Senkyire kindly gave me an interview in Accra in 1971. All information relating to his career which is not otherwise referenced is derived from this interview.
13 GNA Sunyani, Goaso District Files, C. 384.
14 Information relating to B. F. Kusi's career is derived, except where otherwise indicated, from an interview which he kindly gave me in the summer of 1969 in Kumasi.
15 See e.g. the very able analysis of the reasons for the growing inadequacy of native administration in GNA Kumasi, Acc 1672, Relations between Divisional Chiefs and their Youngmen 1943, items 2 and 9.
16 GNA Sunyani, Goaso District Files, Acc 69/1969, p 81.
17 *Loc. cit.* p 46.
18 GNA Sunyani, Sunyani District Files, 585, Chief Commissioner's Confidential Letter 27 Sept. 1950 (and see 584).
19 GNA Sunyani, Goaso District Files, Acc 69/1969, 111.
20 *Loc. cit.* p 105.
21 *Loc. cit,* p 94.
22 *Loc. cit.* p. 97.
23 *Loc. cit.*
24 GNA Sunyani, Goaso District Files, C. 136, 9. And Acc 106/69, 27 Sept. 1951 and 23 Oct. 1951.
25 See *Legislative Assembly Debates*, 1951, 4, 10 Dec. 1951, 646–7. 1952, 1, 18 Feb. 1952, 361; 29 Feb. 1952, 490; 23 April 1952, 1208; 7 March 1952, 1435.: 1952, 1481; 1952, 2, 25 June 1952, 211; 27 June 1952, 266–8; 1 July 1952, 338–9; 4 July 1952, 509 and 511. 1952, 3, 13 Oct. 1952, 351–2 (Cocoa Marketing Board (C.M.B.) funds improperly borrowed by the government). 1953, 1, 11 Feb, 1953, 118–19; 17 Feb. 1953, 283–7, etc.
26 Austin, *Politics in Ghana*, pp 167–8.
27 *Debates*, 1953, 1, 17 Feb. 1953, 285 and 287; 26 March 1953, 1762. 1953, 3, 11 Nov. 1953, 314–15 (Cocoa Purchasing Company (C.P.C.) loans takers instructed to vote against Kusi); 1953, 3, 12 Nov. 1953, 434–40. 1954, 1, 2 March 1954, 1188–94.
28 *Debates*, 1953, 3, 4 Nov. 1953, 56.
29 Austin, *Politics in Ghana*, p 276. The Ghana Congress Party was the official opposition party to the C.P.P. in the south.
30 GNA Sunyani, Goaso District Files, C. 237, 24.
31 Information about Osei is taken from interviews with him in 1969 and 1971.
32 GNA Sunyani, Goaso District Files, C. 237, 29–32.
33 *Report of the Commission of Enquiry into the Affairs of the Cocoa Purchasing Company Ltd* (Government Printer, Accra 1956).
34 Information regarding the C.P.C. loans was obtained by the kindness of the Loans Department of the S.C.M.B. whch has inherited the entitlements of the C.P.C.

35 Asanteman Archives, Manhyia, File 400, Ashanti Farmers Union, Progress Report, 29 July 1955, p 2.
36 *Loc. cit.* p 3.
37 *Loc. cit.* p 6.
38 Austin, *Politics in Ghana*, pp 274–5.
39 *Ibid.* p 276.
40 Asanteman Archives, File 400, Report 29 July 1955, p 5.
41 In addition to the account of Senkyire himself, the following treatment of the negotiations is indebted to interviews kindly given in the summer of 1971 by the first two Regional Commissioners for Brong-Ahafo, B. A. Yeboa-Afari and S. W. Yeboah.
42 *Debates*, 1955, 2, 9 Aug. 1955, 441.
43 *Debates*, 1956–7, 1, 18 May, 1956, 138–41.
44 This useful medieval equivocation is used here as a reminder that, although a durable hegemony within the face-to-face society of a village can hardly subsist *against* the wills of a majority today without the assistance of external force, such a hegemony when it does exist reflects the political influence of socially and economically unequal persons and not necessarily the sentiments of a majority of individuals whose influence is carefully and artificially rendered equal. For a helpful account of medieval balancing of quantitative and qualitative notions of legitimate authority within a community see Alan Gewirth, *Marsilius of Padua and Medieval Political Philosophy* (New York 1951), pp 182–98.
45 GNA Sunyani, Goaso District Files, C. 246.
46 Osei discussed this episode with me in 1969 and 1971. See also *Constituent Assembly Debates*, 13 June 1960, 185.
47 GNA Sunyani, Goaso District Files, Acc 38/1969, Quarterly Report, Jan.–March 1958.
48 *Loc. cit.*
49 GNA Sunyani, Goaso District Files, Acc 38/1969, Quarterly Report, July–Sept. 1958.
50 *Loc. cit.*
51 GNA Sunyani, Goaso District Files, C. 117, 30 Sept. 1958, Regional Commissioner to Prime Minister.
52 *Loc. cit* note 49 above.
53 *Loc. cit.*
54 *Loc cit.* Quarterly Report, Oct.–Dec. 1958.
55 Austin, *Politics in Ghana*, pp 379–80.
56 GNA Sunyani, Goaso District Files, Acc 38/1969, Quarterly Report, Oct.–Dec. 1958.
57 GNA Sunyani, Goaso District Files, C. 439.
58 *Loc. cit.* note 49 above.
59 *Debates*, 1956–7, 1, 138–41, 144–5.
60 *Debates*, xiv, 20 March 1959, 438–60.
61 *Debates*, xv, 11 June 1959, 60.
62 See note 44 above.
63 Austin, *Politics in Ghana*, pp 273–4n.
64 GNA Sunyani, Goaso District Files, Acc 71/1969, 323,
65 GNA Sunyani, Goaso District Files, Acc 44/1969.
66 GNA Sunyani, Goaso District Files, C. 235, 1.
67 GNA Sunyani, Goaso District Files, Acc 50/1969, Quarterly Report, Jan.–March 1956, 178.
68 *Loc. cit.* Kumasi District Jan.–March 1956, 185 etc.
69 *Loc. cit.* April–June 1956, Ahafo Local Council, 190 (7 and 8).
70 *Loc. cit.*
71 GNA Sunyani, Goaso District Files, Acc 136/1969, 34, 10 Aug. 1956.
72 *Loc. cit.*
73 *Loc. cit.* note 69 above.

74 GNA Sunyani, Goaso District Files, Acc 72/1969, 47; and see file minutes of 22 May 1956 and 2 June 1956.
75 GNA Sunyani, Goaso District Files, Acc 38/1969, Oct.–Dec. 1956, Ahafo Native Court C.
76 GNA Sunyani, Goaso District Files, C. 235, 5.
77 *Loc. cit.* 6.
78 *Loc. cit.* 7
79 *Loc. cit.* 8.
80 *Loc. cit.* 10.
81 *Loc. cit.* 3 and 4.
82 *Loc. cit.* 26.
83 *Loc. cit.* 13.
84 GNA Sunyani, Goaso District Files, Acc 72/1969, 81–2.
85 GNA Sunyani, Goaso District Files, 114/1969, 5, 4 June 1956
86 GNA Sunyani, Goaso District Files, C. 235, 12.
87 GNA Sunyani, Goaso District Files, Acc 146/1969, 33.
88 *Loc. cit.* 44.
89 The Mim Chief's oath. For the significance of swearing the stool oath see R. S. Rattray, *Religion and Art in Ashanti* (London 1927), cap XXII and K. A. Busia, *The Position of the Chief in the Modern Political System of Ashanti* (2nd edn., London 1968), cap IV, esp. 75–8. And see chapter 5(*b*) above.
90 GNA Sunyani, Goaso District Files, Acc 146/1969, 52.
91 GNA Sunyani, Goaso District Files, Acc 136/1969, 30, 10 Aug. 1956.
92 GNA Sunyani, Goaso District Files, Acc 50/1969, 199, Jan.–March 1957, Native Courts.
93 GNA Sunyani, Goaso District Files, Acc 48/1969, 56.
94 GNA Sunyani, Goaso District Files, Acc 136/1969, June 1957, 44–5.
95 *Loc. cit.*
96 GNA Sunyani, Goaso District Files, Acc 48/1969, 94 = notes on a meeting of the Secretary to the Regional Commissioner at Ahafo Native Court House, 9 April 1958).
97 GNA Sunyani, Goaso District Files, Acc 136/1969, 159–60(25).
98 *Loc. cit.* 82(40), 28 May 1958.
99 *Loc. cit.* 126(7).
100 *Loc. cit.* 157(8).
101 GNA Sunyani, Goaso District Files, Acc 38/1969, 45(6).
102 *Loc. cit.* note 100 above.
103 *Loc. cit.* note 99 above.
104 The obvious regional disparities are to some extent offset by labour migration. For helpful discussions see John C. Caldwell, *African Rural–Urban Migration. The Movement to Ghana's Towns* (Canberra and London 1969) and Margaret Peil, *The Ghanaian Factory Worker: Industrial Man in Africa* (Cambridge 1972), esp. cap 5. It is extremely difficult to get useful statistics for recruitment to the industrial labour force as a whole by region of origin; but for some suggestive indications see Peil, *ibid.* p 128.
105 For these figures see the article cited in note 3 above.
106 *West Africa*, 2865 (12 May 1972), 602.
107 The contrast drawn here is made most easily with F. G. Bailey, 'The Peasant View of the Bad Life', in Teodor Shanin (ed.), *Peasants and Peasant Societies* (Harmondsworth 1971), pp 299–321 (reprinted from *Advancement of Science*, Dec. 1966, pp 399–409). Professor Bailey's studies of the hill peasantry of Orissa, particularly *Politics and Social Change: Orissa in 1959* (Berkeley, Calif. 1963) and *Tribe, Caste and Nation* (Manchester 1960) have been exceptionally stimulating and suggestive in their portrayal of political relationships in a rural society under pressure to incorporate itself into a much larger political unit. To stress a contrast in the phenomena between Ahafo and the Konds and Oriyas of Orissa is to affirm, not to repudiate, the felicity of the questions which Professor Bailey has asked.

385

Conclusion pp 353–5

1 Patrick Riley (ed.), *The Political Writings of Leibniz* (Cambridge 1972), pp 6–7.
2 Cf. Clifford Geertz, *Peddlers and Princes: Social Development and Economic Change in Two Indonesian Towns* (Chicago 1963), pp 118–19.
3 The taste for photography developed early enough in Ahafo for it to be worthwhile for a photographer to visit Mim as early as 1928 to take photos on a commercial basis. (See GNA Accra, ADM 49/4/2, pp 3, 5 etc., 14 March 1928.)
4 Cf. John Rawls, *A Theory of Justice* (Cambridge, Mass. 1972) and Brian Barry, *Political Argument* (London 1965).

INDEX

aban, see Government
Abengourou, *cercle d'* (Ivory Coast), 151, 373
Abese fetish, 130
Abiri Moro, Aowin invader of Ashanti, 243–4
Aboum, Ahafo town, 29, 48, 90, 119, 211, 266, 339–41, 366
   Aboumhene, 192, 196, 210–11, 230, 239, 266, 277–84, 379
   Aboum river, 79
Aburi, Government agricultural station, 44, 46
Accra, Capital of Ghana, administrative centre, 5, 10, 35–6, 38–9, 45, 50, 54, 80, 83, 104, 112, 144, 161, 164–5, 174, 197, 203, 241, 259, 261, 266, 275–6, 279–82, 284–5, 296, 335, 355, 373, 376, 381
Acheampong, Colonel, Leader of National Redemption Council, 275
Acherensua, Ahafo town, 15, 29, 33, 48, 50, 112, 119, 146, 153, 180, 208, 252, 318–19, 336–9, 341, 358–9, 366, 377 (*and see* schools, secondary)
   Acherensuahene, 184, 188, 233, 328
Achimota, elite school, 83, 138
   visited by Kukuomhene, 147
Adama, B. K., Northern M.P., 108–9
Addai, B. D., unsuccessful parliamentary candidate for Ahafo, 322–3
Administrative Officer, *see* Commissioner, District
Adomako-Sarfo, J., 365
Adu, A. L., D.C. in Goaso, 154, 316, 383
Aduana clan, 23
Agbodeka, Francis, 363
Agona clan, 236
Agriculture, Department of, 45–6, 50, 59, 196, 339
   Cocoa Survey by (1928/9), 63, 76, 116, 361
   Curator of, 48
   Director of, 52

Superintendent of, 50
Ahafo Chiefs Association, 253, 275–85, 381
Ahafo United Association, 316, 320
Ahafo Youth Association, 317, 346, 348, 363
Akan
   concept of citizenship, 11
   contrasted with northerners, 62–3
   cosmology, 16, 183
   culture, 155, 161, 166, 180, 206, 225, 348–9
   history, 208
   marriages, 28
   matriclans, 23
   military organisation, 182, 244
   settlement pattern, 11
   social organisation, 20, 34, 201
   states and political organisation, 23, 24, 34, 36, 160, 169, 176–7, 182, 186, 192, 194, 223, 314
Akim-Kotoku, 20
Akims, 243
   Akim stool, 351
Akokoaso, cocoa village, 356
Akrodie, Ahafo town, 76, 106–7, 127, 130–131, 146, 215, 237, 241, 244, 253, 262, 277, 300, 318, 329, 350, 366
   Akrodiehene, 31, 203, 214, 217–18, 236, 268, 328, 336
Akropong, Ashanti town, 236, 245
   Akroponghene, 230, 236, 245
Akufo-Addo, Mr Justice, 200, 293
Akwaboahene, 53, 55, 80–1, 194, 234, 243, 247, 255–6, 260, 274
   Akwaboa Stool, Kumasi Stool, 128, 131, 173, 193, 243, 247
Allah, 122–3 (*and see* Islam)
American capital, 81
Amponsah, R. R., Minister of Lands (P.P.), 81–2
Ancestors, 21, 192, 194, 205, 209, 212, 230, 241, 243–4, 261, 276, 372 (*and see* Stools)

387

Index

388

Index

Index

Index